Marx
and the Bible

A Critique of
the Philosophy of Oppression

José Porfirio Miranda

SCM PRESS LTD

Translated by John Eagleson from the Spanish
Marx y la biblia, Crítica a la filosofía de la opresión
published 1971 by Ediciones Sigueme, Salamanca

334 00972 3

First British edition 1977
published by SCM Press Ltd
56 Bloomsbury Street, London

© Orbis Books, Maryknoll, New York 1974

Typeset in the United States of America
and printed in Great Britain by
Billing & Sons Ltd
Guildford, London and Worcester

Marx and the Bible

Contents

In the historical Jesus, in the Gospels, in Romans.
The Kingdom. The Spirit of God.

Glory according to the Old and New Testaments. Present
and future. Messianism. Western scientific stubbornness.
Historical meaning and eschaton. All-embracing civilization.
Against the philosophy of oppression and the unchangeability
of nature. The new man. The dialectical mind vs. Greek
contemplation. Economics and philosophy.

Foreword

José Porfirio Miranda's *Marx and the Bible* was born out of real-life experience and passionate study.

Miranda studied theology and economics in Frankfurt, where I met him in 1955.

Later he returned to his native Mexico and engaged in Christian social action among the working class. It was in this context that he dedicated his efforts to a study of Marx's writings.

His studies and his experiences led him to see more and more that the essential meaning of the Bible's message has been eluding us Christians and our organizations. The Bible, especially Exodus and the prophets, is the revelation of the Transcendent God, the Liberator of the oppressed who fights against the oppressors in their behalf.

If Christians had not lost sight of this fundamental datum, Christianity down through the ages could not have become in fact an effective ally of so many structures of economic, social, and political oppression. And modern Christians would not have become the pawns of an emotional and acritical anti-Marxism, which at its most effective is reduced to a classist ideology at cross-purposes with the demands of an authentic Christianity.

But there is a noteworthy phenomenon which occurs. When those Christians who have made a class option for the oppressed and their liberation struggle read Sacred Scripture, they clearly perceive the fundamental datum that Yahweh is the God of liberation who fights against the exploiters. But when they suggest a reading of the Bible with this orientation, they are told that they are not "experts" and that their interpretation is, therefore, of no value. At the same time, because of the gravity and difficulty of their work, the experts in biblical studies form a true aristocracy within the university world of theological sciences; with a few brilliant exceptions, they are conditioned by a series of social factors which make it almost impossible for them to grasp seriously and existentially the Bible's most basic meaning.

Realization of this fact led Miranda to undertake specialized Scripture studies at the Biblical Institute in Rome. He brought to the task all the experience and socio-economic reflection of his years of social action.

The result of this effort of synthesis is *Marx and the Bible*. And it is in this synthesis that the truly singular value of his work lies.

This is not the occasion for a detailed critical evaluation. Taken as a whole I think that his reflections on the Pentateuch and the prophets are both striking and irreversible. On the other hand I believe that his reading of Paul's letter to the Romans needs more reflection and elaboration—not to reject outright the essential elements of this reading, but rather to overcome possible oversimplifications and extrapolations of the Pauline text.

It seems to me that when Paul speaks of the "justice of faith" in contradistinction to the "justice of the law," his point of view is less directly and exclusively "political" than Miranda interprets it. But neither can we deny the historico-political dimension on which the author of *Marx and the Bible* focuses. He has clearly grasped Paul's letter.

"For the created universe awaits with eager expectation for God's sons to be revealed. It was made the victim of frustration, not by its own choice, but because of him who made it so; yet always there was hope because the universe itself is to be freed from the shackles of mortality and enter upon the liberty and splendor of the children of God. Up to the present, we know, the whole created universe groans in all its parts as if in the pangs of childbirth" (Romans 8:19-22).

Perhaps Miranda takes for granted a pure and simple continuity between the prophetic outlook of the Old Testament and the outlook of the New Testament. It seems, however, that in fact there are involved in this continuity complex aspects and problems which need further elaboration. So, for example, with the light of Scripture we cannot describe the concrete phenomena which will characterize the realization of eschatological hope. So, too, the formula describing the balance which will exist between the "here and now" and the "beyond," between temporal life and eternal life in the fulfillment of God's salvation, has not been revealed to us.

But we can say that the "here and now" belongs to the content of hope, because there is a bond between history and eternal life deeper than we can imagine. We cannot deny the tight and indivisible link between the Old Testament and the New.

If the first generations of Christians had broken with the prophets, they would have broken with Jesus himself. Jesus was truly a prophet of Israel, although with a qualitatively superior dimension, and it was for this reason that he lived and died as a victim of the powerful of his time.

The temptation to oppose the New Testament to the Old is very ancient. But it would be unjust to attribute a maneuver of this nature to Paul of Tarsus, a maneuver which would have made Christianity into an exquisitely subtle Hellenic neo-paganism.

Indeed the Magnificat, which serves as a prelude to Luke's Gospel, is enough to stop any attempt at a historico-political or historico-prophetic "neutralization" of the Christian message.

The Lord of Mary, who made her the expectant mother of Jesus "to redeem those who were under the law" (Galatians 4:5), is God the Savior, the Powerful One, of whom it says in the song of the pregnant virgin:

He put down the mighty from their thrones
and raised up the lowly.
He filled the hungry with good things
and sent the rich away empty (Luke 1:46-47, 53-54).

It would be absurd to consider Miranda's *Marx and the Bible* as a kind of unquestionable dogma. On the contrary, it is a powerful appeal to rethink profoundly the essential meaning of the biblico-Christian message.

But the greatest absurdity would be to write this book off *a priori* as being "ideological," in the name of an alleged "neutrality." Such a neutrality would in reality be the product of a ruling class "ideology," against which the Bible unremittingly sets itself.

José María Díez-Alegría

Prologue

The philosophy of oppression, perfected and refined through civilizations as a true culture of injustice, does not achieve its greatest triumph when its propagandists knowingly inculcate it; rather the triumph is achieved when this philosophy has become so deeply rooted in the spirits of the oppressors themselves and their ideologues that they are not even aware of their guilt. Marx himself recognizes that in the capitalist system the oppressor is as alienated as the oppressed.

Thus I wish to make it clear from the very beginning that when I speak of exploiters, I do not wish to assign conscious guilt to all of them nor to all their purveyors of philosophical ideology. Far from it. Rather, I hope that the conscience of people of good will is capable of being shaken up and of challenging itself. Injustice is more a work of the social machinery, of the system of civilization and culture, than it is of people's intentions. "Indeed, the hour is coming," Jesus warned his disciples, "when anyone who kills you will think he is doing a holy duty for God" (John 16:2).

Besides this point it seems necessary to make clear only two others beforehand, although in the chapters that follow they will be obvious to the reader. The first is that I speak of Marx and not of communism. The second is that the author does not believe himself to be outside the social and cultural system criticized here; he only wishes that he might be freed from it himself and that all of us might be freed from it as well.

Introduction

It is well known that many European and North American evaluations of *Populorum progressio* referred to it as "the complete résumé of Marxist and pro-Marxist cliches." But this judgment is not only the resentful position of conservatives. Already in 1951, years before the publication of the encyclical and even before *Mater et Magistra,* Oswald von Nell-Breuning, S.J., a recognized spokesman for Catholic social doctrine in Germany, had this to say in his commentary on no. 100 of *Quadragesimo anno*: "This analysis of economic society and—for what it says concerning the industrialized countries—of society as a whole is the imperishable achievement of Marx. All subsequent critiques of capitalism are based, to one degree or another, on it."[1]

And in 1967 the same author in his article on "The Catholic Church and the Marxist Critique of Capitalism" spells out how "we are all riding on Marx's shoulders."[2] There is no doubt that the encyclicals take their diagnosis of society from Marx, a society divided into classes, in which some are owners of the means of production and others, the proletariat, are able to contribute only their own labor and are forced to submit to the decision-making power of the capitalists. The inevitability of the confrontation between the two classes, affirmed by *Quadragesimo anno,* is also a thesis taken from Marx; the only difference is that Pius XI calls "confrontation" what Marx calls "struggle." The necessity of building a classless society—with the difference that Marx calls it such while the pontifical doctrine terms it a "society free of classes"—is another noteworthy loan. The need to conceive and seek a transformation of structures and institutions and not only a reform of attitudes and persons, as Catholics taught before Marx, is another outstanding and most important example. With the transformability of institutions we also learn from Marx to think with a historical mentality about the social problem; this is perhaps still more important.

To this analysis of Nell-Breuning we could easily add a whole list of passages and arguments from *Populorum progressio* which directly or indirectly are derived from Marx. The list would include paragraphs of the greatest human profundity, those dedicated to the search for "a new humanism which will enable modern man to find himself anew" (*Populorum progressio*, no. 20). The encyclical affirms, "The development of which we speak cannot be limited to mere economic growth. . . . We do not believe in separating the economic from the human" (no. 14). Here it is well to recall Bigo's statement in 1953 about Marx's law concerning fixed capital and free capital: "Here we see Marx's conception of science. It is an understanding of phenomena from the inside. It is directed not toward appearances but toward reality. It presupposes a constant effort, when dealing with the economic reality, to pass . . . from a material viewpoint to a human viewpoint."[3]

When there are so many and such important derivations, recognized not only by liberals but also by the most authoritative Catholic authors, it is disconcerting to find in *Populorum progressio* an attack against what it calls "messianisms laden with promises but fabricators of illusions" (no. 14, original Italian version), for it is clear that the allusion here is to Marxism. It would be more accurate to recognize that it was the messianists who, by risking their lives and even losing them and by renouncing any advantageous social position, struggled for social justice against capitalist oppression long before the Church did. It would be more accurate and truthful to affirm that it was precisely this messianic element, the polarizer of immense proletarian masses, which forced a pope finally to come out in favor of the workers, as any reader of *Rerum novarum* can see. If the risk was much less and the acceptability much greater when the popes finally spoke up, this was because of these messianists. It was they who without assured social status and in the midst of the illegality with which capitalist legislation afflicted them sacrificed everything for the poor and the oppressed. It was they who had to struggle even against the Church itself, which later took from them its ideas of justice.

Of course, in the Western socio-cultural system the Church is not the only institution which has adopted intuitions of Marx without publicly acknowledging it. To cite just one example we need look only to the schools of philosophy and economics in our universities. At one time Marx's contributions to both disciplines were disdainfully considered as less than irrelevant; now there is an overwhelming need to study his theses with great dedication. This change in attitude is today a general fact in the entire West. But institutions have always demonstrated a conspicuous inability to repent, to recognize errors and injustices and remedy them. Thus we must realize that it is not enough merely to take seriously today the Marx whom we scorned yesterday; nor is it enough to execute almost imperceptibly some effectual change. The former preterition was not a mere careless omission. If we are to abandon yesterday's position, we must also revise the whole system of ideas and values which made such a position necessary. Real conversion is needed, not lukewarm concealment of changes which are made underhandedly.

A work like the present one cannot escape the fact that this approach has caused in the Church a situation which, as much as we might dislike it, must be called division. The teaching of Pius XII, John XXIII, and Paul VI that there is no absolute right to ownership unites broad sectors of Catholics, while others espouse paragraphs like no. 15 of *Rerum novarum* or the rejection of violence by Paul VI in Bogota or this teaching of Pius X which makes one marvel: "In the order of human society as established by God there are rulers and ruled, employers and employees, rich and poor, learned and ignorant, nobility and proletariat."[4] These paragraphs were never revoked, yet other teachings have taken a completely different direction. Thus if anyone were to claim to support the papal doctrine in its totality, he would be either insincere or ignorant of the doctrine. This would also be true of anyone who wished to reconcile Vatican II with Pius IX and the Syllabus. The unity is broken and any apologetic in this regard is a lost cause. This is not pluralism but a real and true division with which we must reckon from now on. Michel Blaise puts it clearly: "The unity of the Catholic world is broken."[5] If we are to take seriously and with all their implications some of the most important papal teachings, we cannot promise to arrive at conclusions which are completely reconcilable with all the papal declarations which have been made and not revoked. They are not completely consistent. It would be more humble, although not exactly more favorable to Catholic unity, to follow the directive of Paul VI: "It belongs to the laymen, without waiting passively for orders and directives, to take the initiative freely and to infuse a Christian spirit into the mentality, customs, laws and structures of the community in which they live" (*Populorum progressio,* no. 81).

The situation of the Church little lends itself to triumphalism. Thus the present work is able to point out the ideological causes of capitalist oppression without pretending that these philosophies have not existed and do not now exist in the Church. I fell into this partisan approach in an earlier book, *Hambre y sed de justicia.*

If there were no division in the Church, as certain officious declarations would have it, the leftist sectors would already have left the Church, for they could not tolerate being identified with those who support exploitative social regimes. If they were to be asked why they do not leave, they would have incomparably more right to return the question: Why do the rightists, as a Church of the rich, insist on belonging to an institution which was established to be the Church of the poor?

As regards the method of this work, the initial question which we pose is this: How was it possible that Catholic doctrine defended private ownership of the means of production? The first chapter points out how astonishing this is, given the antecedents in the Bible and the tradition of the first four centuries of Christianity. The rest of the book is a positive effort to understand the mentality, the very way of thinking, which we find in the Bible, for the position to which we have alluded follows a manner of thinking which is common to both Christian theology-philosophy and to Western science, and indeed to Western civilization in general as derived from the Greeks. The question of the dehellenization of Christianity, posed by Leslie Dewart and many others, is much deeper than realized by the scholastics, who suppose that nothing more than snobbism or a merely negative attitude is involved.[6] In its mode of thinking, in its very manner of thinking, the essence of Christianity is at stake. This work is, therefore, a biblical and philosophical study. Private ownership is treated only in the first chapter as an initial example; it is, however, an example which is extremely important in itself and for economic theory.

On the other hand, Marx's critique of Western political economy and philosophy is not for us merely an example. I am explicitly retracting here the position I affirmed in *Hambre y sed de justicia,* that is, that the dialectical mentality is incompatible with a genuine morality. I was deceived by my own superficiality when I read Marx's criticisms of morality. The truth is, as I explain in the last chapter, that it is precisely an acute moral sense which makes thinking dialectical; it makes one unable to resign oneself to a present reality that is without contradictions and that therefore remains forever as it is. Only dialectical philosophy is capable of discovering in past and present reality the inexorable exigency for a more human world. Marx could not relate this exigency with the pantocrator god that the oppressive West adored and continues to adore. I assume his rejection of this idol and of all idols; see chapter 2.

Various Christian authors have already pointed out that Karl Marx belonged to the category of the prophets of Israel and that both his messianism and his passion for justice originated in the Bible.[7] But they point out this connection in order to diminish Marx's importance by saying that he is not original. This is an astonishing procedure which only demonstrates how incapable of conversion Western science is before a prophetic voice: Similarity to the prophets invalidates a message. Here I hope to go beyond the similarity which can be drawn by academically listing parallels between the Bible and Marx. Such a catalogue of multiple coincidences can only produce a superficial understanding of both the Bible and Marx. It could, however, arouse a suspicious aesthetic pleasure by confirming the prevailing culture in its self-esteem and self-titillation because of its juxtapositional genius. I am going to follow another path: I will not attempt to find parallels between the Bible and Marx, but rather simply to understand the Bible. Our method will be the most rigorous and scientific exegesis. If we find coincidences with Marx, we will note them in passing. It is not, however, the number of intersections that matters, but rather the fundamental connection which challenges the whole reality which calls itself Christian civilization. "The West or Christianity, either ... or": This is the conclusion of our study. What Marx criticizes in Western science is the same thing that today prevents it from being challenged by the fact, which is recognized by this science itself, that to a great degree Marx coincides with the Bible. The hardening of the hearts has reached its apex: Only obstinacy is scientific, all conversion is prohibited by objectivity, and whoever sustains the contrary "betrays the West." From the beginning I place myself among these traitors, so that there be not the least doubt concerning my position.

We are at the moment in which Western civilization is becoming aware of itself and therefore is relativizing itself. This is not the relativism of one who can no longer discern between good and evil; rather it is a recognition of the antihuman and profoundly life-destroying power which is part of Western culture. The capitalism criticized by Marx is only the last link (we hope) in a long chain of oppressions, the most perfect link, the best structured link. If we look to the past, however, we see that the beginning of the chain does not coincide with the beginning of Western civilization; the chain began much before that. I agree with the Marxist Koschelava when he says that it is dangerous to make this statement, for there are those who will use it to erect injustice into an innocuous universal principle, a quasi-nature, a property inherent to the human essence, thus exonerating capitalism and distracting us from our struggle against capitalism.[8] The danger is not imaginary. We can see it in the reactionary arguments in defense of private ownership based on a presumed selfish nature of man. We can see it in the homage to a classist society and to the differentiation of income as nature's wise disposition which encourages work based on a so-called congenital laziness of the human being. We are all familiar with these melodies and others equally tender. But to affirm that capitalism carries within it all the age-old evil of exploited humanity is something very different from espousing universal Platonic principles. To assert this is to face historical facts; it is to see the injustice which piles up from generation to generation and finally achieves its most perfect and systematic institutionalization. It is to struggle so that the destruction of capitalism might be the destruction of all injustice. It would be adialectical to imagine capitalism as a species of mushroom which appeared by spontaneous generation without roots in previous history. And it would be dangerous not to distinguish the true essence of this capitalism which oppresses us. If the root of this whole system of injustice is not clearly defined, we could be attacking the effects while passing over the cause. And the root existed long before its capitalistic manifestation, long before it generated the present all-pervading and self-justifying system which enslaves man's id, ego, and superego—in the oppressor as much as or more than in the oppressed.

The transformation of labor into merchandise, labor's fetishization as an object, clearly denounced by Marx as the axis of the capitalist social system, has its roots in Western and Greek philosophy, which was later diversified into various specialized sciences. Marx himself, in his first thesis on Feuerbach, defines the root: "The chief defect. . .is that the thing, reality, sensuousness, is conceived only in the form of the *object* or of *contemplation*."[9] Although he does not explicitly say so, this is the defect not only of the entrepreneurs and economists and philosophers, but also of Western civilization as such. Hans-Georg Gadamer has formulated this idea well: "The knowledge of domination is the knowledge of the modern natural sciences as a whole."[10] The scholastics will find it very difficult to understand that to conceive something as an object implies such evil. They would say that by adding the epithet "persona" to the object they no longer consider it to be an object. Thus we must penetrate deeply into this mentality, into the very way of thinking.

> When modern science says that something is "in itself,". . .this has nothing to do with the ontological difference between the essential and the nonessential. Rather it is determined by a specificially self-conscious power to manipulate and a will to modify. . . . As Max Scheler especially has pointed out, the "in itself" is therefore relative, relative to a specific manner of knowing and willing.[11]

The Greek *technē* cannot be dissociated either from its metaphysics or its ethics.

Our century is definitively challenging the very concept of being, the "in itself," which was the absolute criterion of the Greek mind. This criterion was adopted without question by Western culture (including most importantly "Christian" philosophy and theology) as the indisputable norm of truth. Emmanuel Levinas has summed it up with brilliant accuracy: "A philosophy of power, ontology, as a fundamental philosophy which does not call into question the self, is a philosophy of injustice."[12] This is the "specific manner of knowing and willing" to which Max Scheler refers. Out of the substance of this mental universe were gradually formed the Western sciences and even the very definition which distinguishes between what is scientific and what is not. As Marcuse says:

> The scientific method which led to the ever-more-effective domination of nature thus came to provide the pure concepts as well as the instrumentalities for the ever-more-effective domination of man by man *through* the domination of nature.[13]

It is mere superficiality to think that the workaday phrases of businessmen—"I'm sorry, this is a business, not a charitable institution"; "That's your problem"; "Business is business"; "Please don't get sentimental"; etc.—are isolated bits floating in the soup of a different kind of civilization. They are the cultural system itself; its sciences and philosophies have been saying these same things for centuries, even when the voice takes on an academic tone. For them you are a mere "in itself"; you would be interesting if you were an object to be manipulated. You might even be liberated if you come under their gaze as an object of a "disinterested view of reality." Indeed, Greek philosophy was born to neutralize reality and prevent it from disturbing us, to reduce it to a cosmos in which everything is all right. Contrasting this philosophy with biblical knowledge, one great exegete described it in this way: "The independent gnosis which relies on itself and which lacks 'obedience' inevitably sees its objects as phenomena which are present at hand. It does not need to submit itself to them, to 'hear' them."[14] "For its knowledge to be 'objective' means that participation in what is known is reduced to 'seeing.' "[15]

These observations are made from a biblical point of view, both of the Old Testament and of the New. In general Christian theology has deliberately minimized the fact that Paul assails the wisdom of the Greeks (cf. 1 Cor. 1:22; 2:4-5; "philosophy" in Col. 2:8), although the issue is much more serious than one specific word might indicate. Here we hope to demonstrate this. Moreover, this is a manner of knowing more ancient than Greek civilization; but in Greek wisdom it did find its self-justifying systematization. To consider that capitalist oppression carries with it the weight of thousands of years of injustice and hardening of hearts and obstinacy of spirit changes neither the urgency nor the direction of our struggle. On the contrary, it gives it its true dimensions. What is at stake is, in Teilhardian terms, the qualitative mutation of the human genus and, in Pauline terms, "the new man" (Eph. 4:24), "the new creation" (Gal. 6:15; 2 Cor. 5:17). Marx expresses it by saying that prehistory has ended and the history of man has begun.

Notes to Introduction

1. Oswald von Nell-Breuning, S.J., in *Herders Wörterbuch der Politik,* part 5, col. 240.

2. Oswald von Nell-Breuning, S.J., in *Stimmen der Zeit* 180 (1967): 365-74.

3. Pierre Bigo, *Marxismo y humanismo* (Madrid: ZYX, 1966), p. 194. French edition: *Marxisme et humanisme,* 3rd ed. (Paris: Presses Universitaires de France, 1961).

4. Pius X, "Fin Dalla Prima," December 18, 1903, Motu Propio on Popular Catholic Action, in *All Things in Christ: Encyclicals and Selected Documents of Saint Pius X* (Westminster, Md.: The Newman Press, 1954), p. 208.

5. Michel Blaise, "Une morale chrétienne pour l'action révolutionaire," *Frères du Monde* 51 (1968):55.

6. Leslie Dewart, *The Future of Belief* (New York: Herder and Herder, 1966).

7. For example, the Catholics Christopher Dawson, *The Dynamics of World History* (New York: Sheed and Ward, 1956), pp. 354-56; and Georges M. Martin Cottier, *L'athéisme du jeune Marx* (Paris: J. Vrin, 1959); and the Protestant Karl Löwith, *Weltgeschichte und Heilsgeschehen* (Stuttgart: Kohlhammer, 1953), p. 48.

8. V. Koschelava, *El mito de los dos Marx* (Buenos Aires: Futuro, 1966).

9. Karl Marx and Friedrich Engels, *On Religion* (New York: Schocken Books, 1964), p. 69; italics in the original.

10. Hans-Georg Gadamer, *Wahrheit und Methode,* 2nd. ed. (Tübingen: Mohr, 1965), p. 427.

11. Ibid., p. 426.

12. Emmanuel Levinas, *Totalité et Infini: Essai sur l'exteriorité,* 2nd ed. (The Hague: Nijhoff, 1965), p. 14; cf. *Totality and Infinity: An Essay on Exteriority,* trans. Alphonso Lingis (Pittsburgh: Duquesne University Press; The Hague: Nijhoff, 1969), p. 46.

13. Herbert Marcuse, *One-Dimensional Man* (Boston: Beacon Press, 1964), p. 158.

14. Rudolf Bultmann, *Faith and Understanding,* trans. Louise Pettibone Smith (New York: Harper & Row, 1969), 1:217.

15. Rudolf Bultmann, "ginōskō," *TWNT,* 1:690; cf. *TDNT,* 1:691.

Chapter One

Private Ownership Under Challenge

Before treating the theme of ownership in a strictly economic analysis and in an unimpeded study of the Bible and primitive Christian tradition, it is important to note that by right of ownership the encyclicals understand something completely different from right of ownership as understood in legislation, books, newspapers, and everyday language. What we commonly understand as the right of ownership is the ability to use and even destroy something (*facultas utendi et abutendi*). The encyclicals, on the other hand, following Saint Thomas, understand the right of ownership as "the ability to care for and distribute," as Tomas G. Allaz, O.P., and Pierre Bigo, S.J., have convincingly demonstrated.[1]

The expression which Saint Thomas uses to define the term is *procurare et dispensare*,[2] the correct translation of which is "to care for and distribute," as Allaz rightly says. "This implies," he continues, "both administration and *allotment,* as expressed by the synonyms of *dispensare* used by Saint Thomas and his principal commentators: distribute, attribute, give, hand over, cede, owe, apportion, etc. The antonym is *cumulare* 'to accumulate.' "[3] And the difference between the pontifical definition of the right of ownership and the commonly understood definition is clearly seen in the famous message of Pius XII on June 1, 1941,[4] as well as in *Mater et Magistra,* no. 43, and *Populorum progressio,* no. 23; these statements emphatically place the right of all men to *use* the goods of the earth for their sustenance prior

1

to the right of ownership. The prior right is the right to use, while the right of ownership is one of management and administration—which should be directed toward the *de facto* realization of the prior right of *all* people to *use*. On the other hand, what is commonly understood as the right of ownership is well described by Bigo: "Each one spontaneously considers ownership, not as administration, but as possession. What belongs to me is *ipso facto* given over to my use. This is what the great majority of people think, even Christians."[5] This is in fact how ownership is understood by legislators, journalists, professors, politicians, the man in the street, etc.

These notions of the right of ownership are, therefore, two very different things. The attack of this book against the right of ownership is not directed against the papal doctrine, for this doctrine understands the right of ownership as something completely different from the common notion. (We will consider this doctrine in more detail later.) I do not make this statement apologetically in defense of Catholic social teaching, for the verbal coincidence in the term "right of ownership" has been a most efficacious support to capitalist oppression and the system itself, and this is indefensible. I make the point only as a caution.

Let it be very clear that this is not a question of criticizing "the abuses," while allowing "the thing in itself" to escape unscathed. This is a distinction frequently made by conservatives in their defenses of the system. Here it is a question not only of attacking the prevailing distribution of ownership, but the very right of differentiating ownership, especially of the means of production.

Distribution of Income

The reader who is unfamiliar with economic theory will find the next few pages quite dry, but he is the one who has most need of reading them. They present elementary notions of economics, without which it is difficult, if not impossible, to understand what is meant by distribution of income. Moreover, the injustice of ownership depends, as we shall see, on the injustice of income.

Every year national income is figured by calculating in dollars and cents the sum of all the wages, profits, interest, and rents that the businesses have paid out during the year. Transactions that businesses make among themselves are not considered. All the businesses existing in one country are considered as a whole as if they were one great enterprise—all businesses, whether commercial or banking or industrial or mining or cattle or fishing or theatre or haircutting or any kind of service or anything at all. And then the public (the entire population of the country) is considered at the same time as the buyer of the products of this great enterprise and the employee who all year long receives money from it. For example, the owners of capital receive, from the business, interest for the money which they lent (directly or through banks) for its operation. The owners of the business receive profits. The employees and workers receive wages and salaries. If we add up all that the population receives in money in one year from this great enterprise the total is what is called national income.

Each year this sum must be equal to the sum, in dollars and cents, of the goods and services produced by our great national conglomerate enterprise. This second figure is called the national product. That the first and second figure should be the same is obvious if we bear in mind that one of the items included in the first is profits. If the national income consisted only of interest, rents, and wages, the annual equivalence of the national income with the national product would not be clear. But it is precisely the profits figure that makes up the difference between the national product and the national income, which without that figure would be a total less than that of the national product. It is like the bookkeeping which arranges things so that both sides of an account always add up to the same total. If the totals are not equal, a figure called the balance or the deficit or the surplus or whatever is added to the lesser sum to make up for the difference; thus both figures automatically come out the same. There is no trick.

Every year the national treasury takes a part of the national income and with it causes an equivalent part of the national product to be qualitatively of a specified type (a specified type of goods and services), but this does not change the totals nor the correspondence between the national income and the national product. In the accounting of the national income and the national product, the government businesses are included like the others which have been combined into the great national enterprise. But the government of a country, strictly speaking, does not need to set up its own businesses; it need only order a specific type of goods and services from the already existing great national enterprise.

Naturally, not everything produced in one year is consumed by the population in that year. More is produced than is consumed, and the difference is called the net investment. (A part of what is produced remains as a component element of the great enterprise. If from this figure, which is called the gross national investment, we subtract the depreciation, that is, the wear and tear on what already existed that year, the remainder is called net investment.)

National income is not a sum equal to national consumption. There are people who, even if they wished, could not spend in consumption all the money they receive in a year. They save part of it and thus become holders of capital, either as owners of the means of production (co-owners of the great enterprise) or as lenders of money to the enterprise with or without the mediation of a bank. In the former case they will earn profits the following year. In the latter case they will receive interest, in addition to their salaries, if they continue to work.

If the loan of money to the great enterprise is made through a bank, either juridically or otherwise the holders of capital are co-owners of the bank. And since we said that the banks are a part of the great national enterprise, the result is that the holders of capital are co-owners of the great enterprise. If the banks are not the intermediary, the loan is made through stocks or bonds or other certificates. Directly or indirectly all these make their holders into co-owners of the various businesses, that is, of the great national enterprise.

All the above are elementary notions of economic theory, accepted by all economists and necessary to understand the meaning of the distribution of income. We must be careful to distinguish between distribution of income on the one hand and distribution of wealth on the other. To calculate the latter we would have to appraise the property existing in a country and then see how it is distributed among the population; but the appraisal is so difficult that nobody undertakes the task. On the other hand the distribution of national income is calculable with a great degree of precision by means of national accounting, the general lines of which we have described. For example, in absolute terms we can say that in 1957 there were in Mexico 223,411 families with an average monthly income of 185 pesos, while there were 134,998 families with an average monthly income of 11,592 pesos.[6] In relative terms we can establish that in 1957 83.9 percent of Mexican families together received only 43.5 percent of the national income, while a wealthy 4.9 percent of Mexican families monopolized 36.6 percent of the national income. In other words, there was a privileged 25 percent of the population that monopolized two-thirds of the national income, leaving only one-third of the national income for the remaining 75 percent.[7]

To evaluate the justice or injustice of a situation like this, we will make use of a papal teaching truly focused on reality, truly demonstrating a profound observation of observable facts. It happens that the obvious consequences have not been drawn from this teaching and it seems that such consequences would radically alter the whole of Christian social doctrine. The defense of the worker's right to organize, which is the axis and the novelty of *Rerum novarum,* is based on the reality described in no. 34 of the encyclical (which will be our starting point), namely, the weakness of the workers in entering into a contract. By referring to this idea and to no. 59 of *Populorum progressio,* which is totally in accord with it, I want to point out that the papal teaching which will be our starting point is not secondary, not merely touched on in passing so as not to be omitted altogether.

Let it be granted, then, that, as a rule, workman and employer should make free agreements, and in particular should freely agree as to wages; nevertheless, there is a dictate of nature more imperious and more ancient than any bargain between man and man. . . . If through necessity or fear of a worse evil, the workman accepts harder conditions because an employer or contractor will give him no better, he is the victim of force and injustice (*Rerum novarum,* no. 34).

If this passage from *Rerum novarum* protests, in the name of justice, against the harsh conditions of contracts which the employer imposes on the worker, it naturally presupposes that the employer is keeping for himself a disproportionate share of the income of the business and that in justice he should channel a much greater part of it to the workers. The national accounting of the economists, briefly described above, allows us to bring a macroeconomic dimension to this analysis of Leo XIII. Moreover, it is clear that the pope's intention went beyond the limits of a particular business. The fact that the underprivileged 75 percent of the population of a country accepts, by means of all the pertinent contracts and transactions, the meagre portion of the national income which it is in fact receiving, in no way means that such a distribution is just. Rather, it means that the workers are being permanently robbed, with the support, approval, and sanction of the prevailing juridical system. The national income in a given year is a limited sum; it is not elastic. Insofar as the portion of the national income destined to the working class in that year is increased, to that same degree the portion that remains for the capitalist class as interest or dividends or high salaries is diminished. These two portions are complementary; as one increases the other decreases.

However much one may advocate the legitimacy of the wage system in itself (that is, the system in which some contribute only their labor and are subjected to the decision-making power of others, who own the means of production), it in any case presupposes that both parties to the contract consent to the terms in full freedom. If this free acceptance does not exist, the wage system cannot legitimately and licitly be realized. This is the principle and foundation of *Rerum novarum,* which focuses precisely on the workers' right to organize, for it is only organization which can enable the workers to be in a position in which the strength of the employers does not force them to capitulate before Draconian wage stipulations. Let us suppose that the national workers' organization (that is, the organization of all those who are not owners of capital and instruments of production) could operate effectively. Nothing or no one could make them accept a distribution of the national income which resulted in the underconsumption and disempowerment of the workers and the overconsumption and reinforcement of the capitalists. If in fact they do capitulate, it is because they are "the victim of force and injustice" (*Rerum novarum,* no. 34).

One of the reasons we often do not grasp in all its depth the incessant injustice of this continuous spoliation is that when unions (in the nations where there are unions) obtain an increase in wages, the entrepreneurs recuperate their loss by raising the prices of the goods and services produced by the great national enterprise. Thus the wage increase is merely nominal (that is, in solely monetary terms), since the consuming public, made up principally of the same wage-earning workers who obtained the increase, receives the same quantity of goods and services that they received before the increase. This phenomenon causes the false impression that the national income of a given year is not a limited quantity. And at that moment people's minds become confused and falter. They go no further, as if they were before some kind of mystery which is accessible only to specialists.

But there is no reason why our thinking should move in circles or confusion. What is important with regard to distribution is the distribution of goods and services which are produced each year in the country. Money is only a means to acquire them. The distribution of income in monetary terms is important only as an instrument by which the distribution of the national product is determined. When they raise the prices, the capitalists use their own organization to prevent the wage increase from modifying the prevailing distribution of the national product. We might say that it is one organization against another, but this would be to recognize that the prevailing distribution of real income is only the effect of the violence that the system exercises on the workers. If they could effectively exercise, *as consumers,* their right to organize which by natural law belongs to them, their wage increase would not be converted into a merely nominal one. The portion of the national product which goes into the hands of the workers would effectively and really increase, and inevitably the portion which remained in capitalist hands would decrease, for the total each year is a limited quantity. It should be clear that the workers' right to organize, emphatically asserted by the popes and by all modern legislation, is futile if at the same time the right of the consumers as such to organize is not exercised.

If it is objected that the rise in prices consequent to a rise in salaries is not determined by entrepreneurial organization but by the mechanism of the economy itself, the moral configuration of spoliation is not thereby altered. No one would say that the workers freely accept the national system of contracts and transactions in virtue of which they are kept in a state of perpetual disempowerment and the capitalists in a perpetual situation of privilege. What forces them to capitulate before the system is the prevailing institutional violence which encircles them with hunger.

Let us pass over as evident the police, the army, legislation, and the courts, whose efficacy in defense of the status quo is notorious. Apart from these we have the media of social communication, which, as we know, are controlled by the social classes which are most favored by the prevailing system; the advertising of the corporations is today an indispensable source of financing for the mass media. The media prevent one workers' group from knowing about the initiatives and even the existence of other groups in the same country and even in the same city. They thus prevent them from organizing and even from knowing that they have the right to organize. Paid announcements are not within the reach of the workers, and the boasted right to the press, which our formal democracies claim belongs to all citizens equally, is pure ideology. In fact the freedom of the press belongs to the government, to the entrepreneurs, to the owners of the newspapers, and to those who have the money to buy space. The rest are excluded. Let us also mention the campaigns of calumny, defamation, and disorientation which the mass media wage against any initiative by "agitators" and in this way ingratiate themselves with their financiers and/or the government. Such initiatives do not have at their disposition the means to undertake in their own defense an even remotely comparable campaign. Such a situation is violence, a systematic shackling.

There is also the educational system—both that of the classroom and that of the religious or secular ideologies and axiologies. The educational apparatus is designed to reproduce the prevailing social system. Through it individuals are fashioned to occupy their proper place in the machinery. Thus those who are able to situate themselves well within the functioning social system are held in esteem while the others suffer an inferiority complex. People's very ideals are fabricated from within and thus there occurs in history the most perfect type of slavery there has ever been: that of not only not knowing that one is a slave, but of holding as an ideal of life a situation which objectively is slavery.

But the most inescapable snare is the necessity "to earn a living" in the terms imposed by this social system. So there is no need for chains or bars; the slave who flees will be forced by hunger to return. He cannot think of marriage nor of survival itself if he does not submit and render homage to the conditions imposed by the system. The man has no choice but to accept or to die of hunger—together with his wife and children. This "hidden persuader" (Vance Packard's expression) is worse than all propaganda and ideology, for it sinks its harpoon into the deepest level of the person. The system forces the man to surrender himself, with all his existential weight, to assuring his economic future and to regarding the problems of others as completely foreign to himself. It forces him to surrender himself to the spirit of calculation, to the ideology which says that a man's value depends on his cleverness in situating himself within the system. And he must do this because of the system itself, independently of indoctrination by propaganda or education or ideology; he must do this necessarily, to be someone, to be able to survive, in order not to be crushed by the social machinery. Momentum is given to this infernal apparatus by the ideal of development. And we cannot stop to consider that it is quantitative development, that is, that it means more of the same, more noncommunication among people, more internal enchainment, more systematic control of the workers to that they accept supposedly free contracts, more generalized spoliation, more violence.

One effect of education and the media and the ideologies pertains in a special way to distribution: A general and unchallengeable conviction is created that those who do certain kinds of work ought to receive lower incomes and be content with lower levels of consumption than those who do other kinds of work. A classist society is thereby, in people's minds, canonized as something morally correct, as a situation demanded by justice. Although both ideas are equally false, this conviction should not be confused with the medieval belief that the son of a shoemaker should also be a shoemaker and the son of a prince should be a prince; sociologists call this situation a lack of capillarity or social mobility. Today one can indeed "ascend" the classist ladder and it is even an ideal to do so. The depravity to which I refer is the conviction, apparently ineradicable although entirely mythological, that certain work is forever destined to receive low income and other work is "in itself" worthy of greater remuneration. This conviction is one of the worst violences inflicted on the workers to force them, in the labor contract (and in its indispensable complement, the multiple contract of bargain and sale of consumer goods and services), to submit to the conditions which are favorable to the capitalist class.

In many countries today the scarcity of the labor supply or the repugnance for manual labor is sufficient so that a bricklayer can in fact be paid more per hour than a white-collar worker. If it were not for the obduracy which also comes into play, facts of this nature would be enough to make our conviction collapse. They would indicate that the organization of workers could legitimately impose a wage scale entirely different from the prevailing one.

The economists' attempt to determine objectively what part of a company's output is the result of the workers' labor and what part is a result of the machinery and management not only has been declared a failure; it has also become clear that it was an impossible task. The last attempt was made by the American John Bates Clark in 1899, after the decline of the Cambridge and Vienna schools. But Clark saw very clearly the import of what he was undertaking with his scientific effort. (His book was titled *Distribution of Wealth.*) He was very conscious that if the distribution of income in a company did not correspond to the "value added" which each one had contributed by his work to the production, then our society was nothing more than "institutional robbery."[8]

As well intentioned as it was, Clark's attempt was not successful and could not be successful. The distribution of profits is determined by the prevailing network of forces, not by objective criteria which are reducible to justice. Any economist knows this today, although the majority of them soothe their consciences by means of a juridical positivism, that is, by telling themselves that if the worker accepts and signs the wage contract in the terms in which it is formulated, he does it freely and there is no injustice. But this philosophoumenon is self-serving nonsense, considering the multitude of constrictions, barefaced or masked, to which the workers are subjected. The second jaw of the pincers, that is, the multiple contract for the purchase of consumer goods (on which the amount of *real* income depends) is no more "free" for the workers than the first jaw: No one could convince us that we are free to pay or not to pay what is charged for a loaf of bread. This is determined by the entrepreneurs as a group. You pay it or you die of hunger. This is how the distribution of the real income is made in a country. This is how the 80 percent of the population who receive 36 percent of the national product for their work "freely accepts" their part of the contract. The wealthy 20 percent, on the other hand, receive 64 percent of the pie which we *all* produce in a given year. The worker "is the victim of force and injustice" (*Rerum novarum*, no. 34).

Differentiating Ownership

What has generally been overlooked is that private ownership, to the degree that it constitutes unequal social classes, exists only as a result of this coercive distribution of income, against which the popes have protested in the name of justice. The distribution of ownership is simply the accumulated distribution of income.

Since people with a high income cannot spend in consumption all the money which they receive annually—or they do not wish to, which has the same result in this case—, they therefore save a part of their income. And this part becomes capital of one form or another: They can lend their money to banks in exchange for interest, and the banks in turn lend it to entrepreneurs; they themselves can invest their savings in the means of production, which as entrepreneurs they control; they can buy stocks or bonds; they can lend directly to businesses. In any case this much is very clear: Not one ounce of the capital which exists today could have been generated if the workers of our countries had been able to exercise their natural and inalienable right to organize as workers and consumers. Violence prevented them from exercising it, a violence that is institutional, legal, juridical, pseudomoral, cultural, etc. And thus private ownership continues to be constituted, not only of the means of production, but also of villas, private vacation estates, expensive household furnishings, all the inherited differences which make up social inequality and the classist society.

When the Marshall Plan for war-torn West Germany was begun, Nell-Breuning posed this problem: Who will repay these American loans? Obviously the consumers, for by means of prices the businesses will collect the money necessary to pay the Americans. But at the end of the reconstruction who will be the owners of the factories and all the machinery of production? Obviously the Krupps and the Thyssens and the capitalist class in general. The means of production will be paid for by the workers who labor and consume; but they will be the private property of a handful of families. And so there occurred the German miracle, as it was called, and indeed in fifteen or twenty years the industries, the commercial chains, the automobile and truck fleets, the banks, etc., etc. were reconstructed stronger than ever. The workers paid for all this by enduring high prices for goods and services which could have cost them much less. The workers paid for all of it, and none of it belongs to them. Private ownership is robbery—legalized, institutionalized, civilized, canonized robbery. What could be observed as a laboratory case in fifteen or twenty years of German history is exactly what has happened and day by day continues to happen in the long history of the entire West. The astonishing thing is that the popes and Catholic moralists have not seen this, despite the fact that they have been working from the necessary logical presupposition, that is, the negation of positivism.

It is useless to object by arguing that capital existed before industrialization. It was generated by commerce (either directly or through loans), and the commercial enterprises despoiled their workers and consumers in the way we have mentioned. Or it was amassed on plantations with the work of slaves. Money as well as freedom was thus stolen from the slaves. And no one would think of justifying the fortunes which came from the plantations or mines or estates worked by slaves. As for the so-called "things belonging to no one" (*titulus occupationis rei nullius*), it is clear that they could not become capital in the strict sense without becoming a part of that mechanism of violence which we call the market, whether the consumer market, the wage market, or both. Then there is the right of conquest, but to assert this would be to assert the right of the strongest and thus abandon any difference between right and injustice. The good faith with which the subjects themselves have proceeded, deceived by the positive law of the country, of the time, or of the mores, cannot be used as a defense without advocating a juridical positivism, that is, without advocating that it is the law itself which determines what is good and bad. But in that case there would be no denunciation of present-day injustice, for 99 percent of the exploitation today is legal. The notion that a long-term, uninterrupted possession constitutes a right was invented by the possessors themselves who wished to continue uninterrupted. They say that irreparable damage would occur in society if there were no prescription, yet this is precisely the way that the injustice and spoliation which they or their ancestors committed against the rest of society is made irremediable. The evils to which they refer can be reduced to disturbing order, security, and peace. Order, security, and peace are certainly a worthy objective, but the issue with which we are concerned is not an amoral question of mere efficacy of means, as if any means to achieve order and security and peace could be legitimately employed and the moral relevance of the means did not have to be taken into account. It is pure self-serving conservatism to maintain that spoliation and injustice should continue unremedied as long as peace is achieved. Peace is very good when it is established on justice (cf. Isa. 32:17), not when it serves only to make injustice irremediable.

By differentiating ownership we mean both the ownership of the means of production possessed by a small part of the population and unavailable to the workers as well as of consumer goods which manifest social differences. It is not enough to affirm that all the differentiating ownership which exists today is *de facto* the result of spoliation; this would possibly be to condemn only the "abuses" of something which "in itself" could have been and could be good. In addition to the *de facto* question there is the *de jure* question: Differentiating ownership *could not and cannot* come to be except by means of violence and spoliation; therefore there can be no legitimate differentiating ownership (with the exception of lottery prizes insofar as all who participate by purchasing a ticket consent in true freedom that only one of them will win).

What is astonishing is the curious manner in which the *de jure* question has generally been posed. It has been done by essentializing, detemporalizing, prescinding from the historical origins of ownership (and there is no better way to avoid remorse than to prescind from the past). It is as if the question could be resolved by dully looking at the concept of ownership on the one hand and of legitimacy on the other and discovering that one does not contradict the other and that therefore ownership is not intrinsically evil. This is not to speak of ownership but rather of some mental representation we would like to think is the essence of ownership. The advocates of such a method are willing to concede that all the extramental concretizations of the essence being analyzed have been *de facto* bad; but they assert that this in no way affects the essence itself, which "in itself" can be good. So this is the thinking: The reality which constitutes the empirical datum under examination is recognized as always bad, but the conceptual abstraction made from all these extramental realities turns out to be good "in itself." Does this not clearly indicate that such an abstraction does not correspond to reality?

It is apparent why such a method is used: If we prescind from history as the only *possible* origin of ownership, then we need not pose the decisive question of whether differentiating ownership *can* come to be without violence and spoliation. If we prescind from the historical question, the problem of the possibility of legitimate ownership is reduced to a merely essentialistic issue: Essences descend vertically from a Platonic world; ownership has no genesis; it is not a product of history. Such a mentality came to us from the Greeks, and Marx criticized it in the classical economists: "Political economy starts with the fact of private property, but it does not explain it to us."[9] This is also what is done by the moralist who is an heir of the Greeks: He speaks of ownership with the explicit or tacit presupposition that it was rightly acquired. With this presupposition all his lucubrations are very logical and coherent and he believes he is grasping ownership "in itself," the essence itself of ownership, and not its anecdotal and accidental abuses. But the real problem is completely different: Could differentiating ownership be acquired without these anecdotal and accidental abuses which can be reduced to violence and spoliation?

In reality the accumulation of capital in a few hands could not and cannot be achieved without an institutional violence exercised over wages and prices. The rest of the population would not freely assent to this disempowerment. If they have capitulated before the series of implicit or explicit contracts involved, it is because they had no choice (that is, because of violence) and/or it is because the ideologies, education, and communications media of their respective periods of history have made them unaware that other possibilities even existed (that is, because of the violence of deception).

Biblical and Patristic Testimony

Since at least the sixth century A.D., a bald fact has been systematically excluded from theological and moral consideration: "To give alms" in the Bible is called "to do justice."[10]

To cite just a few of the passages which have resisted all misrepresentation, we mention Prov. 10:2; Tob. 4:10; 12:9; 14:11; Dan. 4:24; and Matt. 6:1-2. These are not the only ones, but these are unequivocal. When our Western translations say "almsgiving," they do not do so in bad faith. Indeed the reality involved is what we call today "almsgiving," and the translations are made for the people of today. But the original says ṣ*edakah*, which signifies "justice." We might also add Ecclus. 3:30, 7:10, and 12:3, the original Hebrew of which we have only recently come to know. Previous centuries knew only the Greek translation, which, like our modern versions, is "almsgiving." With the

same certainty we could also list Ps. 112:3,9; Artur Weiser and
H.J. Kraus dogmatically interpret "justice" (*s^edakah* in Hebrew) in these
two verses as "fidelity-to-the-covenant," but they hold that the Bible
treats no other theme but the covenant. As we shall see later, however,
covenant theology belongs to a relatively late period in the Old
Testament. In Ps. 112, as in the other passages we have cited, the Bible
calls "justice" what we call "almsgiving."

Some exegetes have tried to diminish the importance of this fact.
They argue that the Greek translators of the Old Testament, the famous
Seventy, caused some confusion by translating justice (*s^edakah*) at
times by *eleēmosynē* 'almsgiving,' at other times by *eleos* 'compassion,'
and at others by *dikaiosynē* 'justice.' But, in the first place, this
characteristic of the translation should not distract us from the
fact—which is disconcerting for the West—that the works which we
consider to be of charity and supererogation are in the original Bible
text called works of justice. This is the same *s^edakah* which the whole
Bible considers transgressed when the worker does not receive his wage;
see, for example, Jer. 22:13. In the second place, instead of minimizing
the bald fact we have pointed out, the Greek translation emphasized it
even more: It means that the translators of the Septuagint themselves
were disconcerted.

The act which in the West is called almsgiving for the original Bible
was a restitution that someone makes for something that is not his. The
Fathers of the early Church saw this with great clarity:

> Tell me, how is it that you are rich? From whom did you receive
> your wealth? And he, whom did he receive it from? From his
> grandfather, you say, from his father. By climbing this genealogical
> tree are you able to show the justice of this possession? Of course
> you cannot; rather *its beginning and root have necessarily come out
> of injustice.*[11]

> Do not say, "I am spending what is mine; I am enjoying what is
> mine. In reality it is not yours but another's.[12]

Jerome comments in this way on Jesus' expression "money of
injustice" (Luke 16:9):

> And he very rightly said, "money of injustice," for *all riches come
> from injustice.* Unless one person has lost, another cannot find.
> Therefore I believe that the popular proverb is very true: "The rich
> person is either an unjust person or the heir of one."[13]

Basil the Great thinks the same way:

When someone steals a man's clothes we call him a thief. Should we not give the same name to one who could clothe the naked and does not? The bread in your cupboard belongs to the hungry man; the coat hanging unused in your closet belongs to the man who needs it; the shoes rotting in your closet belong to the man who has no shoes; the money which you hoard up belongs to the poor.[14]

Ambrose teaches the same thing in a formula of unsurpassable exactitude:

You are not making a gift of your possessions to the poor person. *You are handing over to him what is his.*[15]

The defenders of private ownership have used wonders of subterfuge and misrepresentation to escape attack by such an unequivocal and constant tradition, which was only being faithful to Sacred Scripture. But no subtlety is able to whitewash these explicit teachings of Ambrose and Augustine:

God willed that this earth should be the common possession of all and he offered its fruits to all. But avarice distributed the rights of possession (*Avaritia distribuit iura possessionum*).[16]

Iustitia est in subveniendo miseris: Assisting the needy is justice.[17]

Apologists for the status quo attribute this incontrovertible tradition to the imprecision of preachers. By this standard, however, we would also have to eliminate not only the entire patristic tradition but the Bible as well, for there is nothing imprecise about the statements we have considered. On the contrary, they demonstrate on the part of their authors the very clear intention of formulating a well-deliberated idea. The time has come for Christianity to break a long chain of hypocrisy and collusion with the established powers and decide if its message is or is not going to be the same as the Bible's.

It does us no good to think like the Greeks and say that "money of injustice" cannot mean that injustice is inherent in money like a quality, like weight or color, and that therefore we do not comprehend what Jesus means by the term and should let the question rest. It is obvious that Christ did not mean that, nor did Luke, for the simple reason that neither of them was a disciple of Aristotle. The expression in question should be understood in the context of a society divided between rich and poor. "How happy are you who are poor" (Luke 6:20) and "Alas for you who are rich" (Luke 6:24) are not expressions which bless the physical fact of not having money and condemn the physical fact of having money, and neither are the numerous statements in the Psalter and the prophets on behalf of the poor and against the rich. The terms "rich" and "poor" are correlative, and what the blessing and the corresponding curse attack is precisely the difference between the two. It does not seem to Luke (nor to Christ) that this difference can be justified. It is "money of injustice" for, as Jerome understood very well in the paragraph we have quoted, "All riches come from injustice.... The rich person is either an unjust person or the heir of one." Jesus ben Sirach, who in Ecclus. 5:8 uses "unjust riches" with the same sense as the term in Luke 16:9 (and not, certainly, in a determinative sense, which would need the article: *tois chrēmasin tois adikois*), with astonishing perspicacity provides the same explanation:

Many have sinned for the sake of profit; he who hopes to be rich must be ruthless. A peg will stick in the joint between two stones, and sin will wedge itself between selling and buying. (Ecclus. 27:1-2)

Let it not be said that the biblical authors did not understand economics; this is the same ben Sirach who in 3:30, 7:10, and 12:3 in the original Hebrew refers to "almsgiving" as "justice." The underlying conviction is that differentiating ownership, that which makes some rich and some poor within the same society, could not be achieved with the genuine acquiescence of those who were thereby disempowered; it could not and it cannot be achieved without violence and despoliation. The condemnation of the rich in Luke 6:24 and the expression "money of injustice" in Luke 16:9 are based on the same conviction. If this were not so the programmatic battle cry which at the beginning of his Gospel Luke puts on the lips of Jesus' mother herself would be completely incomprehensible: "He has filled the hungry with good things and sent the rich away empty" (Luke 1:53). This verse is generally classified among the incomprehensible, but such an alternative is not very scientific. It is obvious that the statement in question presupposes a definite conviction about the injustice of differentiating wealth, that is, the wealth which in the same society constitutes some people in one class and others in another. The underlying conviction can be none other than the one we have indicated: It is impossible for this wealth to have been acquired without violence and spoliation. To avoid this conclusion regarding what is at the basis of all these scriptural passages, it would be necessary to assert that they do not refer to every type of differentiating wealth, but only to that which was wrongly acquired. The passages would therefore imply that the wealth could have been rightly acquired. But the very strength of the texts is in the intentional universality of the statements, in the nondistinction, precisely in the fact that they do not allow distinctions: "It is easier for a camel to pass through the eye of a needle than for a rich man to enter the kingdom of God" (Mark 10:25; Matt. 19:24; Luke 18:25). It is impossible to interpret this statement as directed against the distribution of differentiating ownership which *de facto* prevails and not against *de jure* differentiating ownership as such. It is impossible to interpret it as directed against the abuses and not against differentiating ownership in itself.

The efforts of certain modern exegetes to negate the authenticity of this logion (Mark 10:25; Matt. 19:24; Luke 18:25) as the words of Christ himself only show how greatly the work of interpretation is influenced by the status which Western civilization bestows on the theologian and on Christianity itself as the official religion. Of this entire teaching they wish to retain as the original nucleus only Mark 10:26, which in substance says, "How difficult it is to be saved." They want us to believe that 10:25 is one example among many and that it was more or less invented by pre-Marcan community preaching, which does not have to be taken literally. But with this maneuver exegesis transgresses the methodological principles which it has scientifically elaborated during many decades of meritorious work. In fact, the absolute impossibility of salvation for the rich is something which no primitive Christian community (before 70 A.D., as Mark's Gospel was written in 70 or 71) would have dared to assert if it were not basing its assertion on the authority of Christ himself. On the other hand, "How difficult it is to be saved" is a theological generality which could have been invented by any community or redactor of that time or any other. Therefore the most serious modern exegetes, from the accredited Joachim Jeremias and the authoritative Walter Grundmann to the very exigent Rudolf Bultmann and Norman Perrin, hold that Mark 10:25 is an authentic saying of the historical Jesus.[18]

Thus the statements of Luke 1:53, 6:24, and 16:9 could be, as regards their formulation, proper to Luke or to his preredactional tradition; as regards the content, however, they faithfully transmit to us the thinking of Christ himself, which we know from Mark 10:25 and many other equally authentic passages like Matt. 11:5-6 (Luke 7:22-23); Luke 6:20; etc.

Thus we can return to our starting point: The fact that differentiating wealth is unacquirable without violence and spoliation is presupposed by the Bible in its pointed anathemas against the rich; therefore almsgiving is nothing more than restitution of what has been stolen, and thus the Bible calls it justice. And we include here the New Testament. Matthew leaves no room for doubt when he explains and thematically attempts to delineate what justice is, that is, what makes some just and others not, in Matt. 25:31-46: "the just" (vv. 37 and 46); "And they will go away to eternal punishment, and the just to eternal life" (v. 46). It all has to do with giving food to the hungry, drink to the thirsty, a home to the stranger, clothing to the naked, etc. The list is given four times so that there can be no mistake. It would be difficult to establish with greater emphasis a definitive and single criterion to distinguish between the just and the unjust. And this justice cannot be reduced without misrepresentation to some kind of "virtue" or supererogation, as we see by the fate which awaits those who do not practice it: "Go away from me with your curse upon you, to the eternal fire prepared for the devil and his angels" (v. 41).

These are all works which the West calls charity, in contradistinction to justice.[19] A frequent methodological error is to believe that the discrepancy is verbal or explicable by the alleged imperfection of biblical morality, which did not know how to distinguish between justice and charity. The discrepancy is a solid, unequivocal fact. To brand the biblical authors as primitive is a value judgment, not objective exegetical work. What is in question is precisely Western morality's alleged superiority to biblical morality. To base oneself on this superiority in order to reduce biblical thought to Western thought is an extraordinarily unscientific methodology, for it prevents one from seeing the difference which exists between the thinking and wishing of the investigator and that of the authors being studied.

We have said that when the Bible calls "justice" what Western culture calls "almsgiving" it is because the private ownership which differentiates the rich from the poor is considered unacquirable without violence and spoliation; the Fathers of the Church also understood this very clearly. The causal dependence which exists between the distribution of ownership and the distribution of income had led us, by economics alone, to the same conclusion. But it would be erroneous to think that this economic fact escaped the biblical authors. Ecclus.

27:1-2, which we have cited, is exceedingly clear: It refers to those who try to enrich themselves through profits, and it points out how this profit occurs in buying and selling. When in 3:30, 7:10, and 12:3 it refers to "almsgiving" as "justice" (s^edakah), the thinking is in perfect congruence with the economic fact to which we have alluded and which, to be sure, has escaped Western moralists and jurists.

In 22:17 Jeremiah condemns this same profit, after describing in v. 14 the luxurious home which King Jehoiakim had built, undoubtedly with such profits. Thus in v. 13 the prophet could specify of what material the property was made: "Shame on the man who builds his house by not-justice and completes its upstairs rooms by not-right." As economic theory demonstrates, profit is the tangible concretization of the difference in incomes. Jeremiah sees very clearly how private ownership arises from this. We refer to the ownership which we have called differentiating.

Amos is equally penetrating in the causal relationships he draws. He, however, refers to no person in particular but to the system itself:

Well then, since you have trampled on the poor man, extorting levies on his wheat—those houses you have built of dressed stone, you will never live in them; and those precious vineyards you have planted, you will never drink their wine.

"Assemble on Samaria's mountain and see what great disorder there is in that city, what oppression is found inside her."

They know nothing of fair dealing—it is Yahweh who speaks—they cram their palaces full with violence and spoliation.

(5:11; 3:9-10)

Here we have, despite all the appearances of elegance and luxury, the true consistency of the property of the rich: violence and spoliation. Their palaces and all that which makes them into a class different from the rest of the population are for Amos concretized oppression, the accumulated materialization of violence and spoliation. When he threatens punishment, Amos is aware that he is proclaiming elementary justice. Because they trampled on the poor and extorted from them levies of wheat, they could build their houses of dressed stone, but they would not inhabit them, for the day of justice is coming.

Micah (3:9-10) alludes to this same characteristic of differentiating ownership as he contemplates the mansions and buildings of Jerusalem:

You who loath justice
and pervert all that is right,
you who build Zion with blood,
Jerusalem with injustice.

The second chapter of Habakkuk attacks profit in both its second (vv. 6b-8) and third (vv. 9-11) stanzas.[20] Then it speaks of the cries of the walls and the beams of the houses which were built with such materials:

For the stone from the very walls cries out, and the beam responds from the framework.

And it continues by taking up the words of Micah:

Trouble is coming to the man who builds a town with blood and founds a city on injustice.

(2:11; 2:12)

It is needless to draw out the list of biblical testimony. Thirty years ago there were those who tried to explain this unanimous understanding of the essence of differentiating ownership by the rural and antiurban origin of the prophets. Today scientific exegesis rejects such subterfuges of interpretation, of which the history of Christianity is full. Any anecdotal or psychological explanation is out of place here, for in the prophetic anathemas there is a lucid understanding that inherited wealth has its economic origin in profit. Moreover, Isaiah and Hosea think the same way as the other prophets, and they are not peasants but city-dwellers. Isaiah is even from the capital, and proud of it.

Before Christianity became compromised with the prevailing social systems, that is, up to the fourth or fifth century A.D., there were never misrepresentations or evasions with regard to the biblical testimony concerning the inescapably unjust origin of differentiating ownership. The patristic passages which we have cited abundantly demonstrate this.

At the beginning of this chapter, I noted that the papal encyclicals' defense of private ownership cannot be quoted to brand as heterodox what I am sustaining. As Allaz and Bigo have demonstrated, the encyclicals understand ownership as something very different. I now wish to add, although I have already touched this in passing, that in their defense the popes obviously presuppose this provision: that the ownership has been legitimately acquired. Thus the papal doctrine on ownership is on a different level, onto which my considerations in no way enter. But the whole doctrine is conditioned by the implicit phrase: provided that the ownership has been legitimately acquired.

If it is objected that the popes presuppose that legitimately acquired ownership *de facto* does exist, I respond that in any case this notion is not the object of their teaching activity but is rather a supposition. Their teachings therefore do not prejudge the possibility of demonstrating that this supposition is false. Both the recent advances in economic science and the understanding that the Bible and the Church Fathers had of the matter demonstrate that the supposition is indeed false.

Legitimacy of the Wage System?

The falsity of this supposition challenges a whole series of conservative theses which exist in Catholic social teaching. Sooner or later a deeper understanding of the diverse elements of this teaching had to reveal the contradiction which was always latent in the teaching. The contradiction is between the genuine intuitions of social reality and those that are not genuine, that is, precisely those theses conditioned by this supposition.

One of the latter, for example, was the legitimacy of the wage system, that is, the social system in which some people are the owners of capital and the means of production while others contribute nothing but their labor to production. When the problem was posed in essentialistic terms, that is, by detemporalizing and dehistoricizing it, there seemed to be no contradiction between, on the one hand, the wage contract agreed to by both parties and, on the other, the concept of legitimacy. The deduction was, therefore, that the wage system is not in itself evil.

But if that capital which makes one person an owner with respect to another, who is merely a worker, is the product of the violence and spoliation which the ancestors of the first exercised on the ancestors of the second, then the whole neoscholastic question about whether the wage contract is in itself intrinsically evil or not becomes a question that is asked too late. Logically and essentialistically speaking, it could be unobjectionable. But the presupposition is not unobjectionable, namely, that the capital was legitimately acquired. This is the fundamental issue which the neoscholastic authors do not examine.

Moreover, the whole papal doctrine on the legitimacy of the wage contract in itself clearly presupposes that in making the contract there is true freedom on both sides. If this condition is not fulfilled, all the successive argumentation is nullified. But the atrocious coercion exercised by the existing social system was discovered by sociologists, psychologists, anthropologists, and economists after the neoscholastic opinion was formulated. There has never existed a socio-cultural system whose refined constrictive power was so capable of entrapping and hooking people on such deep psychic levels as the capitalist sytem. Not only does it make them believe that they are free, but it makes them consider inserting themselves into the system and assisting it to function as a life ideal. For the slaves of old there was at least the interior freedom of knowing that they were slaves; at least in that little corner of their soul they were free. Today the system can allow its slaves to run physically free, because it knows it has subjected them psychologically and ideologically. If by chance they should escape, they have no choice but to return; it is the only way they can survive.

In making these clarifications we are not trying to exonerate the authors of the papal doctrine and their advisers. An elementary sense of justice, that they could have found in the Bible, would have convinced them that no human group freely accepts contractual terms which result in the social disempowerment of that group in relation to the other party to the contract, who thereby become an increasingly privileged and favored class. Jesus' statement about the rich man and the camel passing through a needle's eye should have made them suspect that they were moving on unconscious presuppositions entirely different from his. They should have suspected that in the eyes of the Bible a society divided into classes is evil in itself, not because of the essences involved, but because it is absolutely impossible for such a society to exist without the violence and spoliation that one group exercises on the rest of the population.

The question of whether or not the workers have the natural right to enter into the contract with the business as partners and not simply as wage earners was, in social ethics, posed in essentialistic terms, and this implies that the ownership of the means of production by the entrepreneurs was legitimately acquired, the ownership which situates them as owners with respect to the mass of workers who have nothing more than the strength of their labor. This supposition conditions all the arguments devised by interrelating concepts, definitions, and essences. Once the supposition is demonstrated to be false, the conclusions of such argumentation are completely nullified. This same nullification could also have been arrived at by taking seriously the natural right to organize affirmed by *Rerum novarum,* for the most elementary social ethics holds that for the wage contract to be licit, both parties to the contract must accept it in true and authentic freedom. Only intellectual blindness could lead one to assert that the working-class masses accept the wage system with true freedom, the wage system on which the Western socio-economic system as a whole is based.

Today these masses capitulate because they have no choice if they want to survive and because the educational, legal, religious, ideological, and communications machinery prevents them from knowing even that they have the right to refuse. They capitulate; they would not freely agree to continue as proletariat when they can be the owners of the means of production, not only to the same degree as the entrepreneurs but even more. Before agreeing to work, the workers' organization can demand that the ownership of production pass into their hands. If they do not demand this, it is because the violence of all of Western civilization prevents it. The wage contract is the only path that this civilization leaves open; the workers either are ignorant of even the existence of other paths or they die of hunger if they try to follow them. Thus to suppose that the wage contract is freely accepted by the workers demonstrates only how unconscious the advocates of this position are of the docility with which they themselves obey the directives of the prevailing system. They do not realize that they themselves coproduce the violence which nullifies the conclusions of their lucubrations; and their arguments are indeed invalid, for the condition for their validity is that this violence not exist.

Pius XII's negation of the natural right of workers to participate in profits, management, and ownership has recourse to the nature of the wage contract and the nature of business, which pertains not to public law but to private.[21] But he is obviously supposing that the workers freely accept the wage contract and that the private ownership of capital and the means of production of which the business consists were legitimately acquired. Pius XII would have been offended if anyone had thought that these were not his obvious presuppositions. The reaction of Fr. Gundlach, the author of the pope's addresses on social and juridical matters, would have been the same. But when the defense of the wage system fortifies itself against the irruption of distributive justice by basing itself on the *contractual* nature of business, it thereby lets in precisely the Trojan horse. The nature of the contract demands that there be no force nor deception. But because of the system prevailing throughout the whole of society, there is both force and deception in these contracts, or rather, the less efficacious the deception, the more force there must be.

The mental methodology is what is defective in all the argumentation of these authors. They conceptually isolate business by virtue of "de-finitions" which abstract this business or bit of reality from its social and historical context. Once they have abstracted and pre-scinded from that reality, it is not strange that they do not see the effects of the surrounding historical society on this business. They have created a mental illusion expressly isolated from real society, and then they argue that society does not affect it. Thus they cannot see that the evaluation of the various contributions which are made within business is conditioned by the hierarchy of values which prevails in the society as a whole and which dictates the distribution of national income and therefore of ownership. And this hierarchy of values is both force and deception when it persuades people that it is an incontestable fact that the managers and owners should enjoy greater well-being and a higher social status than those who do mere physical labor. This is especially true when it persuades people that productive collaboration can be achieved only through the wage contract between the possessing class and the dispossessed class.

The whole notion of Western justice and law is fashioned after the contract of bargain and sale, of commutative interchange. This means that the prevailing distribution is accepted as non-revisable; the only thing that is demanded is that the operations of interchange between the subjects be such that each one receives the equivalent of what he gives. *That is, the prevailing distribution must remain as it is. The morality and law of the West are par excellence the ideology of the status quo.* This same notion of commutative justice was applied to the wage contract, as if it were possible to evaluate as merchandise the labor that is a person's life, as if the dedication of the only life I have could be bartered for all the gold in the world, as if there really were some way to establish equivalencies in this area. The abyss of immorality which exists in the Western idea of justice is strictly unfathomable; it sets up as an ideal the systematic profanation and humiliation of the human being.

Moreover, the simple operation of bartering objects, which to the Greeks and scholastics seemed so objectifiable and even quantifiable that they used it as a basis for their original notion of commutative justice, is not nearly so obvious as it appeared to them. Naturally it is not a question of bartering one pound of wheat for another pound of wheat of the same quality, for in that case there would be no reason for the exchange nor would there be any commutative operation. The things which enter into the operation are heterogeneous. Thus the postulated equivalence depends *on the whole hierarchy of values* prevailing in the society, *on the degree of necessity,* which suspends that very freedom without which the contract is no longer a normative example, as the authors themselves say, *and on the labor or effort* which is required to produce the exchangeable objects. The degree of necessity depends on the position of greater or lesser comfort which the party to the contract occupies in society; thus commutative justice itself carries within it the whole problem of distribution. It is pure superficiality to try to define and demarcate questions in which only commutative justice is competent and distributive justice should not be involved.

When the mind is closed to the absolute normativeness of distributive justice, the complexity of the equivalence postulated between nonhomogeneous things often makes moralists and jurists take the easy path: They abide by the price which *de facto* is in force in society at that given moment. And this is to abdicate. To confuse the *de facto* price with the just price is to renounce the task of moral science and to surrender to positivism; it is to accept the right of the strongest. The times in which the god called "supply and demand" was capable of soothing serious consciences were strictly mythological times. Today we know that not even the utopian and nonexistent "state of perfect competition" would guarantee that the prices formed would be just prices. But we also know how a business's greater or lesser capital determines the greater or lesser torrent of advertising and "hidden persuaders" that generate a demand for their product, which is necessary so that they may be able to raise the price. To abide by *de facto* prices or the equivalences accepted by the common understanding of society is to forget that society is under the power of ideologies and educations and advertisings and even fatalisms with regard to the impossibility of eliminating social differences.

The commutative operation is only an instrument of distribution. When we are told that commutative justice consists in the seller's not receiving more or less than what he gives, what do these words mean?

By what criterion do we know that something which is completely heterogeneous to something else is "more" or "less" than that thing? The fixing of wages, as well as of prices, which are the operations allegedly reserved to commutative justice, are the two valves or channels through which there pass the distribution of income and therefore the distribution of ownership (which is, as we have seen, accumulated income). To attempt to establish them without any reference to distributive justice is to overlook the most elementary economic science.

Consequences for the Theory of Law

If the objection is made that a business is an entity of private law and not public law, my first reponse is that "in essence" this might be true, considering the definitions which are used. In any case, however, this doctrine, which Pius XII makes his own, unquestionably presupposes that the private ownership of the business has been legitimately acquired. Pius XII and his advisers Gundlach and Hürth suppose this as the condition which is absolutely necessary for the essential relationships affirmed by them to be applied to reality and to have effective validity. The means of production and the entity itself which possesses them as capital cannot legitimately enter the area reserved to private law if the private ownership did not begin legitimately. But it is historically impossible for differentiating ownership to have come into existence except through violence and spoliation.

With this terminology we are touching on one of the most burning and central problems of the philosophy of law: the distinction between private law and public law. The greatest jurist of this century, Hans Kelsen, has forthrightly denied that such a distinction or demarcation exists.[22] What is of great consequence is that Nazi jurists denied this distinction with equal resolution; they asserted—very much in accord with their despotism—that every matter, regardless of how private it might appear, was of concern to the government.

In classical Roman law the relationship or contract between individuals pertained to private law, while any relationship in which one of the parties was the State (*status rei romanae*) pertained to public law. An explanation involving a theory of the interest at stake was developed to clarify and establish this distinction. It happens, nevertheless, that there are contracts between the State and a private group (for example, a construction company) which according to Roman theory and by definition should be of public law but in reality are governed by principles which are exactly the same as those which are used to judge any transaction between private companies, nor does it seem that it should be otherwise.

To avoid, therefore, the vagueness in which the theory of the interest at stake leaves the matter, a theory involving the nature of the relationship was invented. According to this, there is public law when the relationship between the individuals and the State is one of subordination, that is, when the State acts in its character of sovereign power. But even if these definitions are accepted, García Máynez very rightly objects, "When should the State be considered a sovereign entity and when is it on an equal level with private parties? . . . Is there a firm criterion to establish this?"[23]

In the positivistic approach this question is easily resolved by saying that the State itself decides when it is acting as a sovereign power and when it is not, that is, when a matter is of public law and when it is of private law. But in positivistic terms Kelsen is much more logical when he asserts that everything is public law, since the State itself determines the juridical status of each of its affairs; thus with all correctness it can consider that in affairs between individuals the private persons act as delegates of the State in settling a question, especially if we bear in mind that the law and the law alone gives a contract between private parties legal validity.

The fear of the antipositivists with regard to the great power and despotic all-pervasiveness of the State is very justifiable; our century is perhaps much more aware of these things than previous ones. But I do not think that the distinction between private law and public law is going to be of much help in checking despotism if in the last analysis it is the State itself which draws the dividing line according to its own good pleasure. Moreover if the rich can ravage me daily with impunity through the distribution of income, it does not make much sense to take precautions—theoretical ones at that—to prevent the government from occasionally ravaging me.

The antipositivists insist on the theory involving the nature of the relationship: The State acts as sovereign power when it is the "common good" which is at stake. This is indeed a penetrating clarification, for the common good is not, as a mechanistic approach would have it, simply the sum of individual goods; it is a totality (in a gestalt sense) in which the whole is much greater than the sum of the parts. But even if we accept this clarification, the problem arises again practically intact. It is well to bear in mind that according to the juridical theories of the French Revolution and its triumphant bourgeoisie, the distribution of wealth was a matter that was completely outside the competence of the State and was reduced more than any other to simple private law; it was considered a matter of relationships and transactions between private parties, while the State was concerned specifically and solely with "common good" as such.

Both papal doctrine and Western legislation have declared themselves, at least in principle, in opposition to this juridical conception of the bourgeoisie. Indeed, since *Rerum novarum,* its first significant document, the papal doctrine maintained and has continued to maintain that without any shadow of a doubt it is the State's role to intervene in favor of the weak and needy and not allow the big fish to continue eating the little ones. And the existence of specific labor legislation in Western countries demonstrates just by its presence that the problem of distribution is considered to be not simply a question of private law; if that were so the Napoleonic civil code would be enough to regulate the contracts between worker and employer with the same "impartiality" with which it regulates relationships between other kinds of private persons. The fact that the States have decided to create specific labor legislation demonstrates that they recognize, whether willingly or unwillingly, that the problem of distribution pertains to the State as such; from the beginning the doctrine of the popes has been in agreement with this notion. The redistributive function of taxes has also been generally accepted; the same recognition is implied here.

But all this means that the State acts as sovereign power when it intervenes in distribution. And so we are faced once again with the problem of the distinction between public and private law, which seemed to be so neatly delineated by means of the concept of the "common good." For if the distribution of income (and therefore of wealth) is a problem that pertains to the functions proper to the State, it is thereby recognized that the State acts as sovereign power not only when it defends or promotes the "common good" as such.

Because of these facts—especially the papal position, which in principle and even without drawing out the consequences is against the restriction of the problem of distribution to the realm of private law—it seems to me highly inconsistent to assert that business is merely an entity of private law. As a unit of productive collaboration, business is perhaps the most important and decisive channel through which distribution passes. Just as it is impossible to establish wages and prices by a commutative justice allegedly disconnected from distributive justice, it is also impossible to enclose business in the realm of private law disconnected from public law.

We say this keeping in mind the realities and advances which have been accepted in the West. Willingly or unwillingly, openly or tacitly, the West has had to admit, at least in principle, that it is the role of the State and public law to watch over with a criterion of distributive justice a series of operations which for long and unfortunate centuries were considered to be the exclusive domain of private law and commutative justice. In all this the Bible goes much further and deeper than all the Western jurists; for the Bible law is nothing like the "neutral arbitration" which the Greco-Roman tradition imposed on us, a so-called neutral arbitration whose unimpeded task is to preserve the status quo by overcoming with force whoever challenges it. For the Bible, as we shall see in chapter 4, law consists in finally achieving justice for the poor and oppressed of this world. Completely opposite to the defense of the status quo, the realization of justice not only subverts it, it also demands that we abolish the State and the law. This understanding coincides with that of Marx; the West has tried to cover this over, even by theological means.

Besides those we have mentioned, there have been various asystematic irruptions of the sense of justice, implicit recognitions that the mental system itself of the West is unacceptable (we need not speak here of the real, effective system). In the first place there was the unsettling introduction of the idea of "social justice" by Pius XI (*Divini redemptoris,* no. 52). Then there was Pius XI's exhortation to "modify somewhat the wage contract with elements of a contract of partnership (*Quadragesimo anno,* no. 65). There was John XXIII's insistence that in self-financing enterprises, "at least in the future," the workers should become co-owners (*Mater et Magistra,* nos. 75-77), and this affirmation by Paul VI to employers: "There must be something fundamentally wrong, a radical insufficiency *in the system itself,* if it gives rise to such social reactions."[24] And there is the fundamental rejection by *Populorum progressio* of "material gain [as] the key motive for economic progress, competition as the supreme law of economics" (no. 26).

The first on this list of outbreaks of a sense of justice demonstrates very well that they do not fit into the tradition inherited from the Greeks and made into the backbone of Western civilization: The tractarians simply do not know what to do with the term "social justice." And I do not refer only to the jurists in the universities, who have practically ignored it completely. I refer to the Catholic authors as well. We need only cite the contrasting and disparate definitions of "social justice" offered by, among others, Messner, Calvez and Perrin, Pitarque, Nell-Breuning, and Bigo.[25] In the Western mental system there is no room for the much considered "social justice." Even the most elementary sense of justice is incapable of reaching an understanding and agreement with a system in which distributive injustice, because it is not commutative, dispenses with restitution. All the palliatives which try to cover over this absurdity are only apologies for the status quo. Even the most elementary moral consciousness of justice chokes in the strait jacket of a system in which commutative operations can be considered and regulated without regard to distribution, and this when the distribution of income has no other channels through which to pass than the so-called commutative operations. Thus moral conscience burst forth and postulated an unknown social justice, to see if perhaps that would break the blockade. But it is futile. We must choose between the Western system and justice.

The problem runs deeper. In the Western theologico-philosophical system (and I am not overlooking its many varieties), the social problem is new. I cannot sufficiently emphasize this fact. Derived from Plato and Aristotle, Western culture—whose generative epicenter was and continues to be "Christian" theology-philosophy—has been inevitably aristocratic, privileged, incapable of perceiving the most massive, tragic, and urgent reality of our history. Its humanism was and is a humanism of thought—a mental, aesthetical humanism. And its "man" is an abstraction, a Platonic essence valid *semper et pro semper,* not real flesh-and-blood humanity, a humanity of blood and tears and slavery and humiliations and jail and hunger and untold sufferings. When after agelong resistance and obduracy, this culture finally agreed condescendingly to consider the existence of the social problem, it necessarily had to assign it the place of a footnote, a tangent, a complementary collateral question acceptably marginal to the system. The cultural system had been structured with complete disregard of the social problem; the social problem in no way prevented the system from being monolithic and flawless. And so the system cannot now confront the problem in its true dimensions without destructuring itself completely. Anyone who believes that a total change of attitude is possible without a total change of the mental system does not know what a mental system is.

Notes to Chapter 1

1. Tomás G. Allaz, "El derecho de los postergados," in *La Iglesia, el subdesarrollo y la revolución* (Mexico, D.F.: Nuestro Tiempo, 1968), pp. 200-38; Pierre Bigo, *La doctrine sociale de l'Église* (Paris: Presses Universitaires de France, 1965), pp. 238-47.

2. Thomas Aquinas, *Summa Theologica,* II-II, q. 66, a. 2.

3. Allaz, "Derecho," p. 211.

4. Pius XII, *AAS* 33 (1941), p. 210.

5. Bigo, *Doctrine sociale,* p. 373.

6. Cf. Ifigenia M. de Navarrete, *La distribución del ingreso y el desarrollo económico de México,* no. 10 (Mexico, D.F.: Ediciones de la UNAM, 1960), pp. 79-80.

7. Ibid., no. 11, p. 83.

8. Cf. L. J. Zimmerman, *Geschichte der theoretischen Volkswirtschaftslehre* (Cologne: Bund-Verlag, 1954), pp. 126-53.

9. Karl Marx, *Economic and Philosophic Manuscripts of 1844,* ed. Dirk J. Struik, trans. Martin Milligan (New York: International Publishers, 1964), p. 106.

10. See below pp. 46-47.

11. John Chrysostom, "In 1 Tim," *PG* 62, col. 562-63; the italics are mine.

12. John Chrysostom, "In 1 Cor," *PG* 61, col. 86.

13. Jerome, "Carta 120," *PL* 22, col. 984; the italics are mine.

14. Basil, "Homily on Luke," *PG* 31, col. 277.

15. Ambrose, "De Nabuthe," *PL* 14, col. 747; the italics are mine.

16. Ambrose, *PL* 15, col. 1303.

17. Augustine, "De trinitate," *PL* 42, col. 1046.

18. Joachim Jeremias, *The Parables of Jesus* (New York: Scribner's, 1963), p. 195; Walter Grundmann, *Das Evangelium nach Markus,* 4th ed. (Berlin: Evangelische Verlagsanstalt, 1968), pp. 213-14; Rudolf Bultmann, *The History of the Synoptic Tradition,* trans. John Marsh (Oxford: Blackwell, 1963), p. 105;

Norman Perrin, *Rediscovering the Teaching of Jesus* (London: SCM Press, 1967), p. 143.

19. See below pp. 58-59 and 93-94.

20. See the commentary and translation by Karl Elliger, *Das Buch der zwölf Kleinen Propheten II,* 6th ed., ATDeut 25, 1967, pp. 41-48.

21. Pius XII, Address of May 7, 1949, *AAS* (1949), p. 283; Address of June 3, 1950, *AAS* (1950), p. 485; Address of January 31, 1952, *L'Osservatore Romano,* February 1, 1952.

22. Cf. Hans Kelsen, *Teoría general del estado* (Mexico, D.F.: Editora Nacional, 1965), pp. 105-20; and *Teoría pura del derecho,* 6th ed. (Buenos Aires: Editora Universitaria, 1968), pp. 180-85. English versions: *General Theory of Law and State,* trans. Anders Wedberg (New York: Russell, 1961); *The Pure Theory of Law,* trans. Max Knight (Berkeley and Los Angeles: University of California Press, 1967).

23. Eduardo García Máynez, *Introducción al estudio del derecho,* 16th ed. (Mexico, D.F.: Porrúa, 1969), pp. 134-35.

24. Paul VI, Address to UNIAPAC, June 8, 1964, *Ecclesia* (Madrid), July 4, 1964.

25. Johannes Messner, *Das Natur-Recht,* 4th ed. (Innsbruck: Tyrolia Verlag, 1960), pp. 378-84 and 930-38; English version: *Social Ethics: Natural Law in the Western World,* rev. ed., trans. J. J. Doherty (St. Louis and London: Herder, 1965); Jean-Yves Calvez and Jacques Perrin, *The Church and Social Justice: The Social Teachings of the Popes from Leo XIII to Pius XII (1878-1958)* (Chicago: Henry Regnery, 1961), pp. 133-61; Felipe Pitarque, *Curso de sociología pontificia,* 3rd ed. (Barcelona: Casulleras, 1961), pp. 366-69; Nell-Breuning, *Herders Wörterbuch,* part 2, pp. 35-44; Bigo, *Doctrine sociale,* pp. 219-30.

Chapter Two

The God of the Bible

We are seeking the "way of thinking" proper to the Bible, and if we begin by distinguishing between the God of the Bible and the gods knowable through philosophy, it is because our whole understanding of the Bible and the meaning of revelation depends on this distinction. Beginning here also has the advantage of eliminating once and for all the impression that this book is an attempt to make Marx and the Bible coincide. The reader is not going to find here another book on the "God is dead" theme or on the much-discussed "secularization," nor the nth attempt to "recover" the atheists by making them see that, although they might say that they deny the existence of God, deep down they accept it. We have had more than enough apologetics in recent centuries, and in my opinion the atheist has the right to be an atheist in peace without someone continually interpreting his position as undercover theism. I am not reducing the Bible to Marx nor Marx to the Bible. There have already been enough of these harmonistic efforts. We now establish the fundamental point that the coincidence does not exist. Let us put our cards on the table. I am not attempting to prove anything; I only wish to understand what the Bible says.

But this is exactly what prevents me from sparing the reader from the technical minutiae of exegesis. I do not believe in those who say, "Could you summarize in a few words what the Letter to the Romans says?" If it could have been expressed in a few words, Paul would not have used so many. The reader will have to have his Bible on hand the

35

whole time. This is not a book to be read, but a book to be studied. I apologize for this only partially; some day we will have to give up completely the very common idea that to interpret the Bible is a matter of the mind of the interpreter, since the Scripture has various "meanings" and each adopts the one which "moves" him most or suits him best. Such a belief has been promulgated by conservatives to prevent the Bible from revealing *its* own subversive message. Without recourse to this belief, how could the West, a civilization of injustice, continue to say that the Bible is its sacred book? Once we have established the possibility of different "meanings," each as acceptable as any other, then the Scripture cannot challenge the West. If one of these "meanings" were capable of doing so, nothing obliges us to take it seriously. Each person can legitimately accept the meaning which best suits his own thinking and temperament; that is why there are various meanings. If we find Matthew's assertion that "the gentle. . .shall seize upon the whole earth" (5:5) to sound too earthy, it is easy to "interpret" the statement, saying that it refers to the domain of the heart; and everything continues peacefully as it was.

Here we want to take the Bible seriously. Since many of the "interpretations" have been crystallized in the translations which the reader might have on hand, it is necessary to refer to the original texts when the exact meaning of what we are considering depends on these texts. If I refer to Hebrew or Greek words, it is to explain and justify a translation with the reasons that I will mention in each instance. In any case the presentation will be understandable to those who do not know Greek or Hebrew. The only thing that I am presupposing on the part of the reader is an average university-level education, approximately the same as in the previous chapter.

The Prohibition of Images of Yahweh

As Zimmerli observes, "the invisible spiritual-visible material antithesis, with which we have tried to understand the Second Commandment, originates in an idealist mentality, not in the biblical mentality."[1] He refers to the commandment which in the Decalogue of the biblical text occupies the second place: Exod. 20:4-6; Deut. 5:8-10. Of course, it is images of Yahweh which the commandment prohibits from being made and venerated, as modern Scripture scholars have pointed out,

and not images of other gods, as was believed for a long time. This error
had as a logical consequence the identification of this commandment
with the first, which prohibits having other gods, and thus the
suppression of the Second Commandment in the Christian Decalogue
which became traditional.²

Zimmerli's viewpoint, which is common to modern exegesis, rightly
excludes any facile interpretation of the prohibition of images of
Yahweh which would hold that the prohibition emerged from the
spiritual-material antinomy and that the commandment in question
hoped to prevent the Israelites from forgetting the spirituality of
Yahweh.

It is not that scientific exegesis denies the difference between spirit
and matter or asserts that the God of the Bible is material. It does not
put into the least doubt the validity of these concepts of Christian
dogmatics and philosophy. It only asserts that that is not what the
Bible wishes to teach when it emphatically prohibits the making of
images of Yahweh. The reason given to us in Deut. 4:12 for the
prohibition is that when Yahweh revealed himself, "you heard the
sound of words, but saw no shape; there was only a voice." Hearing is as
material (or spiritual) as sight; indeed psychology teaches us that sight
is more immaterial. When in Gen. 3:8 the Yahwist tells us that Adam
and Eve heard Yahweh's footsteps as he walked through the Garden of
Eden (and there is a similar passage in 2 Sam. 5:24), the least that we
can say is that the matter of the immateriality of Yahweh was not
important enough to the biblical authors for them to proclaim a
commandment about it. And when in Exod. 33:23 Yahweh assures
Moses that Moses may see Yahweh's back but not his face, it is obvious
that what the Bible tells us does not coincide with our concern to
distinguish between the material and the immaterial, though this
concern may be quite valid. I will go even further: The dogmatic
demonstration of the spirituality of God can be made deductively with
biblical arguments and is perfectly legitimate and irrefutable; but this is
not the concern of the biblical authors when, convinced as they are of
the true nature of the God of Israel, they emphatically prohibit the
making of images of him, for example, in Deut. 4:9-28.³

Besides the hypothesis of interpretation which contrasts the material
image with an immaterial God to explain the prohibition of images,
another hypothesis has been proposed: The commandment was to

prevent the worshippers from confusing the representation with what was being represented. This hypothesis supposes that we are a very superior people and that they were in such a primitive stage of the development of the human mind that they confused or might confuse the representation with what was being represented. I do not hesitate to cast aside this facile hypothesis, which today is accepted by no serious exegete. Von Rad and Ouellette as well as the noted specialists in the Decalogue Stamm and Andrew have established that no people of that period confused or identified the image with the divinity which it represented.[4] They were perfectly able to distinguish between the god whom they worshipped and the statue or image of the god, just as we are. Neither Yahweh nor Moses nor the sacred authors had any reason to caution against a confusion which would not have occurred to anyone.

There is also a third hypothesis: The Bible wishes to emphasize the transcendence of God. Note here the hermeneutical mechanism operative in this progression of explanations, each coming to the aid of the previous one when it can no longer be sustained: The unadmitted tendency is to keep the Bible from saying anything that we do not already know. The pretext is to proceed "from the already known," according to the methodological precept of Aristotle; the result is to "reduce" the biblical message to eternal truths already deductively known within our own system.

Coming to the point, what, in this case, is meant by "transcendence"? It was not necessary to teach that God cannot be identified with things, for no one was tempted to think that he could be. Does the word "transcendence" in the hypothesis in question mean something more than the nonidentification of God with things? If so, what? And with what scriptural basis is it asserted that this something more is the intention in the Second Commandment? Of course God is transcendent, but the biblical prohibition of images of Yahweh does not speak of transcendence; rather it affirms a close relationship, that of the voice (cf. Deut. 4:12), which penetrates very deeply into a person and does not put God far from the world and people.

There is a passage which has a meaning very different from what we usually understand by transcendence, yet it probably has something to do with our problem. In Gen. 1:26 God says, "Let us make man in our image and likeness." And in the following verse he says, "So God created man in his own image; in the image of God he created him; male and female he created them." There exists, therefore, in this world something which, according to the Bible, is indeed the image of God. I am not against the idea of transcendence if we understand it in a way which faithfully accords with Scripture, but let us agree that this teaching of Genesis on the image of God is quite far from what we usually understand by transcendence.

Perhaps we were on the wrong trail when we compared Gen. 1:26-27 with the prohibition of images of Yahweh, for the problem is made even more difficult when we see that Deut. 4:16 also prohibits representing Yahweh by a human figure or image, and in Rom. 1:23 Paul shows that he is convinced that this prohibition is of great importance. If God himself made man in his own image, why should it be forbidden to represent God through an image, even when it is human?

The reason which Deut. 4:12 gives us is definitive: "You heard the sound of words [*debarim*] but you saw no shape; there was only a voice."

This passage might increase our perplexity. But if we have looked to Gen. 1:26-27, we must also consider Gen. 9:6. Its lapidary formula gives us a clue for understanding why the first passage so greatly emphasized the idea that God created man in his own image: "He who sheds man's blood shall have his blood shed by man, for in the image of God man was made." This passage must have some relationship with our problem, for here we have the command "You shall not kill" of what we call the Decalogue and Deut. 4:13 calls "the Ten Words" (*debarim*), immediately after telling us in 4:12, "You heard only the sound of words." But the problem remains: Why is there a prohibition of images of God, even human images, if the Bible insists that man is the image of God? Evidently there is a great difference between a real man and an image, even if it has a human figure. The image does not speak; it enjoins no commandment, no imperative; it does not prohibit murder. The real man does; and the Bible does indeed consider the real man, the flesh-and-blood man, to be the true and legitimate image of God.

If this line of reasoning is not mistaken, it also explains why Paul, in his pregnant statement in Rom. 1:18-32 (which in vv. 22-23 deepens our understanding of Deut. 4:15-19) begins by speaking against "the injustice of men who *by their injustice* are suppressing the truth" (v. 18). As we see in v. 25, Paul is speaking of "the truth of God," the true essence of God. And Paul asserts that by their injustice men are suppressing this truth of God. If he had said that they were suppressing it with falsity or lies or error or a lack of logic, there would be nothing noteworthy about his statement; but he says that it is by injustice that they are suppressing this truth. Perhaps this idea is related to 2 Cor. 4:2 and 5:11, where he says that his message is directed to the conscience; the point is that to try to grasp his message with some other faculty of the soul is necessarily to falsify it.

Let us for the moment leave aside the other passages which seem to be related to the prohibition of images of Yahweh and keep to the reason for this prohibition which is put forth by Deut. 4:12, namely, the contrast between seeing and hearing (to be sure, it is a question of hearing "the Ten Words," according to Deut. 4:13). If we take this reason seriously, the God of the Bible cannot be grasped as a neuter theme; he stops being God the moment his injunction ceases. And man has many resources at his disposal to cause this command to come to an end. He need only objectify God in some way. At that moment God is no longer God. Man has made him into an idol; God no longer commands man.

The relationship which is established between the God of the Bible and man has this special characteristic: Man enters into it only insofar as he himself effectuates it. If man breaks off the relationship, if in any way he neutralizes his being-commanded, it is no longer God whom he worships, it is no longer Yahweh. According to ontology, God first exists and then later enjoins his imperative; but I wonder if the ontological viewpoint is adequate for understanding the central message of revelation. This imperative, nonneutralizable relationship is essential to the God of the Bible; it is his way of existence, in contrast to the other gods. He is the only nonobjectifiable God.

In Rom. 1:18-32 Paul is very conscious of this difference. But he adds something of utmost importance. Otto Michel correctly observes, "Israel was obliged to submit to the voice, to the sound of the words, and renounce all images. . . . For Paul the Gentiles are under the same obligation as Israel."[5] At first sight it seems that this is a completely arbitrary demand on Paul's part, but in reality it is the moment in which his theo-logy reaches, in its simplicity, its greatest depth. When in

Rom. 1:23 Paul reproaches the Gentiles for representing the divinity in a human image, he evidently does not believe that the prohibition of Deut. 4:16 is a merely positive precept binding only on Israel. Rather, it is a question of something essential, for the God known by the Gentiles (*gnontes ton Theon*, Rom. 1:21) is the same Yahweh, the God of Israel, to represent whom, to objectify whom is to break off the imperative relationship. And without this relationship God ceases to be God and is made into an idol. Paul explicitly affirms that the Gentiles knew the true God; it is after he says that they exchanged him for images (vv. 22-27) that he concludes that "they refused to acknowledge God" (v. 28).

For our purposes the most striking thing about the passage is that the Gentiles knew this same God of Israel. Paul evidently supposes that they knew him in the moral imperative of justice, outside of which he is no longer God. As we see in Rom. 2:14-15, "When Gentiles who do not have the law naturally fulfill what is prescribed by the law, without having the law they are the law for themselves, as those who show that they have the work of the law written in their hearts. Their consciences and their conflicting judgments which accuse or defend are called as witnesses." And in Rom. 2:29 we read, "The real Jew is the one who is inwardly a Jew, and the real circumcision is in the heart—something not of the letter but of the spirit; such a man receives his commendation not from men but from God."

It is apparent that this notion is what is being considered in Rom. 1 as well, because *gnontes ton Theon* of v. 21 is taken up again in v. 32 by *to dikaiōma tou Theou epignontes*; that is, "knowing God" is taken up again in "knowing well enough God's demand for justice."[6] Also *dikaiōma* is the same term that is used in 2:26 and this makes it possible to understand why "by their injustice they are suppressing the truth [of God]" (1:18). It is important to note that in Deut. 4:14 (Septuagint), *dikaiōma* in the plural is used as a synonym of "the Ten Words" of Deut. 4:13. This God, perceived essentially as a demand for justice, ceases to be God at the moment in which he is objectified into any representation and thus ceases to command.

When Otto Kuss interprets Rom. 1:18-32 by saying that Paul accuses the Gentiles of "conscious idolatry" or of "knowingly idolizing," he touches on an important point, namely, guilt.[7] But frankly the term "conscious idolatry" seems meaningless to me. Without doubt Paul says that they are inexcusable (v. 20c) and deserve to die (v. 32), and he knowingly and consciously develops the thesis that all the transgressions which he enumerates in the passage stem from idolatry. But he does not affirm, nor even insinuate, that the guilt of idolatry consists in consciously worshipping as God something that is not God. The verb *(met)ēllaxan* (vv. 23, 25, 26) 'exchanging,' 'confusing,' rather suggests the contrary. The same is true of *emataiothēsan en tois dialogismois autōn* 'all their thinking has ended in futility' (v. 21).

To be sure, he in no way accuses them of rusticity or of an inferior level of culture which is incapable of, as the philosophers say, "rising to the metaphysical level." On the contrary, in v. 22 he levels his aim on the Greco-Roman culture, the most advanced of its day, and says, *phaskontes einai sophoi emōranthēsan* 'they boast of their wisdom, but they have made fools of themselves.' Certainly he is not indicating crudeness or natural stupidity as the cause of idolatry, for then it would not be blameworthy. But in any case "knowingly idolizing" seems impossible to me, and in the text there is no indication that that is what Paul means.

In v. 25 he says, "They have given up the truth of God for a lie," they confused the true nature of God with deception, the true God with a false one.[8] This operation, which fixes God by objectifying him, is a deception. God thus no longer commands us; he loses his ethical essence, and ceases to be God. But this is a self-deception by which we drive away the imperative. In v. 18 Paul attributes this self-deception to "the injustice of men who by their injustice are suppressing the truth." It is the human disposition of injustice which makes us neutralize the command in which, and only in which, God is God.

I mentioned a moment ago that the most striking thing about this passage is that, according to Paul, this true God known by the Gentiles is the same God of Israel, the one spoken of in Deut. 4 and in the commandment of the Decalogue which prohibits images of Yahweh. I repeat: The God of the Bible does not "be" first and later reveal himself. He *is* only in the word which commands, Deuteronomy tells us. "And the word was God," the Fourth Evangelist says (John 1:1). I do not think there is any other way to understand what Paul means when he unhesitatingly says that the pagans have knowledge of the true God and just as emphatically says that they have become idolaters. As Kuss has said, "Paul does not say that the Gentiles are able to know the invisible God, but that they have known him."[9]

As we shall see, the biblical authors are extremely aware that their God is not to be confused, that he is radically different from any other god. Without exaggeration it could be said that the Bible speaks of nothing but this difference. The study of the prohibition of the images of Yahweh which we have made is only a step, but I think it is a decisive one. Allow me to summarize the results of this study with the philosophical statements formulated by Bultmann more than forty years ago. They confirm what we have said, for they reflect a deep understanding of biblical books and passages different from the ones we have studied. The question is this: What does it mean to speak of God?

If by "to speak of God" we mean "to speak about God," it means absolutely nothing; it would suppose placing oneself outside of that which is spoken about, in which case it would no longer be God. The meaning of propositions of universal validity consists precisely in that they prescind from the concrete situation which is spoken of. But to situate myself outside of the demand which God makes on my concrete existence is to speak of something else, not of God. The antithesis between materialism and idealism is totally irrelevant in the matter, for both philosophies are constructed by prescinding from my concrete existence. I am enclosed in the world as one object among others. World views only enable man to be distracted from his own responsibility. I understand myself as an instance of the general rule, and automatically I shake off the obligation of taking seriously the moment in which for me God is reality. It does not help if I consider myself a subject in the midst of objects, for this subject continues to be regarded from outside. Nor is the matter corrected if the "world view" is theistic or Christian and considers everything as founded in God and the laws and forces of the cosmos as having their origin in God; God is still regarded as an object, and the relationship between God and man is still contemplated from outside as much as before. This world, with its god and all, is still as atheistic as before. Only when God commands me and obliges me can I really speak of God.[10]

By citing these penetrating reflections of Bultmann, first published in 1925, we are collaterally preparing material for a particular question of some importance: Is this biblical manner of knowing God thus because it is the biblical manner of *knowing* or because it is a question of knowing *God*? I will not now deal with this question, which seems to me most relevant for an investigation of the origin of the dialectical mentality, but I will say that the question can also be formulated in this way: Is Kierkegaard the ultimate origin of existentialism or is it the God of the Bible as unmistakably contrasted to all the other gods? The relationship between dialectics and existentialism can be seen in Ernst Bloch and in Sartre.[11] Surely the biblical way of knowing, a focal point of the Bible's irreconcilability with Western civilization, is characteristic of all knowledge in the Bible.[12] But is it due to the Hebrew culture and mentality or is it that the whole Hebrew mind and attitude were engraved with the self-revelation of a God whose being is to command us and who therefore cannot be neutralized into any objectification without ceasing to be God?

To Know Yahweh

To understand the reason for the prohibition of images of Yahweh is only a first step, though a decisive one. The command in which God is God is not just any injunction whatsoever, with no defined content. Even more, the depth of this uncompromising and antiontological actualism is impossible without a defined content.

Fortunately the Bible treats this question thematically, allowing no room for divergencies in interpretation:

Shame on the man who builds his house by not-justice,
and completes its upstairs rooms by not-right,
who makes his fellow man work for nothing,
without paying him his wages,
who says, "I will build myself an imposing palace
with spacious rooms upstairs,"
who sets windows in it,
panels it with cedar, and paints it vermilion.
Are you more of a king
for outrivalling others with cedar?
Your father ate and drank like you,
but *he practiced justice and right*;
this is good.
He defended the cause of the poor and the needy;
this is good.
Is not this what it means to know me? It is
Yahweh who speaks.

(Jer. 22:13-16)

Here we have the explicit definition of what it is to know Yahweh. To know Yahweh is to achieve justice for the poor. Nothing authorizes us to introduce a cause-effect relationship between "to know Yahweh" and "to practice justice." Nor are we authorized to introduce categories like "sign" or "manifestation of." The Bible is well acquainted with these categories, and when it means them, it says so. A fundamental hermeneutical principle is at stake here: What possibility are we leaving to the sacred authors of affirming a strict identification if, whenever they attempt it, we "interpretatively" put in our categories of "sign of" or "cause" or "manifestation," which imply duality? If we were to use this procedure the biblical authors could never tell us anything which our theology did not already know.

As G. J. Botterweck observes in his careful monograph on the knowledge of God in the Bible, this passage of Jeremiah expresses what all the prophets understand by knowing Yahweh, that is, interhuman justice.[13] In Hosea we read:

There is no goodness, no compassion,
no knowledge of God in the country,
only perjury and lies, slaughter, theft,
adultery and violence, murder after murder.

(Hos. 4:1b-2)

This antithesis between "knowledge of God" and interhuman crimes demonstrates that the former is naturally understood to mean "justice among men." We also see the parallelism or synonymous relationship between "knowledge of God" and "goodness and compassion." The synonymy between to-know-Yahweh and interhuman justice is here so taken for granted that this prophet of the early eighth century B.C. includes in his testimony all the previous centuries of Israelite tradition. As H. W. Wolff points out, Hosea indifferently uses his own formula, "knowledge of Yahweh" (2:22; 5:4; 6:3), and that of the Priestly tradition, "knowledge of God" (4:1; 6:6; cf. 4:6).[14] This demonstrates that the identification to which I have been referring was made in the early periods of Israel's history. It goes back at least to the tenth century, which is sufficient for us, for the most ancient biblical books, that is, the Yahwistic work, were not composed before that time.

In the verse following the text we have cited from Hosea, we read, "Therefore the country is in mourning, and all who live in it pine away" (4:3). "Therefore" means because of the interhuman crimes just referred to. Three verses later Hosea takes up the idea again: "My people perish for lack of knowledge" (4:6), obviously for lack of the knowledge-of-Yahweh which he has just mentioned. The direct cause of the internecine destruction of the people is the lack of knowledge of

Yahweh, that is, simply speaking, the prevailing injustice. In chapter 6 he repeats this same theme of the self-destruction of the people, at least in its general lines of cruel relationships among men:

What am I to do with you, Ephraim?
What am I to do with you, Judah?
Your compassion is like a morning cloud,
like the dew that quickly disappears.
Therefore I have torn them to pieces through the prophets,
I slaughtered them with the words from my mouth,
since what I want is compassion, not sacrifice;
knowledge of God, not holocausts.

(Hos. 6:4-6)[15]

If the meaning of "compassion" in vv. 4 and 6 were not already clear in itself (*ḥesed* in the Hebrew; *eleos* in the Septuagint), in vv. 8-9 we see what kind of crimes Hosea lashes out against for their lack of compassion: murder, robbery, bloodshed.

H. W. Hertzberg very correctly comments: "Justice and right, this is the key in which the words of Amos are tuned. Goodness and to-know-God, these are characteristic of Hosea. Just as the first pair of concepts designate for the hearers of Amos' message the conduct that they are obliged to observe among themselves, in the same way Hosea's two terms indicate the behavior the Israelites should follow in the praxis of their lives. One impedes his own understanding if he thinks here of what we understand today as 'loving and knowing God,' that is, an activity between man and God."[16] H. J. Kraus summarizes the question in the same way: "Amos, Hosea, Isaiah, and Micah know only one decisive theme: justice and right."[17] The same idea is found in the splendid monograph of Sigmund Mowinckel, *Die Erkenntnis Gottes bei den alttestamentlichen Propheten.* Mowinckel insists on a point which we too have pointed out: The prophets are conscious that they do not have anything new to tell Israel about the knowledge of Yahweh; the content of their message does not originate in some vision which is inaccessible to common mortals.[18]

Let us dwell for a moment on Hos. 6:6, which I have just cited. It is quoted at crucial points by the redactor of Matthew, in 9:13 and 12:7, and is the key to this Gospel. In these passages it is seen very clearly that the New Testament understood *ḥesed* as interhuman compassion, as the translators of the Septuagint also understood very well. Indeed the strict synonymic parallelism in Hos. 6:6 between compassion and to-know-God and their corresponding contrast with sacrifice and holocausts abundantly demonstrate the meaning that the knowledge of God is understood to have with regard to interhuman relationships. This is also seen in the explicit definition of Jer. 22:16: "He defended the cause of the poor and the needy; is not this what it means to know me? It is Yahweh who speaks." The translation of *ḥesed* as *eleos* is perfect, and although we are aware of the paternalistic degeneration that the word "compassion" has suffered in the last twenty centuries, it is still the best single word to translate *ḥesed*. It is less subject to ambiguity than "love," "fidelity," etc., terms which have been used to correct the "mistake" of the Septuagint so that *ḥesed* would mean a vertical "religious" relationship—a meaning alien to this term. (To have compassion on God was evidently an idea too baroque even for the spiritualizing exegeses.) In the Hebrew Bible *ḥesed* appears together with justice (*ṣᵉdakah*) and/or right (*mišpaṭ*) in synonymic parallelism or in hendiadys in the following instances: Jer. 9:23; Isa. 16:5; Mic. 6:8; Hos. 2:21-22; 6:6; 10:12; 12:7; Zech. 7:9; Pss. 25:9-10; 33:5; 36:6-7; 36:11; 40:11; 85:11; 88:12-13; 89:15; 98:2-3; 103:17; 119:62-64.

It is difficult to imagine a more convincing proof in favor of the Septuagint translation. This is a compassion strictly related to a sense of justice. In the passages we have cited we see that it is a compassion-for-the-poor-and-oppressed, which can be identified with the indignation felt before the violation of the rights of the weak. This biblical attitude might strike Western canons as not particularly edifying; it begins with a Yahweh who because of his compassion for the enslaved assailed the oppressors "with raised hand and outstretched arm" (Deut. 4:34; 5:15; 7:19; 26:8; Exod. 6:6; Ps. 136:12; etc.) and ends with a Jesus of Nazareth who, according to Matt. 23, insults the scribes and Pharisees seven times with the title of "hypocrites," calling them "blind" five times and "stupid" once (v. 17), and in his condemnation not hesitating to teach the values of "justice, compassion, and goodness" (v. 23). But frankly I do not see how there can be an authentic compassion for the oppressed without there being at the same time indignation against the oppressor. Nor do I see how a genuine sense of justice can be described with greater depth than by the expression "com-passion for the needy."

Moreover, Hos. 6:6 thematically and intentionally contrasts "knowledge-of-God" with acts of religion. The thesis is taken up again in Prov. 21:3 with these words: "Do what is justice and right; that is more pleasing to Yahweh than sacrifice." Hos. 6:6 is a concentrated expression of the prophets' classic rebuke: "I will not accept your offerings and sacred ceremonies; what I demand is that you do justice to the poor and needy" (See Hos. 8:13; Amos 5:21-25; Isa. 1:11-17; Mic. 6:6-8; Jer. 6:18-21; 7:4-7; 11-15, 21-22; Isa. 43:23-24; Isa. 58:2, 6-10; etc.). The meaning of "to know Yahweh" is thus all the more clear, almost like a technical term: to have compassion for the needy and to do justice for them. For Wolff both $s^e dakah$ and $hesed$ are pregnantly summarized in the knowledge of God of Hos. 6:6.[19] According to him the antinomy between Hos. 4:1 and 4:2 demonstrates "that alongside an 'ethical' zone there is no mention of a second, heterogeneous 'religious' zone, as if union with God were something else alongside union with one's neighbor."[20] This exclusion of "alsoism" is perfectly accurate, but I think that in all this there is much greater depth than a simple negation of juxtapositions. There is even more here than a simple technical term would lead us to believe. Note that the teaching that we are studying does not depend on the use of the verb "to know": "Turn again, then, to your God, hold fast to compassion and justice" (Hos. 12:7).[21] And note also the well-known verse Hos. 10:12: "Sow justice for yourselves, reap a harvest of compassion, break up your fallow ground: it is time to go seeking Yahweh" (*lamed* as a sign of the accusative).[22]

Whether it is to know, to seek, or to turn to, what we are being told is of unimagined seriousness and depth. The God who does not allow himself to be objectified, because only in the immediate command of conscience is he God, clearly specifies that he is knowable exclusively in the cry of the poor and the weak who seek justice. To know God directly is impossible, not because of the limitations of human understanding but rather, on the contrary, because Yahweh's total transcendence, his irreducible and unconfused otherness, would thereby disappear. Our ability to accept him in man goes beyond any comprehension which can thematize and encompass its object. Transcendence does not mean only an unimaginable and inconceivable God, but a God who is accessible only in the act of justice.

If the Transcendent is posited as the poor and the orphan, then the metaphysical relationship with God cannot be realized by prescinding from people and things. If we perceive otherness as a defect, then we cannot see that only an absolutely irreducible Other—that of the word which speaks to me—is able to break through the solitude of my

concepts and my ontological objectifications. In the intelligibility of
the representation, I dominate what is being thought, and the distinction between myself and the object is erased; only moral conscience
goes out of itself when confronted with the cry of the weak and the
needy. It alone transcends. The relationship with God is always,
essentially, contact through a distance; the infinity of transcendence
consists in this. "He defended the cause of the poor and the needy. . . . Is
not this what it means to know me? It is Yahweh who speaks" (Jer.
22:16). The true God is not something that we can grasp or contemplate or thematize. True transcendence situates us beyond the categories of being and all the extrapolations of being. Yahweh is not
among the entities nor the existings nor in univocal being nor in
analogous being, but rather in the implacable moral imperative of
justice.

Thus the famous chapter 2 of Hosea asserts that Yahweh will
betroth Israel in justice and right and compassion and goodness so that
it might know Yahweh (Hos. 2:21-22). It has been often noted that
this passage is parallel to Jer. 31:34: "There will be no further need for
neighbor to try to teach neighbor, or brother to say to brother, 'Learn
to know Yahweh!' No, they all will know me, from the smallest to the
greatest. It is Yahweh who speaks."[23] But it is often forgotten that in
22:16, which we have considered, Jeremiah had explicitly defined what
it is to know Yahweh. Only by keeping this in mind is it possible to
understand why Hosea uses "justice and right" to indicate the contents
of the nuptial dowry (Hos. 2:21-22)! The idea is quite bizarre if we do
not keep in mind what we have been considering, namely, that Yahweh
is known only in the human act of achieving justice and compassion for
the neighbor. In Hos. 2:21-22 the Hebrew preposition b^e affects what
the bridegroom must give for the betrothal to be accomplished.[24] Hos.
2:19 says, "I will take the names of the Baals off her lips, their names
shall never be uttered again." On the other hand in vv. 21-25, after
Yahweh endows Israel with justice and right and compassion and
goodness, then he can be known by Israel and she can say to him, "You
are my God." And thus ends the chapter.

In order to understand Hos. 2:21-22, good method demanded that
we compare it with Hos. 4:1-2 and 6:6, for they too associate
knowledge-of-God and compassion. But in 4:1-2 and 6:6 these terms
describe acts of man, not of Yahweh. In 2:21-22 Yahweh as bride-

groom endows Israel with compassion; this attitude is not Yahweh's but Israel's. This is confirmed by the juxtaposition of justice and right with compassion, for it is inconceivable that the attitude of Yahweh *as bridegroom* should consist in justice and right toward the bride Israel. If Hosea's message criticizes the people for their lack of compassion and justice and right (10:12; 12:7; 4:1-2; 6:6) and of knowledge of God, in 2:21-22 he can say only that Yahweh endows the people with all this. The last *waw* of v. 22 can be only consecutive or final: "in order that you know Yahweh" or "in such a way that you know Yahweh." Thus the sublime hope of Hos. 2 coincides with that of Jer. 31:34: The whole people will know Yahweh. But we must bear strictly in mind what Jer. 22:16 has told us about the nature of the knowledge of Yahweh. The same hope is expressed in Trito-Isaiah: "Your people shall all be righteous" (Isa. 60:21).

Although Hos. 14:4 does not treat the knowledge of Yahweh as a theme, it nevertheless demonstrates it: "What we have made with our own hands we will never again call gods; for you are the one in whom orphans find compassion." The theme is very similar to that of Hos. 2, for in 2:19 Yahweh says, "I will take the names of the Baals off her lips, their names shall never be uttered again." The acute sense of justice and compassion, by which according to 2:21-22 Israel will be able to know Yahweh, is the same that in 14:4 distinguishes Yahweh from the other gods. The only difference is that Yahweh is defined as "the one in whom orphans find compassion." As Wolff says, this hemistich is the *confessio veri Dei* coming after the hemistich of renunciation: "What we have made with our hands we will never again call gods."[25] What we have said is well confirmed by the fact that other interpretations have to amputate the hemistich Hos. 14:4d by declaring it a gloss or by making it parenthetical. As Rudolph observes, these solutions are convenient but unsatisfactory because they do not explain the insertion of *this* gloss exactly at this spot.[26] Rudolph's solution is equally unsatisfactory; he modifies the consonantal text itself to read *tamin* 'perfect' instead of *yatom* 'orphan.' For his part, Wolff affirms that both the vocabulary and the idea are of Hosea, but he makes the hemistich parenthetical![27]

We will not dwell any longer on Hosea. Although I have already said that his testimony, from the beginning of the eighth century, is applicable to the entire previous biblical tradition, it is important to recognize that not only Hosea and Jeremiah take it for granted that to know God and to do justice to the needy are the same thing.

In Isa. it is equally apparent, for example, in 11:1-9. As Botterweck accurately points out, in the expression "knowledge and fear of Yahweh" (Isa. 11:2d), the objective genitive pertains to both knowledge and fear.[28] Indeed, knowledge and fear are here the same thing. Because of his knowledge of Yahweh, the Messiah will defend the poor with justice and the needy with equity; he will strike down the violent with the rod of his mouth and will kill the unjust with the breath of his lips. Justice will be his loincloth and good faith the belt around his hips" (Isa. 11:4-5). Among the Messiah's gifts (v. 2) the knowledge of Yahweh is decisive in the eyes of Isaiah; this is demonstrated in the final recapitulation, which makes a "bracketing": "They shall not hurt or destroy on all my holy mountain, *because* as the waters fill the sea, so shall the land be filled with the knowledge of Yahweh" (v. 9). This verse alone is sufficient to document the fact that the knowledge of Yahweh and the realization of justice are understood to be the same thing. It is well to keep in mind that the peace spoken of in vv. 6-8 is, according to Isaiah, the fruit of justice: "The work of justice will be peace, the effect of right will be quietness and confidence forever. My people will live in a peaceful home, in safe houses, in quiet dwellings" (Isa. 32:17-18).

The citation of Isa. 11:9 in Hab. 2:14 is indeed eloquent; the exegetes' reactions show us that "knowledge of Yahweh" absolutely cannot be understood if we do not realize that it is a strict synonym for the realization of justice. The common practice is to declare Hab. 2:14 a gloss,[29] or to do the same with at least the word "knowledge,"[30] or to avoid the problem by saying that the quotation does not have "any particular bearing on the subject."[31] But such solutions do not resolve anything, for we still have to explain the connection the glossator found between the thought of the text of Habakkuk and that of Isa. 11:9. And if indeed there is a connection in the thought then there is no reason to deny Habakkuk the idea of quoting Isaiah, for in the preceding verses he quotes previous prophecy, as can be seen by the citation of Mic. 3:10 in Hab. 2:12 and of Jer. 51:58 in Hab. 2:13. If in certain cases a solution of the problem by its elimination is inadequate it is especially so in this case. We must confront the text.

After vv. 1-5, chapter 2 of Habakkuk contains five condemnations:

vv. 6b-8; 9-11; 12-14; 15-17; 18-20.[32] Horst has very clearly pointed out the antithetical-vindictive structure of each of these five units: The punitive counterstroke is qualitatively of the same kind as the crime enunciated in the warning, "Trouble is coming to you who do such and such a thing." This intrinsic correspondence is the key idea of each of the five stanzas. Hab. 2:14 describes as an overflowing of the knowledge of Yahweh the punitive counterstroke to the crime formulated in this way: "Trouble is coming to the man who builds a town with blood and founds a city on injustice" (Hab. 2:12). The antithetical structure obliges us to consider Hab. 2:14 strictly as an overflowing of the sense of justice on the peoples which have been oppressed and enslaved by the Babylonian emperor—an overflowing of justice which would put an end to Babylonian domination (v. 13).

The technical nature of the term "knowledge of Yahweh" which we see in Hosea is here even more accentuated, more schematized and formalized. When he cites Isa. 11:9, Habakkuk presupposes that his hearers unequivocally understand this verse to mean an abundance of the sense of justice: "They shall not hurt or destroy, . . . *because* as the waters fill the sea, so shall the land be filled with the knowledge of Yahweh." "They shall not hurt or destory" is the idea which leads Habakkuk to cite this passage. But this overflowing of justice is called "to-know-Yahweh."

This identification also appears in chapter 1 of Isaiah. The chapter consists of three great rebukes, preceded by the title (v. 1) and followed by the short final section (vv. 29-31), which is a unit in itself.[33] The three rebukes are profoundly parallel in substance: They describe the sin of Judah and Jerusalem in various figures and allusions and the corresponding great punishment: vv. 2-9; 10-20; 21-28.

The theme of the third is this: "How the faithful city has become a whore, once the home of justice where right dwelt (v. 21). . . . They show no justice to the orphan, the cause of the widow is never heard (v. 23). . . . Justice shall redeem Zion and right her repentant people (v. 27). . . . Those who abandon Yahweh shall perish (v. 28)."

The theme of the second is this: "Your New Moons and your pilgrimates I hate with all my soul (v. 14). . . . Search for justice, help the oppressed; do justice to the orphan, plead for the widow (v. 17). . . . If you refuse and rebel, you shall be devoured by the sword (v. 20)."

The first rebuke describes the punishment more extensively (vv. 5-9), but the sin which the other two describe expressly in terms of injustice is formulated by the first in this way: "The ox *knows* its owner and the ass its master's stall; but Israel, my own people, has no *knowledge*, no discernment" (v. 3).

The parallelism of the three rebukes seems conclusive: What the second and the third call a lack of justice and right, the first calls a lack of knowledge of Yahweh. This is exactly the same terminology, negatively expressed, as that of Isa. 11:2, 9.

The Reason for Anticultus

Jeremiah, Isaiah, Habakkuk, and especially Hosea constitute sufficient testimony to a very particular knowledge of God. This knowledge is not a tradition within the Bible, but rather the biblical tradition itself, the irreducible novelty of the message of the Bible. It involves the unconfused difference between Yahweh and all the other gods, the unique consciousness the biblical authors have of the fact that the true God revealed himself to Israel. Before we proceed it is well to consider more deeply this central reality of revelation; only because it is central can we comprehend the radicalism and intransigence of the prophets. The anticultic polemic of the prophets is often studied as an isolated problem of limited importance, as if to prevent it from contaminating "other" teachings.

Let us express our point preventively: To hear or interpret the anticultic invective of the prophets as the oratorical impulse of a well-intentioned preacher whose assertions should be taken with a grain of salt is, in the first place, scientifically unfounded, because the same could be done with the whole Bible and there is no textual reason to prefer the anticultic passages. But second and more important, to interpret in this way is to adopt precisely the hermeneutical position in which understanding becomes impossible. If we consider the prophets to be exaggerating, we suppose ourselves to know Yahweh and revelation better than they. We reserve to ourselves the right to discriminate between what is exaggeration and what is not. And then the Bible really cannot modify our hierarchy of values, which means that it cannot tell us anything new.

With regard to Jesus' criticism of the ritual purifications—"You put

aside the commandment of God to maintain the tradition of men"
(Mark 7:8)—the Jewish exegete C. G. Montefiore offers his countercriticism: Jesus does not demonstrate that ritual observance is the cause
of their disobedience of God.[34] The Pharisees could have refuted Jesus'
statement with a simple "also," that is, "you should do one just as
much as the other." The similarity between this Jewish countercriticism
and the customary arguments of Christian morality and dogma is
obvious. In "alsoist" terms, Montefiore is irrefutable, and Jesus is the
one who is in error. Indeed not one syllable of the Gospel passage
(Mark 7:1-23; Matt. 15:1-20) gives us reason to believe that by
observing the purifications the Pharisees were lacking in charity to
anyone. The ritual question is to be considered in itself. And even if
Jesus had referred to the fact that some Jews abandoned the will of
God by using ritual observances as a pretext, he could be refuted with
equal facility: There is no reason to criticize the *use* of ritual by basing
your arguments on the *abuses.* Montefiore's countercriticism aims at
the most vulnerable point: As long as Jesus does not indicate the causal
connection between abandoning the will of God on the one hand and
ritual on the other his criticism is unfounded.

In an apologetic approach we would tend to concentrate on the fact
that Jesus attacks ritual by calling it "the tradition of men." But this
observation does not help us with regard to Montefiore. How does
human tradition hinder us in our fulfillment of the will of God?
Moreover, a few verses later, in Mark 7:15, Jesus attacks cultic precepts
which are explicitly given in the Pentateuch in Lev. 11 and Deut. 14.
And it does not help to say that the divinity of Jesus gives him the
authority to abolish divine laws, for here he does not speak as one
abolishing them nor as one attacking already abolished laws. Rather he
argues as an ordinary person would in the anticultic tradition of the
prophets. Scientifically the exegetical explanation has to be valid for
the anticultic polemic of the prophets as well as for that of Jesus; they
are of the same kind and one is the continuation of the other. Nothing
in the texts gives us the authorization to distinguish between them.

In this matter it is useless to try to distinguish between the Old
Testament situation and that created by the coming of Jesus. In Matt.
22:10-14; 13:24-30, 36-43, 47-50; 7:21-23, we see that the Gospel of
Matthew is directed to Christians; it apostrophizes those who already
proclaim Jesus as "Lord, Lord" and "in his name" perform miracles

and "prophesy" (7:21-23); he rejects them when they are "doers of injustice" (7:23). This is exactly the same reason why Yahweh rejects his worshippers in Isa. 1:10-20. Matthew addresses Christians, and his polemic against the temple, the Sabbath, and the sacrifices (Matt. 12:5-7) pertains to Christians. Matt. 5:23-24 without any doubt has to do with Christians for it (like all the antitheses in 5:21-48) involves the "greater justice" which must distinguish the followers of Jesus from the Jews (cf. 5:20). And we need not consider at length 1 Cor. 11:20-22, where Paul clearly asserts, "It is not the Lord's Supper that you are eating," when he finds out that in the Christian community of Corinth some go hungry while others are gorged.

In this matter if there are those who wish to distinguish between the Old and the New Testaments it is because they have not understood the reason for the anticultus of the prophets. And indeed this is exactly what occurred in the case of Montefiore. If he does not understand the anticultic polemic of Jesus, it is because he has not grasped the reason for the polemic of the prophets. We return to this point because it is here that the difference between the God of the Bible and all the other gods becomes unconcealable.

The customary apologetic argument is that "the prophets do not condemn cultus as such." It is thereby deduced that they anathematized only a certain kind of cultus or a certain way of rendering cultus and that they thus tended to reform the cultus or to demand the appropriate internal dispositions. This is how the prophetic anathemas are reduced to pious exhortations of spiritual guidance. But to know that the prophets did not condemn "cultus as such" we need not even open the Bible; it is enough to know that they were not Greeks or scholastics. The thesis under consideration has no more to do with the Bible than its opposite: "The prophets do not approve of cultus as such." If we decide to look at the Bible the first thing we must establish is that the prophets were quite unconcerned about "cultus as such." But we also must establish that it is impossible to reduce their anticultus to a demand for the correct dispositions in the worshipper or a demand for a reform of the cultus or a demand "to do one just as much as the other." See Amos 5:21-25:

> 21 I hate and despise your feasts,
>   I take no pleasure in your solemn festivals.
> 22 When you offer me holocausts,

I reject your oblations,
and refuse to look at your sacrifices of fattened cattle.
23 Let me have no more of the din of your chanting,
no more of your strumming on harps.
24 But let right [*miŝpat*] flow like a river
and justice [*s^edakah*] like an unfailing stream.
25 Did you bring me sacrifice and oblations in the desert
for all those forty years, House of Israel?

Here Yahweh does not demand interhuman justice "besides" cultus;
nor does he require that the cultus be reformed; nor is he asking that
the cultus be maintained but with better internal dispositions. What he
says can be summarized in this way: *I do not want cultus, but rather
interhuman justice.* Whatever we do to interpret this message in some
other way is pure subterfuge. Nor would it be objective to summarize
his message as if he said simply, "I do not want cultus." This phrase is
inseparable from what follows and what indeed carries the emphasis:
but rather interhuman justice. This is the very message of Isa. 1:10-20;
Hos. 5:1, 2, 6; 6:6; 8:13; Amos 4:4-5; Mic 6:6-8; Jer. 6:18-21; 7:4-7,
11:15, 21-22; Isa. 43:23-24; 58:2, 6-10. The message is the same
whether in the eighth century or in the seventh century or in the
postexilic period. I am not going to transcribe these passages; I insist
only on one point which is more explicit in Isa. 1:10-20 than in other
passages, namely, that prayer is also rejected:

Hear the word of Yahweh. . . .
11 What are your endless sacrifices to me?
says Yahweh.
I am sick of holocausts of rams
and the fat of calves.
The blood of bulls and of goats revolts me.
12 When you come to present yourselves before me,
who asked you to trample over my courts?
13 Bring me your worthless offerings no more,
the smoke of them fills me with disgust.
New Moons, sabbaths, assemblies—
I cannot endure festival and solemnity.[35]
14 Your New Moons and your pilgrimages
I hate with all my soul.
They lie heavy on me,
I am tired of bearing them.
15 When you stretch out your hands,
I turn my eyes away.

You may multiply your prayers,
I shall not listen.
Your hands are covered with blood,
¹⁶ wash, make yourselves clean.
Take your wrong-doing out of my sight.
Cease to do evil.
¹⁷ Learn to do good,
search for justice [*mišpaṭ*],
help the oppressed [or stop the oppressor] ;
do justice to the orphan,
plead for the widow.

(Isa. 1:11-17).

Let it be clearly understood that v. 15, which puts prayer in a list among the most diverse expressions of cultus, excludes the possibility of finding the God of the Bible by means of prayers. Now is the moment to take up again Montefiore's objection, which is that of all the harmonists of past and present: In what way does cultus hinder the prophets (or Yahweh)? It is very well that they should demand interhuman justice, but there is no reason that they should pose the dilemma between justice and cultus, between prayer-to-God and compassion on the poor.

What is certain is that the prophets do indeed pose this dilemma and with an unavoidable seriousness. In the whole Bible there is no message more serious and central than this, for on it depends our understanding of the difference between the one true God and all the other gods which we men create with our images or philosophies or theologies or religions. The dilemma between justice and cultus occurs because while there is injustice among a people worship and prayer do not have Yahweh as their object even though we have the formal and sincere "intention" of addressing ourselves to the true God. To know Yahweh is to do justice and compassion and right to the needy. If it were a question of a god accessible through direct knowledge, that is, of a nontranscendent god, there would be no dilemma. The essence of the idol is in this: We can approach it directly. It is entity, it is being itself; it is not the implacable moral imperative of justice.

The objection of naturalism and horizontalism, which should rather be directed in the first place against the entire Bible, passes over the only decisive point of revelation: *The question is not whether someone is seeking God or not, but whether he is seeking him where God himself said that he is.* This is the point of radical irreconcilability between

Greek and Western philosophy on the one hand and biblical revelation on the other: "Ontology, as a fundamental philosophy which does not call into question the self, is a philosophy of injustice."[36] If we are able to prescind from the cry of the poor who seek justice by objectifying God and believing that, because he is being, he is there as always, since being is objective and does not depend on any considerations of our minds nor on what we can or cannot do, at that very moment he is no longer God but an idol. And this is what happened to Christianity from the time it fell into the hands of Greek philosophy. When we demand the dehellenization of Christianity, what we are demanding is that idolatry not be imposed on us, for we do not wish to know any other god than the God of Jesus Christ.

There is an apparently obvious religious objection to the anticultus of the prophets: If there can be cultus only when there is justice, then there will never be cultus, for justice will never be realized. But we must in any case make one thing clear: The prophets were convinced that justice would indeed be achieved on earth (and this conviction was shared by Jesus, Paul, John, the Synoptics, the Yahwist, the Deuteronomist, the Priestly tradition, the entire Psalter, and the author of the Letter to the Hebrews). Thus cultus will be acceptable to the prophets at the time when justice has been achieved: Isa. 2:2-4 (cf. Isa. 4, Isa. 32, Isa. 9, and Isa. 11); Mic. 4:1-8; Hos. 14:2-3 (cf. Hos. 2:21-25); Zeph. 3:9-13. Note the grand message of the last part of the book of Ezekiel about the return of the glory of Yahweh to the temple; but this will occur when there are no longer hearts of stone (Ezek. 36:26). Only then— says Yahweh—"I will be your God." Note also the burning hopes of Zechariah in relation to the temple; but they will be realized when "Injustice" (*hariš'ah*) has been torn out from the holy land and carried to the land of Šin'ar (Zech. 5:5-11). *It is not a matter of excluding cultus but rather of this very clear message: first justice and then cultus.*

The objection we have been considering reveals a hermeneutical option in the deepest sense, and here Marx does indeed have something to say: Whoever is capable of resigning himself to the fact that justice will never be realized is incapable of taking the prophets seriously. Everything that they wrote, did, and said stems precisely from the fact that they did not resign themselves to injustice. To avoid problems, one can classify as utopian all the hope of the Old and New Testaments and the God who by his very essence originated this hope. But then one would have to hold to a Christ-of-private-faith, for the historical Jesus, Paul, John, and the Synoptics were convinced that the kingdom of God absolutely had to be realized. And on earth, of course.

And finally let us touch on the last objection to the anticultus of the prophets: If the people withdraw from cultus they will have even less hope of learning justice, for it is only contact with God which will teach them justice. As is obvious from what we have been saying, those who put forth this objection have not understood the reason for the anticultus. Basing themselves on the one thing that the Bible has to reveal to us—that is, the difference between Yahweh and the other gods—the prophets deny the entire presupposition of such an objection, namely, that cultus and prayer could put the people in contact with Yahweh while injustice exists on earth. The formal and sincere intention of "addressing ourselves" to Yahweh while prescinding from the cry of the needy does not make Yahweh accept and value this "as if" we were addressing ourselves to him when really we are addressing not him, but rather an idol which we decide to call Yahweh. "When you stretch out your hands, I turn my eyes away. You may multiply your prayers, I shall not listen. . . . Search for justice, and help the oppressed [or stop the oppressor]; do justice to the orphan, plead for the widow" (Isa. 1:15, 17).

It is precisely this juridical fiction of the "as if" which Jeremiah combats among the false prophets and priests of the reform undertaken by King Josiah. Jeremiah untiringly calls this reform a "lie": cf. Jer. 7:4-8, 21-23; 8:8-12; 14:11-16; 23:25-29; etc. The reform of Josiah was as well intentioned as all those undertaken by Christianity in our times. On the one hand it adopted the concern of the eighth-century prophets for the poor, the orphan, and the widow; but on the other, with regard to cultus it did not deem it prudent to wait until justice could be achieved. This is exactly the mentality we find behind the objection which we have been considering. Since it does not understand the difference between Yahweh and the other gods it does not consider that this harmonistic approach gets caught up in a vicious circle. It leads us to believe that we can enter into contact with Yahweh while prescinding from the beseeching cry of the poor and the needy.[37]

The fact seems to me to be today beyond doubt: The eighth century prophets were no longer around to oppose Josiah's reformism and the superficiality of the priests and scribes, but Jeremiah did understand how all this manifestation of good will directly hindered the people from knowing the true nature of the God of Israel. Smend is correct: If Jeremiah rejected the reform of Josiah—for the message of the prophets cannot be accepted through reforms or "integrations"—"much less can it be supposed that Amos would have acted differently."[38] The anticultic polemic of the prophets was "a battle against the exponents of a false conception of God."[39] In his detailed analysis Dobbie states that the contrast between the Josianic priests and the prophets goes beyond temperamental or professional animosity. It stems from mutually exclusive conceptions of religion.[40]

What is at the bottom of all this is a different God. And the difference goes far beyond all metaphysical questions. Only thus can we explain the Bible's lack of interest in the problem of whether or not the other gods exist. Such a question moves on the level of being, while the God of the Bible is known in the implacable moral imperative of justice.[41]

What is most significant here is that whether the other gods are entities or not is of no concern to the biblical authors. Otherwise the exegetes would not still be so perplexed by the question. The unique character of the God of Israel is irreducible to ontological questions, no matter how many efforts and analogies the philosophy derived from the Greeks might make in the belief that it can understand everything in terms of being. The Western absolutization of the ontological point of view makes us believe that this instrument of cognition is superior to that of the Bible. But we do not consider how presumptuous and even ridiculous it is to suppose that we know God better than Moses and the prophets did. And, most importantly, we do not consider that it was not because of an ethnologically specific mentality or culture that Israel knew God as it did, but it was rather because of the unconfused specificity of the one true God that a special way of knowing come into existence so that this specificity might be known.

The continuity between the Old and the New Testaments is so striking on this decisive point that it can be explained only by the peculiar nature of God himself, who revealed himself to the authors of both the New Testament and the Old. We need only compare the statements of Jeremiah, Hosea, Habakkuk, and Isaiah in regard to "knowing Yahweh," which we have already considered, with the words of John: "My dear people, let us love one another, since love is from

God and everyone who loves is born of God and knows God. Anyone who fails to love has not known God, because God is love" (1 John 4:7-8).

As Blass and Debrunner observe, the aorist tense in "has not known God" is the gnomic aorist, that is, it is absolutely valid and does not have a temporal sense.[42] Moreover, both the "anyone who fails to love" of v. 8 and the "everyone who loves" of v. 7 take for granted that the object is "his neighbor," since the initial imperative, "Let us love one another," strikes the theme of the paragraph. As Bultmann comments, "The imperative of the initial *agapōmen allēlous* leaves no doubt concerning whether *pas ho agapōn* refers to the love of neighbor, although no object is added."[43] We find the same omission of the object in 3:18; here, because of the preceding verse, there is no doubt that to love means to love one another.[44] In the fact that "to love one's neighbor" is expressed simply by "to love" Meinertz even sees a proof of how the commandment to love one's neighbor ought to dominate our whole life.[45]

So the thesis of 1 John 4:7-8 can be summarized thus: He who loves his neighbor knows God; he who does not love his neighbor does not know God. And we know that this is not a question of a romantic, very general love-of-neighbor, as is often believed, but rather it is the same teaching which we have seen in the Old Testament, as is shown by the identification between love and justice:

Everyone who loves is born of God. (1 John 4:7)
Everyone who does justice is born of him. (1 John 2:29)

The meaning of Johannine love is quite apparent in the following paragraph:

If a man who was rich enough in this world's goods
saw that one of his brothers was in need,
but closed his heart to him,
how could the love of God be living in him?
My children,
our love is not to be just words or mere talk,
but something real and active.

(1 John 3:17-18)

One of the most disastrous errors in the history of Christianity is to have tried—under the influence of Greek definitions—to differentiate between love and justice.[46]

If we keep in mind the Johannine meaning of love of neighbor, which is quite clear from the passages we have just compared, then the thesis of 1 John 4:7-8—he who loves his neighbor knows God; he who does not love his neighbor does not know God—is precisely the same as that of Jer. 22:16: "He defended the cause of the poor and the needy.... Is not this what it means to know me? It is Yahweh who speaks."[47] The sense of justice is the only love that truly gets to the heart of the matter. With great intuition Bigo points this out: "The supreme delicacy of charity is to recognize the right of the person being given to";[48] *because of this recognition, love is love* and not a humiliating paternalism, which because of who knows what mental depravities came to be confused with love, even though we can all see that it is an oppressive insult to the neighbor. Love which is not an acute sense of justice and an authentic suffering-with-my-outraged-brother, such love *does not transcend.* It is satisfied with itself although with its words it denies that it is so; and thus it remains in itself and does not transcend. If it is not equivalent to saying, "You have a complete right to this and I am not condescending to you in any way," then not even the genuine love between man and woman is able to transcend.[49]

Allow me to repeat the words of Bigo: "The supreme delicacy of charity is to recognize the right of the person being given to." And I add that without this so-called delicacy what we have is paternalism, the injurious attitude of one who "lowers himself" to inferior beings who do not deserve such condescension (*Herablassung*, as the Germans say). Love is not love without a passion for justice. The love that the Bible knows is love-justice, and this is so from the Yahwist to the Letters of John, as we see in 1 John 3:17-18, which we are considering, and in a comparison of 1 John 4:7 and 2:29. I can only make my own this paragraph of the Marxist Koschelava:

> Is it not the height of absurdity to call "humanistic" the anthropological theory which recognizes oppression and alienation as the inevitable fate of man and at the same time brands as "antihumanistic" the science of the emancipation of every kind of oppression and the abolition of alienation? When have the hypocritical sighs for the unenviable lot of mankind become more human than in the heroic and selfless struggle for the genuine equality of men?[50]

It is not delicacy to recognize the right of our neighbor, as if such a recognition "added" something to a love which already substantially existed without it. Not to see our neighbor as capable of suffering injustice is not to take him seriously. Even phenomenologically speaking, the person is not a person for me except insofar as he is capable of suffering injustice.

It is striking that the precept of Lev. 19:18—"You must love your neighbor as yourself"—which plays such a central role in the preaching of Jesus and in the whole New Testament, is given in its original vital place as a synthesis of a series of prohibitions which all concern the most rigorous justice. Lev. 19:11-18a includes prohibitions against swearing with intent to deceive (vv. 11-12), keeping back a hired man's wages (v. 13), treating the deaf with contempt (v. 14), perverting justice by favoring the poor or by subservience to the great (v. 15), spreading slander (v. 16), nursing hatred or cherishing anger (vv. 17-18a); the final synthesis of all this is to love one's neighbor as oneself (v. 18b). It is difficult to present more clearly the biblical identification between love and justice. What is certain is that, according to Luke 10:25-37, the one time that Jesus explained the meaning of "You must love your neighbor as yourself," he put forth not just any man but a man who had suffered injustice and violence and needed help from someone who was able to have "com-passion on him" (vv. 33, 37), in the sense of "compassion" (Greek *eleos*) which in the previous section I explained with reference to Hosea.

And for Matthew the law and the prophets are synthesized both in the formula "Love your neighbor as yourself" (Matt. 22:39-40) as well as in the formula "Whatever you want men to do to you, do this to them" (Matt. 7:12). For anyone without systematic preconceptions, the latter formula must appear to be a norm of the most elementary justice. ("As yourself" is the measure, not the motiviation, as Bultmann believes; in a rare moment of superficiality, he reduces this golden rule to naive egoism.[51]) Indeed in all laws this rule is the norm of equality; and equality is a matter of justice. There is no problem here except for ideological systems which try to distinguish between love and justice because they do not understand that true love discovers that it is unjust that our neighbor should suffer. Only authentic love can feel that everything that our neighbor suffers is an intolerable injustice.

Let us return to John. It is of this love that 1 John 4:7-8 affirms that he who loves his neighbor knows God and he who does not love his neighbor does not know God. This is exactly the decisive teaching of

Jer. 22:16 and of all the prophets. And just as in this teaching we find
the deepest reason for the anticultus of the prophets, in the same way
John uses this thesis as the basis for his rejection of all "direct" access
to God:

No one has ever seen God;
but if we love one another
God dwells in us
and his love is complete in us.

(1 John 4:12)

God is love
and anyone who lives in love lives in God,
and God lives in him.

(1 John 4:16)

A man who does not love the brother whom he can see cannot love
God, whom he has never seen.

(1 John 4:20)

My dear people,
let us love one another since love is from God
and everyone who loves is born of God and knows God.
Anyone who fails to love has not known God,
because God is love.

(1 John 4:7-8)

From these passages it is clear that the direct inaccessibility of God
should not be understood as in Greek philosophy, that is, that what is
immaterial is unknowable to the sight and to the other senses because
they are material, but is knowable to the intellect which is immaterial.
John does not reduce himself simply to "no one has ever seen him,"
but rather also affirms that they "have not *known* God." John's
intention is clearly directed to maintaining that God is knowable only
through one's neighbor. It is not enough to say that God is knowable
only through transforming revelation, which was the thesis of the
gnostics.[52] Unquestionably we are speaking of a God who is God only
in the revealing of himself, *in the* commanding. But this revelation and
command is not direct. It is possible *only through the neighbor who
must be loved* (love understood here in the sense we have indicated,
that is, love-justice). For John what is in question is not the limitations
and defects of our cognitive organs with regard to some object of a
category too elevated for them, an object which would be knowable

to some superhuman intellect. In John's thesis there is not even a shadow of this epistemological problem. For John the question is rather that God is not God when we try to approach him while avoiding our neighbor. This is precisely the anticultic teaching of the prophets: I do not want cultus, but rather interhuman justice.

Therefore, this is not a revealing that is a transmission of previously unpossessed data or knowledge; this is not a revealing which can be prescinded from, once these data or knowledge are transmitted, as if it were a means which already had achieved its end. Such is the case with Greek science and with all Western sciences without exception, beginning with philosophy and theology, from which the rest historically branched out as if from a trunk. In the Greco-Western approach to knowledge, the other and the others can disappear once they have fulfilled their informative or instructive task. Their contribution is absorbed by the self; it is summarized in and replaced by a representation or an affirmation, made by the self, of the extramental existence of a something. This is a transcendental affirmation of being. This operation is, in any case, an exercise of the self. It involves the disappearance of the radical otherness which, falling under the power of the thinker, loses its resistance as an exterior being. There is truth, I do not deny it: the correspondence between the intellect and the thing. But it is the intellect which possesses this same truth and makes it its own; truth becomes part of the self.

In contrast, the God of the Bible must always be present as the Other. His exteriority and otherness cannot cease without his ceasing. The pluralism constituted by the self and the Other needs, in order to exist, the movement and the attitude of the self with regard to the Other. This movement and attitude is not a species of the genus called "relationship," that is, it cannot be converted into a "theme" for an objective understanding liberated from this confrontation with the Other. In other words this movement and attitude is impervious to "reflection." Levinas brilliantly observes, the famous "impossibility of total reflection must not be posited negatively as the finitude and imperfection of a knowing subject which prevent it from reaching complete truth, but rather as the surplus of the social relation, where the subjectivity remains in face of. . . . "[53]

But this irreducible otherness, this "traumatism of astonishment" [*traumatisme de l'étonnement*] [54] is maintained only in the appeal of our neighbor who cries for justice. Without this cry we have an imagined god, not the real God. What is truly real, that is, that which is not at my disposal and does not succumb to my powers of affirmation or representation, is this imperative alone, this term of an understanding which finally penetrates beyond the object.[55] What is truly real is not that which offers itself to me to the extent that I discover it. This reality would in that case depend on my subjectivity, as in fact objects qua objects do depend on it. The cry of the poor, the widow, the orphan, and the alien is truly foreign to this world of objects. It is heterogeneous to this world; their cry is not commensurate with the objects nor with the forces that prevail in this world of objects. Its strength resides precisely in its weakness and its foreignness in this world. By this effective transcendence it judges me and this whole world.

> This gaze that supplicates and demands, that can supplicate only because it demands, deprived of everything because entitled to everything, and which one recognizes in giving (as one "puts the things in question in giving")—this gaze is precisely the epiphany of the face as a face.[56]

The God of the Bible does not affect us as something which must be overcome, encompassed, dominated, but rather precisely as the other, the entirely other, independently of us, as the one who, beyond any relationship which we can establish with him, reappears as absolute.[57] My spontaneity no longer has the last word; I am no longer alone. "All other experience is conceptual, that is, it becomes mine and depends on me." The God of the Bible, on the other hand, withdraws in the measure that my consciousness approaches him. Our relationships are irreversible; he judges me always. This impossibility of taking him unto myself is the very life of moral conscience. I am no longer alone. His demand, insofar as I heed it, increases my responsibility. I am always in relationship with another. But this relationship does not have the structure that formal logic finds in all relationships. The terms remain absolute in spite of their relationship.[58] It is the relationship which is called the moral imperative of justice. It is absolutely insuppressible. To affirm this imperative is the only way of totally rejecting idealism. To objectify this imperative is to reabsorb it into the self and to become alone again. It is to cut off transcendence, no matter how much we "ontologically" paint windows in the four walls of our prison. There is exteriority only in the cry of the oppressed who cries out for justice.

The best way of summarizing what we have said in this chapter appears in an especially archaic passage of Deuteronomy. By a most careful linguistic analysis Norbert Lohfink has discovered that this passage served as the background document for the redactor who composed Deut. 5:1 to 6:25, which is where we find the Decalogue.[59]

Knowledge and Praxis

The archaic passage of which we are speaking is Deut. 10:12-11:17. Its theme is stated as a title in the very beginning: "to love and serve Yahweh your God with all your heart and soul" (10:12). As Lohfink points out, it, was here that there originated the formulation of Deut. 6:4-5, which came to be and still is the most famous formulation of the Great Commandment. We should not forget for a moment that this is the theme of 10:12-11:17. The theology of this passage takes on all the greater importance in the measure that the original formulation of the Decalogue (approximately deducible from a comparison between the Decalogue of Exod. 20 and that of Deut. 5) itself manifests Deuteronomic, language. Jepsen has pointed this out.[60] For the last commandment in particular Moran has shown that the formulation of Deut. 5 is more ancient than that of Exod. 20.[61] Of course the vocabulary of the primitive Decalogue (deducible from the comparison we have mentioned) also shows a predeuteronomic origin which is possibly very ancient,[62] but the overall conflation with its theological characteristics seems to be Deuteronomic. In this case Lohfink's thesis obliges us to seek the source of inspiration of the theology of the Decalogue in Deut. 10:12-11:17.

Of all this long and ancient passage the part of greatest theological import, with a content most rooted in the primordial tradition of the liberation from Egypt, the part which seems to be most capable of generating the theology that we find today in the Decalogue, is Deut. 10:16-19. The initial "so" (*waw*, of logical consequence) leads us to keep in mind that vv. 16-19 is dealing with the Great Commandment stated in v. 12: to love Yahweh. This is also obvious because Deut. 30:6 repeats that the circumcision of the heart (of which 10:16 speaks) is "so that you will love Yahweh your God with all your heart and soul" (cf. 10:12). Moreover, the antiquity of Deut. 10:16-19 is evident in the expression "God of gods" (v. 17).[63] Our passage reads thus:

¹⁶ Circumcise your heart then
   and be obstinate no longer
¹⁷ *for* Yahweh your God is God of gods
   and Lord of lords,
   and great God, triumphant and terrible,
   never partial, never to be bribed.
¹⁸ It is he who sees justice done for the
   orphan and the widow,
   who loves the stranger and gives him food and clothing.
¹⁹ Love the stranger *then,*
   for you were strangers in the land of Egypt.

By the preceding context and the "then" (Hebrew *waw*) of v. 16 we
see that the circumcision of the heart is in order to be able to love
Yahweh and to hold him alone as God. Vv. 17-18, with the initial
"for," thus tell us this: The reason circumcision of the heart is needed
in order to have Yahweh exclusively as God is that only Yahweh does
justice to the forsaken. (The parallelism of this with John is striking: 1
John 4:7-8 establishes the "let us love one another" on the fact that
God is love, and in 1 John 3:17-18 it is pointed out to us that love is
love-of-the-needy.)

Note that Deut. 10:17-18 is in the indicative, while vv. 16 and 19 are
imperative. From the indicative and essentialistic nucleus (vv. 17-18)
the passage derives two imperatives: to circumcise the heart (v. 16) and
to love the stranger (v. 19). The logical derivation (cf. the two
conjunctions I have italicized) is made in the first case by means of a
."for" (Hebrew *ki*, v. 17), which gives the reason for the imperative of
circumcising the heart in order to know Yahweh. In the second case it
is by means of a "then" (Hebrew *waw*, v. 19),⁶⁴ which deduces from
the same indicative and essentialistic nucleus of vv. 17-18 the imperative of loving the forsaken.

Both imperatives, that of v. 16 and that of v. 19, are based on the
fact that Yahweh is, among all the gods, the only one who does justice
to the forsaken. I think that the synonymy is clear: To love the
forsaken is the way to circumcise the heart so as to be able to love
Yahweh exclusively. If this were not so, v. 19 would have no reason to
exist. The mandate of v. 16 and its reason in vv. 17-18 would be
enough. If "love the forsaken" is added it is becaùse the circumcision of
the heart either consists in this or it cannot be achieved without this. If
vv. 17-18 is giving reasons to circumcise the heart, the conclusion

(v. 19) should be "Circumcise, then, your hearts." But instead of this it tells us, "Love, then, the forsaken." The structure of Deut. 10:16-19 gives us, therefore, the same penetrating theology as Jer. 22:16: "He defended the cause of the poor and the needy. . . . Is not this what it means to know me? It is Yahweh who speaks."

In fact, the indisposition of the heart which Deut. 10 calls uncircumcision (and is referred to in the same way in Jer. 4:4 in contrast to the "right and justice" of Jer. 4:2), in Jer. 5:23 is described as "a rebellious, unruly heart." Jer. 5:27-28 explains its meaning:

Like a cage full of birds
so are their houses full of loot;
they have grown rich and powerful because of it,
fat and sleek.
They support the unrighteous cause,
they have no respect for justice,
for orphans' rights, to support them;
they do not uphold the cause of the poor.

If Deut. 10 was the document which inspired the redactor who composed Deut. 5, the theology which we have just seen in Deut. 10:16-19 ought to give us direction for understanding the Decalogue. The foundation of everything, "I am Yahweh your God who brought you out of the land of Egypt" (Deut. 5:6; Exod. 20:2), is the essential characterization of Yahweh as the one god whom we cannot have as God except in justice to our neighbor, because he is the God who revealed himself by doing justice. The monolatrous exclusivity of Yahweh (Deut. 5:7; Exod 20:3) does not mean cultus but rather interhuman justice. Thus there is the prohibition against representing Yahweh in an image (Deut. 5:8-10; Exod. 20:4-6; cf. above, the first section of this chapter). The mandate of the Sabbath speaks not of cultus but of rest for men (Deut. 5:12-15; Exod. 20:8-10), as Jepsen correctly notes: "Neither in the original form nor in the amplifications is there any mention of cultus but rather only rest. . . . The concern is not God but men. The Sabbath was made for man" (Mark 2:27)."[65] The previous commandment (Deut. 5:11; Exod. 20:7) prohibits the perjury which deceives the neighbor.[66] I do not have to emphasize that adultery is interhuman injustice.

As for the last commandment (Deut. 5:21; Exod. 20:17) we need only read it to dismiss the sexual-ascetic meaning that moral tradition bestowed on the Latin word *concupiscentia*. Lyonnet is correct when after a detailed study he concludes, "Revera in ipso decalogo sensus est de quovis desiderio contra iustitiam" ("Truly in the Decalogue itself the meaning is any desire which goes against justice").[67] We need only read the commandment: "You shall not covet your neighbor's house. You shall not covet your neighbor's wife, or his servant, man or woman, or his ox, or his donkey, or anything that is his" (Exod. 20:17). Because of the suppression of the prohibition of images in the Christian Decalogue this last commandment was divided in two in order to complete the number.[68] Because of this, the prohibition against coveting our neighbor's wife was more easily understood to be a prohibition independent of that against coveting the things that the neighbor possesses for his daily life. Only thus was it possible to think that antisexual motivations played some role in the Decalogue.

In the Decalogue of the Bible there is nothing but the practical sense of interhuman justice, of authentic compassion,[69] in which, and only in which, the true God reveals himself as absolutely not to be confused with other gods. Everything is said in the introductory verse: "I am Yahweh your God who brought you out of the land of Egypt" (Deut. 5:6; Exod. 20:2). The first two commandments wish only to present this God as unconfused (Deut. 5:7-10; Exod. 20:3-6); in the last eight the imperative of justice in which this God reveals himself as different from all the other gods is made inescapable.

The composition of Luke 10:25-37 demonstrates that this was also the understanding of the Decalogue in the New Testament, for, although v. 27 states the commandment of loving God and the commandment of loving the neighbor as two, the concretization of both in "Go, and do the same yourself" (v. 37) is concentrated in having compassion on the neighbor in need (v. 37a) as the Good Samaritan did (v. 33).

The thinking of Matthew is equally clear. Matt. 22:37-40 summarizes "the law and the prophets" in the two great commandments stated as two (to love God, vv. 37-38; to love our neighbor, v. 39). But Matthew likewise summarizes "the law and the prophets" in "Whatever you want men to do to you, do this to them" (7:12). He takes it for granted that the God of Israel is loved in the love of neighbor.

In Mark the rich young man wants to know *everything* which must be observed to win eternal life (10:17). The initial response of Christ, "You know the commandments," apparently has this scope: *tas entolas*

(v. 19), all the commandments which must be observed to win eternal life. And then Christ enumerates commandments of justice and love among men. He takes it for granted that this is where God is loved.

As for John, after what we have seen it is not necessary to explain more. And with regard to Paul, even today it would be difficult to formulate better than he the thesis that in one thing, in one imperative, not in two which later converge or support each other or are deduced one from the other, but in one imperative the whole law is found: "The *whole* of the law is summarized in a *single* command: 'Love your neighbor as yourself' " (Gal. 5:14). Paul himself provides the emphasis and the italics through his collocation and selection of the words: *ho gar pas nomos en heni logō peplērōtai, ktl.* Only an exegesis which confuses its own method with that of jurisprudence could forget this verse when reading the catalogue of "vices" in Gal. 5:19-21. Clearly these "vices" are of concern to Paul insofar as they hinder love of neighbor; thus he puts v. 14 at the head of the passage. And the "virtues" listed in vv. 22-23 are of concern to him only insofar as they constitute true love of neighbor. To take them out of the context in which Paul very explicitly places them and to try to understand them according to what the dictionary definitions say about them would be to set up words as idols. It would be voluntarily to become again a slave to the letter and to relapse precisely into captivity to the law, against which Paul contends with his Letter to the Galatians and with his entire work.

In this passage there is total clarity, but there is perhaps another passage which is still more eloquent, 1 Cor. 8:1-3, in which he does not make explicit, but rather takes for granted, as if it were obvious, that to love God and to love our neighbor are the same. No one denies that in this whole context the theme is intentionally love of neighbor. But suddenly we are struck by v. 3: "But any man who loves God is known by him." Paul is confuting gnosis and asserts of it that "knowledge gives self-importance; it is love that makes the building grow" (v. 1); then vv. 2 and 3 continue this contrast between gnosis and agape. He says of gnosis, "A man may imagine he understands something, but still not understand anything in the way he ought to" (v. 2). On the other hand, he says of charity, "But any man who loves God is known by him" (v. 3).

All the exegetes have rightly taken heed of the change from the active to the passive voice.[70] Indeed, this is the intentional and explicit point that Paul wants to make: With regard to knowledge (gnosis), everything depends, not on our knowing, but on our being known by God. But this surprising twist, intentionally made by Paul, has prevented the exegetes from being surprised by how naturally v. 3, calling it "love of God," continues to contrast love of neighbor with gnosis. He who has gnosis knows nothing. On the other hand, for him who loves his neighbor it is not that he knows but that he has been known by God, which is the only important thing. For our Western tradition the greatest surprise should consist in the fact that love of neighbor is called love of God. Paul does not even dwell on this; he presupposes it as taken completely for granted. (V. 3 cannot be speaking of love-of-God in the vertical sense, for this is what the gnostics say that they have; and Paul was not going to concede to them that by this they were known by God.)

Notes to Chapter 2

1. Walther Zimmerli, *Gottes Offenbarung: Gesammelte Aufsätze zum Alten Testamenten* (Munich: Kaiser, 1963), p. 244.
2. Ibid., pp. 234-48.
3. See the commentary of Pierre Buis and Jacques Leclercq, *Le Deutéronome* (Paris: Gabalda, 1963), pp. 57-61.
4. Gerhard von Rad, "Some Aspects of the Old Testament World-View," *The Problem of the Hexateuch and Other Essays,* trans. E. W. Truman Dicken (New York: McGraw-Hill, 1966), pp. 144-65; Jean Ouellette, "Le deuxième commandement et le rôle de l'image," *RB* 74, no. 4 (October 1967):504-16; J. J. Stamm and M. E. Andrew, *The Ten Commandments in Recent Research* (Naperville, Ill.: Allenson, 1967).
5. Otto Michel, *Der Brief an die Römer,* 4th ed., Meyers Komm (Göttingen: Vandenhoeck, 1966), p. 66.
6. Cf. ibid.: *Rechtsforderung.* See also "dikaiōma" in Walter Bauer, *A Greek-English Lexicon of the New Testament,* trans. and adapted by William F. Arndt and F. Wilbur Gingrich, 4th ed. (Chicago: University of Chicago Press; Cambridge: The University Press, 1952).
7. Otto Kuss, *Der Römerbrief,* 2nd ed. (Regensburg: Pustet, 1963), pp. 47-48 and 50.
8. This is the meaning here of the preposition *en.* See Paul Althaus, *Der Brief an die Römer,* in NeuTestD 6, 1966; Franz-J. Leenhardt, *L'épitre de saint Paul aux romains* (Neuchâtel: Delachaux, 1957), p. 40: "Eux encore ont substitué le

mensonge à la verité divine." English version: *The Epistle to the Romans: A Commentary* (Cleveland: World Publishing Company, 1961). See also Michel, *Römer*, and Kuss, *Römerbrief*, especially p. 49.

9. Kuss, *Römerbrief*, pp. 38-39.
10. Bultmann, *Faith and Understanding*, 1:53-65.
11. Ernst Bloch, *Das Prinzip Hoffnung*, 2nd. ed. (Frankfurt: Suhrkamp, 1969); Jean Paul Sartre, *Critique de la raison dialectique* (Paris: Gallimard, 1960).
12. Cf. Bultmann, "ginōskō," *TDNT*, 1:696-701.
13. G. Johannes Botterweck, *"Gott Erkennen" im Sprachgebrauch des Alten Testaments* (Bonn: Peter Hanstein, 1951), p. 44.
14. Hans Walter Wolff, *Dodekapropheton I Hosea*, 2nd. ed., BiKomm 14/1 (Neukirchen: Neukirchener Verlag, 1965), p. 84.
15. Regarding the text and the meaning of v. 5, cf. ibid., pp. 135, 152-53, and Wilhelm Rudolph, *Hosea*, in KommAT (Gütersloh: Mohr, 1966), pp. 132-33 and 139. The variant readings are of little importance to our concern.
16. Hans Wilhelm Hertzberg, *Prophet und Gott*, Bz FöchrTH, 28/3 (1923), pp. 23-24.
17. Hans-Joachim Kraus, *Die prophetische Verkündigung des Rechts in Israel* (Zollikon: Evangelischer Verlag, 1957), p. 29.
18. Oslo: Universistets-Forlaget, 1941, p. 9.
19. Hans Walter Wolff, " 'Wissen um Gott' bei Hosea als Urform von Theologie," *EvTh* 12 (1952-53): 533-34.
20. Wolff, *Dodekapropheton I*, ad loc.
21. Rudolph, *Hosea*, p. 222. We must respect the original text; there is no reason to modify it so that it says *bᵉ' ohaleyka teseb*.
22. Cf. William Rainey Harper, *Amos and Hosea*, International Critical Commentary 19 (Edinburgh: Clark, 1936), p. 355; Theodore Henry Robinson and Friedrich Horst, *Die zwölf kleinen Propheten*, 3rd. ed., HBAT 14 (Tübingen: Mohr, 1964), p. 40; *Gesenius' Hebrew Grammar*, 2nd Eng. ed. (Oxford: Clarendon Press, 1910), 117n.
23. Cf. Rudolph, *Hosea*, p. 82; Wolff, *Dodekapropheton I*, p. 65; Artur Weiser, *Das Buch der zwölf kleinen Propheten II*, 5th ed., ATDeut 24 (Göttingen: Vandenhoeck, 1967), p. 34.
24. Cf. Rudolph, *Hosea*, pp. 80-81, and Wolff, *Dodekapropheton I*, pp. 63-64. For his part, Harper (*Amos and Hosea*, p. 242) finds this to be "a bizarre arrangement of thought" and states that "in righteousness and in judgment" are an interpolated gloss. This is very bad methodology.
25. Wolff, *Dodekapropheton I*, p. 304.
26. Rudolph, *Hosea*, p. 248.
27. Wolff, *Dodekapropheton I*, p. 304.
28. Botterweck, *"Gott Erkennen,"* pp. 49-50.
29. See Karl Elliger, *Das Buch der zwölf kleinen Propheten II*, in ATDeut 25, 6th ed., 1967, 46ff.
30. See Robinson-Horst, *Zwölf kleinen Propheten*, p. 178.
31. William Hayes Ward, *Habakkuk*, International Critical Commentary 20 (Edinburgh: Clark, 1911), p. 17.

32. See ibid., pp. 15-18; and Robinson-Horst, *Zwölf kleinen Propheten*, 180-83. Elliger alters the consonantic text of v. 5 and puts the first condemnation there; thus he counts six condemnations in the chapter.

33. See Otto Kaiser, *Isaiah 1-12: A Commentary* (Philadelphia: The Westminster Press, 1972), pp. 5-21.

34. C. G. Montefiore, *The Synoptic Gospels* (London: Macmillan, 1927), 1:146.

35. Cf. Rud. Kittel, *Biblia hebraica* (Stuttgart: Privileg. Wurtt. Bibelanstalt, 1937).

36. Levinas, *Totalité et Infini*, p. 14; cf. *Totality and Infinity*, p. 46.

37. The ultrabalanced Wilhelm Rudolph definitively asserts that Jeremiah rejected the reform of Josiah. Regarding Jer. 7:21-28, see his commentary *Jeremia*, 3rd. ed., HBAT 12 (Tübingen: Mohr, 1968), p. 57. John Skinner had already seen this very clearly in 1926 (*Prophecy and Religion* [London: Cambridge University Press, 1926], p. 106). And Ed. König had noted it twenty years earlier ("Der Jeremiasspruch 7, 21-23," *ThStKr* 79 (1906):327-93. Other authors are in agreement: Christopher R. North, "Sacrifice in the Old Testament," *ExpTim* 47, no. 6 (March 1936):252; Paul Volz, *Der Prophet Jeremia* (Leipzig: A. Deichertsche, 1922), pp. 101-04; R. Hentschke, "Die Stellung der vorexilischen Schriftpropheten zum Kultus," *BZAltW* 75 (1957):114-115; Robert Dobbie, "Deuteronomy and the Prophetic Attitude to Sacrifice," *ScJourTh* 12, no. 1 (March 1959):68-82, especially p. 74; R. Smend, "Das Nein des Amos," *EvTh* 23 (1963):404-23.

38. Smend, "Amos," p. 422.

39. Hentschke, "Stellung," p. 52.

40. Dobbie, *Deuteronomy*, p. 70.

41. The problem of the monotheism or the nonmonotheism of the Bible has occasioned many doubts, and this fact itself is what is most significant. See Walther Eichrodt, *Theology of the Old Testament*, trans. J. A. Baker (London: SCM Press, 1961), 1:220-27; B. Balscheit, "Alter und Aufkommen des Monotheismus in der israelitischen Religion," *BZAltW* 69 (1938); H. H. Rowley, "The Antiquity of Israelite Monotheism," *ExpTim* 61, no. 11 (August 1950):333-34; von Rad, *Old Testament Theology*, 1:210-212. Regarding Ps. 95:3; 97:7; and 1 Kings 18:27 von Rad observes, "The designation of the gods as 'nothing' has not as yet to be understood in the sense of a basic denial of their existence: it can also be a way of rendering them contemptible" (ibid., p. 212n.). It is often asserted that monotheism in the strict sense was proper to the end of the exile—in the theology of Deutero-Isaiah. But the most recent and authoritative commentary has this to say with regard to Isa. 41:24: "The declaration that the gods are nothing is related to their action ('your work is nothing'; v. 29, 'their works are vain'), just as their claim, here declared to be nothing, is also related to activity.... Here the ontological question whether these gods exist, whether 'there are such,' is entirely wide of the mark and has to be left out of account if the trial speeches are to be properly understood.... If ... Deutero-Isaiah had proclaimed that these gods were non-existent, he would have been talking at cross purposes with the situation in which his compatriots found themselves. In such a

state of affairs, to teach monotheism *per se* would have been empty words" (Claus Westermann, *Isaiah 40-66: A Commentary* [Philadelphia: The Westminster Press, 1969], p. 86).

42. F. Blass and A. Debrunner, *A Greek Grammar of the New Testament*, 3rd. ed. (Chicago: University of Chicago Press, 1967), n. 333. The atemporal intention is apparent, notwithstanding Rudolf Schnackenburg, *Die Johannesbriefe*, 3rd. ed. (Freiburg: Herder, 1965), 229, n. 1.

43. Bultmann, *Die drei Johannesbriefe*, MeyersKomm (Göttingen: Vandenhoeck, 1967), p. 70.

44. Schnackenburg, *Johannesbriefe*, p. 201 ad 3, 18. He very correctly cites James 1:25; 2:12, 15-17, and Test-XII Gad 6:1.

45. Max Meinertz, *Theologie des Neuen Testamentes* (Bonn: Hanstein Verlag, 1950), 2:304.

46. Cf. above chapter 1.

47. Cf. above "To Know Yahweh," pp. 44-53.

48. Bigo, *Doctrine sociale*, p. 378.

49. As Levinas observes, "Le rapport qui, dans la volupté, s'établit entre les amants, foncièrement réfractaire à l'universalisation, est tout le contraire du rapport social. Il exclut le tiers, il demeure intimité, solitude à deux, société close, le nonpublic par excellence" *(Totalité et Infini*, p. 242). "Si aimer, c'est aimer l'amour que l'Aimée me porte, aimer est aussi s'aimer dans l'amour et retourner ainsi à soi. L'amour ne transcende pas sans équivoque.... Il se complaît, il est plaisir et égoïsme à deux" (ibid., p. 244). "Solitude qui ne nie pas seulement, qui n'oublie pas seulement le monde. L'action commune du sentant et du senti que la volupté accomplit, clôture, ferme, scelle la société du couple" (ibid., p. 243) [cf. *Totality and Infinity*, pp. 264-65, 266, 265]. By this it is not denied that such a love might be very healthy, but that it is able to transcend.

50. Koschelava, *El mito de los dos Marx*, p. 57.

51. Bultmann, *Synoptic Tradition*, p. 103. Even better, see Josef Schmid, *Das Evangelium nach Matthäus*, 3rd ed. (Regensburg: Pustet, 1956), p. 148.

52. Cf. Rudolf Bultmann, "Untersuchungen zum Johannesevangelium," *ZNeuW* 29 (1930):169-92; Bultmann, *The Gospel of John: A Commentary*, trans. G. R. Beasley-Murray et al. (Philadelphia: The Westminster Press, 1971), pp. 54-55; Schnackenburg, *Johannesbriefe*; Wilhelm Michaelis, "horaō," in *TDNT*, 5:315-67.

53. Levinas, *Totalité et Infini*, p. 196; cf. *Totality and Infinity*, p. 221.

54. Levinas, *Totality and Infinity*, p. 73.

55. Cf. ibid.

56. Ibid., p. 75.

57. Ibid., pp. 89-90.

58. Ibid., pp. 180-81.

59. Norbert Lohfink, *Das Hauptgebot*, AnBi 20 (Rome: PIB, 1963), pp. 227-31.

60. Alfred Jepsen, "Beiträge zur Auslegung und Geschichte des Dekalogs," *ZAltW* 79 (1967):227-304, especially pp. 281-84.

61. William L. Moran, "The Conclusion of the Decalogue (Ex 20, 17=Dt 5, 21)," *CBQ* 29, no. 4 (October 1967):543-54.

62. Cf. Jepsen, "Beiträge," p. 300.

63. Concerning the archaism of this theology see Mitchell Dahood, *Psalms II*, Anchor Bible 17 (Garden City, New York: Doubleday, 1968), p. 269, with regard to Ps. 82; and Hans-Joachim Kraus, *Psalmen II*, BiKomm 15, 3rd. ed. (Neukirchen Kreis Moers: Verlag der Buchhandlung des Erziehungsvereins, 1966), p. 570.

64. Paul Joüon in his *Grammaire de l'hébreu biblique*, 2nd ed. (Rome: PIB, 1947), 119e, gives v. 19 as an example of the inverse perfect of logical consequence.

65. Jepsen, "Beiträge," p. 293.

66. Ibid., p. 295: "Du darfst keinen Meineid leisten und damit die Wahrheit verleugnen."

67. Cf. Stanislao Lyonnet, *Exegesis epistulae ad romanos cap V-VIII*, 2nd ed. (Rome: PIB, 1966), p. 103.

68. Cf. above p. 36.

69. Cf. above pp. 45-46.

70. See for example Bultmann, "ginōskō," in *TDNT*, 1:709: Heinz-Dietrich Wendland, *Die Briefe an die Korinther*, in NeuTestD 7 (Göttingen: Vandenhoeck, 1968), p. 67; Jacques Dupont, *Gnosis*, 2nd ed. (Paris: Gabalda, 1960), p. 104.

Chapter Three

God's Intervention in History

Since creation is a theme which is intelligible in ontological terms and reducible to categories of cause and effect, of entity and nonentity, of being and nonbeing, the West has centered the difference between the God of the Bible and the God of philosophy on the fact that the former is the creator and the latter is not. But with respect to the Bible this constitutes such a modification of emphasis that it is tantamount to falsification. In the view of the Bible, Yahweh is the God who breaks into human history to liberate the oppressed. Von Rad has correctly pointed out the subordinate and reinforcing role that the theme of "Yahweh Creator" plays, for example, in Amos 4:13, if we do not make the error of reading this verse separately from Amos 4:1-12. The same is evident in Pss. 89; 136; 148; 33; and 74, if we read them in their entirety as they are meant to be read. Yahweh intervenes in human history in the demand for justice, but this demand becomes much stronger and more irresistible if he makes it as the creator of heaven and earth, for then the power of this God who intervenes to achieve justice is immense. The same can be seen in Amos 5:8-9 and Amos 9:5-6, if they are read in context.[1]

Even after the exile, the biblical authors always used the theme of creation as a theological resource to put into relief Yahweh's interventions which rescue from oppression and injustice. Not only are the two themes not juxtaposed, it is not even enough to say that it is a question of emphasis, as if the characterization of Yahweh as creator were "also"

77

there, although less accentuated. Yahweh is presented as creator to give importance to his intervention on behalf of justice. See Isa. 43:1-2; Isa. 51:7-14 (vv. 9b-10); Isa. 42:5-7; Isa. 44:24-28.

Isa. 42:5-7 should be sufficient example. Following the first canticle referring to the servant of Yahweh, it has Yahweh saying:

Thus says God, Yahweh,
he who created the heavens and spread them out,
who gave shape to the earth and what comes from it,
who gave breath to its people
and life to the creatures that move in it:
I, Yahweh, have called you to serve the cause of justice;
I have taken you by the hand and formed you;
I have appointed you as covenant of the people and light of nations,
to open the eyes of the blind,
to free captives from prison,
and those who live in darkness from the dungeon.

Yahweh's intervention in our history has only one purpose. Here it is explicit: "to serve the cause of justice."[2] To recall that the God who intervenes in this way is the creator of all things and all peoples gives both an enormous force to his intervention on behalf of justice and also a universal scope. But the intention of saving from injustice and oppression is the determinant of the entire description which Yahweh makes of himself.

The God of the Exodus

As von Rad has pointed out, Genesis is the prologue, the prehistory, the preparation for the essential fact: the liberation of the slaves from Egypt.[3] In Exod. 6:2-8 the Priestly text programmatically and for the first time uses the formula "I am Yahweh," which will be the unifying thread running throughout all the marvels of the Exodus and all the legislation down to the priest-prophet Ezekiel and Deutero-Isaiah. With regard to this passage, Elliger accurately states:

We immediately see that the decisive phase of history as the action of God begins here in the fact that God reveals himself to Moses with his name Yahweh, while he had appeared to the Fathers only as El-Shaddai .... And God will immediately reveal his most proper and characteristic essence in the fact of "bringing out," "freeing," "releasing," "saving," "with arm outstretched and great judgments" the oppressed people.[4]

I cannot emphasize enough the importance, as qualitative revelation, which this historical intervention has for all the times the Bible says, "I am Yahweh" or "You will know that I am Yahweh." It is difficult to imagine that the biblical author could have done more to accentuate its importance than to tell us that God himself changed his name at that moment (Exod. 6:3) and then add:

Say this to the sons of Israel, "I am Yahweh *and therefore* I will free you of the burdens which the Egyptians lay on you. I will release you from slavery to them, and with raised arm and my great justices I will deliver you. I will adopt you as my own people, and I will be your God. Then you shall know that I am Yahweh your God, he who has freed you from the Egyptians' burdens."

(Exod. 6:6-7)[5]

There is an intentional bracketing of the phrases between the "I am Yahweh" of v. 6 and the "You shall know that I am Yahweh" of v. 7. This bracketing, precisely at the moment in which the writer adopts a new name for God, indicates that the "bracketed" phrases describe the type of action which is linked to the new name: Yahweh. Notwithstanding how some exegetes would have it, it is impossible that "You shall know that I am Yahweh" should mean to recognize Yahweh by his actions in the time of the Patriarchs; for at that time he was not called Yahweh, according to the Priestly text. Neither Zimmerli nor Elliger, who have made exhaustive separate studies of the "I am Yahweh" formulas and its variations, finds that its *Sitz im Leben* has anything to do with the theology of the covenant.[6] Exod. 6:6-7 shows very clearly that the formulas using "to know" belong to the same tradition as the simpler formulas. This is an important point in the investigation, and it has been demonstrated quite adequately by Zimmerli.[7]

Following Elliger we can list in the following way all the formulas of this type which appear in the Bible:

1. I am Yahweh
2. I am Yahweh, your God
3. I, Yahweh, am your God
4. I am Yahweh who brought you out of Egypt. . .
5. I am Yahweh, your God, who brought you out of Egypt. . .
6. You shall know that I am Yahweh
7. You shall know that I am Yahweh, your God
8. You shall know that I, Yahweh, am your God.[8]

Elliger examines formulas 1 and 2 in their contexts. He calls the first *Hoheitsformel* (formula of nobility or sovereignty: "I am Yahweh"); the second he calls *Huldformel* (formula of clemency: "I am Yahweh, your God"). But he concludes his study with the recognition that they do not carry different theological contents: In the shorter formula "Your God" is understood.[9] The same should be said about the difference between formulas 6 and 7 and also 4 and 5.

It might be thought that the formulas with an explicit reference to history (nos. 4 and 5) constitute a group apart, different from the rest. Indeed Rolf Rendtorff believes that the short formula "I am Yahweh" is a later abbreviation of the historical formulations, which seem to him to be the most ancient and original.[10] But as Zimmerli points out, the Yahwist had already used the short formula in Exod. 7:17: "In this you shall know that I am Yahweh"; thus it is not a late expression.[11] The point is that neither the short formulas nor the long ones attempt to make a statement of a historical nature concerning a subject, Yahweh, whose essence remains to a certain degree unexplored. "Israel knows that it can call out 'in the name of Yahweh' and will be heard."[12] He who adores another God, however, "may invoke him," but "he never replies; he never saves anyone in trouble" (Isa. 46:7). The difference is reduced to the fact that the short formulas reveal Yahweh, as it were, more markedly in what he is; the others refer more to history or the historical event in which Yahweh manifested what he is. But the difference loses all importance because what was manifested is precisely that which characterizes Yahweh in contrast with the other gods. The more the historical event is emphasized, the more this qualitative characterization stands out. The best demonstration of this is the continuous substitution in the Bible of one formula for another.

To interpret the "I am Yahweh who brought you out of Egypt" formulas as an elicitation of the observance of the commandments because of gratitude seems to me to be not only forced but unsupportable. As Zimmerli has pointed out, they belong to the same tradition as "You shall know that I am Yahweh." In Num. 14:35; Ezek. 5:13; 6:12-13, 14; 7:9; 12:15-16; 15:7; 21:10; 22:22; and 24:24 we see this "I am Yahweh" as an historical intervention of outraged chastisement *against Israel*. Between these interventions and the saving ones of the "You shall know that I am Yahweh" formula, there is a perfectly consistent and organic relationship. The salvation of the oppressed is in both cases effected against the unjust. Among a people in which injustice reigns, it is always Yahweh-justice who reveals himself by intervening. The laws which are based on the formulas which we are studying accord with this notion without any need for distortion. For example, "Let none of you wrong his neighbor, but fear your God; for I am Yahweh, your God" (Lev. 25:17). With the verb "to fear" inserted here, it is completely aprioristic to assert that these formulas elicit obedience through gratitude. Rather we see clearly the continuity of all these formulas with that of Exod. 6:6-7, where for the first time the name of Yahweh is revealed in the Priestly tradition: I am Yahweh, and *therefore* I will free the oppressed. As Zimmerli enumerates, Ezekiel uses phrases such as the following 78 times: "You shall know that I am Yahweh when I do such and such a thing. . . ."[13] For example, "They shall know that I am Yahweh when I break their yokestraps and release them from the hand of their captors" (Ezek. 34:27). It seems to me that the continuity among all these formulas is obvious: He who reveals himself by intervening in our history is always Yahweh as savior of the oppressed and punisher of the oppressors.

Israel learned this in the event of the liberation from Egypt. Hosea says it clearly: "I am Yahweh, your God, since the days in the land of Egypt; you know no God but me, there is no other savior besides me" (Hos. 13:4). The identical nature of the argument of this early eighth century text with that of the famous polemics against idolatry in Deutero-Isaiah at the end of the sixth century is striking. Because this continuity has been forgotten, these passages have often been wrongly understood. We read, "There is no other god besides me; a just God and a savior, there is none apart from me" (Isa. 45:21). In his attack on idolatry Hosea asserted that only Yahweh is the savior, and Hosea based this assertion on the fact of the liberation from Egypt, which had occurred five centuries before. Deutero-Isaiah considers this same justice to be realized in the shattering of the Babylonian yoke. According to him, the fact that justice has come to the oppressed is enough to know with certainty that it is indeed Yahweh:

The poor and needy ask for water, and there is none,
their tongue is parched with thirst.
I, Yahweh, will answer them,
I, the God of Israel, will not abandon them.

(Isa. 41:17)

so that men may see and know,
may all observe and understand
that the hand of Yahweh has done this,
that the Holy one of Israel has created it.

(Isa. 41:20)

The plain fact is that Cyrus arose and demolished the Babylonian empire. This is enough for Deutero-Isaiah to have Yahweh say:

It was I who roused him for justice' sake
I levelled the way for him.
He will rebuild my city,
will bring my exiles back.

(Isa. 45:13)

The conclusion in Isa. 45:21—"a just God and a savior there is none apart from me"—with which Deutero-Isaiah takes up the words of Hosea appears again in Isa. 45:24 formulated in this way: "They will say, 'In Yahweh alone are justice and strength.' " Note that Isa. 45:21 adds "just" to the "savior" of Hos. 13:4. This is clearly not to alter the meaning, but rather to reinforce it by highlighting its decisive characterization. Because of this characterization the events are seen as unmistakably the work of Yahweh and not of other gods. The entire argument against other gods depends on this unequivocal qualitative distinction. The worshipper of another god "may invoke him but he never replies; he never saves anyone in trouble" (Isa. 46:7). On the other hand, "Listen to me, faint hearts, who feel far from justice. I bring my justice near, already it is close, my salvation will not be late" (46:12-13).

Let us state again that the simple fact is that by defeating the Babylonians ("Chaldeans") Cyrus liberated all the peoples which had been exiled and subjugated by Nebuchadnezzar. This is enough for the prophet of Yahweh:

Thus says Yahweh,
your redeemer,
the Holy One of Israel:
For your sake I send an army against Babylon;
I will knock down the prison bars
and the Chaldeans will break into laments.

(Isa. 43:14)

Isa. 46:13, which we have just cited, deals with the justice of Yahweh in the full sense of the term; it cannot be asserted that Paul coined the expression "justice of God." The passages which we have considered demonstrate that this justice is a saving justice. (Note also the synonymic parallelism between justice and salvation in Isa. 45:21; 46:13; 45:8; 51:5; 51:6; 51:8; 56:1; 59:17; 61:10; Ps. 98:2; 65:6; 71:15; Rom. 1:16-17; 8:10; 5:21; 5:18; 5:17; 10:9-10.) But in Isa. 49:26 we see that this same justice is fiercely punitive against the oppressors. All the efforts of Lyonnet, Beaucamp, and Cazelles to avoid a justice of God which is vindictive against the unjust collide against Isa. 10:22; Ps. 36:11-13; 97:6, 3; Isa. 59:16-17; Wisd. 5:18, 13).[14] These efforts arise from a widely held error: It is believed that irreligiosity or sins of any sort are being avenged and punished. It seems to these exegetes—in my opinion, rightly—that it is not worthy of God to avenge such things. But exegetically this is a pseudo-problem, for according to the Bible the sin against which God intervenes (including the intervention called the Last Judgment) is specific: It is injustice and the oppression of the weak by the powerful.

As Hertzberg, Zimmerli, and Westermann observe, the entire message of Deutero-Isaiah is a response on the part of Yahweh to the cry of an oppressed people: "My destiny is hidden from Yahweh, my right [*mišpaṭi*] is ignored by my God" (Isa. 40:27).[15] This formulation is characteristic of those who suffer injustice, as can be seen, for example, in Ps. 35:23: "Awake, arise and do justice (*lemišpaṭi*) to me, my God, my Lord, hear my complaint [*leribi*]." We see this also in Ps. 140:13: "I know Yahweh will do justice [*din*] to the poor, right [*mišpaṭ*] to the needy." This is the same formulation as in Ps. 146:7: Yahweh is he who "does justice (*mišpaṭ*) to the oppressed, gives food to the hungry." In this same regard see Ps. 13:2; 22:25; 27:9; 37:5-6; 30:8; 44:25; 69:18; 88:15; 102:3; 104:29. As Hertzberg accurately points out, "*Mišpaṭ* consists in doing justice to the poor, neither more nor less."[16]

Yahweh's response to the people's cry is liberation from the Babylonian captivity. "You shall then know that I am Yahweh, and that those who hope in me will not be put to shame" (Isa. 49:23).

> that men may know from the rising to the setting of the sun
> that, apart from me, there is no other.
> I am Yahweh, and there is no other. . . .
> Send justice like a dew, you heavens,
> and let the clouds rain it down.
> Let the earth open

for salvation to spring up.
Let justice, too, spring forth,
which I, Yahweh, have created.

(Isa. 45:6, 8)

If this were not the precise meaning behind Deutero-Isaiah's attacks against idolatry, then Duhm's derisive objection to them would be quite well taken. With regard to Isa. 41:21-29, Duhm says:

This is an outstanding example of the genuine poetic and religious naïveté with which Deutero-Isaiah thinks and speaks. Any believer of another religion would have refuted him and would have laughed at his assertion that only in the Israelite religion were there predictions .... But our prophet has not the least bit of self-criticism; he believes that just by speaking his convictions they are proven.[17]

Duhm is presupposing that Deutero-Isaiah is using the "prediction and fulfillment" schema as it is used in Western apologetical treatises.

But the fact involved was the liberation from the Babylonian captivity, and the pivot of the argumentation is this:

Who predicted this from the beginning so we might know it,
who foretold it long ago so we might say:
    "He is just" [*ṣaddik*]?
No one predicted it,
no, no one proclaimed it,
no, no one heard you speak.

(Isa. 41:26)

What the writer is trying to demonstrate is not that Yahweh alone can predict events, but rather that *the content of the predictions was justice*. The only God who in the past had shown that his sole concern was justice for the oppressed was Yahweh. He was the only one whose revelatory intervention in human history had consisted in an immense act of justice. At the moment when someone—whether Cyrus or someone else—does justice to the poor and despised, this is the God who inspires and guides him. Of course, if we decide to translate *ṣaddik* in Isa. 41:26 by *richtig* (Duhm) or *es stimmt* or *c'est vrai* or *it is right*, then we have a simple case of prediction and fulfillment, and the blessed one of Deutero-Isaiah shows nothing specifically peculiar to Yahweh. But *ṣaddik* means "just" and qualifies Yahweh, as can be seen in "a just [*ṣaddik*] God and a savior, there is none apart from me" (Isa. 45:21). And the fact that Deutero-Isaiah modifies the phrase of Hos.

13:4 with this very adjective proves that it is on this that his attention
is fixed. Our astonishment is all the greater when we see that the
translation "it is right" is devised for Isa. 41:26 when there is no
parallel instance of the same meaning, and when Isa. 45:21 (where
Duhm rightly translates *gerechter*) constitutes a very strict parallel:

Who foretold this
and revealed it in the past?
Was it not I, Yahweh?
There is no other god besides me,
a just God and a savior,
there is none apart from me.
(Isa. 45:21)

Who predicted this from the beginning so we might know it,
Who foretold it long ago so we might say, "He is just"?
(Isa. 41:26)

If exegesis had not been so allergic to Ps. 37, it would have found
there a definition of the meaning of "to be just": "The just man has
compassion and gives" (Ps. 37:21). With regard to Hos. 6:6 we have
already seen that what is involved is intervening on behalf of the poor;
this is what "compassion" means.[18] But there is really no need
for a comparison with other authors; the meaning of "justice" in
Deutero-Isaiah is the same, as we can see even in the few passages we
have considered. The synonymy between "just" and "savior" in Isa.
45:21 is sufficiently eloquent, as well as the "justice" of 45:13, which
consists in freeing captives, and that of 42:6-7, which depends on
releasing prisoners. Moreover, in chapter 41 itself, before the adjective
ṣaddik is used in v. 26, the substantive "justice" is mentioned in v. 10.
And between the two passages we find a most illustrative description:

The poor and the needy ask for water,
and there is none,
their tongue is parched with thirst.
I, Yahweh, will answer them,
I, the God of Israel, will not abandon them.
(Isa. 41:17)

Zimmerli is completely correct when he sees in all this monolatrous
polemic of Deutero-Isaiah a continuation and deepening of the
epiphany of Yahweh which is condensed in the formulas "I am
Yahweh" and "I am Yahweh, your God," and which is the main thread
throughout the entire Old Testament.[19] Concerning Isa. 48:12b—"I am

the same" (*'ani-hu*, as in 43:13)—Zimmerli states, "This is an assertion of self-opening, a revealing word in which the self as self allows itself to be known."[20] Zimmerli's testimony is all the more valuable because he confines his study to a formal level, without broaching the question of the qualitative content by which Yahweh identifies himself. For the question of content we can best refer to the words of Jepsen. He points out that there is a synonymic parallelism in Isa. 51:1:

> You who pursue justice,
> you who seek Yahweh,

and that Trito-Isaiah understood this synonymy perfectly well:

> They are to be called oaks of justice,
> plantation of Yahweh.

(Isa. 61:3)

> Justice will go before you,
> and the glory of Yahweh behind you.

(Isa. 58:8)

He convincingly concludes, "According to this we should speak of *ṣedaḳah* [justice] as the very essence of Yahweh."[21]

By keeping this notion in mind we can understand the meaning of Isa. 48:12b: "I am the same; what I was at the beginning, I am at the end." Therefore Deutero-Isaiah adds "just" (Isa. 45:21) to the formula of Hos. 13:4, which takes it for granted. We can even mark out the bridge between Hosea and Deutero-Isaiah: With regard to the Davidic branch, who "will practice right and justice in the land" (Jer. 23:5), Jeremiah coined the remarkable proper name "Yahweh-our-justice" (23:6) and added:

> So, then, the days are coming—it is Yahweh who speaks—when people will no longer say, "As Yahweh lives who brought the sons of Israel out of the land of Egypt!" but, "As Yahweh lives who led back and brought home the descendants of the House of Israel out of the land of the North and from all the countries to which he had dispersed them, to live on their own soil."

(Jer. 23:7-8)

Hosea asserted that only Yahweh is a savior and he based his assertion on the event of the liberation from Egypt. Deutero-Isaiah considers this same justice to be realized in the breaking of the Babylonian subjugation; but before it had even happened, Jeremiah had already prophetically made this application.[22] He did this perfectly conscious that it is this justice which identifies Yahweh. And this justice is, of course, related to the formula "justice and right" (v. 5), which is accepted by all exegetes as having a social meaning in favor of the poor and oppressed.

Thus we can understand that for the Yahweh of Jer. 9:23 "to know me" means "to know that I, Yahweh, am he who achieves compassion, righteousness, and justice on the earth." It is noteworthy here that the verb "to know" has Yahweh for its object twice, once as direct complement, "to know me," and another (without repeating the verb) immediately after as subject of the preposition which is known: "that I, Yahweh, am he who achieves...." Zimmerli has pointed out this difficult construction in relation to Jer. 24:7: "to know me that I am Yahweh."[23] Undoubtedly the second object is to add a refinement which is not sufficiently expressed in the simple accusative "me." But the construction gives the impression that both objects are the same, and moreover, that to know the first means, carefully considered, to know the second. In other words, to know Yahweh means to know that Yahweh is he who achieves compassion and right and justice on the earth (Jer. 9:23). According to Jer. 24:7 this is the meaning of knowing "me," of knowing "that I am Yahweh."

Besides Jeremiah, the bridge between Hosea and Deutero-Isaiah has another important pillar in the very midst of the exile. In a verse which we have already considered, Ezekiel says,

They shall know that I am Yahweh
when I break their yokestraps
and release them from the hand of their captors.

(Ezek. 34:27)

Therefore we cannot confuse the theology of history found in the Bible with the theology of providence which the West has inherited from the Greco-Romans. The latter is static, for it contemplates instants as isolated points; moreover, it is not specific. For the Bible, not just any good and praiseworthy event, but rather the realization of justice is the intervention of Yahweh. The God of the Bible has a plan; he has resolved to change our world into a world of justice. In history, within history, there is an *eschaton*, an *ultimum*, toward which all the partial realizations of justice are directed. Here I must point out that this *ultimum*, this *novum*, also characterizes the philosophy of Marx. We shall return to this later.

In the message of Deutero-Isaiah the passages referring to the liberation of Israel by Cyrus have an obvious particularistic mark. But even this message composed in and for such concrete and determined circumstances nevertheless insistently looks toward the realization of justice in the whole world: see Isa. 42:1, 6; 45:20-22; 49:6; 51:4-8; 54:2-3; 55:5. The following passage concerning the servant will serve as an example of the others:

> It is not enough for you to be my servant and restore the tribes of Jacob and convert [or "bring back"] the survivors of Israel;
> I will make you the light of the nations so that my salvation may reach to the ends of the earth.
>
> (Isa. 49:6)

The Plan of Yahweh

The tradition initiated in Exod. 6:6-7 of the Priestly text has led us to Deutero-Isaiah. Here I want to point out expressly that it also leads, as we shall see, to the Gospel according to John with its absolute "I am" statements taken literally from Isa. 41:4; 43:10, 25; 46:4; 48:12; 51:12; 52:6, according to the Septuagint translation; in John these passages are in 8:24, 28, 58, and 13:9.

The Yahwistic tradition does not change Yahweh's name at the moment of his intervention to free the slaves. In this tradition, however, the fact that Genesis constitutes a mere prologue to Exodus is even truer and more profound. To study the Yahwistic tradition separately has two advantages: (1) It provides a powerful confirmation of what we have seen, for the two traditions converge in a notable manner; (2) the Yahwistic tradition leads us to Paul, just as the Priestly tradition leads us to John.

The equivalent of the Priestly Exod. 6:6-7 is Exod. 3:7-9 in the Yahwistic tradition:

> And Yahweh said, "I have seen, I have indeed seen the affliction of my people in Egypt. I have heard their cry to be free of their slave-drivers. Yes, I am well aware of their sufferings. Therefore I have gone down to deliver them out of the hand of the Egyptians and bring them up out of that land to a land rich and broad, a land where milk and honey flow. . . . And now the cry of the sons of Israel has come to me, and I have witnessed the way in which the Egyptians oppress them.

In these lines the "cry" of the oppressed appears twice. Gunkel has noted that this is "a technical term for the cry due to injustice inflicted."[24] And Sarna says, "The Hebrew root *ṣaʿaq/zaʿaq* indicates the anguished cry of the oppressed, the agonized plea of the victim for help in some great injustice. . . . The 'outcry' of Sodom, then, implies above all, heinous moral and social corruption, an arrogant disregard of elementary human rights, a cynical insensitivity to the sufferings of others."[25] The technical nature of the term is apparent in Gen. 4:10; Job 34:28; 19:7; Hab. 1:2; 2 Kings 8:3; Isa. 19:20; 46:7; 5:7; Jer. 20:8; Ps. 9:13; 34:18; 77:2; 88:2; 107:6, 28. As an illustrative example, see Exod. 22:21-22, where coincidentally "cry" appears twice, as in Exod. 3:7-9; "affliction" and "hear" also occur: "You must not afflict the widow or the orphan; if you afflict them and they cry out to me, I shall hear their cry."

Given the Yahwist's insistence on this "cry," it seems to me that we must completely exclude the possibility that Yahweh's "descent" to "deliver" in Exod. 3:7-9 should be attributed to the fact that it is "my people" who cry out. The exegesis which tries to make his intervention depend completely on a promise or pact—as if God would not have intervened against injustice if he had not officially promised to do so beforehand—contradicts with this kind of positivism the deepest and most radical conviction of the Old Testament authors. For them evil is evil whether or not there have been official prohibitions; crime is crime whether or not there have been covenants or promises.

"Listen to the sound of your brother's blood, crying out to me from the earth" (Gen. 4:10), Yahweh says, and this is before there were covenants, patriarchs, promises, and commandments. It is often forgotten that this passage is the first instance in which the sagas collected by the Yahwist allow him a little leeway to express his own theo-logy. In this verse it is immediately apparent that Genesis was written completely under the inspiration of Exodus and as a prologue to the irruption of Yahweh's justice, which, in saving a people from oppression, would determine history. Exegesis today has clarified this central thread: The Yahwist decided to write a prehistory of the Exodus in order to explain the origin of sin and in order that a sinful world might feel the need for the intervention of Yahweh and for the election of a people which would have the mission of abolishing sin in the world.[26] This contribution of exegesis is most important, but it is necessary to clarify that the sin whose origin is being explained is the sin of Cain; it is not just any sin nor is it sin in general. As von Rad rightly points out, the story of Cain and Abel is the first account of man outside of Paradise, of real man, historical humanity for whose redemption Yahweh would intervene.[27] The prologue for Exodus is this: "Listen to the sound of your brother's blood, crying out to me from the earth." The story of Adam is told only so that we might know that man was not this way from the beginning, that God did not create him fratricidal; he became such by his own will.

Sarna has very clearly pointed out that in the story of Cain and Abel the Yahwist was fundamentally writing as redactor and not merely as chronicler. Writing of Gen. 4:2, 8-11, he says:

> No less than seven times the obvious fact is stressed that Abel was Cain's brother; yet the very nature of the biblical Creation story automatically excludes any other possibility. The reason for this stress becomes clear when we recall Cain's response to the divine questioning. "The Lord said to Cain, 'Where is your brother Abel?' And he said, 'I do not know. Am I my brother's keeper?' " (4:9). The Bible wishes to establish emphatically the moral principle that man *is* indeed his brother's keeper and that all homicide is at the same time fratricide.[28]

The redactor obviously wants the reader to answer "yes" to the question, "Am I my brother's keeper?"

But there is much more than this involved here. Yahweh's question to Cain is intentionally parallel to the one he has just addressed to Adam. From "Where are you?" (3:9) we pass to "Where is your brother?" (4:9). The dialogue begun in 3:9 does not lead to a curse upon man, but rather upon the earth (3:17), while that begun in 4:9 ends in the first curse directed against man: "Be cursed you rather than the earth that opened its mouth to receive your brother's blood at your hands" (4:11). I do not think we can doubt the redactional intention of the Yahwist, who by all that went before prepared the reader for this incomparable explosion. The specificity of Adam's sin has still not been clarified in spite of all exegetical efforts; this is clear evidence that it was of no concern to the Yahwist. He was concerned with interhuman injustice, incarnate in Cain. The earth (*ha'adamah* 'soil') in 4:11 is mentioned in order to provide a link with the earth (*ha'adamah*) which had been cursed in 3:17. Only in Abraham (the personification of Israel) will "all the tribes of the earth" (*ha'adamah*) be "blessed" (Gen. 12:3).

Here we have the whole redactional meaning of Genesis; it introduces us to the history of the people of Israel, whose mission will be to lift the curse pronounced upon man in 4:11. Thus in Gen. 18:17-33 the author takes striking redactional liberties, as we shall see; he relates the "outcry" of 4:10 (Gen. 18:20, 21) to the hope that in Abraham "all the tribes of the earth will be blessed" (Gen. 18:18; cf. 12:3). And indeed he has Abraham trying to block Yahweh's path (18:23) when Yahweh comes to destroy Sodom after having heard the "outcry" of the oppressed arising from it (18:20-21). The reason why this super-theologian does not change Yahweh's name in Exod. 3:7-9 is this: The God who intervenes in Genesis is the same Yahweh who hears the cry of all those who suffer injustice.

With regard to Paul's thesis that death entered the world because of the sin of one man (Rom. 5:12) and that death is the wages of sin (Rom. 6:23), von Rad makes an observation which allows us to emphasize still more the importance of the story of Cain and Abel for the Yahwist.[29] The threat of Gen. 2:17—"On the day you eat of that tree you shall surely die"—was simply a threat which was never fulfilled; it brought the threat of instant death into the perspective. The punishment for the transgression is extravagantly divided into that of the serpent (Gen. 3:14-15), that of the woman (Gen. 3:16), and that of the man (Gen. 3:17-19). And it is clear that none of the three effective punishments consists in death, neither as instant death nor as the human condition of mortality. The woman's punishment is to be her pains in procreation and her subjugation to man. That of the man is the curse of the earth and the need to work. If in the collateral and accessory mention of "until you return to the soil, as you were taken from it, for dust you are and to dust you shall return," we wished to find the fulfillment of the punishment threatened in 2:17, even so this mortality would affect only the male, for the determinative intention of Gen. 3:14-19 is to distinguish accurately among the punishment of the serpent, the woman, and the man. (Moreover this is clearly not the case since death should appear as the most central and important element and not simply as a related issue of secondary importance.)

Therefore, von Rad concludes, "the old Testament does not teach that death as such is the penalty of sin." But this conclusion overlooks the fact that the Yahwist connects without any break the account which we have just analyzed with that of Cain and Abel. If, as we have seen, this connection established a causal relationship so that it would not be thought that fratricide was connatural to man as made by God, then it is obvious that in the redactional intention of the Yahwist neither was death a part of mankind's destiny from the beginning. It is most interesting that, as von Rad has pointed out, Gen. 2-3 leaves the question of death enshrouded in a cloud of vagueness. Gen. 4:1-11, on the other hand, is totally unequivocal: Death entered history in the form of fratricide. The punishment threatened in Gen. 2:17 is carried out for the first time in Gen. 4:8. And any reader who can manage to approach these chapters with that difficult freshness of one who knows nothing about what is being said will be left in doubt as to whether in the Yahwist's intention the original sinner was Adam or Cain, for the first man cursed by God was Cain, not Adam.

Any reader can see this. Recently scientific exegesis has been able to penetrate the question more deeply.[30] In Hebrew *'adam* with the article (*ha'adam*) means "man." Without the article it means Adam, for proper names never have the definite article. The first time that *'adam* appears without the article is Gen. 4:25. Therefore in the famous narrative of Gen. 2-3, which we have come to call the account of original sin, there is no question of a concrete man, but rather of "man" in general. And indeed all the modern translations and commentaries translate the term as "the man." This means that here the Yahwist is not trying to write concrete history but rather is philosophizing on man in general with the help of pre-Israelite sagas. Thus Cain is the first concrete man, and human history begins with Gen. 4:1-11. "Listen to the sound of your brother's blood, crying out to me from the earth" (Gen. 4:10) is the essential presentation of the God who intervenes in this history. And this was before there were covenants, patriarchs, promises, and commandments.

The Yahwist is perfectly explicit in Gen. 18:17-33 when he delineates the contrast between 12:3 ("In you all the tribes of the earth shall be blessed") and 4:11 ("Be cursed you rather than the earth"). Gunkel recognizes that there is a radical difference between Gen. 18:17-33 and all the other Yahwistic narratives of Genesis.[31] Before incorporating into his work the pre-Yahwistic tale of Gen. 19:1-28, the Yahwist presents (with regard to the same event, the destruction of Sodom) an entire theology regarding the intervention of Yahweh, human history, and the mission of Israel in its midst. The greatest indication of redactional freedom is the interior reflection of Yahweh: "Shall I conceal from Abraham...?" (18:17). Noth correctly states, "For the Yahwist, Sodom certainly represents not only the indigenous Canaanites but at the same time the people of the whole world." And referring to the passage as a whole he adds, "Here we have the oldest discussion known to us of the subject of the justice of God in the sphere of the Old Testament."[32] Given the freedom with which the Yahwist theologizes here, Noth concludes that this passage "deserves special and serious attention in the analysis of [Yahwistic] theology."[33]

The method of *Redaktionsgeschichte*, which became completely conscious of itself only in 1954, leads me to say that Noth's assertion cannot be sufficiently emphasized. The key to the entire Yahwistic work, from Genesis to Numbers, but very especially Genesis, is in this passage in which the redactor undertakes to express his own theology. As von Rad has said, it reveals to us the intention and spirit with which these legendary accounts were collected and assembled and with which they should be read and understood.[34] Unfortunately, neither Noth nor von Rad has carried out this formal programmatic observation.

When Wellhausen and Gunkel felt the need to state that even Gen. 18:18-19 ("justice and right") were interpolated verses, they were not lacking in intuitive sensitivity. To accept this passage as authentic is definitively to challenge the "religious" interpretation of the Old Testament (and therefore the New Testament). It is to have to recognize that the absolute centrality of justice is not the late invention of various gentlemen called prophets, but that the most ancient of the Old Testament authors wrote his own work to affirm that doing justice to the oppressed was *the* purpose of Yahweh's intervention in human history.

Indeed, even the most supernaturalistic exegetes recognize that *ṣ^edakah umiṡpaṭ* ("justice and right") is the most clearly technical term that the Old Testament uses to signify justice for the poor and oppressed, social justice. Therefore I will not quote and analyze the passages in which the term appears. The nonspecialized reader has only to read them to establish that indeed "justice and right" or "right and justice" (*miṡpaṭ uṣ^edakah*) means justice for the poor and needy.[35] In all there are thirty-one instances. This is clearly a hendiadys, that is, an expression in which the two words are meant to signify only one thing. Moreover, the Old Testament uses these two words twenty-three times in strict synonymic parallelism.[36] We find the same parallelism eleven other times but with *ṣedek* instead of *ṣ^edaḵah* (they have the same root and are interchangeable in the Old Testament).[37] In addition to these thirty-four synonymic parallelisms, the two roots *šphṭ* and *ṣdḵ* appear paired together in thirty-two other instances.[38]

Because of the thirty-four cases of strict synonymic parallelism which we have enumerated, we cannot consider this hendiadys as an ordinary one. In the ordinary hendiadys the two paired concepts are not in themselves synonymous: "cups and gold"="golden cups." On the other hand, in this case no matter what prebiblical history and semantics of the two roots in the Semitic languages might have been, the expression *mišpaṭ uṣ^edaḵah* (or *ṣ^edaḵah umišpaṭ*) carries only one idea by means of the joining of two synonymous terms; either one of these terms might, in a given instance, fulfill the same function as the entire hendiadys. It is the same as in the French expressions *us et coutumes, à ses risques et péril, en son lieu et place*, the German *die Art und Weise*, the Latin *mysterium vere et proprie dictum*, which is preserved in the Italian *una tragedia vera e propia*, the English *the mode and manner*, and the Spanish *de modo y manera que. . ., con tasa y medida, simple y sencillamente*. We see how "to achieve *mišpaṭ*" in Jer. 5:1 is the same as "to achieve *mišpaṭ uṣ^edaḵah*" in Jer. 22:3; 22:15; 9:23. Likewise the union of this hendiadys with *ḥesed* 'compassion' in Hos. 2:21 and Ps. 33:5 can be substituted for simply *ṣ^edaḵah* together with *ḥesed* in Hos. 10:12; Ps. 36:11; and Ps. 103:17; or for simply *mišpaṭ* together with *ḥesed* in Hos. 6:5b-6; 12:7; and Mic. 6:8. Moreover, the translators of the Septuagint, who customarily translate *ṣ^edaḵah* as *dikaiosynē* and *mišpaṭ* as some substantive derived from the Greek verb *krinō* (*krima* 180 times, *krisis* 142 times), in 48 instances use the root of *dikaiosynē* to translate *mišpaṭ*, an indication that they considered it a synonym of *ṣ^edaḵah*.

But, I repeat, what we have in Gen. 18:19 is the entire hendiadys. There is no exegete who is unaware that this expression means social justice, accomplished on behalf of the oppressed, the poor, the widow, and the orphan. Gen. 18:18-19 says:

> Abraham will become a great nation and in him all the tribes of the earth will be blessed, *because* I have singled him out to command his sons and his household after him to keep the way of Yahweh by observing "justice and right" *in order that* Yahweh might carry out for Abraham what he has promised him.

These verses deliberately interpret the promise made in Gen. 12:3: "In you all the tribes of the earth will be blessed." Gunkel has seen very clearly the meaning of these two verses: "Yahweh desires above all 'justice and right,' and only if Israel maintains this 'way of Yahweh' will Yahweh fulfill his promises in it."[39] Therefore Gunkel wishes to expurgate the verses. He argues that in the sagas of Genesis Yahweh's promises do not depend on conditions, as they do here. But this is reasoning from the *sola gratia* of dogmatics; it is not exegetical analysis. We have already seen that exegetes now know that in this passage the Yahwist is not transmitting preredactional sagas or accounts, but rather is elaborating the theology for interpreting them and giving them meaning. The difference which Gunkel points out is not reason to cut out this passage, but rather to give it complete preference when we are trying to understand the work of the Yahwist. Moreover, the gratuitous beneficence of Yahweh's love for mankind consists, according to the Yahwist, precisely in Yahweh's breaking into our history to achieve a justice which all previous history had shown that men were not able to achieve. All the tribes of the earth will be blessed in Abraham "because" Yahweh "has singled out" the people of Israel to teach the whole world how to achieve "justice and right."

Gunkel claims to find an interpolative Deuteronomist hand in Gen. 18:17-19, but, in the first place, the vocabulary itself excludes this possibility: The interpolations, retouches, and glosses in the Pentateuch are either of the Deuteronomist or of the Priestly schools. But the expression *sᵉdakah umišpaṭ* does not appear even once in Deuteronomy or in the Priestly text (cf. above, the list of passages in which it occurs). To postulate for this passage alone a glossator of another school who left no trace in any other part of the Pentateuch would be to postulate a marvel.

In the second place, we can see—to select only a few of the passages which we could cite—in Ps. 9:5-13, in Job 19:7, and in Isa. 5:7 the reason why "justice and right" in Gen. 18:19 is inseparable from the "outcry" of Gen. 18:20-21: It is precisely this cry of the poor and the oppressed which pleads that "justice and right" be done. Authors as diverse as Isaiah, the compiler of the book of Job, and the poet of Ps. 9 attest to the fact that this relationship is intrinsic and obligatory. And it is very ancient, as we can see. In this passage it is precisely because Yahweh intervenes to heed the cry of the oppressed that he cannot conceal his plan from Abraham, since Abraham was chosen to bring about justice and right in the world. We cannot cut out Gen. 18:19 without also extirpating Gen. 18:20-21. But if we eliminate vv. 20-21 then we must also eliminate the rest of the passage (vv. 22-33), for vv. 20-21 tells us the reason for Yahweh's intervention against Sodom. The historical question is of no concern to us at this moment. We are concerned with the Yahwist's version of the sin of Sodom. In any case, it is well to note that the Yahwist had the same idea of Sodom's sin as had Isaiah (Isa. 1:10, 15, 17), Jeremiah (Jer. 23:14), and Ezekiel: "The crime of your sister Sodom was luxury, opulence, complacency; such were the sins of Sodom and her daughters. They never helped the poor and the needy" (Ezek. 16:49). Such a situation "cries" to heaven (Gen. 18:20-21), and thus the idea of achieving "justice and right" (Gen. 18:19). Not only is the entire passage Gen. 18:17-33 of one piece, but it is precisely v. 19, "justice and right," which is the axis of the entire passage.

In the third place, however, the most important point is that Gen. 18:25 describes Yahweh as "the judge of the whole earth." And the whole Old Testament knows that the judge's task is "to do justice and right." This is precisely the expression we find in Gen. 18:19, which, therefore, is inseparable from the text which follows. We will take up this matter in the next chapter. Here we cite simply as an example:

God, give your own judgment to the king,
your own justice to the royal son,
so that he may rule your people with justice
and your poor with right.

(Ps. 72:1-2)

In the passages which we have listed above and in those where justice and right appear in hendiadys or synonymic parallelism, practically all those which refer to God represent him as judge. The true basis of the doubts concerning Gen. 18:19 has been the fact that exegesis did not take Gen. 18:22-33 seriously for what it is, namely, the key to the Yahwist's theo-logy: Yahweh is the God who intervenes in history to destroy the unjust ($r^e\check{s}a\,\text{'}im$, in v. 23 and twice in v. 25) and to save the oppressed from the injustice which they suffer and which unfailingly cries out to heaven. This is the only God whom the Bible knows, from Gen. 4:1-11 to Matt. 25:31-46. The "just" of Gen. 18:23, 24a, 24b, 25a, 25b, 26, 28 are the same as those of Matt. 25:37, 46. But underneath the exegetical doubts was the prejudice which did not want to translate *ṣaddik* as "just," but rather as "justified," and did not want to translate *ṣᵉdaḳah* as "justice," but rather as "justification." By dismissing from the start the possibility that the only purpose for God's intervention in our history is to achieve justice on earth, one can then consider as pharisaical the Psalms—and there is a striking number of them—which divide men into the just and unjust, the Psalms which speak only of the secular hope that Yahweh will at last one day eliminate the unjust from the earth and that this world will be changed into a history of justice.

The paradigm of the abomination was Ps. 37. "The just" appear in vv. 12, 16, 17, 21, 25, 29, 30, 32, 39; and "the unjust" in vv. 10, 12, 14, 16, 17, 20, 21, 28, 32, 34, 38, 40. How difficult it must have been for exegesis to acknowledge that Ps. 37:14 describes the unjust (*rᵉ̌šaʿim*) as men who "bend their bow to strike down the poor and needy" and that Ps. 37:21 describes the just man (*ṣaddik*) as he who "has compassion and gives." But now we see that the Psalter has exactly the same idea of Yahweh as the Yahwist. And note that the Yahwist calls Yahweh "judge," not only in Gen. 18:17-33, but also in Gen. 16:5 ("Let Yahweh judge between me and you"); he saves Noah from the flood simply because he is "the only just man of this generation," according to Gen. 7:1. This same idea also distinguishes Gen. 4:1-11. Moreover, in the remarkable prelude regarding the person of Moses, which the author places before Moses' vocation and the primordial revelation of Yahweh, the qualifier "unjust" *(rašaʿ)* appears again as the unequivocal qualifier of the person who commits injustice against his neighbor (see Exod. 2:13 in the second of the three scenes which make up the prelude in Exod. 2:11-20). As we shall see shortly, *rašaʿ* can mean nothing else in Exod. 9:27 (also Yahwistic).

It is striking that the three scenes narrated in Exod. 2:11-20 go well beyond the merely anecdotal and try to explain why God chose Moses. The organic nature of the entire passage is governed by the initial statement: "Moses, a man by now, set out at this time to visit his brothers, and he saw what a hard life they were having" (Exod. 2:11a). This is the same "seeing" which in the fundamental revelation of the Bible (Exod. 3:7-9) is the reason for the intervention of Yahweh in human history: "I have seen the affliction. . . . Yes, I have seen the oppression." We would be letting literary genres obfuscate things for us

if we were to think that the first two scenes have the purpose only of
narratively transferring Moses from Egypt to Midian, as if they were an
"etiological account" to make his presence in Midian plausible. This is
not the case. These passages insist that Moses had to flee because
already by that time his only concern was for justice. This is so much
the case that, contradicting all verisimilitude, the first scene after Moses
arrives at Midian is a third intervention in defense of the weak: "Moses
came to their defense" (Exod. 2:17b). The theme of justice is the
strand which unites the three accounts.

In contrast with the passages which are parallel in literary genre
(Gen. 24:11ff. and 29:2ff.), here it is the stranger who undertakes the
action of justice: "An Egyptian delivered us out of the hand of...,"
say the girls in Exod. 2:19. This is exactly the expression Yahweh will
use in revealing himself: "Yes, I am well aware of their sufferings, and I
have gone down to deliver them out of the hand of the Egyptians"
[*l^{e}haṣṣilo miyyad* 'deliver out of the hand of'] (Exod. 3:8). The words
of Exod. 2:19 are said to Jethro, and in Exod. 18 *haṣṣil miyyad* will be
repeated no less than five times in a description, also in the Midianitic
tradition, of the already achieved liberation of the people by Yahweh.
This enables this same Jethro to recognize that "Yahweh is the greatest
of all the gods" (Exod. 18:11). Because of his eagerness for justice,
Moses had to flee Egypt; because of his eagerness for justice he met
Jethro: The Yahwist used a specific content to fill the etiological-
biographical connections (Exod. 2:11-20) which were necessary to the
thread of the story; he had to present a qualified Moses.

The revelation of Yahweh in Exod. 3:7-9 has been the focal point of
the polarization with regard to the entire Yahwistic text. When in
Exod. 9:27 the Yahwist has the Pharaoh recognize that he and his
people are "the unjust" (*har^{e}ša'im*) and that Yahweh is "the just"
(*haṣṣaddik*), the meaning of these terms has to be consistent with Gen.
18:17-33 and Exod. 2:13. Together the Priestly and Yahwistic documents exhaust the Hebrew vocabulary to tell us that this was a matter
of true injustice: "oppression," "abuse," "hard life," "affliction,"
"slavery."[40] There is no doubt about the meaning of "unjust" in Exod.
9:27 after such irate insistence on the fact that this was a matter of real
injustice and not some "declaratory" injustice pronounced by some
nonexistent tribunal as the result of some nonexistent trial (*rib-
pattern*). We should keep in mind that this long string of "afflictions,"

"oppressions," "abuses," etc. makes those who suffer them "cry out" to Yahweh (in the technical sense of the term) an equally striking number of times.[41] It would be quite extraordinary for a "declaratory" injustice to provoke such an outcry. Yahweh is just, because he has compassion on those who suffer and intervenes to deliver them from oppression; the Pharaoh and his people are unjust because they oppress and harass and abuse and enslave.

The author of Ps. 82 moves within the same very ancient tradition when he challenges the other gods by contrasting them to Yahweh:
Defend [*šiftu*] the poor and the orphan,
do justice to the destitute and the helpless.
Rescue the poor and the needy,
deliver them from the hand [*haṣṣil miyyad*] of the unjust [*rešaʿim*].
(Ps. 82:3-4)
It is not a mere coincidence that Ps. 82 uses the same expression, *haṣṣil miyyad*, with which Yahweh revealed himself to Moses in Exod. 3:8. It is the same expression insistently repeated five times in Exod. 18:1-10 so that an impartial witness might recognize that "Yahweh is greater than all the gods" (Exod. 18:11); and this is the recognition that Ps. 82 also is trying to achieve.[42] The Psalm was composed previous to the period of the monarchy, and so it is, therefore, more ancient than the Yahwist. But we must not forget that in Gen. 18:17-33 the Yahwist situates the historical mission of Israel within the specific purpose of God's intervention in human history: To make the whole world observe "justice and right," which is to rescue the poor and the helpless from the hand of the oppressors. Thus the intervention of Yahweh is no longer fragmented; it becomes a plan for the realization of which he has chosen Israel. In this way there begins the history of "the just" (as opposed to the *rešaʿim*), whose unceasing recurrence in the Psalter has left the impression on some exegetes that they were some band or party or association.[43] What we do indeed have in the Psalter is the perfect awareness of the continuous and organic nature of Yahweh's intervention as a plan to achieve justice and right on the entire earth.

But the term does not refer to parties. The *rešaʿim*, whom both the Yahwist and Ps. 82 describe as those from whose hands the weak and oppressed must be delivered, are inevitably conceived as enemies of Yahweh (Ps. 21:9; 66:3; 83:3; 89:11, 52; 92:10; 110:1, 2). The more we understand Yahweh's intervention as a continuity in human history, a continuity which meets with opposition, so much the more does this characterization make sense. Therefore the $r^e \check{s}a\text{'}im$ are also represented as members of an army (Ps. 3:7; 27:3; 55:19; 56:2; 59:5; 62:4). It is supposed, and rightly so, that because of their mercilessness and their injustices they are an obstacle to the achievement of justice in the world, an obstacle to Yahweh's plan; they fight against Yahweh.

Given the abundance of items offered us by the Psalter for understanding who the $r^e \check{s}a\text{'}im$ are, I think we are at the Archimedean point of our interpretation of the Psalter. The importance of the meaning of the term is decisive, for on it depends the meaning of the much-considered "justice of the just," and on this depend the most central questions in the interpretation of the New Testament. Indeed, certain characterizations of the $r^e \check{s}a\text{'}im$, as persecutors of the poor, enemies of the just, doers of iniquity (*'awen*), have been inexplicably relativized in exegesis; thus "the poor," for example, is said to refer to a pious association which calls itself by this name, and so the $r^e \check{s}a\text{'}im$ are opponents of this association whenever the Psalter says that they persecute and exploit the poor.

At this point one feels that he has no solid ground under his feet; all the words have interdependent variable values, and we cannot know what any of them really means. As Gunkel has pointed out, "We should proceed methodically in exactly the opposite direction";[44] we should not use as our reference point the half-dozen passages where the Psalmist does not make the meaning of his expressions explicit because he supposes it to be already known. Since in these passages, "absolutely" speaking and prescinding from the context, each word has various "possible" meanings, it contradicts every reasonable principle of objectivity to insist on one of these "possible" meanings and then claim that it is applicable in all the other instances in which the word occurs. The only scientific approach is to get the meaning from those passages in which there can be no doubt, and then use this meaning in reading the other passages where the meaning of the word in question is not made explicit.

Gunkel himself describes the erroneous methodology which led Mowinckel to understand "doers of *'awen*" as magic enchanters or practicers of witchcraft.[45] Not even in Isa. 58:9 should Gunkel take his challenge seriously; we need only read vv. 6-10 to see that the idea of magic is entirely impossible. The passage speaks of breaking the enslaving yoke, of giving food to the hungry, shelter to the homeless, clothing to the naked, relief to the oppressed. To say that the "pointing of the finger" on the part of the enemies implies magic is going too far. This is "a gesture of contempt," as Bright says.[46] But to assert that because in Isa. 58:9 *'awen* is near "pointing of the finger," it therefore always means witchcraft, and on this basis to interpret all the "doers of *'awen*" in the Psalter, this indeed is beyond reason.

We must be perfectly clear about our method. For example, let us take the word *dal* ("needy"). It occurs five times in the Psalter (Ps. 41:1; 82:3, 4; 72:13; 113:7). Ps. 72 says that the king will have pity on the poor and the needy and will save their lives because their blood is precious in the eyes of the king (vv. 12-14). The meaning of *dal* seems here as unequivocal as in the other passages where the term occurs. In Ps. 72:12-14, however, there is no mention of orphans or unhappy women or times of famine; but it would be methodologically unacceptable to use this circumstance to invent some pious congregation called "the poor and the needy" and to maintain that the king will be its protector. If the Psalter consisted only of these three verses (Ps. 72:12-14), perhaps such a possibility would be conceivable in "absolute" terms, on an equal footing with many other possibilities which could be imagined. One of them, of course, is that these are in fact poor people and in fact needy people.

But we have a way to overcome our doubts. Ps. 113 blesses Yahweh because he raises the needy from the dust (v. 7) and because he gives sons to the barren woman (v. 9). We must conceive of the *dal* of v. 7 to be as realistically poor as the woman of v. 9 is barren. Ps. 41 states that happy is the man who cares for the poor and the needy; if disaster strikes God will come to his help (v. 1). There is no doubt about the meaning. So too since Ps. 82:3-4 speaks of saving "the poor and the orphan" from the hand of the *reša'im*, it is not pious associations that the author has in mind. The orphan is he who has no parents, and the poor person is he who has no money.

As regards the substantive *reša'im*, the accumulation of descriptive elements in the Psalter is so unequivocal that, even if the other words which frequently occur in relationship with *reša'im* were truly of variable significance, they would nevertheless acquire a clear outline simply by their relationship with *reša'im*. It is like identifying some unknown quantity on whose value all the others depend. Here the interpretation comes up against solid rock, not slippery ground. What single word we should use to translate the term $r^e\check{s}a'im$ is a subordinate question. What is important is what manner of conduct, according to the Psalter, characterizes these people. They are those who practice *violence* against the weak (Ps. 11:5; 18:49; 25:19; 27:12; 72:14; 86:14; 140:2, 5, 12; "men of violence" in 18:49 and 140 in synonymy with *raša'*); they exploit the *orphan* (Ps. 10:14-15; 82:3-4; 94:3, 6; 146:9) and the *widow* (94:3, 6; 146:9); they are *bloodthirsty* (5:7; 26:9; 51:16; 55:24; 59:3; 72:14; 94:21; 119:19), *oppressors* (62:11; 72:4; 73:8; 119:121, 122, 134; 146:7), *exploiters* (35:10); they are *cunning* (10:7; 72:14); they tell *lies* to their neighbor (12:3; 24:4; 26:4; 41:7; 144:8, 11) and *deceive* him (5:7; 40:5; 58:4; 62:5; 28:3) through *fraud* and *trickery* (5:7; 10:7; 24:4; 35:20; 36:4; 43:1; 50:19; 52:6; 55:24; 109:2); they accept *bribes* (26:10); they *do not pay back* what they borrow (37:21); they are *unmerciful* in the fullest sense of the word (12:1; 43:1; 109:16); they practice *injustice* (37:1; 43:1; 64:7; 89:23; 107:42; 125:3).[47]

It is objectively impossible to relativize this series of data or to spiritualize it in some figurative sense. The conduct of the $r^e\check{s}a'im$ is simple injustice from which the weak and helpless need to be saved. To encompass all this I know of no qualifier more appropriate than "unjust," in its strongest sense. When the context is that of a judicial institution and litigation, the $r^e\check{s}a'im$ are declared to be unjust because they are so; their injustice does not consist in having been declared unjust.

"Sinners" is an equivocal translation, unless it is supposed that the only sin is injustice. The translators of the Septuagint did suppose this, for they were well versed in the Bible, but our modern languages do not. "Atheists" is not adequate either, although they are indeed atheists;[48] the Bible does not describe them by their vertical relationship with God but by their horizontal relationship with their neighbor. Nor is "impious" an accurate rendering, since in our modern languages it distracts attention toward the religious dimension; but the history of this translation in the Vulgate deserves a monograph on the degeneration that the word "piety" has suffered. Originally *impius* meant pitiless, lacking in compassion, which is surprisingly in accord with the root of the conduct of the $r^e\check{s}a'im$ as the Bible describes them. It is noteworthy that at one time "pious works" unequivocally meant actions on behalf of one's neighbor, but today they are practically equivalent to prayers and religious exercises. The term "pious" has suffered from the same process of evasion. The whole history of Christianity is involved in this.

The list of descriptive traits mentioned above corroborates the meaning of "doers of *'awen*," which is already quite obvious in Ps. 5:6-7 from the synonymic parallelism with "bloodthirsty and fraudulent man"; in Ps. 14:4 from the expression "those who devour the people" (cf. Mic. 3:3; Isa. 9:11; Hab. 1:13; Jer. 10:25; 30:16; Prov. 30:14); in Ps. 28:3 from the quasi-definition "who talk of peace to their neighbors while malice is in their hearts"; in Ps. 58:3 from the synonymy with "bloodthirsty men"; in Ps. 94:4 because it is they, according to v. 6, who "kill the widow and stranger and murder the orphans"; in Ps. 101:8 because it is they, according to v. 7, who "commit fraud and tell lies"; etc. Thus "iniquity" is a good translation for *'awen*, as long as we do not trivialize it. It is practically synonymous with *reša'* (the quality of the *reša'im*), which appears in Ps. 5:5; 10:15; 45:8; 84:11; 125:3; and 141:4.

The term "unjust" (in singular or plural) occurs in the Psalter eighty-two times, while "just" (in singular or plural) occurs fifty-two times. We need look only at Ps. 37, Ps. 1, and Ps. 9 to see that the *reša'im* and the *ṣaddiķim* are correlatives; thus by establishing the meaning of "unjust," we know by contrast the meaning of "just." So we see that in Gen. 18:17-33 the "just" one is he who is not numbered among the "unjust." But it would be exegetically out of focus to forget that both in the Psalter and in the Yahwistic document Yahweh's intervention on behalf of justice is the true theme; and it is in function of this intervention that it is important to belong or not to belong to the army of the unjust. Yahweh breaks into our world to achieve justice; for this reason and only for this reason is there such an insistence on not belonging to the group which will be destroyed by Yahweh's intervention. In the kingdom of justice, which God will establish in the world, there will be not even one of the *reša'im*: "In your people all will be just; they will possess the land forever" (Isa. 60:21). Ps. 37 itself expresses this with incomparable exactitude:

> The unjust will perish once and for all
> and the children of the wicked shall be expelled;
> the just will have the land for their own,
> and make it their home forever.

(Ps. 37:28-29)

Neither the Psalter nor the Old Testament nor the New Testament can be understood in a static way. Everything in them must be seen in the light of *the* intervention of Yahweh, which is one alone and has as its only purpose the achievement of the definitive rule of justice. When Matthew has Christ say, "Blessed are the gentle, because they shall possess the earth" (Matt. 5:5), the ultraterrestrial interpretation which tries to situate the kingdom in the beyond becomes impossible. Paul says that the observers of the law will not "inherit *the world*," but that those who by faith are converted into the just will do so: "The promise of inheriting the world was not made to Abraham and his descendants on account of the law, but on account of the justice of faith" (Rom. 4:13). Both Nestle and Merk have noticed that here Paul makes his own the Yahwist's hope in Gen. 18:18. The "kingdom of heaven" does not mean a kingdom in the sky, but rather "the kingdom of God," as all modern commentators agree, since in this expression they find the classic circumlocution of late Judaism which in this way avoids naming the name of God. The passages in Paul and Luke which speak of an extraterrestrial "paradise" (Luke 23:43; 2 Cor. 12:4) or of "the bosom of Abraham" (Luke 16:23) or of a proximate "being with Christ" (Phil. 1:23), etc. allude to a provisional situation which will last only until Christ returns to earth to establish the kingdom of God definitively and perfectly.[49]

Theodor Zahn rightly states, "After the Beatitudes of Matt. 5:3-10 it is obvious that the reward (mentioned in 5:12) will be given to the disciples only in the kingdom which must be established on earth." "Your reward is great in heaven" does not mean that they will be rewarded in heaven "as if it said *hoti misthon polyn* (or *plērē*) *lēpsesthe en tois ouranois.*" What it does say is that men's actions enter into the knowledge of God, or "in figurative language, that they ascend to God in heaven and there accumulate like a treasure," not that we will enjoy them there.[50] "Your prayers and offerings have gone up like a remembrance before the presence of God," says Luke in Acts 10:4, and this is also the exact idea of Luke 6:23; 12:33; Matt. 5:12; 6:20; 1 Pet. 1:4-8. It must be noted that this idea already existed in the Old Testament (cf. Tob. 12:12-15) and that the New Testament offers no textual basis for asserting that there is any difference on this point. We see that the resurrection of the dead will arrive with the kingdom in Isa. 26:19; Hos. 13:14; Dan. 12:2; Ezek. 37:12, 14. But we cannot take seriously the absolute centrality of the resurrection of the body in the New Testament if the kingdom of justice is not established on earth.

This is not to deny the "beyond" nor eternal blessedness, but rather to take them with complete seriousness, for once we affirm the resurrection *of the bodies*, even the most conservative theology needs a corporeal place to put them. I have no difficulty in accepting a "heavenly Jerusalem"; but we must make it very clear that this heavenly Jerusalem, made up of the apostles and the martyrs and the just who have died, "will come down from heaven" to the earth, according to Rev. 21:2 and 10, and that it therefore is the same provisional place which I have just mentioned with regard to Luke and Paul.

The apocalyptic description of this kingdom which has come down from heaven continues to Rev. 22:5, where it ends by saying, "They will reign forever and ever." Rev. 5:10 had already explained to us that the just "will reign on earth." I do not see what objection can be brought forth against this idea, even by a dogmatics which is not at all concerned with biblical normativeness, since it is expressly recognized that the earth itself will be completely transformed (cf. Isa. 65:17) and that "the last enemy to be destroyed is death" (1 Cor. 15:26). All the objections and "cosmological or anthropological curiosities" to which this biblical earthly kingdom might give rise are equally or more applicable if we imagine a heavenly kingdom (once we have accepted the resurrection of the body). Moreover, all the assertions and predications that dogmatics might well make about heaven can equally be made about the transformed earth. And thus the reluctance of traditionalism to accept what is being maintained in this book is reduced to a verbal question.

When Matt. 25:34 says to "the just" (vv. 37, 46), "Take for your heritage the kingdom prepared for you," this is the same kingdom which according to Matt. 12:28, "already arrived" (aorist tense) on earth. The Evangelist insists that the field in which this kingdom takes root "is the world" (Matt. 13:38), that Christ will return to this kingdom to gather out from it all "those who do iniquity" (Matt. 13:41), and that "then the just will shine like the sun in the kingdom of their Father. Listen, anyone who has ears" (Matt. 13:43).

We should not be surprised by the continuity stretching from the Yahwist to Paul, Matthew, and John, since the central verse of the Letter to the Romans (3:21) expressly informs us that the justice of

God revealed in the Gospel is not merely any justice of God, but precisely that "made known through the law and the prophets."

Notes to Chapter 3

1. Cf. von Rad, "The Theological Problem of the Old Testament Doctrine of Creation," in *Problem of the Hexateuch*, pp. 131-43.

2. *B^{e}ṣedek*: Christopher R. North, *The Second Isaiah* (Oxford: Clarendon, 1964), pp. 155 and 111-112: "for a saving purpose." Gesenius in the *Handwörterbuch* concerning the preposition *b^e*: *begründende Bedeutung,* or *auf etwas hin.*

3. Von Rad, "Creation," p. 139.

4. Karl Elliger, "Sinn und Ursprung der priesterlichen Geschichtserzählung" (1952) in *Kleine Schriften zum Alten Testament* (Munich: Kaiser Verlag, 1966), p. 178.

5. See Joüon, *Grammaire*, 119e; "Je suis Jéhovah! et (en conséquence) je vous ferai sortir. . . ." This is the same *waw* of logical consequence that the majority of translations overlook, but which can be seen in Gen. 20:11; Isa. 6:7; 2 Sam. 3:21; 1 Kings 2:31; Judg. 6:16; Deut. 2:6; 2:28; 10:19.

6. Cf. Walther Zimmerli, "Ich bin Jahwe" (1953), in *Gottes Offenbarung: Gesammelte Aufsätze zum Alten Testamenten* (Munich: Kaiser Verlag, 1963), pp. 11-40; Zimmerli, "Erkenntnis Gottes nach dem Buche Ezechiel" (1954), *Gesammelte Aufsätze*, pp. 41-119; Zimmerli, "Das Wort des göttlichen Selbsterweises" (1957), *Gesammelte Aufsätze*, (pp. 120-32); Karl Elliger, "Ich bin der Herr-euer Gott" (1955), in *Kleine Schriften*, pp. 211-31.

7. Zimmerli, "Erkenntnis Gottes," pp. 54-78.

8. It should be noted that the difference between nos. 2 and 3 is the work of the Masoretes who punctuated the original text over a thousand years after it was written. This is also the case in the difference between nos. 7 and 8. As Elliger has pointed out, there is often a discrepancy between the Septuagint and the Masoretes on these two points ("Ich bin der Herr," pp. 220-23).

9. Elliger, "Ich bin der Herr," pp. 228-30.

10. Rolf Rendtorff, "Die Offenbarungsvorstellungen im Alten Testament," *Ker Dog* 1 (1961), pp. 21-41.

11. Zimmerli, " 'Offenbarung' im Alten Testament," *EvTh* 22 (1962), pp. 15-31.

12. Ibid., p. 25.

13. Zimmerli, *Gesammelte Aufsätze*, pp. 43-44.

14. Stanislao Lyonnet, *De peccato et redemptione* (Rome: PIB, 1960), 2: 100-03 and 108; Lyonnet, *Exegesis epistulae ad romanos cap. I ad IV*, 3rd ed. (Rome: PIB, 1963), pp. 80-107d; E. Beaucamp, "La justice de Yahve et l'Économie de l'alliance," *StBiFr* 2 (1960-61). H. Cazelles, "A propos de quelques textes difficiles. . .," *RB* 58, no. 2 (April 1951): 169-88.

15. Hans Wilhelm Hertzberg, "Die Entwicklung des Begriffes mišpaṭ im AT," *ZAltW* 40 (1922): 256-87; 41 (1923):35. Walther Zimmerli, "pais Theou," in *TDNT*, 5: 669. Westermann, *Isaiah 40-66*, p. 59.

16. Hertzberg, "Entwicklung," p. 34.

17. Bernhard Duhm, *Das Buch Jesaja*, 5th ed. (Göttingen: Vandenhoeck, 1968), p. 307.

18. See above pp. 45-47.

19. Zimmerli, *Gesammelte Aufsätze*, pp. 69-70 and 22-23.

20. Zimmerli, "Offenbarung," *EvTh* 22 (1962):21-22.

21. Alfred Jepsen, "Ṣdḳ und ṣdḳh im Alten Testament," in *Festschrift Hertzberg* (1965), pp. 78-97, especially p. 86.

22. Cf. Rudolph, *Jeremia*, pp. 145-48.

23. Zimmerli, *Gesammelte Aufsätze*, pp. 73ff.

24. H. Gunkel, *Genesis*, 7th ed. (Göttingen: Vandenhoeck, 1966), pp. 44, 202.

25. Nahum M. Sarna, *Understanding Genesis* (New York: McGraw Hill, 1966), p. 145.

26. See the bibliography in Sarna, *Understanding Genesis*, pp. 235-45; and Henricus Renckens, *Israel's Concept of the Beginning* (New York: Herder, 1964), chapters 22-24.

27. Gerhard von Rad, *Genesis: A Commentary*, trans. John H. Marks (London: SCM, 1961), p. 105.

28. Sarna, *Understanding Genesis*, pp. 30-31.

29. Cf. von Rad, "zaô ktl," *TDNT*, 2:844 and n. 85.

30. Cf. E. A. Speiser, *Genesis*, Anchor Bible 1 (Garden City, New York: Doubleday, 1964), p. 18 ad Gen. 2:22. And cf. the Catholic Claude Tresmontant in Roger Garaudy, *Perspectives de l'homme*, 3rd ed. (Paris: Presses Universitaires de France, 1961).

31. Gunkel, *Genesis*, p. 202.

32. Martin Noth, *Überlieferungsgeschichte des Pentateuch* (Stuttgart: Kohlhammer, 1948), pp. 258-59; cf. Noth, *A History of Pentateuchal Traditions*, trans. Bernhard W. Anderson (Englewood Cliffs, N.J.: Prentice-Hall, 1972), pp. 238-39.

33. Noth, *Überlieferungsgeschichte*, p. 259; Noth, *History*, p. 239.

34. Von Rad, *Genesis*, p. 204 and cf. p. 160.

35. Gen. 18:19; 2 Sam. 8:15; 1 Kings 10:9; Isa. 9:6; 33:5; Jer. 4:2; 9:23; 22:3, 15; 23:5; 33:15; Hos. 2:21; Ezek. 18:5, 19, 21, 27; 33:14, 16, 19; 45:9; Ps. 33:5; 89:15; 97:2; 99:4; 119:121; Prov. 1:3; 2:9; 21:3; Eccles. 5:7; 1 Chron. 18:14; 2 Chron. 9:8.

36. Isa. 1:27; 5:7, 16; 28:17; 32:16; 54:17; 56:1; 59:9, 14; Amos 5:7, 24; 6:12; Mic. 7:9; Ps. 36:7; 37:6; 72:1; 99:4; 103:6; 106:3; Job 35:2; 37:23; Prov. 8:20; 16:8.

37. Deut. 16:18, Isa. 1:21; 16:5; 26:9; 32:1; Jer. 22:13; Ps. 9:5; 72:2; 94:15; Job 8:3; 29:14.

38. Lev. 19:15; Deut. 1:16; 16:18; 25:1; 1 Sam. 12:7; 2 Sam. 15:4; 1 Kings

108   *Marx and the Bible*

8:32; Isa. 1:26; 11:4; 16:5; 43:26; 51:5; 59:4; Jer. 11:20; Ezek. 23:45; Ps. 7:9, 12; 9:5, 9; 35:24; 50:6; 51:6; 58:2, 12; 82:3; 96:13; 98:9; Job 9:15; Prov. 8:16; 31:9; Eccles. 3:17; 2 Chron. 6:23.

39. Gunkel, *Genesis,* p. 202.
40. Exod. 1:11-14, 16; 2:11; 3:7, 8, 16, 17; 5:7-14; 5:16-19; 6:5-6; 6:9; 13:4; 14:10; etc.
41. Exod. 2:23; 3:7, 9; 5:8, 15; 11:6; 12:30; 14:10, 15.
42. Regarding the antiquity of Ps. 82 see Dahood, *Psalms II,* p. 269; and Kraus, *Psalmen II,* p. 570.
43. See the bibliographical review in Johann Jakob Stamm, "Ein Vierteljahrhundert Psalmenforschung," *Theologische Rundschau NF* 23 (1955): 50-60. Cf. also William Oscar Emil Oesterley, *The Psalms* (London: SPCK, 1953), pp. 56-66.
44. Gunkel, *Einleitung in die Psalmen,* 2nd. ed. (Göttingen: Vandenhoeck, 1966), pp. 202, 201 n. 4.
45. Ibid., pp. 200-11.
46. *Peake's Commentary on the Bible,* Matthew Black and H.H. Rowley, eds. (London: Thomas Nelson, 1964), p. 531 ad loc. Gesenius ad voc. and Duhm ad loc. are of the same opinion.
47. Regarding the substantive *'awᵉlah,* cf. Franciscus Zorell, *Lexicon Hebraicum et Aramaicum Veteris. Testamentum* (Rome: PIB, 1959), p. 579: "iniustitia," and see its meaning in Mic. 3:10 and Hab. 2:12.
48. See above chapter 2.
49. Cf. Joachim Jeremias, "paradeisos," *TDNT,* 5:769-70; "hadēs," *TDNT,* 1:148-49; "geenna," *TDNT,* 1:657-58; *Parables of Jesus,* p. 185; and the Catholic Paul Hoffmann, *Die Toten in Christus* (Münster: Aschendorff, 1966).
50. Theodor Zahn, *Das Evangelium des Matthäus,* 3rd ed. (Leipzig: A. Deichertsche, 1910), p. 197.

Chapter Four

Law and Civilization

God's intervention in our history has the unified and organic character of a coherent plan, the stubborn continuity of someone who has decided to accomplish something. Its last act is what we are accustomed to call "the Last Judgment."

But when we say "judgment," exegetically we come up against the Hebrew term *mišpaṭ*. And it is on this term; it seems to me, that our interpretation of the entire Bible, and the New Testament in particular, depends (subject to what we have said in the first part of chapter 2 concerning the unmistakable characteristic of the God of the Bible). This same word, *mišpaṭ*, means law, judicial act, right, justice, extra-judicial intervention for justice' sake, and, what is most important and yet has not been adequately considered, it also designates the content of what we customarily call "Last Judgment." What the Last Judgment will be depends on what *mišpaṭ* means. Paul, John, and the Synoptics suppose this meaning to be understood. "Last" has the sense of "Finally!" "At last!" "This is what all mankind has been awaiting for thousands and thousands of years!"

Methodologically we will put to one side the historico-cultural question regarding the West's differentiation among the different meanings of *mišpaṭ*, namely, whether or not this differentiation represented progress with respect to a mentality and a consciousness which insisted on seeing these various meanings as identical. Of course, in any hypoth-

109

esis this identification tends to keep, for example, the law or a judicial proceeding from becoming absolutized as an autonomous value which thus becomes capable of the worst injustices. The tendency to absolutize the law and the judicial process is obviously more ancient than the West, and indeed the prophets, Christ, and Paul rebelled against this tendency. We are here dealing with perhaps the most serious problem of the philosophy of law.

For now I am concerned with the methodological question of scientific exegesis. Western translators consider it praiseworthy when they introduce distinctions among the various uses of *mišpat* by employing different terms. But methodologically there is nothing that authorizes us to project different meanings on one word (or on the root *špht*, from which *mišpat* is formed), for these differences originate in our own culture, our own history, and our own language. It is *for us* that justice, judgment, law, right, intervention for justice' sake, etc. have different meanings. But the West has been so ingenuous as to set itself up as the absolute criterion and to assert that, independently of all cultural discrepancies, these meanings which to the West seem different are *in themselves* different. This is indeed an unusual coincidence: That which is absolute and independent of all cultural variation coincides exactly with Western culture. According to our mentality these meanings have very little to do with each other, or at least they are not the same; but to suppose that the biblical authors saw it the same way would be methodologically unacceptable. If these meanings were not the same for them we would have to say that in Hebrew the word *mišpat* was equivocal. But to attribute this equivocality to the Bible would be to base ourselves entirely on our own culture and our own language, not on the Bible.

Unquestionably the Western versions have to translate *mišpat* at times by "salvation of the poor," at times by "righteousness," at times by "justice," etc. The scientific task should be to try to understand why these ideas are expressed as one in the word *mišpat* in the Bible; it should not avoid the problem by having facile recourse to the assertion of equivocality. Otherwise, the peculiarities of our language and our culture are stretched like a veil between Scripture and us; this keeps from its intended hearers a biblical message which could challenge our moral codes and our entire civilization.

Judgment or Justice?

Before considering the meaning of *mišpaṭ* in the Hebrew itself, it would be illustrative to see how the translators of the Septuagint reacted to the term, given the linguistic means at their disposition. The first thing that they perceived was, in all probability, that the verb of the Hebrew root *šphṭ*, that is, the verb *šaphaṭ*, was often used in the sense of the Greek verb *krinein*, which in our languages is the equivalent of "to judge." Therefore as a general rule they tried to translate Hebrew words which had the root *šphṭ* with terms having the Greek root *krin*. For the verb itself, they always used *krinein*, except for thirteen times in which they used *diakrinein*, which has the same root.[1] To translate *šopheṭ*, which is the substantivized participle of the Hebrew verb *šaphaṭ*, they consequently used the Greek substantive *kritēs* ("judge") or the participle *krinōn* ("judging" or "he who judges"). Logically they looked to the same Greek root to find some substantive of thing to translate the Hebrew substantive *mišpaṭ*. They found *krima* and *krisis*; they used the former 180 times and the latter 142, although it is difficult to determine by what criterion or nuance they preferred one to the other. Up to this point, nevertheless, their approach was quite consistent.

We begin to see the illustrative aspect of their reaction when we note that twenty-seven times they translated the Hebrew verb *šaphaṭ* or its above-mentioned participle by means of the root of *dikaiosynē* ("justice"), which they had apparently reserved for the Greek version of the Hebrew root *ṣdk*. We find the verb *ekdikein* ("to do justice to someone," "to avenge him") as the Greek version of *šaphaṭ* in 1 Sam. 3:13; 2 Chron. 28:8; Obad. 21; Ezek. 7:7, 27; 16:38; 20:4; 23:24, 45. We find *dikazein* ("to pass judgment," "to do justice") as the Greek version of the same Hebrew verb in 1 Sam. 7:6, 15, 16, 17, 8:5, 6, 20; 12:7; 24:13, 16. And for the participle *šopheṭ* we find the Greek substantive *dikastēs* ("vindicator") in Exod. 2:14; Josh. 8:33; 23:2; 24:1; 1 Sam. 8:1, 2; 24:16; Isa. 3:2. These twenty-seven instances of turning to the root of *dikaisoynē* are significant, for they are symptomatic of the fact that in the Hebrew verb *šaphaṭ* the translators of the Septuagint saw not exactly the neutral function connoted by our "to judge," but rather to do justice to someone who in one way or another has been oppressed. But even more eloquent is the fact that forty-eight times in their translation of *mišpaṭ*, they abandon the Greek root *krin,* which they had set as a rule, and turn to the root of *dikaiosynē.*[2] The change for this substantive of thing is more frequent, because the substantive refers to the result, namely, justice, and not so much to the action itself. In all, therefore, the Greek translators had to abandon the root *krin* seventy-five times to reproduce with greater fidelity the meaning of the Hebrew root *špṭ* by means of the explicit mention of justice.

As we have seen, in the Hebrew itself the roots *špṭ* and *ṣdḳ* appear ninety-seven times linked in the closest fashion known to the Hebrew language: either in the internal accusative form or a similar phrase, in synonymic parallelism, or in the classical hendiadys *mišpaṭ uṣ^e daḳah.*[3] Herntrich rightly comments, "These two words of very different origin came to be regarded as virtually synonymous."[4] The meaning of the verb *šaphaṭ* is therefore much more specific than our Western verb "to judge," for, as Herntrich adds, "even in texts like Gen. 16:5, in which by the preposition *ben* [that is, "between"] the root *špṭ* undoubtedly has a juridical meaning, one can see that it is not the verdict as such which is important but rather the elimination of an injury in which the violation of justice consisted."[5] It is impossible to emphasize sufficiently how important this conclusion of the analysis is for our understanding of what the Bible awaits when it waits for the Last Judgment.

Herntrich's assertion seems completely accurate to me; nevertheless I think we should consider the matter more deeply. We do not deny that in some cases the Hebrew terms which we customarily translate by "judge," "to judge," or "judgment" do indeed refer to the judicial institution. But there are Hebrew expressions from which it is necessary to conclude that the root *špṭ* and the three above-mentioned words do not necessarily imply a reference to the judicial institution nor is their truly proper meaning "to judge."

We find the term *šophetim* (the so-called "judges") used to designate the avenging chiefs who liberated Israel from the oppression of the powerful invading peoples (Judg. 2:16-19; 3:10; 4:4; 10:2-3; 11:27; 12:7-14; 15:20; 16:31). Throughout the entire book there is no instance of a judicial act ascribed to these chiefs raised up by God, and yet each is called *šopheṭ.* To assert that all the verses which designate them in this way are later interpolations still does not solve the problem, for why then did it occur to a Deuteronomic redactor to call them this when it is clear that they never exercised judicial functions?[6]

The cited passages are each preceded by the fact that a king or a foreign nation subjugated the Israelites for a certain number of years. At the end of this period the Israelites "cried out" to Yahweh.[7] And then Yahweh raised up a man from among them who delivered them from oppression, and he was a *šophet* of Israel. This all leads us to believe that the original meaning of *šaphat* is "to save from oppression" and not "to judge."

Our suspicion becomes certainty when we consider the construction of the verb in 2 Sam. 18:19; 2 Sam. 18:31; and 1 Sam. 24:16: "I must run and tell the good news to the king [David] that Yahweh has delivered him from the hand of [*šephato miyyad . . .*] his enemies" (2 Sam. 18:19). It is impossible to use the verb "to judge" here. The correct meaning of *šaphat* cannot be "to judge," for "judge me from your hand" is a meaningless phrase. The Hebrew verb means a liberation for justice' sake and nothing else. When the reference is to the judicial institution and when it is not must be deduced from the context, for the presence of the root *špht* does not in itself imply it.

In Ps. 10:18 the use of *lišpot yatom wadak* ("to deliver or save the orphan and the needy") is another case in which no one would think of using the verb "to judge." In no way could it mean that Yahweh comes to judge the orphan and the needy, but rather that he comes to save them from injustice, to deliver them from oppression. It would be preposterously farfetched to think that first he judges them and afterwards, having found them innocent, he does them justice by delivering them from their oppressors.

Ps. 72:4 expresses the desire that the king "save [*špht*] the poor . . . and crush their oppressors"; with no amount of subtlety could we understand this to mean a desire that the king come and judge them first and, after seeing that they are right, then repel the aggressor. Therefore, the true meaning of *šaphat* is not "to judge," but rather "to do justice to the weak and oppressed." The verb *šaphat* is also used in Ps. 96:13 and 98:9, but if we translate it by "to judge," we cannot understand why the earth rejoices because he is coming to judge it; what it says is that the earth rejoices because he is coming to save it, *šaphat*.

We might conjecture that a *šophet* came to be understood as a "judge" because the intervention for justice' sake of one who saves another from oppression has at the same time a favorable result for the oppressed and an unfavorable one for the oppressor; he has to settle between two contending parties. But even this conjecture is inadequate, for the biblical *šophet* is not an impartial, neutral arbiter who is thereby a savior. Every defender of the oppressed defends him from another, and his action has, therefore, a double edge; but this does not mean that the proper and always operative meaning of the Hebrew word is not precisely to defend from injustice. This meaning is also seen in the very frequent synonymic parallelism of *šaphat* with "to save" (the root is *yṣʿ*) and the clear interchangeability of the two verbs, for example, in Ezek. 34:22; Ps. 35:24; Ps. 43:1; Ps. 67:5; Ps. 75:3; Ps. 96:13; Ps. 98:9.

In a general anthropological approach we could have already supposed as obvious that when in human history the function of judge or of what later came to be called judge was conceived, it was exclusively to help those who because of their weakness could not defend themselves; the others did not need it. But because of the biblical usage of the root *špht*, such a theory is no longer mere theory and conjecture. The original meaning of the verb *šaphat* cannot be "to judge," because "judge me from your hand" is nonsense. *Šophet* did not first mean "judge," and then later, after it was seen that justice was done, come to be synonymous with liberator or savior. The opposite is true. The original and authentic meaning has nothing to do with judicial institutions; it is applied to, among many other things, judicial intervention, because it is supposed that this intervention saves the needy from injustice. And even in this case what the author understands by *šophet* is "defender of the oppressed." Whether he considers him invested with an official capacity or he prescinds from this institutional investiture is secondary.

The original meaning we have seen for the verb *šaphat* is the same for the corresponding root in Akkadian, Egyptian, and Ugaritic.[8] The importance of the discovery of this meaning for the philosophy of law seems to me inestimable; but it will be better to consider this when we treat the problem of law directly. What is of concern to us in the present context is to establish that when the Bible speaks of Yahweh as "Judge" or of the Judgment whose subject is Yahweh, it has in mind precisely the meaning which we have seen for the root *špht*: to save the oppressed from injustice. This is the meaning of the Last Judgment awaited down through all the centuries of expectation in the Old and New Testaments.

Fensham summarizes Ps. 82 quite accurately: "God challenges the gods to give justice (stem *šaphaṭ*) to orphans and the poor and to save the wretched from the power of the evildoers [*reša'im*]. The gods fail to accomplish this command and the verdict of death is pronounced over them. The last verse of the Psalm brings to God the victorious command to give justice to the world. Out of this we may deduce that the only One who can give justice and deliverance to the weak is God."[9] But the Psalmist's criterion for distinguishing Yahweh from the other gods is not the institutional character of judge, although he uses the verb *šaphaṭ*; rather it is the ability to protect the poor against the injustice of the powerful.

Ps. 94 also appeals to Yahweh as "judge of the world" (vv. 1-2), but the meaning of this characterization is obvious in the following verses. The Psalmist calls for this help against the "unjust" (vv. 3-4) who "kill the widow and stranger and murder the orphans" (vv. 4-6).

Ps. 58 is completely parallel to Ps. 82, except that it is not Yahweh but the Psalmist who apostrophizes the other gods.[10] He addresses them directly:

Do you truly pronounce justice, gods,
do you do justice [verb *šaphaṭ*] to mankind?

(Ps. 58:2)

Then there follows a description of the evil of the "unjust" of the earth (vv. 4-6). The whole force of this passage is that the Psalmist attributes this predominance of injustice on the earth to the amoral indifference of the gods who do not intervene to abolish it. He goes on to ask Yahweh to intervene and crush the *reša'im* without restraint. Then the just will rejoice and people will say that there is a God who "judges" over the earth (v. 12). The meaning of the verb *šaphaṭ* and of the "Judgment" which the Old Testament awaits from Yahweh seems unequivocal: to save the world from the oppression of the unjust. The judicial institutional investiture is of very secondary importance.

In Ps. 7 we find the same anguished petition addressed to Yahweh as him who "judges [*šaphaṭ*] the peoples" (v. 9), namely, "that the evil of the unjust should come to an end" (v. 10). This is the meaning of the *mišpaṭ* mentioned in v. 7, and this is why Yahweh is "the liberator who brings justice" (*šophet ṣaddik*) in v. 12.

Ps. 35 also expressly mentions *mišpaṭ* (v. 23) and invokes Yahweh's liberating intervention (verb *šaphaṭ*): "Deliver me [*šaphṭeni*] according

to your justice, Yahweh, my God" (v. 24). But this invocation is based on
the description of the "Yahweh Judge" given in v. 10: "Yahweh, who
can compare with you in rescuing the poor man from the stronger, the
needy from the man who exploits him?"

Ps. 9 also proclaims Yahweh as "judge of justice" (v. 5), but it
specifically refers to crushing the unjust (vv. 6, 17, 18); this "judicial"
(?) activity is based on the fact that Yahweh "does not ignore the cry
of the poor" (v. 13), and "Yahweh is a stronghold for the oppressed"
(v. 10).

Like Ps. 82, Ps. 10 also concludes by calling out to Yahweh to come
"to judge" (*lišpoṭ*) in v. 18. The definitive struggle against the *reša'im* is
on the first level, vv. 2, 3, 4, 13, 15, and the trait which makes them
unjust is mentioned by name (*reša'*) in v. 15, which asks Yahweh to
make it "disappear from the earth." In Ps. 10 there may be all the
gratitude which the cultivators of "literary genres" might want, but the
last verse, precisely the one in which the desire for Yahweh's *šaphaṭ* is
expressed, remains like a lance through our heart: "to do justice to the
orphan and the oppressed, so that earthborn man may strike fear no
longer."

If our learned exegesis cannot perceive the infinite yearning of these
Hebrews of thirty centuries ago who desired justice for all future
centuries, then our learned exegesis is not worth much. The Psalter not
only gives us the true meaning of what was later schematically called
the Last Judgment; it also reveals the great antiquity of the roots of the
eschatology which some exegetes have tried to neutralize by character-
izing it as a later phenomenon. Eschatology was not invented by the
prophets nor by postexilic Israel. It was already inextricably rooted in
Yahweh's revelation of himself in the liberation of the Exodus.[11] The
God whom the Yahwist knows is, from the beginning, "the judge
[*šophēṭ*] of the whole earth" (Gen. 18:25), who intervenes in our
history against the "unjust" (Gen. 18:23, 25a, 25b) because he hears
the "outcry" of the oppressed (Gen. 18:20-21); he chooses Israel so
that "justice and right" might be achieved among all the nations of the
earth (Gen. 18:17-19). The total, world-wide realization of this "Judgment" was pending from the first moment in which Yahweh revealed
himself to Moses.

Of utmost importance for our understanding of the New Testament's expectation of the Last Judgment is the hymn of confidence

called Ps. 62. The apex of the composition is in the last two verses
(12-13): Because of his power and compassion Yahweh "will repay man
as his works deserve." The meaning of this technical term is always *in
malam partem,* as we can see in Ps. 28:4; 31:24; Job 34:11; Jer. 17:10.
It is directed against the *reša'im,* and it clearly deals with the definitive
intervention of Yahweh as "judge." When *mišpat* is foreseen, what is
really foreseen is that Yahweh will eliminate the unjust from the earth.
Thus Ps. 62, a hymn to instill confidence, rightly says, "Do not rely on
oppression, put no empty hopes in exploitation" (v. 11). Do put your
hopes in Yahweh, however, because Yahweh is the savior of all the
exploited and oppressed. "In God alone there is rest for my soul, from
him comes my salvation" (v. 2). And note how the expressions "rock,"
"fortress," "refuge," "salvation" are repeated in vv. 2, 3, 7, 8. This is
the essence of the "Judgment" ("He will repay man as his works
deserve," v. 13).

The combination of "power" and "compassion" in vv. 12-13 has
long disconcerted the exegetes. I refer to Dahood's study regarding Ps.
18:28: "Indeed you are the Strong One who saves the poor."[12] The one
who delivers the helpless from oppression must have power. And
compassion is the motivation, in the sense which we saw in Hos. 6:6
(cf. above pp. 45-47). This is illustrated in Ps. 86, which mentions
Yahweh's compassion seven times in vv. 3, 5, 13, and 15, either with
the root *ḥsd, rḥm,* or *ḥnn;* but the whole idea is summarized in the first
verse: Yahweh answers me *"because* I am poor and needy" (Ps. 86:1).
If, as some believe, the author of this verse was not really poor, it is all
the more significant that he had to present himself as poor for Yahweh
to hear him. Yahweh's compassion is specifically to be in solidarity
with the needy. The linking of "power" and "compassion," by which
Yahweh "will repay man as his works deserve" according to Ps.
62:12-13, disconcerted some exegetes only because they had not seen
that the Last Judgment consisted in the final liberation of the poor and
the oppressed, the definitive realization of justice on earth.

The Last Judgment which Paul awaits in Rom. 2:5-12, where he
cites Ps. 62:13, is of the same nature. In reality the only detailed
description which the New Testament gives us of the Last Judgment is
in Matt. 25:31-46, which coincides point by point with what we have
seen in the Old Testament: elimination of the "unjust," possession of
the kingdom solely by the "just," that is, by those who give food to the

hungry, drink to the thirsty, etc. There is no basis for imagining that the other New Testament authors conceived the Judgment in terms different from those of Matthew. Although it is not a description, Rom. 2:5-12, corroborates this unanimity. On the one side are the men "of constancy in good words"; on the other are "the men of discord . . . who trust in injustice" (Rom. 2:7-8). There would never have been any obscurity in these expressions if exegetes had kept in mind that they refer to the same Last Judgment that Matthew describes in 25:31-46. The expression "good works" in Rom. 2:7 (reemphasized in 2:10 by "to do good") is a rigorous technical term used to designate precisely those actions described in Matt. 25:31-46.[13] The technical nature of the term can be seen in 2 Cor. 9:8; Rom. 13:3; 1 Tim. 2:10; 5:10a, 10b, 25; 6:18; 2 Tim. 2:21; 3:17; Eph. 2:10; Col. 1:10; Titus 1:16; 2:14; 3:1, 8, 14; 2 Thess. 2:17.

As regards the expression *hoi ex eritheias* in Rom. 2:8, which I have just translated as "the men of discord," Otto Michel renders it in this way: "The men who have made discord and rancor the content of their lives."[14] Indeed, in Phil. 1:15-17 Paul uses the word *eritheia* as a synonym for *eris*, which everyone translates as "discord" or "dissension." To confirm this meaning, the word is contrasted to *agapē*. The other three times that Paul uses the term *erithia* (=*eritheia*), it clearly means "discord" (2 Cor. 12:20; Gal. 5:20; and Phil. 2:3). And the term appears in the New Testament only two other times, James 3:14, 16, manifestly with the same meaning. Therefore, according to Rom. 2:5-12, the separating of mankind into "doers of good works" on one side and "men of discord . . . who trust in injustice" on the other is the same conception of the Last Judgment that we see in Matt. 25:31-46 and the whole Old Testament.

Some exegetes, however, suggest that God's eschatological intervention is based not so much on the idea of "Yahweh the Judge" as it is on that of "Yahweh the Warrior." They support their suggestion by the fact that many passages allude to the Last Judgment as "the day of Yahweh" (for example, Isa. 13:6, 9; Amos 5:18); the original vital context of this phrase is definitely "the wars of Yahweh" and the conception of Yahweh as a war hero. In any case it is true that the New Testament refers to the Last Judgment by means of expressions like "the day of judgment" (for example, Matt. 10:15; 11:22, 24; 12:36), "the day of the Lord" (for example, Acts 2:20; cf. Joel 3:2), "the last day" (John 6:39, 40, 44, 54; 7:37; 11:24; 12:48), "the day of the anger and the revelation of the just judgment of God" (Rom. 2:6).

Thus we are obliged to study the relationship between "Yahweh the Judge" and "Yahweh the Warrior," for today we know that the expression "the day of Yahweh," translated by the Septuagint as "the day of the Lord," pertained to the wars of Yahweh.[15] All the monographs agree that "Yahweh the Warrior" is a very ancient concept in Israel, perhaps more ancient than "Yahweh the Judge." This is documented by the Song of Deborah (Judg. 5), which is from the twelfth century B.C. at the latest. The monographs, nevertheless, have not compared this concept with Ps. 82 ("Yahweh the Judge"), which is also premonarchic, nor have they kept in mind that the Yahwist in Gen. 4:1-11; 7:1; 16:5; 18:17-33 supposes that the concept of Yahweh as "Judge" is unquestionably traditional and established. We will focus on "Yahweh the Warrior," which is already the meaning of the designation "Yahweh Sabaoth" (="Yahweh of hosts"), and leave aside for the moment the question of anteriority. An independent investigation has the advantage of corroborating what we have learned from our study of the root *šphṭ*.

Von Rad cites Ps. 147 as thoroughly typical of the holy war:[16]

The strength of the war horse means nothing to Yahweh,
it is not infantry that interests him.
Yahweh is interested only in those who fear him,
in those who rely on his compassion.

(Ps. 147:10-11)

This is undoubtedly a war, but v. 6 specifies what kind of war: "Yahweh lifts up the needy, and strikes the unjust (*rešaʿim*) into the dust."[17] We find, therefore, in Yahweh the Warrior the same compassion specifically for the poor and the helpless which we have just seen in Ps. 62:12-13 as proper to Yahweh-the-Last-Judge. His bellicosity is at the service of compassion for the needy in Ps. 147, just as the "power" of the *šopheṭ* was at the service of compassion in Ps. 62. We see the same thing in Ps. 143:12, "In his compassion he destroys my enemies," and this formula is paradoxical only for those who do not accept the biblical sense of compassion. The term refers to Yahweh's solidarity with the poor and against the oppressors for justice' sake. Quell is completely correct when he writes, "It is a mistake to translate it [*ḥesed*] as 'love,' since it differs from *'ahab*, etc. in the fact that it . . . always [denotes] a volitional attitude orientated to the concept of right."[18]

Completely parallel to Ps. 147 with its warrior profile in vv. 10-11 is Ps. 33:16-18; here v. 5 gives us the same key: "Yahweh loves justice and right; Yahweh's compassion fills the earth."

Among the most typical war Psalms we find Ps. 18, which describes Yahweh as "letting his arrows fly and scattering his enemies" (v. 15). In v. 14 it attributes a war cry to him; in v. 16 it speaks of "the menacing blast of your nostrils' breath," and in v. 11 it even has Yahweh riding a mount. But v. 28 tells us what the *casus belli* is:

You are the one who saves the poor people
and humiliates eyes that are haughty.[19]

Ps. 74:13-14 characterizes Yahweh as a battle hero; we need not dwell on the description. In v. 21 we see what war is being spoken of: "That the hard-pressed not be defrauded; that the poor and the needy praise your name." And we see the same meaning in v. 12: "You are he who achieves liberations [salvations] throughout the earth." The salvations or liberations of Yahweh the Warrior are condensed in Zeph. 3:17 in the title *gibbor yoši'a* ("liberator hero"). We do not resolve anything by translating *yešu'oth* in Ps. 74:12 as "victories" and *yoši'a* in Zeph. 3:17 as "victorious," for this does not explain why a root meaning "to save" was used to designate these victories. But Ps. 74 itself tells us without circumlocution in v. 21: It is speaking of the helpless (*dak*), the poor (*'ani*), and the needy (*'ebyon*), as in Ps. 82. The war is to save them. Zephaniah is even more persistent in specifying this: "Trouble is coming to the rebellious, the defiled, the oppressive city!" (3:1). It is clear from the beginning: The war is against oppression. After the great assault, "in your midst I will leave the poor and needy people, and those who are left in Israel will seek refuge in the name of Yahweh. They will commit no injustice, will tell no lies, and the perjured tongue will no longer be found in their mouths. But they will be able to graze and rest with no one to disturb them" (Zeph. 3:12-13). In vv. 3, 5, 11, and 18 we see that, in contrast to Yahweh who is "just," it is the powerful ones who are the unjust, those who devour and terrorize the people. This is the war of the "savior hero" (v. 17).

"The day of Yahweh" is mentioned twice in chapter 13 of Isaiah (vv. 6, 9), and like few others this chapter is dedicated to the theme of war. In v. 11 it makes clear the target that the battle is directed against:

"I will punish the world for its evil-doing, and the unjust [*rešaʿim*] for their crimes, to put an end to the insolence of arrogant men and humble the pride of the despots."

Jer. 6:1-9 proclaims the holy war (v. 4), and vv. 6-7 sums it all up:
For thus says Yahweh of the armies:
Cut down the trees,
throw up an earthwork outside Jerusalem.
She is the city that is visited:
There is nothing but oppression in her.
As water comes from a well,
so wickedness comes from her.
Violence and exploitation are what you hear in her,
suffering and wounds are always before me.

As von Rad has correctly pointed out, Deut. 9:1-6 is a thoroughly martial passage.[20] What has not been sufficiently clarified is that the passage itself specifies the reason for the war: "It is for their injustice [*berišʿath*] that Yahweh defeats these nations for you" (v. 4, repeated in v. 5). What Yahweh wars against is the *rešaʿ*, that is, that which makes the *rešaʿim* to be *rešaʿim*. *Rešaʿ* of Deut. 9:27 is the same as *rišʿah* of 9:4, 5; 25:2. Lohfink objects to von Rad that the introduction of *sedakah* in Deut. 9:1-6 means that the ideology of the holy war no longer holds; but in doing this he overlooks the one essential element of Yahweh's war: It is a struggle against injustice and for the triumph of justice.[21]

In this passage the suppostion is that the nations which inhabited Palestine were committing injustice (just as the Yahwist, Isaiah, Jeremiah, and Ezekiel supposed that the inhabitants of Sodom perpetrated injustice which "cried out" to heaven); since *rišʿah* is in contrast to *sedakah* in the reflections on the war of conquest, it can have no other meaning than that which we have seen that *rešaʿim* and "justice" have in Ps. 147, Ps. 33, Isa. 13, Zeph. 3, and Ps. 18. The martial passage Deut. 9:1-6 says to Israel on Yahweh's behalf: Not because of your justice but because of the injustice of these nations do I defeat these nations for you. Since Deuteronomy uses the word *sedakah* very seldom (five times in all, three of which are in this passage), its significance in Deuteronomic theology can be clarified by Deut. 24:12-13: "If the man [to whom you have lent money] is poor, you are not to go to bed with his pledge in your possession; you must return it to him at sunset so that he can sleep in his cloak and bless you; and it

will be justice on your part in the sight of Yahweh your God." It seems
clear that in the tradition of Deut. 9:1-6 the Israelites' conquest of
Palestine is justified by the injustices which the aborigines were supposed to be committing; in the same way the Priestly document
explains the flood by the fact that "the earth had filled with violence"
(Gen. 6:11, 13), that is, with injustice, according to the Yahwist (cf.
Gen. 7:1).

Isa. 10:1-4 also appeals to Yahweh's war (vv. 3-4), and the combatted enemy is described in this way:

> Woe to the legislators of infamous laws,
> to those who issue tyrannical decrees,
> who refuse justice to the needy
> and cheat the poor among my people of their
>   right [mišpaṭ],
> who make widows their prey
> and rob the orphan.

(vv. 1-2)

There is no break in continuity between the crime described in this
way and the threat of war: "What will you do on the day of punishment, when, from far off, destruction comes?" (v. 3).

Ps. 103 is likewise military, speaking of "all the armies" of Yahweh
(v. 21) and of his angels, his "mighty heroes" (v. 20). But in v. 6 this
warrior Yahweh is described as follows: "He who does justices
[ṣᵉdaḳoth] is Yahweh, and acts of justice to all the oppressed." The
motivation is compassion, as we see in vv. 4, 8, 11, 17, that is, ḥesed,
translated by *eleos* all four times and in Hebrew used as a synonym of
rḥm in vv. 4, 8, 13a, and 13b. As we have seen, this is compassion for
the oppressed, compassion proper to him who fights with raised hand
and outstretched arm.

To continue this survey in detail would be quite time-consuming, for
there is hardly a biblical passage describing Yahweh as warrior which
fails to mention the poor and the oppressed as those for whose
liberation Yahweh makes war on the oppressors and the unjust. I will
schematically enumerate them so that the reader can examine them if
he wishes. In Jer. 51 the militant aspect can be seen in v. 27; that the
war is against injustice and oppression can be seen in vv. 10, 13, 24,
34-36, 46, and 49. In Hab. 3 we see war in vv. 8, 11; justice in
vv. 13b-14. In Isa. 45, war is in v. 12c; justice in v. 13. Obadiah has war
in v. 15; justice in v. 10. In Isa. 51 there is war in v. 9; justice in vv. 4-8.

Jer. 6: war in vv. 4-6a; justice in vv. 6b-7. Amos 5: war in v. 18; justice in the whole chapter. Ezek. 7: war in the whole chapter; justice in vv. 11, 23, 24. Isa. 31: war in v. 4c: justice in v. 2b. Joel 4: war in v. 9, justice in vv. 2, 3, 19.

We can summarize. If the hope of a Last Judgment (a hope absolutely central to the New Testament, even, with all due respect to Bultmann, in Paul and John) is derived more from the idea of "Yahweh the Warrior" than from that of "Yahweh the Judge," the meaning of these two terms is nevertheless the same: the elimination of all oppressors, liberation and justice for all the oppressed. The hope is for the definitive establishment of the kingdom of justice on earth. This is the justice of God, not of men, for it is supposed (and is expressly verified) that men have not been able to achieve justice. This is also Paul's theology, but we will consider this later.

Before proceeding let us consider the question of whether "Yahweh the Warrior" or "Yahweh the Judge" is the anterior term. In the first place it is a fact that these two representations of Yahweh converge, not only with respect to content, but also with respect to representations. The great final war spoken of in Joel 4 ("the day of Yahweh" in v. 14 and "proclaim the holy war" in v. 9) takes place entirely in "the valley of Yahweh-judges" (vv. 2, 12; this is the meaning of $Y^e ho\check{s}a$-$pha\underline{t}$). Here we see that "Yahweh the Warrior" is totally identified with "Yahweh the Judge" in the most explicit Old Testament thematization of the Last Judgment.

Ps. 68 is outstanding as a hymn to Yahweh-the-War-Hero, with its abundant naturalistic and mythic echoes: Yahweh is the "Rider of the clouds" (v. 5), who "suffocated the serpent" (v. 23); "the war chariots of Yahweh are in the thousands" (v. 18), "when you set out at the head of your people and marched across the desert" (v. 8), etc. Let us note the explicitness with which it tells us what all this paraphernalia is for:

Father of orphans, defender of widows,
such is Yahweh in his holy dwelling;
Yahweh gives the forsaken a permanent home,
frees the prisoners and gives them wealth.

(Ps. 68:6-7)

There would be no way to explain why the orphans and widows were involved in a matter such as this if we did not recognize that all this military armor is the garment of the one essential Yahweh: the Yahweh who is implacably indignant against all injustice, the Yahweh-

Judge in the sense of *šophet* and "judging" which we have seen. Therefore the Psalm begins by saying, "The unjust [*reša'im*] perish when Yahweh approaches, and the just [*ṣaddiķim*] rejoice" (vv. 3-4). Here we find the same division of the world, proper to the final "judging" and executed by Yahweh-of-the-armies. It seems to me that we must deduce not only that the military manner is a garment of the essential Yahweh described in Ps. 82 and Gen. 18, but that we can even say that Yahweh-Warrior is simply at the disposition of Yahweh-Judge.

Deut. 33:21 calls Yahweh's wars simply "justices": Gad "executed the justices of Yahweh and his acts of justice on Israel." Here we can grasp to the quick the question of anteriority. The plural "justices" occurs only in Judg. 5:11; 1 Sam. 12:7; Ps. 103:6; Mic. 6:5; Dan. 9:16. Also, because of the parallelism with the plural *mišpaṭim*, it is practically certain that in Deut. 33:21 the plural "justices" should be read. 1 Sam. 12:7-8 links the "justices of Yahweh" to the "outcry" of the oppressed;[22] because of that first "outcry" of the Israelites enslaved by Egypt there is unleashed that whole series of "justices of Yahweh" which deliver them from oppression and establish them in a land without slavery. Mic. 6:1-8 is an especially fertile passage, for it argues from the "justices of Yahweh" achieved in that same history to conclude that this God is not to be adored with cultus and sacrifices but rather with *mišpaṭ* and compassion (vv. 6-8). Robinson wants to separate Mic. 6:1-5 from Mic. 6:6-8 because he has not understood this argumentation; he states that the first passage is addressed to Israel, while the second is addressed to the whole world.[23] His arguments are not convincing, for it is precisely by the "justices" which delivered Israel from slavery that Yahweh revealed his essence to the whole world. It is precisely because Yahweh is in justice that no one can reach him except through justice and compassion toward the needy.

The most ancient Old Testament composition, the Song of Deborah, is a war hymn par excellence; its protagonist is Yahweh as war hero (see Judg. 5:4-5, 13, 23, 31). By its very antiquity it demonstrates not only that Yahweh-Warrior is at the disposition of Yahweh-Doer-of-Justice, but that the latter "conception" is even more ancient than the former:

There they extol Yahweh's justices,
the justices of his reign in Israel.

(Judg. 5:11)

We resolve nothing by translating *ṣedakah* in some other way, for example, as "victories" or "favors," for there would still remain the question of why the author chose to designate "victories" with the term "justices." If the nature of Yahweh taken for granted in Ps. 82 and by the Yahwist (Gen. 4:10; 7:1; 16:5; 18:17-33; Exod. 3:7-9) were not presupposed, then the expression in Judg. 5:11 could not have occurred. I repeat that the only thing that exegesis accomplishes by translating the justices of Yahweh as "graces" or "favors" is to resign itself to superficiality and to the impossibility of ever receiving the message of the Bible. So, for example, Otto Kuss, after recognizing that God's justice is a central concept in Paul's message and designates the true driving force behind God's saving intervention, goes on to say that the word "justice" is an "extremely inadequate, even erroneous" manner of describing it and that it would have been "much clearer and simpler" to use the concept of "goodness" or "love" or "compassion."[24] But if we have already decided to reduce the Bible to our own conception of Christianity, then the most central expressions of the Bible seem to be fatally erroneous. With this kind of armor we will never receive the only thing that Scripture wants to tell us: that God comes to achieve the justice awaited by human history for thousands of years.

The conception of Yahweh as "judge" (in the sense of *šophet* which we have described) is more ancient, more profound, and more essential than that of Yahweh as warrior. Moreover, it is the former which gives the latter its true meaning. Note the concise expression in the Song of Moses:

When I have whetted my flashing sword
and my hand takes up *mišpat*.
(Deut. 32:41)

It could not be more clearly expressed that the military activity is at the service of the achievement of justice on behalf of the oppressed, which is the activity proper to the verb *šaphat*. The entire Song of Moses exalts this characteristic of Yahweh's military activity. Such is the meaning of the metaphor "Rock," which appears six times (Deut. 32:4, 15, 18, 30, 31, 37, and in Ps. 18:3, 32); we have already seen that this term means the defense and protection of the "poor people" (Ps. 18:28). It also appears in Ps. 62:3, 7, and 8 as meaning a defense against those who rely on oppression and spoliation (v. 11). "Rock" has the same meaning in Isa. 17:10; 26:4; 30:29; etc. Salvador Carrillo very rightly says of Deut. 32:36, "The richness of his thought is synthesized in the verses 'he will do justice' and 'he will have mercy,' arranged in chiasmatic form, thus requiring that they be interpreted in synonymic parallelism."[25] Regarding the very obscure Hebrew formulation in the last part of v. 36, Carrillo (following P. Saydon) throws some light on the question with his translation "helpless and forsaken."[26] This rendering corresponds perfectly with the justice and compassion of v. 36a, and the idea of v. 36b is thus, "until there is no longer anyone either helpless or forsaken." Then the "judgment," which according to v. 41 Yahweh wields like a sword, will be final. According to v. 4, "All his ways are *mišpat.*"

That such an outstanding war hymn considers *mišpat* and compassion as the reason for everything is a datum of utmost importance. It demonstrates that the original meaning of Yahweh-Warrior referred to war against oppression and injustice and that Yahweh intervened in Israel's favor only because it was oppressed. This explains why the prophets could declare Yahweh's war against Israel when it became an unjust and oppressive people. According to Ps. 103, the Yahweh of war (vv. 21, 20) is described in this way: "He who does justices is Yahweh, and *mišpatim* to all the oppressed." Because of this linking in a war song of justice with "judgments" it is impossible to translate the *sidkoth* of Judg. 5:11 as "victories" (or any other evasive term) and equally impossible to use the translation "justifications" in the military passage Deut. 9:1-6.[27] We must not forget that *sidkoth umišpatim* is the plural of *sᵉdakah umišpat*, which is acknowledged as a technical term for social justice.

Soggin quite rightly shows that Mic. 3:5 is sufficient to demonstrate the very common preprophetic occurrence of the idea that the war of Yahweh can also be directed against Israel.[28] With all due respect to von Rad,[29] Amos 5:18 is indeed important:

Trouble for those who are waiting so longingly
for the day of Yahweh!
What will this day of Yahweh mean for you?
It will mean darkness, not light.

This is the most ancient text in which the expression "the day of Yahweh" appears, and as such it very expressly documents two things at once: (1) that eschatology not only is not postexilic, but that it is not even from the time of Amos (the first half of the eighth century) nor was it invented by the prophets, and (2) that the preprophetic tradition awaited the "judgment" and the war of Yahweh as the great saving event which would deliver them from all oppressions. But Amos 5 denies that Israel can expect this day with joy, because in the meantime Israel has changed from oppressed to oppressor; therefore the Last Judgment would be disastrous and destructive for it. But before Amos, in Amos, and after Amos, this definitive intervention of Yahweh is expected as the liberation of the oppressed and the establishment of justice on earth. The intentional reversal which Joel 4:9-10 makes of Isa. 2:2-5 (Mic. 4:1-4) is illustrative. What in Isa. 2 (and Mic. 4) was the establishment of justice and peace for the benefit of all nations, in Joel 4 is a devastating war against all the nations which oppressed Israel (oppressions indicated with a fiery finger in Joel 4:3, 5, 6, 19). But the ardent hope for peace and justice is not therefore any less (cf. Joel 4:16b, 18). And the eschatological idea of judgment and war is still exactly the same: the establishment of definitive justice.

Methodologically it is important to note that the link between Judgment-War and the injustice which it attacks recurs both in contexts favorable to Israel and in contexts unfavorable to Israel, both against a nation and against social strata within a nation (which we have seen in abundance, for example, in Zeph. 3 and Isa. 10), both when the oppressed one is a people and when it is an individual (cf., for example, Pss. 18 and 103). The invariable characteristic of all these possibilities is the connection between Justice-War and the injustices punished by it. We see that such an essential connection is not an invention of the prophets when confronted by the social injustices of Israel, because Jer. 51, Hab. 3, Isa. 45, Obadiah, Isa. 51, and Joel 4 proclaim Judgment-War *on behalf of Israel.* If we accept that the war of Yahweh in Jer. 6, Amos 5, Ezek. 7, and Isa. 31 is *against Israel,* then the only common denominator is the fact that the war of Yahweh is, in essence, against injustices and oppressions. Such unmistakable specificity concerning the war of Yahweh is exactly the sense of *mišpat*; in the words of Hertzberg which we have already cited, "*Mišpat* consists in doing justice to the poor, neither more nor less." According to the Old and the New Testaments, this is also the meaning of the definitive *mišpat*, the so-called Last Judgment.

Thus when the Fourth Evangelist sees in Jesus Christ the arrival of the definitive age in which men will love one another and there will therefore be no one who oppresses his neighbor, he can affirm that

Judgment is now being realized (John 12:31; 16:11; 5:24). The meaning of "[the believer] does not come to judgment, but has passed from death to life" in John 5:24 is explicitly spelled out for us by the same author in 1 John 3:14: "We know that we have passed from death to life because we love our brothers." And the meaning of John 12:31–"Now is judgment being passed on this world; now the prince of this world is to be overthrown"–is clear if we keep in mind what John 8:44 tells us about the prince of this world: "He was a murderer from the start" (and noting too that "to hate your brother is to be a murderer," according to 1 John 3:15).

Thus Judgment consists in the elimination from the world of all who do not love their neighbor. As Bultmann observes in his consideration of the variant of 1 John 3:17 in 4:20, "hatred" is the designation for a simple lack of compassion, enmity, or the mercilessness which we have seen as characteristic of the *reša'im*.[30] In the Old Testament and in Matt. 25:31-46; 13:38-43; and Rom. 2:5-12, the essence of the Last Judgment is rooted in the elimination of mercilessness and in the exclusive possession of the earth by the just. And this is precisely what John sees is being achieved from the moment when Jesus Christ begins to act in this world. Thus he asserts that "Judgment is now" (John 12:31), for the head and father (cf. John 8:33 and 1 John 3:8-10) of those who do not love their neighbor will be at this moment expelled from this world. We have already seen that the true meaning of the verb *šaphat* is to save from the hand of the unjust.[31] But there are many who do not want to understand it in this way. Thus the Johannine Christ clarifies the notion very explicitly: "I did not come to judge the world but to save the world" (John 12:47 and 3:17). Even in the Apocalypse it is made explicit that the just "will reign on earth" (Rev. 5:10). And this is not simply a question of the millenium, for "the second death has no power over them" (Rev. 20:6) and on earth "they will reign forever and ever" (Rev. 22:5).

Matthew also is convinced that in Christ's works themselves *mišpat* began to be realized (Matt. 12:18, 20). In spite of the opposition and persecution of the Pharisees (vv. 14, 15), Christ persists in doing good for all those in need (v. 15), knowing that in this way "he would proclaim *mišpat* to the nations" (v. 18), "till he has led *mišpat* to victory" (v. 20). Büchsel has very rightly pointed out that in these two verses of Matthew, *krisis* is the translation of *mišpat; krisis* is also used in the Septuagint version of the Deutero-Isaianic passage cited in Matthew; it means "the right (of the poor)."[32] Schniewind's interpretation is along the same lines.[33] And in his excellent monograph, Gerhard Barth points out that in this passage Matthew is referring to the works of Christ on behalf of the poor mentioned in Matt. 11:2-5: The good news is given to the poor.[34]

But it must also be noted that in this same chapter (Matt. 12), of ineffable theological richness, the redactor uses the word *krisis* three other times (vv. 36, 41, 42), and in all five instances he acts on his own initiative. In the last three it is universally accepted that he is speaking of the Last Judgment. We need not try to determine whether in Isa. 42:1-4 Deutero-Isaiah, cited by Matthew, was thinking of the final *mišpaṭ*; it seems clear to me, however, that he was, since he explicitly states the intention of achieving justice for all the nations (Isa. 42:1, 3, 4, 6). But in 12:20 Matthew powerfully reformulates Isa. 42:4 to read "till he has led *mišpaṭ* to victory," and he then goes on to use the same word three times in the sense of Last Judgment; these facts inevitably oblige us to think that according to Matthew the triumph of *mišpaṭ* will be the Last Judgment. If not, there is no explanation for Matthew's modification of the Septuagintal content of Isa. 42:4, which makes it so much more vigorous. The conclusion of Gundry's exhaustive study is that Matthew's formulation cannot be documented in the Masoretic text nor in that of the Targums, nor in Peshitta, nor in the Septuagint, nor in the other Greek translations.[35] Matthew created it according to his own stamp.

In Christ's works of justice on behalf of the poor and helpless, Matthew sees—as does John—the definitive realization of Judgment: "till he has led *mišpaṭ* to victory." This is confirmed in Matt. 8:17, where the mission of this same Deutero-Isaianic servant (identified with Christ) consists in "taking away" our pains and our sufferings. This rendering contradicts the customary interpretation of Isa. 53, according to which he does not "take away," but rather "takes on himself." Matthew is so convinced of the presentness of the Judgment during the time of Christ that on his own account he adds a series of resurrections of the dead in Matt. 27:52-53.

The characteristic division of humanity, which is proper to the Last Judgment, is explicitly described by John with the same criterion which we have seen in the Old and the New Testaments: "good works," in the technical sense of the term.[36]

This is the judgment:
The light came into the world
and men loved darkness more than the light
because their works were evil.

(John 3:19)

This verse, as well as John 5:24 (clarified by 1 John 3:14) and John 12:31 (clarified by John 8:44 and 1 John 3:8-15), necessarily suppose that the Judgment executed by Jesus Christ must be understood in the qualitatively unmistakable sense which the Judgment of Yahweh has, according to the Old Testament. For this reason, that is, in order to achieve this specificity of contents, not in order to obtain an external formal authority, the Johannine Christ insists that his "Judgment" is qualitatively the same as his Father's:

I can do nothing by myself;
I can only judge as I hear,
and my judgment is just,
because my aim is to do not my own will,
but the will of him who sent me.

(John 5:30)

You judge according to the flesh;
I judge no one,
and if I judge, my judgment is true,
because I am not alone,
but I and the one who sent me (are here).

(John 8:15-16)

In the same sense see John 12:47-50. "He who sent me" is for John a qualitative characterization which has strength only as a reference to the Yahweh of the Old Testament. If this were not so, his arguments would move in a perpetual vicious circle. Note the intention to express an identification in this passage:

"In your Law it is written
that the testimony of two witnesses is valid.
I am testifying on my own behalf,
and the Father who sent me is my witness too."
They asked him, "Where is your Father?"
Jesus answered,
"You do not know me, nor do you know my Father;
if you did know me, you would know my Father as well."
He spoke these words in the Treasury, while teaching in the Temple,
No one arrested him, because his time had not yet come.

(John 8:17-20)

What John is complaining about is that the Jews do not know the God of the Old Testament. If they did know him, they would understand perfectly well that the Father is in Christ's works and signs, for these are the characteristic works on behalf of all those in need and all those who suffer. This is why he insists: After referring to Christ's "good works" (John 10:32; remember that this is a technical term), it says, "If I am not doing the works *of my Father,* do not believe me" (John 10:37).

We see that his intention is indeed one of qualification and identification in John 8:41 ("You are doing the works of your Father") and John 8:39 ("If you are Abraham's children, do the works of Abraham. As it is, you want to kill me"). Thus it is clear that he intends to give an unequivocal characterization when he says,

If I am not doing the works *of my Father,*
do not believe me.
But if I am doing them,
and you do not believe me,
believe then the works I do,
so that you will know
that the Father is in me and I am in the Father.

(John 10:37-38)

We need not prejudge the legitimacy or the demonstrative force of the argument *de miraculis* or the use which the apologetic treatises make of the miracles of Jesus in this connection. But to understand these Johannine paragraphs we must realize that this is not the argument which they use. Their purpose is to point out the distinctive character of the God of Israel:

The works my Father has given me to carry out,
these same works of mine
testify that the Father has sent me.

(John 5:36)

I tell you most solemnly,
the Son can do nothing by himself;
he can do only what he sees the Father doing;
and whatever the Father does the Son likewise does.
For the Father loves the Son
and shows him everything he does.

(John 5:19-20)

In the latter passage the intention of the adverb "likewise" (*homoios*) is to grasp the quality, the distinctive note, the unmistakable character of the works which characterize Yahweh. The insistence is unceasing: As long as they do not understand this unequivocal difference, everything is futile.

Neither he nor his parents sinned,
but rather so that the works *of God* might be
    displayed in him.
I must carry out the works of *the one who sent me.*

(John 9:3-4)

Have I been with you all this time, Philip,
and you still do not know me?
To have seen me is to have seen the Father,
so how can you say, "Let us see the Father"?
Do you not believe
that I am in the Father and the Father is in me?
The words I say to you I do not speak as from myself;
it is the Father, dwelling in me, who is doing *his* works.
You must believe me when I say
that I am in the Father and the Father is in me;
believe it on the evidence of the works,
if for no other reason.

(John 14:9-11)

We have already seen in Deutero-Isaiah the same argumentation based on the qualitative and essential difference of the one God who is concerned with achieving justice on earth.[37] We saw that exegesis is mistaken if it tries to find there apologetical arguments based on the power to perform miracles or the power to predict events. The identification which Deutero-Isaiah discovers between the God who breaks the Babylonian captivity and the God who, seven centuries before, had freed the slaves from Egypt is a qualitative one: that of the one God who is defined by justice. Six centuries after the liberation from Babylon, John wrote a Gospel consciously based on the same essential difference of the one true God. Even if there were no other proofs, this would be demonstrated by the deliberate adoption of the "I am" formulas in an absolute sense (John 8:24, 28; 13:19, to mention simply the indisputable ones). As Feuillet has shown, the extrabiblical literature has no exact correspondent to this. On the other hand the Septuagint invariably translates the *'ani-hu* of Isa. 41:4; 43:10, 25; 46:4; 48:12; 51:12; and 52:6 by the absolute "I am."[38] The presence of an *'ani-hu* (Septuagint: *egō eimi*) in the Song of Moses, which we have studied in connection with the war hymns of Yahweh, is not a coincidence. We will come back to this point.

What is clear is that, as Rengstorf and Schnackenburg have pointed out, if we do not grasp the intention of qualification and identification in the "works *of my Father*" formulas, the Gospel of John openly contradicts itself.[39] On the one hand, John 2:18 and 6:30 (like the Synoptics, Mark 8:11-12; Matt. 12:38; 16:1-4; Luke 11:16, 29) express a rejection of the Jewish, human petition for "signs" which would authenticate and "authorize" Jesus. On the other hand, it can be said that the whole Fourth Gospel establishes a basis for faith and "believing" on the "signs" and "works" of Jesus (John 1:50; 2:11, 23; 4:48; 6:14; 4:39, 53-54; 7:31; 9:16b, 35-39; 10:41-42; 5:36; 11:40; 11:47-48a; 12:18-19, 37; 14:7-14; 20:30-31). The point is that Jesus never says "my works." And the greatest superficiality which exegesis can show is to try to find some spiritual or ascetic fruit in this by supposing that it is because of humility that he does not do so. These are the works of the Yahweh of the Old Testament.

They did not remember his hand
and the time he saved them from oppression,
when he did wonders [Septuagint: *sēmeia*] in Egypt.

(Ps. 78:42-43)

So that they too would put their confidence in Yahweh,
and not forget the works [Septuagint: *erga*] of Yahweh.

(Ps. 78:7)

Because they had not believed [*episteusan*] in Yahweh
nor hoped in his salvation

(Ps. 78:22)

The confluence of *sēmeia, erga,* and *pisteuein,* which are the three key terms in the Fourth Gospel, cannot be explained by mere coincidence. The works of Yahweh-Warrior, who redeemed the Israelites from Egyptian oppression, are also translated by *erga* in Ps. 106:13; 105:1. They are called *sēmeia* in Ps. 105:27. And it speaks of believing in Yahweh, with the verb *pisteuein,* in Ps. 106:12, 24. We have seen that Yahweh's war is a mere garment of Yahweh's *mišpaṭ.* If John adopts these three terms to tell us of the life of Jesus, it is because he is seeing that Judgment is being achieved during the life of Jesus himself. But he is very conscious that "judging" can be misunderstood if its Old Testament meaning is not kept in mind. And so he makes this clarification: "God did not send his Son into the world to judge the world, but so that the world might be saved by him" (John 3:17).

This statement would flagrantly contradict the innumerable times in which he asserts that he did come to judge, if we were to forget that in

O

3:17 and 12:47 John makes every effort to make us understand the Old Testament meaning of "judging." We have already seen that Judgment + War has the meaning of "savior from injustice" in the Song of Moses (Deut. 32).[40] In v. 4 it speaks to us of "the Rock ·whose works [*erga*] are perfect because all his ways are *mišpaṭ*." And in v. 39 he is identified as the Deutero-Isaian Yahweh: "See now that it is I." Salvador Carrillo holds that Deut. 32 is of the Deutero-Isaianic school.[41]

"Then you will know that it is I" (John 8:28) is a formula that leaves no doubt about John's intention, namely, that in Jesus Yahweh is revealed just as he was revealed in the liberation from the Babylonian captivity. Compare these two verses:

So that (*hina*) you may believe (*pisteusēte*), when it happens, that it is I.

So that (*hina*) you may know and believe (*pisteusēte*) and understand that it is I.

The first formulation is from John (13:19); the second is from Deutero-Isaiah (43:10). But they are perfectly interchangeable. "It is I, do not fear" in John 6:20 bears a relation to "I am Yahweh, your God; I am holding you by the right hand; I tell you, 'Do not be afraid, I will help you'" in Isa. 41:13 (cf. also Isa. 43:1-3; 44:2-3; 51:9-10). But let me repeat: John's intention is that Yahweh be revealed in Jesus. I do not deny the legitimacy of the ontological problem concerning the divinity of Jesus Christ, but the fact that John does not affirm his divinity on any of these highly appropriate occasions shows that he is pursuing another objective which is much more important for him.

With great objectivity Feuillet shows that in all these passages much more than Christ's messiahship is involved, and yet Christ's divinity is not affirmed.[42] John wants Yahweh to be revealed to us *in Jesus*; he wants revelation effectively to happen; he is not concerned that our understanding be enriched with new data. Any other issue is a distraction. The moment we ontologize we obstruct the summons of the word; we make revelation impossible. And John's intention is the same as that of the historical Jesus. I say this with regard to the problem of the messianic consciousness of Jesus or the problem of whether or not he was conscious of his divinity. What Jesus wanted was effectively to reveal Yahweh to us. The intention to reveal destroys and rends and pierces at last the curtain of ontology (whose inevitable juxtaposition of beings—even of the so-called spiritual ones—demonstrates its visual origin): "To have seen me is to have seen the Father" (John 14:9); "whoever sees me, sees the one who sent me" (John 12:45).

When he gives the reason for this, John expresses a simple qualitative identification which is thoroughly deontologized: "You must believe me when I say that I am in the Father and the Father is in me; believe it on the evidence of the works, if for no other reason" (John 14:11). The de-entified quality of these works which reveal the Father will continue to be active in the world even when Jesus ontologically is no longer in the world: "I tell you most solemnly, whoever believes in me will perform the same works as I do myself; he will perform even greater works, for I am going to the Father" (John 14:12). And then he specifies what works he is speaking about: "If you love me, keep my commandments" (John 14:15). (This is the commandment which he spelled out in 13:34: "Love one another, as I have loved you so that you might love one another.")

It has been a mistake to think of the *terminus ad quem,* the "where to," when Jesus tells us that he is "going away." What he wants to emphasize is that he is going away and the Christians will remain behind in his place: The Spirit will show the world how wrong it was about justice "because I am going to the Father and you will see me no more" (John 16:10). Speaking with the Father he says, "I am not in the world any longer, but they are in the world, and I am coming to you" (John 17:11). The predominant concern is "I will not leave you orphans" (John 14:18). The expression "knowing . . . that he had come from God and was returning to God" (John 13:3) conveys the idea of completion: It is finished; the work that he personally could achieve on earth has ended.

John insistently indicates that in the action of washing his disciples' feet (13:1-18), Jesus was perfectly conscious that the Father had put everything in his hands. John is not emphasizing a contrast between Jesus' great power and this lowly action in order to extol humility. Rather in this action Jesus believes that he is passing on his entire message; he is achieving everything that God placed in his hands; the realization of his entire task depends on their understanding this action. And the meaning is explicitly stated in 13:14-15: "I have given you an example so that you may do what I have done." Therefore "if we love one another, God *dwells in us*" (1 John 4:12), just as Jesus said, "It is the Father, *dwelling* in me, who is doing his works" (John 14:10). He insists, "Believe it on the evidence of the works" (John 14:11), and tells us, "Whoever believes in me will perform the same works as I do myself; he will perform even greater works, for I am going to the Father" (John 14:12). Revelation will continue to be present and active in these works of love of neighbor, the revelation of the one true God. Thus, when he is asked, "Lord, what is all this about? Do you intend to show yourself to us and not to the world?" (John 14:22), Jesus does give an answer indeed: "If anyone loves me he will keep my word, and my Father will love him, and we shall come to him and *we shall dwell in him*" (John 14:23). Jesus will indeed be shown to the world, but qualitatively, unmistakably, that is, in the works of love-of-neighbor of those who have understood and keep the word of Christ, for his word is "Love one another."

Schnackenburg is correct when he says that John 10:38 and 14:11 demonstrate that the words of Jesus are more important for believing than his works and signs.[43] And Haenchen rightly stresses the meaning of John 8:30-31: Only if you dwell in my word will you be *truly* (*alēthōs*) my disciples.[44] But let us not forget John 13:35: "By this everyone will know that you are my disciples: if you love one another." These passages also demonstrate that in order for Yahweh to be revealed effectively *in Jesus Christ* the efficacy of the works must be of the same kind as the efficacy of the word, namely, the unmistakable revelation of the God who does not let himself be neutralized, because he is God only in the imperative of justice.[45]

"He who rejects me and refuses my words has his judge already: The word itself that I have spoken will be his judge on the last day" (John 12:48). And then he adds that this word is his Father's and not his own (v. 49). Thus he can insist on the salvific meaning of such a "judging" word (v. 50), precisely because the "judging" must be understood as the *mišpaṭ* of Yahweh in its specific Old Testament sense. Haenchen has seen this very well: Jesus does not say his own words, but rather those of the Father (John 3:34; 7:16; 8:26, 38, 40; 14:10, 24; 17:8); Jesus does not do his own works, but rather those of the Father (4:34; 5:17, 19-20; 5:30, 36; 8:28; 14:10; 17:4, 14); Jesus does not do his own will, but rather that of the Father (4:34; 5:30; 6:38; 10:25, 37); he who rejects Jesus rejects the Father (5:23, 44; 7:18; 8:50, 54).[46] The total transparency of the event called Jesus of Nazareth is the condition for revelation effectively to occur in that event. All ontological opaqueness must be eliminated, whether of the world-view type or of the historico-salvific type.

How the intransigent presentness of Judgment can be correlated with the certainty of a future parousia is a question which we shall leave for the next chapter. Here we want to establish that the meaning of *mišpaṭ* as the elimination of oppression and the realization of justice is not only maintained but is even accentuated in the definitive *mišpaṭ* affirmed by the whole Bible. There is an *ultimum* in human history, and this *ultimum* is defined and characterized, as in Marx, by the complete realization of justice on earth.

The Law

Mišpaṭ is the defense of the weak, the liberation of the oppressed, doing justice to the poor. The fact that laws were originally called *mišpaṭim* (for example, in Exod. 21:1; Exod. 15:25b; cf. also Exod. 18:13-27, to cite only strata of the most widely acknowledged antiquity) is a datum of incalculable importance, for it indicates the intention and original meaning of the legislation. In the philosophy of law as well as in the theology of authority and above all in biblical exegesis, we are thereby given the criterion for discerning when later legislators were really in accord with the will of God. (In the philosophy of law we discern when they were in accord with the profound meaning of human history, which at a given moment decided to create positive law.)

Or, on the other hand, we can determine when legislators mythicized law and authority by setting them up as an entity-in-itself, which in the best of cases lacks obligatoriness and in the worst (which is not infrequently) becomes an instrument of oppression and injustice. The prophets and Christ practiced this discernment. And it is clear they did this, not so that by their words we might assemble another equally mythical structure, but so that the moral imperative of justice in which God is revealed might be made inescapable. *Mišpaṭ* is the only theophany of Yahweh. And it does not cease; it always reappears afresh in the face of the neighbor who pleads for justice. But note that with Christ it reappears demanding to be the definitive justice, *eschaton*. The Gospel is radically unintelligible without this demand. All the agelong hopes and tears and afflictions of human history resonate in the demand for the *mišpaṭ* which yearns to be ultimate. Since the coming of Christ, the only justice possible is definitive justice.

Because of the contributions of Wellhausen, Gressmann, von Rad, and Noth, the exegesis of the Pentateuch has progressed from the simple distinction of sources (Yahwist, Priestly, Deuteronomic, and, perhaps, Elohist) to a distinction among traditions which cut across the sources themselves. The resistance, growing less every day, against this great step forward of biblical science is a passing phenomenon,[47] as was the opposition to the distinction of sources at the beginning of the century. There are two different traditions in the Pentateuch: one libertarian and Exodic (in this manner we could refer to the *Auszugs- und Landnahmetradition*); the other Sinaitic. In geographical terminology, one tradition is of Kadesh, the other of Sinai. Num. 10:29ff. (which reintroduces us into the territory of Kadesh, from which Exod. 19 had inexplicably taken us) achieves nothing in its effort to make the Sinai excursion narratively plausible except to demonstrate clearly that the Sinaitic tradition is the latest of all the themes of the Pentateuch.[48]

With map in hand Wellhausen was the first to point out the unlikelihood of this Sinaitic digression, which breaks the itinerary.[49] Later Gressmann in a detailed study confirmed that "the excursion of the Israelites toward Sinai was unknown in the most ancient tradition."[50] The investigations of von Rad and Noth have strenghtened this conclusion; they also added that the linking of the laws with the Sinaitic tradition was a redactional and editorial operation of an even later date than the insertion of the Sinaitic excursion into the Pentateuchal account.[51] Indeed, there is considerable unanimity in indicating Exod. 24:9-11 (the sacred banquet with Yahweh on the mountain top) as one of the most ancient traditions regarding the covenant. But "neither in this passage, nor in sections attributable to similar strands of the narrative, is anything mentioned about laws"; on the other hand, Exod. 24:3-8, which links covenant and law, is acknowledged to be later.[52] The redactional operation which linked the code of laws (Exod. 21:1-23:19) to the Sinaitic account cannot be dated in a period previous to Deuteronomy, for the Deuteronomic passage (Exod. 23:20-33) had already been inserted into the Sinaitic account before the code was added. Otherwise we cannot explain why they left the Deuteronomic passage where it is, since it treats a theme (Yahweh's protective activity in the conquest of the land) which in the thread of the account is dealt with only after arriving at Exod. 33.[53]

But the problem arises when we remember that the code (Exod. 21:1-23:19), although it was inserted very late in the place it has today, was composed long before the Yahwist sat down to write. As far as I know this opinion is held by all scholars. Alt, for example, dates the composition "in the generations between the entry and the foundation of the Israelite Kingdoms."[54] And we need only read Exod. 22:19a ("Anyone who sacrifices to other gods shall be anathema") to agree with von Rad that it "appears to be in form and content alike an older version of the corresponding commandment in the Decalogue."[55] There is also the fact that in the whole code there is no reference to institutions of the State; we can therefore assume that it was composed before the establishment of the State.

We can formulate the problem in this way: If the Sinaitic account is a late insertion and the laws existed much before it, what was the original connection between the laws and Yahweh? We are not concerned here with the problem posed by Gerstenberger and Fohrer concerning the patriarchal and tribal form of the first rules of conduct of prehistoric Israel.[56] We are concerned with the original theologization of the laws.

It seems to me that von Rad is inconsistent, with enormous consequences for Old Testament theology, when he asserts, "In all circumstances the close connexion between commandments and covenant must be kept in view."[57] In a parallel fashion, if Noth recognizes that the connection between the laws and the Sinaitic tradition was quite late, he is inconsistent when he becomes indignant with Pss. 1, 19, and 119, which sing of the law without mentioning the covenant.[58] Of course Noth's scientific integrity is exemplary in his resistance to the very common exegetical temptation of reading covenant where there is none. If our investigation is to be objective and not a search for theological self-satisfaction disconnected from the texts, then Noth's assertion seems elementary to me: In Pss. 1, 19, and 119, "whose theme is very particularly 'the law,' the word 'covenant' nowhere occurs, which is especially remarkable in Ps. 119 with its wealth of words. But in these didactic Psalms which seek to put the meaning of 'the law' in the correct light, there is no single reference even indirectly to the covenant." However, the books of popular spirituality, written by theologians and not exegetes, have infected von Rad and Noth with the uncritically assumed psychological need of connecting the law with the covenant. This connection is flagrantly inconsistent with the data scientifically discovered by von Rad and Noth themselves. Why do we have to look at the law through the eyes of the covenant when it is a fact that covenant theology came into existence in the seventh century and the original theologization of the law came into existence at least five centuries earlier?

Today we can assert with certainty (although it might give scandal) that the covenant was *not* the form in which the law originally was connected with Yahweh.[59]

The combative covenantist Norbert Lohfink has recently had to concede, "Historically Israel's relation to Yahweh was not at first expressed as a treaty. The treaty analogy was introduced gradually as an explanation, as a literary expression, as a ritual and formal expression. . . . In those parts of JE [Yahwist-Elohist] which are definitely ancient there is no sign of the actual literary form of a treaty."[60] He adds that the most ancient paraenetical stratum of Deuteronomy (Deut. 10:12-11:17) "bears out the hypothesis that the form was not introduced at first, since its [Deuteronomy's] most ancient strata do not have the form."[61] Although he does not say so, Lohfink thus implicitly retracts his thesis of 1963. And indeed he could not do otherwise. The entire conception of the Old Testament which the theology professors, the spiritual writers, and the *New* Testament exegetes have fashioned for themselves and now profess has to be radically modified if it can be demonstrated that the idea of the covenant is from the seventh century. Nor need we mention the Pauline exegesis which, by basing itself on this federalist interpretation, understands the "justice of God" as "fidelity to the pact," nor the Johannine exegesis which bases itself on an Old Testament *ḥesed* also understood as fidelity to the covenant. Both "justice" and "compassion" are central to the Bible and are found long before the introduction of the theology of the covenant. *Ḥesed* is *what* Yahweh promises to Abraham, according to Mic. 7:20. In no way does it consist in fulfilling what was promised. In general we can say that *ḥesed* does not consist in observing the pact; rather those who enter into the pact mutually promise *ḥesed* to each other. It is astonishing that even in Deuteronomy *ḥesed* could have been interpreted as fidelity to the covenant. In this book, which is the book of the covenant par excellence, *ḥesed* appears only in 5:10; 7:9, 12, which are acknowledged to be late re-redactions.

McCarthy and Vriezen (and Zimmerli, cf. above) have shown that the well-known formulas of presentation, of Yahweh's self-presentation, are not covenant formulas as many had believed, following Mendenhall.[62] Smend has definitively shown that the expression "they will be my people and I will be their God" originally had nothing to do with covenant. Moreover, when the eighth-century prophets announced Yahweh's rejection of Israel (an announcement central to all of them), they never based their message on Israel's nonfulfillment of the covenant; this striking fact is convincing proof that covenant theology was introduced at a later date. This datum was sufficient to demonstrate this fact even before there appeared the modern studies to which I refer.

Perhaps what led many astray was the presence of the word "covenant" nine times in the prophetic writings of the eighth century. But Amos 1:9 speaks of a covenant between Tyre and other nations; Isa. 28:15 of a covenant with death; Hos. 6:7 and 10:4 of a pact between the king and the people; Hos. 12:2 of a covenant with Assyria; Isa. 24:5 of the covenant of Noah (cf. Gen. 9:16); Isa. 33:8 of that of Ariel. Hos. 8:1-3 is the work of a later redactor who compiled the diverse passages Hos. 8:4-7; Hos. 8:8-10; Hos. 8:11-13; and Hos. 8:14 and then used the idea of covenant to give to the compilation an adequate prologue in the form of a brief account of prophetic vocation; but this redactor did not see that the reasons ingenuously given for the imminent ruin are too general: Israel rejected the good; it rebelled against the law; it transgressed the covenant. Any theologian of the Deuteronomic period could have devised such reasons. Fohrer understood this very well: "Hos. 8:1-3 is a late word."[63] As for Hos. 2:20, this is about a covenant with animals.

With regard to Jeremiah, the matter has been settled by a specialist in questions of the covenant, the impartial witness Norbert Lohfink: "In the expression 'new covenant,' the word 'covenant' is simply a cipher which emphasizes the typological character and in reality negates precisely what makes a covenant a covenant."[64] In any case, Jeremiah is contemporary to the Deuteronomic reform and is not an exception to what I have indicated, namely, that in the eighth century the existence of the covenant was unknown.

As Zimmerli has shown, the Sinaitic covenant does not appear in the Priestly document.[65] When the word is used it refers to the covenant of Noah or Abraham. And in these cases, as Noth himself has observed, the word "covenant" is "a decorative feature of the narrative which serves to give to a divine promise a solemn form."[66] To clarify this complete nonessentiality of the word "covenant" in Jeremiah and the Priestly document to which Lohfink and Noth respectively refer, consider this parallel question: Is anyone really thinking of some testament when he uses the expression "the writings of the New Testament"? It is simply an abbreviation, a label without content. Moreover, no one would think that the Priestly document connects the laws to the pact of Abraham. And yet this document continuously speaks of laws.

We are, therefore, still faced with the question: What was the original connection between the laws and Yahweh? Recourse to the theologoumenon of the covenant has for years provided a kind of potpourri into which one could throw everything. Everything was "reduced" (in both senses of the term) to covenant. Nötscher very rightly accuses the "Amtsschimmel" of this. And above all this procedure spared the labor of investigating. It was a veil which kept us from looking at the Bible head on and asking the deeper question: What was the original connection between the laws and Yahweh? And the particular area of concern is that although the misleading custom of referring to the "code of the covenant" still prevails, Exod. 21:1-23:19 existed before the theology of the covenant and there is no trace of the covenant in it. The reasons for these laws are of another kind, and, indeed, the reasons are already connected with Yahweh.

For some time scholars believed, following Alt, that the original connection between the laws and Yahweh resided in the form, that is, in the apodictic form of command: "Do this" or "Do not do this."[67] According to Alt's terminology, the casuistic (=conditional) form was originally extra-Israelite: "If anyone does this, he will die" or "If anyone does this, he will be punished in such and such a way." Exegetes hold different opinions regarding which of the two classes the participial form pertains to (for example, "He who does this will die") and which the curse form pertains to ("Accursed be he who does such and such a thing"). According to Alt they are apodictic. For some time, I repeat, it was believed that the form of the apodictic command had been the first and original connection between the laws and Yahweh. (To save space, I ask the reader that he have his Bible open to the well known code of Exod. 21:1-23:19.) Alt himself, however, had this to say about Exod. 21:13, which is not apodictic: "No one would doubt that this 'I' is Yahweh."[68] While Alt does not say so, it is striking that this is precisely the same "I" as in Exod. 23:7 and especially as in Exod. 22:26; and this latter verse is inseparable from 22:20-26, which contains three laws in casuistic form.

When he came to Exod. 22:10 (very clearly "Yahweh"), Alt sensed that it was departing from his schema, and thus he declared it to be a later interpolation. But then his theory began to move in circles. In order for Exod. 22:10 to be extra-Israelite (and it had to be, since it was not apodictic) Alt had to make the word "Yahweh" secondary. This is a question of method: Of course it is secondary with respect to the pre-Israelite state of the law in question. But this is not the problem, since practically all the Old Testament laws, or almost all, have a pre-Israelite and extra-Israelite history (We need only read the Code of Hammurabi). The problem is this: According to what theological conception was a law adopted by Israel? In Exod. 22:10 the word "Yahweh" is precisely the seal of the Israelization of this law.

In any case it is noteworthy that Alt's investigation, begun with a completely formal criterion (the apodictic form), found in the authentically original laws of Israel a common denominator of content. R. Bach, who painstakingly continued Alt's theory, came up against, for example, the casuistic law of Exod. 22:25, whose similarity of content with the apodictic laws is inconcealable; he contrived this escape: "Its origin as an apodictic law does not succeed in hiding itself under a thin casuistic stylization."[69] And again, with regard to Exod. 22:24, Bach says, "Indeed the formulation is casuistic, but the 'I' of Yahweh, the enjoinder in the second person, and the concern for the neighbor clearly show that this belongs to the sphere of the apodictic laws."[70] Fundamentally this procedure demonstrates that Alt's theory, according to its own internal logic, demands to be abandoned: What comes up again and again as the true common denominator is the content, not the form. The conclusion authorized by the textual analyses is not Bach's but rather the following: All the biblical legislation originally had the purpose of looking after the rights of the neighbor, and for this purpose Israel adopted the already existing laws (for instance, in Canaan) which seemed the most just, whether they were conditional or apodictic.

Alt's theory enjoyed much success, but it can no longer be sustained because of the extra-Israelite apodictic texts cited by Gevirtz and Kilian.[71] Even von Rad, accepting Alt's thesis without question, had observed very accurately, "There is no indication that Israel rated this originally Canaanite law [he refers to the casuistic] any differently from her own hereditary sacral law [he refers to the apodictic]."[72] Gevirtz summarizes his own investigation in this way: Apodictic laws and casuistic laws existed before and outside of Israel; apodictic laws and casuistic laws regulated both the civic and the ritual spheres. If the difference between apodictic and casuistic has any significance, it is not in either the content or the origin.[73] Alt undervalues the casuistic laws because they seem to him to be very secular and worldly, very much within the framework of "the normal jurisdiction."[74] He does not find them to be sufficiently "religious."

This is the moment to recall that the laws contained in the code of Exod. 21:1-23:19 carry the title of *mišpaṭim*, that is, "judgments." Alt's position regarding the *mišpaṭim* should lead us to reexamine the religious finality which we assign a priori to God's intervention in human history. Amos, whom Bach fruitlessly tried to reduce to apodictic legislation, shows a marked interest in the "judgments" which were held at the city gates (Amos 2:7; 5:10, 15). The same is true of the other prophets and the Psalms (Isa. 1:26; 29:21; Jer. 22:1-3; Mic. 3:11; Ps. 94:20; 122:5; etc.). What is certain is that these "judgments" (cf. Exod. 21:1) are the most ancient laws which the Old Testament transmits to us and that it is precisely in them that we find the first Yahwization.

The undoubtedly historical nucleus of Exod. 18 is this: If some of the laws (cf. vv. 16, 20) came from Moses in person, he legislated them and used them in function of the "normal jurisdiction," that is, "to do justice between a man and his neighbor" (v. 16), as Moses himself says using the verb *šaphaṭ*. This scene in which Moses legislates (cf. vv. 16, 20) is an account of the institution of the first judges by Moses. Let us keep in mind here the distinction which modern science has made between the tradition of Kadesh and that of Sinai. Any impartial reader who goes through Exodus from beginning to end will see when he reads Exod. 18 that Israel already has laws before there is any mention of Sinai and would have them even if Sinai were never mentioned at all.

If we keep in mind that the Sinaitic account (Exod. 19-Num. 10) is a much later narrative insertion, then the conclusion is unequivocal: Israel's adoption of laws was originally connected with the libertarian (Exodic) tradition and the laws were adopted "in order to do justice between a man and his neighbor." Their primigenial theologization must be sought here. The fact that legislation did indeed occur in the context described in Exod. 18 is all the more certain since it must have been very clear to any redactor of the Pentateuch that this legislation is in blatant contradiction to the tradition of Exod. 19ff., which connects the legislation to Sinai. It was to the Sinai tradition that the latest redactors gave preference for reasons which today it is difficult for us to determine with any certainty; if they did not eliminate the laws in Exod. 18:16, 20 it is because these laws are iron-hard facts which could not be manipulated.

It is natural that the erratic fragment Exod. 15:25b ("There it was he gave them statutes and *mišpat*, there that he put them to the test") should float adrift in the Pentateuchal sea after such unrestrained redactional manipulations by the later editors. But as von Rad rightly observes, this short phrase definitely belongs to the Exodic tradition since it contains an etiology of the geographical name Massah (Hebrew *Massah*, like the verb *nasah* 'to tempt,' with a preformative *M*) in *nissahu* 'he tempted him,' 'he tried him.'[75] And Massah is in the territory of Kadesh. Even though it may be erratic, this fragment of seven Hebrew words constitutes convincing testimony that the original legislation was rooted in the Exodic tradition, not the Sinaitic. If we read the book of Exodus from beginning to end, we see that this fragment is also the first mention of a legislative act in the historical account of the Bible, and here the law is called *mišpat*. This fact is of utmost importance, and it corroborates what we saw in Exod. 18.

Ps. 105, which throughout its forty-five verses offers us a complete lesson in sacred history enlarged in a quite leisurely manner, exhaustively demonstrates that the Sinaitic covenant was not part of the Exodic-libertarian tradition. At this point von Rad's thesis seems to me indisputable, especially since the Psalm with great joy refers to the Abrahamic covenant (vv. 8-9), the oath made to Isaac (v. 9b), the covenant with Jacob (vv. 10-11), the story of Joseph (vv. 16-25), the Mosaic liberation by means of the plagues (vv. 26-38), the crossing of the desert (vv. 39-41), and the possession of the land of Palestine (v. 44). What von Rad did not point out is that in this "historical creed" the law is quite indivisibly connected with the Exodic-libertarian tradition.[76] The synonymic parallelism of v. 5 is very eloquent:

Remember the marvels he did:
his wonders and the *mišpatim* from his mouth.

The marvels he did are like the whole in the first hemistich; the synonymic parallelism obliges us to understand the second part as two chapters which together make up the whole of the marvels, first the wonders or feats as deeds, second the mišpaṭim of his mouth. If it spoke only of the mišpaṭim, they could also be understood as actions; but since they are "from his mouth," there is no doubt that they are laws. The laws belong to the great liberating benefaction. And the last verse of the Psalm, which intentionally rounds it off, expresses with its prominent final conjunction ba'ᵃbur the conclusive crowning point of the libertarian marvels extensively considered in the forty-four preceding verses: "*for the purpose* that they observe his statutes and keep his laws." This last verse belongs to the great benefaction, it is part of the historical account, it is its apex. Covenant theology would have to translate ba'ᵃbur as a conditional particle, but no lexicographer could go along with this translation. The observance of the laws in this Psalm is not conceived as the human counterpart which responds to the divine beneficence, but rather as the last act of the great libertarian intervention with which Yahweh makes justice a reality in the world. Eveything is grace; the Psalm is of one piece.

We are led to believe that the laws were understood as the indispensable prolongation, the complete realization of this same great act of justice by the position of Exod. 15:25b at the end of the liberation from the Red Sea and the crossing of the desert (Exod. 15:1-25a). Keeping in mind Ps. 105, I cannot insist enough in this regard on the fact that the well-known Ps. 119 calls laws both "marvels" (vv. 18, 27) and mišpaṭim (vv. 7, 13, 20, 30, 39, 75, 91, 102, 106, 108, 120, 121, 132, 137, 149, 156, 160, 164). We have already seen that elsewhere they are also called mišpaṭim (Exod. 21:1), but that *the same author*, and as careful and ingenious a one as the composer of Ps. 119, should use mišpaṭ to designate the deeds of Yahweh (v. 52), the direct intervention for justice' sake which is invoked against the unjust (v. 84), and also the laws, strikingly corroborates our previous conclusions: The only meaning of law is to do justice, in the strictest, most social sense of the word. The central thesis of this Psalm, which has been so misunderstood, is this: "All your commandments are justice" (v. 172). And there is no doubt that it is the justice which saves the poor and the oppressed, for we find the technical term "justice and right" in v. 121 and "compassion" in vv. 41, 64, 76, 88, 124, 149, and 159. Therefore, like Ps. 105:5 and 45, Ps. 119 also counts the laws among the "marvels" (vv. 18, 27). Thus the present position of Exod. 15:25b seems to me to be much less erratic than we have been accustomed to think.

The "historical creeds," which von Rad so accurately isolated (one of these is Ps. 105), also understand the laws as an indispensable part of the great act of justice which is the liberation from Egyptian slavery. But we must not break off these creeds before they are finished, as von Rad does. As an example, let us consider the best known of these passages, Deut. 6:20-25:

20 In times to come, when your son asks you, "What is the meaning of the precepts, these statutes, and these *mišpaṭim* that Yahweh our God has laid down for you?"

21 You shall tell your son, "Once we were Pharaoh's slaves in Egypt, and Yahweh brought us out of Egypt by his mighty hand.

22 Before our eyes Yahweh worked great and terrible signs and wonders against Pharaoh and all his house.

23 And he brought us out from there to lead us into the land he swore to our fathers he would give us.

24 And Yahweh commanded us to observe all these statutes, to fear Yahweh our God for our own good forever so that we might live as on this day.

25 And for us justice will be to take care to observe all these commandments before Yahweh our God as he has directed us."

This passage is of one piece. Its whole effort is directed toward showing that unless justice is concretized in laws, the liberating intervention which Yahweh accomplished remains truncated. He rescued us from Egypt to make us "live," but precisely for this reason the laws were indispensable, for without laws there can be no justice. Deuteronomy itself makes this explicit in 16:20: "Justice, justice you must seek so that you might live." The laws are an indispensable part of his benefaction; "for our own good," this historical creed expressly says.

It seems strange to me that von Rad wants to cut the passage off at its best part, that is, in v. 24, where it begins to mention the laws,[77] especially since von Rad himself in his *Old Testament Theology* recognizes that "Israel understood the revelation of the commandments as a saving event of the first rank, and celebrated it as such."[78] The laws pertain to the account as an indivisible part of it, since the justice initiated in the liberation from slavery could not be completely realized without laws. The "historical creeds" demonstrate not only that the

Sinaitic tradition and the whole idea of covenant were completely unknown to the Exodic tradition; they show also that the legislation originally belonged to the Exodic, libertarian tradition. And this is seen to be true both by the distinction of literary traditions and by the content. The basic idea is this: It does us no good to be delivered from foreign oppression if within the people itself there continue to be oppressions and injustices.

Von Rad's very accurate thesis that the Exodic, libertarian tradition knows nothing of the Sinaitic tradition finds a more conspicuous verification in the text of the laws than in the historical creeds cited by him as proof. For example,

You must not pervert justice in dealing with a stranger or an orphan, nor take a widow's garment in pledge. Remember that you were a slave in Egypt and that Yahweh your God redeemed you from there. That is why I lay this charge on you.

(Deut. 24:17-18)

The intrinsic, direct, original radication of the law is here, in the Exodic-libertarian tradition. It is not simply a fortuitous connection which centuries later put the laws in external contact with the Sinaitic tradition in a mere juxtaposition resulting from compilation. For the law which I have just cited, Sinai simply did not exist. Note this other instance:

You must not afflict and you must not oppress the stranger, for you were strangers in the land of Egypt.

(Exod. 22:20)

This reasoning expresses the idea completely: The injustice which they suffered is recalled; the hunger for justice which they had then is revived; and this hunger for justice is now applied to the cases in which it is the Israelites who can commit injustice. To see here the covenant or congeneric ideas would be an operation of theological self-satisfaction in which we get out of a text exactly what we put into it, just as we could do with any other text even if it contradicted this one. However, the passage which follows the cited text identifies the demand for justice with the essential characterization of Yahweh:

You must not afflict the widow or the orphan; if you afflict them and they cry out to me, surely I shall hear their cry; my anger will flare and I shall kill you with the sword. Your own wives will be widows, your own children orphans.

(Exod. 22:21-23)

The only thing that these verses do is to put before the conscience the same Yahweh who with the plagues in Egypt delivered the slaves from oppression. This is the Yahweh who was revealed in a self-defining way in Exod. 3:7-9; in both passages we find the "affliction," the "outcry," the "hearing." There follow two additional laws regarding loans, which are based on the misery of the exploited man himself; the passage concludes, "He will cry out to me and I will hear him, because I am compassionate" (Exod. 22:25).

As von Rad has rightly pointed out, just as the later Sinaitic tradition has its well-known theophany, so too the Exodic-libertarian tradition has its own unmistakable theophany: Exod. 3 for the Yahwist, Exod. 6 for the Priestly document.[79] The most authentic and primordial theologization of the laws was made by connecting them with the characteristic essence of the God called Yahweh as he revealed himself when he broke into human history to save the oppressed from injustice. The laws in Exod. 22:20-26, which we have been analyzing, are a paradigmatic example of this. "Affliction" in 3:7 (theophany) and in 22:20 (law); "oppression" in 3:9 (theophany) and in 22:20 (law); "outcry" in 3:7, 9 and in 22:22 (thrice), 26; "hear" in 3:7 and in 22:22, 26; "my people" in 3:7 and in 22:24; "Egypt" in 3:7, 8, 9 and in 22:20. And still the law, to make Yahweh's essential characteristic even clearer, summarizes everything at the end: "because I am compassionate" (with the root *ḥnn*, so that no one can fall back on the idea of covenant). As we have seen, this is a compassion with raised hand and outstretched arm. Noth observes that what is prescribed in 22:24-26 regarding loans is irreconcilable with the urban economic system of the pre-Israelite oriental cultures.[80] Thus it is legitimate to deduce that the content is proper to Israel and that all speculation concerning conditional or apodictic form is irrelevant when the content is original to Israel.

I repeat, von Rad's thesis that the Sinaitic tradition was completely unknown to the Exodic-libertarian tradition is much more convincingly demonstrated with the legal texts than with the historical creeds; and it is strange that von Rad does not cite them since he himself, in his demonstration of the existence of a twofold tradition, affirms that legislation was present (Exod. 18:16, 20; 15:25b) in the Exodic tradition.[81] To be brief I will not make comparisons, as we did with Exod. 22:20-26, between Exod. 3:7-9 and the following legal texts: Exod.

23:9; Lev. 19:33-34; Deut. 15:12-15; Deut. 24:17-18; Deut. 24:19-22; Lev. 19:35-36; Lev. 25:35-38; Lev. 25:39-42; Lev. 25:47-55; Deut. 16:9-12. All these texts abundantly show that the laws originally and intrinsically had their roots in the theophany of the Kadesh tradition and knew nothing of the Sinaitic tradition.

Von Rad and Noth have very correctly and commendably undertaken to demonstrate this complete disparity between the two traditions; it is one of the great ironies of the history of exegesis that von Rad and Noth have interpreted the laws in function of the covenant and Sinai.[82] In the whole Psalter Noth can discover only two verses which link the covenant and the law (Ps. 50:16; 78:10). They prove only that the Sinaitic tradition, although it originated in a very late period, did also exist. What is striking is that Noth, to be logical, should have declared the entire Psalter to be decadent, as he does with Pss. 1, 19, and 119 because they speak of the law without reference to the covenant. Moreover—and this is serious both for Noth and for von Rad's entire Old Testament theology—only an understanding of the primigenial meaning of the law allows us to relate the Pentateuch with the prophets. And the quality of any interpretation of the Old Testament is proven by its ability to relate these two sets of biblical writings, for it is scientifically acknowledged today that the prophets not only had no intention of innovating, but rather, on the contrary, were conscious of appealing to the most ancient and genuine part of tradition. In his meticulous monograph on Ps. 119, Deissler arrives at this conclusion: "There can be no doubt that the Psalmist regards and defines the genuine Torah with the eyes of the prophets."[83]

Jer. 16:11 shows a notable consistency with Ps. 119 taken as a whole. Ps. 119:2 is a continuation of Jer. 29:13. The idea of Ps. 119:111 is the same as that of Jer. 15:16. Ps. 119:23 coincides with the description in Jer. 36:12. Ps. 119:136 is clearly consistent with Jer. 13:17; 16:11. The condition of the just and the hope and petition for punishment for the oppressors in Ps. 119:84, 85, and 126 are typical of the entire Psalter and of the Yahwist;[84] and although it might scandalize exegetes who believe they possess a "superior religion," they are also typical of the most authentic Jeremiah (18:23; 20:11-13).

Ps. 119:119 basically coincides with Ezek. 22:18-19. And Ps. 119:176 is a condensed summary of Ezek. 34. The substance of Isa. 6:10 is in Ps. 119:70. We find the content of the plea of Ps. 119:36-37 in Isa. 33:14-16. The idea of Ps. 119:119 is the same as that of Isa. 1:22, 25. The synonymic parallelism of Ps. 119:127 moves along the "paths of *mišpaṭ*" of Isa. 40:14. Ps. 119:52 includes the same consolation as in Isa. 51:8b. In v. 142 the Psalmist intones the same canticle of jubilation and hope that is developed in Isa. 51:6.

I said above that v. 172 ("All your commandments are justice") is the key to Ps. 119.[85] In fact, this formulation reveals that the expression "the commandments of your justice," which runs throughout the Psalm (vv. 7, 62, 75, 106, 123, 137, 138, 142, 144, 160, 164), refers to justice as the content of the law. The Deuteronomic redactor sustains the same thesis, which is vital to him: "What great nation is there that has precepts and statutes as just (*ṣaddiḳim*) as this whole law which I give you today?" (Deut. 4:8). But Ps. 119:172 seems to penetrate more deeply: "All your commandments are justice." This is a definition of content. For the author of Ps. 119, "to observe the commandments" (vv. 8, 33, 44, 51, 60, 67, 69, 80, 106, 115) is synonymous with "to achieve right and justice" (v. 121), and this hendiadys is the classical prophetic justice on behalf of the weak and oppressed. From the beginning (v. 3) "to walk along the paths" of the law is synonymous with not committing injustice (*'aw*e*lah*). The clearly social meaning of this *'aw*e*lah* can be seen in Hab. 2:12 and Mic. 3:10, and all the lexicons translate it straightforwardly as "injustice." As we have already seen, to count the laws among the "marvels" (Ps. 119:18, 27) which liberated the people from the oppression of Egypt indicates that the only meaning of the law is to do justice in the strictest and most social sense of the word. One must have a hunger and thirst for justice, as a hermeneutical prerequisite, to participate in the extraordinary outburst of rejoicing that there is in this phrase: "Your justice is [the] definitive justice" (Ps. 119:142). It seems to me that this is the only way we can translate the Hebrew expression *ṣidḳatheḳa ṣedeḳ l*e*'olam*. Otherwise it becomes an insipid tautology: Your justice is always justice.

If we first translate the Psalm so that it expresses truisms, then it is very easy to criticize the same Psalm and dismiss it as decadent. But looking at it objectively, why would the author exult over such platitudes? The Psalm does not refer to justice as a divine property in heaven, but rather justice achieved here below through the laws introduced by God. It is precisely for this reason that the Psalm sings of these laws as a part and the apex of the divine intervention in our history, whose only meaning is to establish on earth the justice which never fails, which is never again interrupted. This intervention is the fulfillment of the yearning of the poor and oppressed from among all mankind. It seems to me to be impossible to understand the Bible if we do not perceive the irrepressible message of hope in the expression *lᵉʻolam* (the Septuagint translates this as *eis ton aiōna, heōs aiōnos*, or the adjective *aiōnois*). This is the concrete justice of God, the definitive reign of justice that arrives at last, which will not end ever again. This alone is authentic "living," according to Ps. 119:17, 25, 37, 40, 50, 93, 107, 149, 154, 156, 159, 175.[86]

For the Pauline concept of "justice of God," I do not see how one can scientifically postulate a meaning different from the one in the Psalter (which is the same as that of the entire Old Testament), when we see that the Psalter employs the term twenty-four times (Ps. 5:9; 24:5; 31:2; 36:7, 11; 40:11; 51:16; 69:28; 71:2, 15, 16, 24; 72:1; 88:13; 89:17; 98:2; 103:17; 111:3; 119:40, 142; 143:1, 11; 145:7). *Paul's revolutionary and absolutely central message, that justice has been achieved without the law, would lack all force if this were not precisely the same justice that the law hoped to realize; this is the revolutionary and unprecedented core of his message.*[87]

Besides the eight verses mentioned above in which Ps. 119 derives authentic "living" from the law, the following passages of the Old Testament also do the same: Deut. 4:1; 5:33; 6:24; 8:1; 30:15-20; 32:47; Lev. 18:5; Ezek 20:11; Ecclus. 15:15-17. Thus the meaning of "life" or "everlasting life" in the New Testament is the same as in the Old, for otherwise we could not explain why it too connects this "living" with the law (cf. Mark 10:17-19; Matt. 19:16-20; Luke 18:18-20; John 5:39-40; John 7:38; Rom. 7:10; Gal. 3:21; etc.). To deny that the law produces life has force as a negation only insofar as it assumes the same meaning of "life" as those who affirm that it does produce life: "If we had been given a law capable of giving life, then truly justice would come from the law" (Gal. 3:21), "but now without the law God's justice which was made known through the law and the prophets has been revealed" (Rom. 3:21). It is scientifically unacceptable to attribute to coincidence the association of the three concepts of "justice," "life," and "law" in Paul as well as in Ps. 119 (and the entire Psalter).

Note this prayer against the *rᵉšaʻim:*

Deny them further access to your justice,
blot them out of the book of life,
strike them off the roll of the just.

(Ps. 69:28-29)

The justice which Yahweh will achieve on earth is here, as it were, hypostatized (as also in Romans, Galatians, Philippians, and 2 Cor. 5:21), or, rather, concretized, like a precinct, like a kingdom into which one can enter, like a new reality with social dimensions in human history. It is the definitive era of justice, a new world in which there will no longer be injustices. Only this is truly "life," according to the entire Bible. Trito-Isaiah says it in this way: "In your people all will be just; they will definitively [*le'olam*] possess the land" (Isa. 60:21). And Zephaniah says, "Those who are left [*še'erit*] in Israel will commit no injustice" (Zeph. 3:13).[88] Both these prophets and Ps. 69 depend on Isaiah for his idea of the "remnant" (Isa. 7:3 and 10:21), about which he says, "Those who are left [*hanniš'ear*] in Zion, and remain in Jerusalem, shall be called holy; all shall be noted down for life in Jerusalem" (Isa. 4:3). An earthly reign of justice in which there is no longer any oppression, in which we love one another, this alone is really "living." "We know that we have passed from death to life because we love our brothers; he who does not love remains in death" (1 John 3:14). This is exactly the same idea of "life" we find in tiny Ps. 133:

How good, how delightful it is
for all to live together like brothers, . . .
copious as a Hermon dew
falling on the heights of Zion,
because there Yahweh confers his blessing,
everlasting life [*hayyim 'ad-ha 'olam*].

The meaning of "your justice is definitive justice" in Ps. 119:142 is the same, but it is justice as the fruit and result of the law, for "all your commandments are justice" (v. 172). The exegetes who accuse the Psalter of nomism should bear in mind that the prophets regard the law in exactly the same way as does Ps. 119. We can see this in a verse of Deutero-Isaiah which is very rich in meaning:

For the sake of his justice it was Yahweh's will
to exalt and glorify his law.

(Isa. 42:21)

And this is not an isolated verse; this is the meaning of the law for the prophets:

If only you had been alert to my commands
your peace would have been like a river,
and your justice like the waves of the sea.

(Isa. 48:18)

Pay attention, you peoples, to my voice,
listen to me, you nations,
for from me comes the law
and my *mišpaṭ* to be the light of the nations;
in an instant I establish my justice,
my salvation shall appear.

(Isa. 51:4-5)

The law is the justice and right which save. The parallelism between law and *mišpaṭ* is the same which, as we have seen, indicated the true meaning that the law originally had in Israel. This can also be seen in Isa. 51:7-8 and Zeph. 3:4-5. Let us listen to Micah:

From Zion the law will go out,
and the word of Yahweh from Jerusalem:
He will do justice [verb *šphṭ*] among many peoples,
and rectify powerful and far-off nations;
they will hammer their swords into ploughshares,
their spears into sickles;
nation will not lift sword against nation
there will be no more training for war.

(Mic. 4:2-3)

In a noneschatological context, we see the meaning of the law for Isaiah:

Woe to those who . . . justify the unjust (*rašaʻ*)
and cheat the just of their justice . . .
because they rejected the law of Yahweh of the armies
and despised the word of the Holy One of Israel.

(Isa. 5:23-24)

For his part Amos compares the sin of Judah with the sin of Israel, and in both it is unquestionably the same sin. With regard to Judah, he says: "Because they despised the law of Yahweh and failed to keep his commandments. . . . " And with regard to Israel: "Because they sell the just man for money, and the poor man for a pair of sandals, they trample the head of the needy in the dust and twist the path of the humble" (Amos 2:4-8).

We need not extend the list of prophetic testimonies which, like the Psalter and the entire Exodic tradition, in the law see exclusively the justice realized on behalf of the oppressed. Let us conclude with Zechariah:

Practice authentic justice [*mišpaṭ* and the verb *šaphaṭ*].
Let each achieve compassion and mercy with his brother;
do not oppress the widow and the orphan,
the stranger and the poor man;
let no one secretly plan evil against his neighbor.
Buy they refused to obey,
they turned a petulant shoulder,
they stopped their ears rather than hear the law
and the words which Yahweh of the armies
sent by his spirit
through the prophets of old.

(Zech. 7:9-12)

We thus see very clearly the authentic meaning of the law, but these texts also demonstrate that the tradition of the law is not that of the covenant. The legal texts themselves have already shown us, as much or more than von Rad's historical creeds, that in fact the Exodic-libertarian tradition knows nothing of the Sinai tradition, which is much later. But at the same time they have demonstrated that the legislation was originally rooted in the Exodic-libertarian tradition. The authentic law of Yahweh was the continuation and crowning point of the great act for justice' sake with which God intervened in our history to free the oppressed and establish justice on earth. This is the teaching that determined the composition which joined Exod. 18:1-12 with Exod. 18:13-27. Knierim's article is a magnificent study, if we except the break that he makes after v. 12, for he thus leaves unconnected precisely those two scenes which the redactor wanted to unite.[89] The second will not be understood prescinding from the first. I can understand the second part of the chapter as preredactional tradition: Moses gave laws to accomplish justice between a man and his neighbor when he instituted the judges.[90] This is the preredactional element in the narrative; but we might add, if we like, that the tradition said that Moses did all this on the advice of his father-in-law, the priest of Midian.

But the first part (vv. 1-11), which repeats the verb *ḥaṣṣil* five times ("to free," as in Ps. 82:4) in vv. 4, 8, 9, 10a, and 10b, is a redactional summary of the entire Exodus account, as redactional as the well-known summaries of miracles in the Synoptic Gospels. The conclusion,

"Now I know that Yahweh is the greatest of all the gods" (v. 11), is on the lips of the same much-impressed Jethro on whose advice Moses then institutes judges and legislates; this is a profoundly theological composition. "Because *mišpaṭ* belongs to God" (Deut. 1:17), the Deuteronomist rightly comments when he recounts all this to us again.[91] The law and judgment belong to Yahweh, according to the redactor of Exod. 18, but precisely to the Yahweh who liberates from the oppression of Egypt.

We have seen from the legal texts we have considered that, in fact, this is the Yahweh who originates laws; this is he who presents himself with the demand for their fulfillment. If Jethro's intervention in Exod. 18:13-27 is preredactional, then the redactor needed a Jethro very deeply impressed by the Yahweh who breaks into history for justice' sake as the one who ends slaveries. If Jethro's intervention in Exod. 18:13-27 is not preredactional, then this impartial non-Israelite, profoundly impressed by Yahweh the liberator, serves the redactor as a compositional resource to root the laws and the judgments, contentwise, in the same great act for justice' sake. Every mention of God in the second part of the chapter would be out of place if this were not the God described and acknowledged in the first part of the chapter. Only a God who is distinguished from the other gods because he does indeed do justice has anything to do with the legislation and the administration of justice. Deutero-Isaiah very rightly says, "For the sake of his justice it was Yahweh's will to exalt and glorify his law" (Isa. 42:21).

But the radication of the original laws in the Exodic-libertarian tradition constitutes a criterion for determining their authenticity, just as the primigenial designation of the laws with the name *mišpaṭ* did. Not just any type of laws can be based in the Yahweh who intervenes to save the poor and the oppressed from injustice. Nor is just any mandate of authority (whether sacred or profane) a true concretization of the will of God. The conclusion to which we were led by the use of *mišpaṭ* as the primigenial term for law finds in the literary analysis of the Pentateuchal traditions an independent confirmation which renders this conclusion highly convincing. Authority is authority in the measure that it makes us discover the will of God. Authority cannot make something into the will of God which was not the will of God.

It was very natural—as the history of Christianity and the legislation of all peoples demonstrates—that the later Israelite legislators should be tempted to justify all sorts of precepts by invoking the Yahweh who saves the poor and the oppressed from injustice. This was the artifice which generated the whole of Deuteronomy as legislation, for the idea of Deut. 10:12-11:17 (which is the most ancient paraenetical portion[92]) occurs again in the crucial "historical creed" of Deut. 26, thus "bracketing" all the legislation of Deut. 12-25. We have already seen that in the other "historical creeds" the fulfillment of the law is not conceived as a human reciprocation, but rather as the indispensable continuation and apex of Yahweh's intervention which liberates from slavery. In Deut. 26 we must not overlook either the verses 10a and 13a[bbcd], as von Rad does. The redactor expressly indicates (in vv. 10b and 13a[a])that they belong to the text which the Israelite should recite when offering the first fruits. They are an indivisible part of the same "creed." The tithing of the first fruits is not brought for Yahweh. Nor is the offering or the fulfillment of the laws understood as the human correspondence to the divine beneficence, but rather as a part and realization of the same great beneficence. The obvious sense of Deut. 12:11-12, 17-19; 16:11-12, 14; 26:10b-12 is that the people of Israel cannot enjoy the land which Yahweh gave them if they do not enjoy it with the orphan, the widow, the stranger, and the Levite, that is, with all the dispossessed. The Levite is introduced as a beneficiary precisely because he is poor. The preredactional "creed" includes in this same realization of Yahweh's work the observance of the precepts (26:13). And the meaning of these precepts is to enable all the needy to participate in the wealth of the land. All this is the great work of Yahweh. The accumulation of Egyptian outrages and the "outcry" and the "Yahweh hears" and the "raised hand and outstretched arm" in 26:6-8 lead into the "stranger, widow, and orphan" of v. 13 with the observance of the laws, within the predeuteronomic recitative itself. This is exactly the same idea as in Exod. 22:20-33, where the remembrance of Egypt was the basis for the protection of the helpless.

The artifice of the Deuteronomist redactor does not lie in including the Levite nor in making the laws of 26:13 a part of Yahweh's work, but rather in encompassing between Deut. 10-11 and Deut. 26 every kind of law (Deut. 12-25), even those which have nothing to do with the Yahweh who acts for justice and legislates only for defense of the needy.

Christ and the prophets, Paul and the four Evangelists understood this artifice of the later legislators very clearly. With regard to cultus, the Catholic Tresmontant, after citing Hos. 6:6; Amos 5:21-24; Mic. 6:6-8, and Jer. 7:21-23, says this: "All this, as has long since been pointed out, is manifestly contrary to what Leviticus teaches."[93] We need not dwell on this point, for we have already studied the anticultus of the prophets, of Jesus Christ, and of the New Testament.[94] They simply consider as nullified all the laws whose content cannot be based on the "I am Yahweh who delivered you from the slavery of Egypt." Amos and Jeremiah say this explicitly:

Did you bring me sacrifices and oblations in the desert
for all those forty years, House of Israel?

(Amos 5:25)

For when I brought your fathers out of Egypt I gave them no orders,
I said nothing to them, about holocausts and sacrifices.

(Jer. 7:22)

With regard to the non-cultic area, R. Bach's careful juridical study of Amos shows that Amos 2:6 and 8:6 are incompatible with Exod. 21:2-6 and Deut. 15:12-18 (cf. 2 Kings 4:1 and Neh. 5:1ff.).[95] Although these laws moderated slavery, they resigned themselves to slavery in a certain form. According to Amos, even this compromise cannot be reconciled with the Yahweh who broke into history to release the slaves. Here we have a dialectic in the authentically Marxian sense, and indeed, right within the content of the laws. Any fixing, any bridling of the divine deslaving irruption, is unfaithful, according to Amos, to the plan of that implacable irruption, which is the only possible basis for the laws.

Jesus adopts the same position in Mark 10:5 with regard to Deut. 24:1ff. The law took regulatory precautions, accepting the divorce of a woman by her husband as an irremediable fact. For Jesus even this resignation, which is prejudicial to the woman, is unfaithful to the single divine intention which gives authority to the laws. The protection of the weak is an imperative always in force, a responsibility which we cannot discharge by means of the letter of a law. And if the law constitutes a fixing and a bridling of the divine intervention which liberates the helpless, then this law militates against the will of God. Jesus' absolute prohibition of divorce is to protect the woman from masculine desertion and arbitrariness. (Let us say in passing that if today we were to use that prohibition in a way prejudicial to the same people in whose defense Jesus formulated it, we would be guilty of the same idolization-of-the-law which Jesus combatted; we would be perpetrating the same human sacrifices on the altar of the same Huitzilopoztli hypostatized in words.)

Here we must repeat what we said above.[96] The New Testament understands the entire "law and the prophets" as a pure and implacable "love your neighbor." This—when put into practice—involves the same distinction in the law as was made by the prophets when they rebelled against the artifice of the later legislators who added precepts having a content which could not be based in the Yahweh who frees slaves from oppression. The only true laws are *mišpat*. It was Jeremiah who spelled out this distinction:

> Even the stork in the sky
> knows the appropriate season,
> turtledove, swallow, crane,
> observe their time of migration;
> but my people do not know
> the justice [*mišpat*] of Yahweh.
> How dare you say, "We are wise
> and we possess the law of Yahweh,"
> when it is clear that it has been falsified
> by the lying pen of the scribes?
> The wise shall be confounded, they will be struck down,
> they will be taken prisoners.
> They rejected the word of Yahweh,
> so what use is their wisdom to them?
> Therefore I will give your wives to foreigners,
> your fields to conquerors:
> for all, least no less than greatest,
> are out for profit,
> prophet no less than priest
> all practice fraud.
>
> (Jer. 8:7-9)

It is legitimate to point out the parallel between this passage and the distinction made by Jesus: "The important part of the law: justice (*krisin=mišpat*), compassion, and goodness" (Matt. 23:23) ("right, mercy, and faithfulness," according to Bonnard; "right, compassion, and loyalty," according to Lohmeyer and J. Schmid). So, too, Paul, although he rejects the law, as is well known, in Rom. 8:4 says that Christ died "in order that the content of justice of the law might be achieved in us."

But perhaps the best testimony regarding the original meaning of the biblical laws, regarding the fact that they were meant to continue and crown the intervention of Yahweh the liberator for justice' sake, is offered to us—unintentionally, of course—by the Deuteronomic redactor's artifice itself. To justify the entire legislative corpus of Deut. 12-25, he felt compelled to "bracket" it between Deut. 10-11 on the one side and Deut. 26 on the other. In Jer. 8:7-9 we see that he did not succeed in deceiving Jeremiah. The exegetes whom I have already cited hold that in this passage the prophet is referring to the Deuteronomic scribes, for it was these who, with the best intentions in the world, believed that the solution of Israel's crisis lay in King Josiah's reformism.[97] But Jeremiah understood things by content, not by compositional literary "brackets." This alone is "to know Yahweh."

Civilization

Sooner or later genuine exegesis has to ask, with regard to all the prophets, the question which Würthwein poses with regard to Amos:

But what is the meaning of the fact that Amos exposes interhuman injustices? In the last analysis these are crimes which occur among all the peoples of the world in the most varied circumstances; and we always end up by finding a *modus vivendi* with them without much squeamishness. Is not Amos assigning them too much importance when he sees in them the cause of the great approaching disaster?[98]

This question must be posed with regard to all the prophets, as we can deduce from assertions such as the following one of Kraus: "Amos, Hosea, Isaiah, and Micah know but one decisive theme: justice and right."[99] How do we explain why the prophets considered the lack of social justice as the only cause for the disaster and rejection of Israel? I think that our customary theology and exegesis have the vague presentiment that such a question, taken seriously, would lead to horrifying conclusions for the West and for Christianity. This is the only way I can explain why customary exegesis and theology generally evade the question, or if they do formulate it, they trivialize it.

But before addressing this important question, it would be well to call to mind a fundamental passage from Paul which in a very similar way is customarily avoided by exegesis, perhaps because it too would demand the formulation of a question identical to Würthwein's. It is the description of the injustice prevailing in the pagan world (Rom.

1:28-32), a description understood by Rom. 2:1-3:20 to be equally applicable to the Jewish world. The structural form itself might lead us to suspect that, since Rom. 1:18-3:20 is the compositional basis for the Letter to the Romans, the seriousness with which we deal with this passage is decisive for our understanding of the whole letter and consequently of the whole Pauline message.

28 Since they refused to acknowledge God, God has given them over to their own wicked minds to do what is not proper, steeped in every injustice:

29 perversity, ambition, corruption, puffed up with envy, murder, discord, treachery, and spite;

30 libelers, slanderers, theoabominable, arrogant, boastful [*hyperēphanous*], insolent, enterprising in wickedness, disobedient to their parents,

31 without brains, loyalty, love, or mercy;

32 they know well enough God's demand for justice, that those who do such things are deserving of death—and yet they do them; and what is worse, encourage others to do the same.

(Rom. 1:28-32)

This is the passage which demands the formulation of a question identical to Würthwein's, but first let me say something about my translation. The qualifier *theostygeis* never, whether in the Bible or outside the Bible, means hater of God or of the gods. It always, without even one exception, has a passive meaning in the Greek language, that is, "abominable to God or to the gods." The effort of certain exegetes to give it an active meaning does not seem to me to be exegetical. Both philology and context indicate that the passage describes only actions of men toward other men. In an identical context, Ecclus. 10:7 tells us, "Pride [*hyperēphania*] is abominable to the Lord and to men, and injustice [*adikia*] is abhorrent to both." And in Prov. 8:13 Yahweh says, "I hate arrogance and pride [*hyperēphanian*], wicked behavior and a lying mouth." And we see the same idea, developed more extensively, in Prov. 6:16-18; cf. also Isa. 2:12. *Theostygeis* is passive, although my translation as "theoabominable" may not be recommendable for reasons of literary aesthetics.

A few more words about the translation. I have placed a colon at the end of v. 28, because of all these concepts the only one which Paul had already mentioned is injustice (*adikia*, in v. 18), and indeed he mentions it twice. We can suppose then that this is what Paul now goes on to spell out and investigate in detail in vv. 29-31. Since in the entire passage (1:18-3:20) *adikia* is the predominant concept (1:18a, 18b, 29; 2:8; 3:5), in 1:28-32 it cannot be put on the same level as the concepts listed immediately after it. Moreover, the description in 1:29-31 substantially coincides with the one of the "unjust" which we found in the Psalter.[100] Therefore, for the concepts listed in 1:29-31, "injustice" in 1:28 serves as the comprehensive title. This is true especially because 1:18 had affirmed the oppressive influence of *adikia* on the knowledge of truth,[101] and the whole intention in 1:28 is to let loose the immanent recoil which this not-knowing exercises, throwing men into the power of *adikia*. This power of *adikia* is detailed in 1:29-31. Let us add that *adikia* reappears in 2:7-8 in the division at the Last Judgment between the men of "constancy in good works" and "the men of discord . . . who trust in injustice"; as we have seen, the designation of the latter group coincides in content with the Psalter's description of the "unjust."[102]

Note that this Psalmodic description is taken up by Paul in Rom. 3:12-18; there, to extend to the Jewish world the same picture that he has drawn for the pagan world, he asserts that the Old Testament itself affirms that the Jews (3:19) have not achieved justice (3:10). And Paul introduces this synthesized Psalmodic description with "There is not a just man, not even one" (3:10). Neither in the Hebrew nor in the Septuagint do we find this formulation in Ps. 14:1, 3 (=Ps. 53:2, 4); and this is the passage which Paul clearly is citing when he redacts this introduction, for "there is not . . . not even one" is an unmistakable expression. What Paul reformulates on his own account is precisely "just man," instead of the Hebrew "doer of good" and the Septuagint's "doer of goodness [*chrēstotēta*]." And to the degree that this reformulation is spontaneous it is all the more decisive for demonstrating what Paul understands by justice.

On the other hand, the identification between *adikia* in Rom. 1:29 and not-just in Rom. 3:10 is fully intentional, for (excepting the *adikia* of 3:5, where all exegetes agree that he is already speaking of the Jews) the *adikia* of 1:18 encompasses the entire passage 1:18-3:20, as we can see by the "brackets" in 1:17 and 3:21 (in both, the revelation of the justice of God). Thus in 1:18-3:20 it is the anger of God which comes down upon the injustice of men in an immanent punishment. We can be saved from this anger only by the coming of the "justice of God" as a new reality of social dimensions in human history.[103] This is the only way we can understand the "because" (*gar*) of 1:18, connected with the "But now" (*Nyni de*) of 3:21, after the thesis is set forth in 1:16-17: *Because* in it the justice of God is revealed, *therefore* the Gospel is salvation. Salvation is understood as to-save-from-the-anger (see Rom. 5:9; 1 Thess. 5:9; 1:10). The thesis of Rom. 1:16-17 is demonstrated (*gar*, 1:18) *by the fact* that the anger is already operative in the whole world (1:18-3:20), *but now* the justice of God has been made known (3:21ff.).

Thus Rom. 3:21 is not a simple repetition of 1:17 after a contrasting rhetorical passage. Rom. 3:21 is the indispensable second part of the demonstration of the thesis of 1:16-17. Only because the justice of God is revealed in it is the Gospel salvation, *because* the anger is already operative in the world, but now the justice which saves us from the anger has been made known to us.

Exegesis has been impaired by forgetting that 2 Cor. 5:21 is historically the first time that Paul uses the expression "justice of God"; and indeed he uses it to tell us that the whole issue is "that we might become the justice of God in Christ." If evangelization and faith make us to *be* the justice of God, it is obvious that this saves us from the anger that has been concretized in history in terms of interhuman injustice. It saves us by making us to be no longer injustice but justice.

Let us move then to Rom. 1:28-32, which I have translated above. What is the meaning of the great emphasis put on interhuman injustices which occur every day in every place and with which we always end up by finding a *modus vivendi* without much astonishment? And above all, what is the meaning of the statement that "those who do such things are deserving of death"? Neither in the Old Testament, nor in the New, nor in any legislation in all of human history are there any laws which punish envy, arrogance, slander, pride, ambition, or cold-heartedness by death.[104] Catholic moral theology does not even catalogue them "in themselves" as "mortal" sins; thus the evasive interpretation of "deserving of death" by using the concept of spiritual death does not resolve the problem. And to understand the Pauline *thanatos* as something different from real, physical death is a hypothesis which does not even deserve the effort of refutation.[105]

We are still faced with Würthwein's great question, and it is as traumatic with reference to the prophets as it is with reference to Paul.

Zimmerli has said that von Rad's response to the general prophetic question tends to cast the suspicion of charlatanism on the prophets.[106] The same conclusion would be reached by the exegesis which interprets Rom. 1:18-3:20 as "rhetorical." But this great passage is in every sense basic to Paul's message. To overlook the problem is tantamount to overlooking Paul of Tarsus. And there are many ways to consider Paul as a charlatan; the most exact way is the implicit: to overlook him.

Von Rad very accurately establishes two points: (1) The prophets unleash a frontal attack against the oppressions of the poor, against injustices; (2) according to the prophets, Israel has failed Yahweh totally. When this outstanding exegete goes on to try to convince us that these two things have nothing to do with each other, then he produces commonplace theology, the theology conditioned by the "establishment" of Western civilization.[107] If there is anything striking about the prophetic proclamations of Yahweh's rejection of Israel it is that Israel's total failure with regard to Yahweh consists precisely in its oppression of the poor and its interhuman injustices:

Woe to those who add house to house
and join field to field
until there is no more room
and they are the sole inhabitants of the land.
Yahweh of the armies has sworn this in my hearing:
"Their many houses shall be brought to ruin,
their magnificent palaces will be left uninhabited."

(Isa. 5:8-9)

The relationship between cause (injustices) and effect (ruin) is immediate. To fail Yahweh consists in the monopolizing of the houses and fields by the rich. The crime and the punishment are expressed here without intermediary terms. The theological "interpretations" which we might want to insert between v. 8 and v. 9 will be our own thinking, not Isaiah's.

Let us hear what Amos has to say to the rich ladies of Israel:

Listen to these words, you cows of Bashan
living in the mountain of Samaria,
oppressing the poor,
crushing the needy,
saying to your husbands, "Bring us something to drink":
The Lord Yahweh swears by his holiness
that the days are coming to you now

when you will be dragged out with hooks,
and your children with prongs.
By breaches in the wall then you will go out,
one behind the other
to be driven all the way to Hermon.
It is Yahweh who speaks.

(Amos 4:1-3)

In a passage like this it is impossible to doubt that the direct cause of
Israel's rejection by Yahweh is injustice, the exploitation of the poor
and the needy. Let us see if Micah thinks any differently:

Now listen to this, you leaders of Jacob,
rulers of Israel,
you who loathe justice [*mišpaṭ*]
and pervert all that is right,
you who build Zion with blood
and Jerusalem with injustice.
The leaders pronounce their judgment for bribes,
the priests preach for money,
the prophets make divinations for a fee.
And yet they rely on Yahweh, saying,
"Is not Yahweh in our midst?
Nothing can happen to us!"
Because of this, since the fault is yours,
Zion will be ploughed like a field,
Jerusalem will be a heap of rubble,
and the mountain of the temple a wooded height.

(Mic. 3:9-12)

The immediacy of the woeful conclusion is striking. The schemas or
entelechies which we might want to read between the crime and the
punishment break precisely that immediate relationship which the
prophets have undertaken to emphasize. Hosea provides a lapidary
formulation of this direct causation:

You have ploughed injustice,
reaped iniquity,
and eaten the produce of fraud.

(Hos. 10:13)

Let us now listen to Jeremiah:
"You have eyes and heart for nothing
but your own profit,
for shedding innocent blood
and perpetrating oppression and extortion."

Therefore Yahweh says this about Jehoiakim,
son of Josiah, king of Judah:
"Raise no dirge for him:
'Alas, oh brother! Alas, oh sister!'
Raise no dirge for him:
'Mourn for his highness, mourn for his majesty.'
He will receive the funeral honors of a donkey,
—dragged away and thrown
out of the gates of Jerusalem."

(Jer. 22:17-19)

The same immediate relationship can be seen between Amos 3:9-10 (injustices) and Amos 3:11 (Yahweh's catastrophic rejection of Israel), between Amos 8:4-6 and Amos 8:7-14, between the crime of Amos 5:11a (trampling on the poor) and the punishment of Amos 5:11b ("Those houses you have built of dressed stone, you will never live in them; and those precious vineyards you have planted, you will never drink their wine"). We see the same immediacy between the injustice against the poor, the widows, and the orphans in Isa. 10:1-2 and the devastation in Isa. 10:3-4; we see the same direct relationship between the interhuman crimes of Jer. 9:3-5 and the threat of Jer. 9:6. For the sake of brevity I will not quote these texts nor extend the list.

Israel's injustices to the poor and needy are the direct and exclusive reason for Israel's rejection by Yahweh. What basis do the prophets have for sustaining a thesis of such incalculable consequences? According to Würthwein, Amos bases himself on the law: "None of the enumerated accusations of social outrages and violations of rights is lacking in substantial affinity with the collections of Old Testament laws."[108]

"Substantial affinity" is a very carefully selected term. I think it is important to note this: If the prophets were concerned with the laws as such, they would cite them textually at least occasionally or they would refer at least occasionally to the content itself of the law as we know it from the collections in the Pentateuch. And if the formulation should not coincide with that which has come down to us in these collections, at least we could unequivocally establish the formal intention of citing them. The absence of formal citations of legal texts and the absence of even the desire to cite them exclude any explanation of the prophetic anathema for reasons of legalism. Substantial affinity does not mean that according to the prophets the reason for Yahweh's rejection of Israel is that Israel violated the law, regardless of its content. It is not for reasons of nonobservance but for reasons of injustice that Yahweh rejects Israel. In Isa. 42:21; 48:18; 51:4-5; 51:7-8; Zeph. 3:4-5; Mic. 4:2-3; Amos 2:4-8; Isa. 5:23-24; and Zech. 7:9-12, which we have already considered,[109] it is clear that for the prophets the law is important only because of its content of justice. Thus, when they proclaim that Yahweh rejects Israel, the law as law does not serve them as a point of support subsistent in itself. The law as such has no substance for them. Argumentatively it is a transparent datum, not a screen. They base themselves on the fact of injustice, not on the fact that injustice may be legally prohibited.

We are still faced with the fundamental question: Why proclaim that Israel's election is destroyed, basing the proclamation on crimes always committed by all mankind and to which history has always been able to accommodate itself? Taken in its true proportions, Würthwein's question seems to me to be the most important exegetical question that can be asked, for Paul goes beyond the borders of the People of Israel and extends the problem to the whole of human civilization; he thus puts at stake the interpretation of the New Testament as well as the Old.

Citing Amos 2:9-12; 4:6-7; Isa. 1:2-3; 5:1-2; Mic. 6:1-2; Hos. 11:1-2; Jer. 2:1-2, von Rad holds that the prophets appeal to history, that is, to Yahweh's intervention on behalf of Israel, and that with these historical facts they now justify Yahweh's anathema against Israel. The observation is accurate: They base their anathema on the Exodic-libertarian tradition and not the Sinai tradition. But this explanation does not really differ from Würthwein's one of the "substantial affinity" between the prophetic rebuke and the laws. As we have seen in the preceding section, what is authentic in the laws is rooted in the Exodic-libertarian tradition, not in the Sinai tradition. The "oppressions" denounced in Amos 3:9 and 4:1 are the same as those mentioned (as prohibited, not as denounced) in the laws of Exod. 22:20-33; Deut. 24:14; and Lev. 19:13, as Würthwein points out. But the law itself uses the history of the liberation from Egypt in its argumentation.[110] Amos' appeal to history is not separable from that content of justice in which the prophets and the laws have their affinity. Nor is it accurate to say with von Rad that in fact the prophets work with a "completely new" conception of the law.[111] The law itself extends the threat of punishment to all of Israel:

You must not be harsh with the widow or with the orphan. If you are harsh with them and they cry out to me, I shall surely hear their cry. My anger will flare and I shall kill you with the sword. Your own wives will be widows and your own children orphans.

(Exod. 22:21-23)

The interest and usury denounced in Amos 8:6 are prohibited in Lev. 25:37-38, but, quite contrary to how von Rad would have it, here the prophet omits explicit mention of the Exodic tradition as a justification for the threat, while the law does explicitly mention the liberation from Egypt. The same thing occurs with Amos 8:5 and Lev. 19:36. And so on with the others. Von Rad tried to distinguish between history and the law as bases for the prophetic anathema because in his analysis of the traditions of the Hexateuch he did not see that the original legislation pertained to the Exodic tradition, both in literary stratum and in content.

Nevertheless, the observation that the prophetic anathema is based on the Exodic-libertarian tradition does lead us toward the true response. The prophets performed no "bold piece of hermeneutic"[112] when they proclaimed the rejection of Israel on the basis of crimes which mankind has always committed and with which history has always entered into compromise. In doing this they were really basing the rejection of Israel on the fact that Israel had frustrated the only reason for its election. In Gen. 18 the Yahwist had stated this one reason quite explicitly: "justice and right" for all mankind. And Isaiah also explicitly spells out why Yahweh will lay waste his selected vineyard, his chosen planting, that is, "the House of Israel" and "the men of Judah": because "he expected right [*mišpaṭ*] from them, but found murder; he expected justice [*sᵉdakah*], but found only a cry of distress" (Isa. 5:7). This is the same "cry" that the Yahwist connected with "justice and right" in Gen. 18 when he told us what Israel's universal mission was according to Yahweh.

In a few words the response to Würthwein's momentous question is this: The injustice, the mercilessness, the oppression, and the exploitation to which all cultures have learned to resign themselves are precisely what Yahweh wants to abolish in the world. The great purpose of God's intervention in human history is definitively to eliminate all this injustice and enmity which many Christians, it would appear, find so normal. If the people chosen solely for the purpose of teaching the world justice (Gen. 18:19) has become a concretization of injustice (cf. Mic. 3:10; Hab. 2:12; Amos 3:9-11; 6:8; 5:11; Jer. 5:1-5; 8:7-9; Isa. 5:1-7; 5:8-9), this is a betrayal of all the human beings who have suffered and are suffering. *For this reason* (cf. Amos 3:2 and Gen. 18:19: "to know" = "to elect") the prophets proclaim the devastation of this people. Because Israel totally failed Yahwah, the oppressed of the whole earth continue to "cry out" in vain.

Israel, however, was not the last instance of Yahweh's choice being betrayed by the chosen ones themselves. "He defended the cause of the poor and the needy.... Is not this what it means to know me? It is Yahweh who speaks" (Jer. 22:16). "To know me" is "to know that I am Yahweh, he who achieves compassion, right, and justice on the earth; yes, these are what please me" (Jer. 9:23). The prophets saw very clearly that if Israel no longer could distinguish Yahweh from the other gods, then its historical mission had ended. It was necessary to disconnect definitively the name of Yahweh from the people called Israel: "I will reduce them to a ruined country, with no inhabitants" (Jer. 34:22).

Why is there such an outrage about injustices and crimes which have always been committed? The desperation of a Jeremiah (cf. 20:7-9) is undoubtedly due to his realization that in the bottom of their hearts his countrymen asked themselves this same question when they saw that he could speak only of "violence and spoliation," exactly as the first of the prophets had denounced those who "cram their palaces full with violence and spoliation" (Amos 3:10;[113] see also Jer. 6:7; Hab. 1:3; Ezek. 45:9; Isa. 16:4-5; 59:7; 60:18). This is the question which "normal" people, surprised at the prophet's outrage, ask themselves; therefore, "The word of Yahweh has become for me infamy and derision all day long" (Jer. 20:8).

Paul's case is identical. What he denounces in the Jews and Gentiles as "deserving of death" (Rom. 1:32) is what has always occurred among all peoples.[114] But he "is not ashamed of the Gospel" (Rom. 1:16), for he knows that in the Gospel is revealed the justice of God which saves precisely from all this *adikia*. Not only is Paul aware that this *adikia* exists among all people; the basis of his message is to show that this *adikia* does indeed reign among all peoples (Rom. 1:18-3:20). There is no equivocation in Paul's position. The "sin" of which he will speak in chapters 4-11 (the word "sin" appears forty-five times in these eight chapters; in the four Gospels it appears forty-one times) acquires its permanent meaning the first time that it appears, namely, in Rom. 3:9 as a summary of the *adikia* of the Jews and the Gentiles: "We have already proven that Jews and Greeks are all under sin."[115] To understand the "sin" of the following chapters in any other way is to forget the structure of the letter, which has for its basis the description of *adikia* in 1:18-3:20. The only thing that he had "already proven" previous to 3:9 was that *adikia* ruled over both the Jews and the Gentiles; this is what he now calls "to be under sin." And the description which he goes on to extract from the Psalter as a confirmation of his statement (3:10-18) carries the heading "There is not a just man, not even one," a heading in which "no just man" replaces the "no doer of goodness" of the Septuagint (that Paul does indeed *substitute* this is seen in Rom. 3:12). Thus, the only thing he understands as "sin," with respect to content, is injustice, injustice as constituted by all the characteristics which we saw in the Psalter as descriptive of the $r^{e\check{s}}a\check{}im$;[116] nor must we forget that "not to fear God" and "not to seek God" should be understood as the "not to know God" which we studied in chapter 2. In Rom. 1:18-32 Paul himself has described how the culpable ignorance of God by its own immanent recoil throws mankind into the growing power of injustice.[117]

As we have already seen with regard to the "vices" listed in Gal. 5:19-21 (and, similarly, the "virtues" in Gal. 5:22-23),[118] it would be an equally fundamental exegetical error to take the sexual "exchanges" of Rom. 1:24-27 out of context and absolutize every word in these verses as if they were articles of a juridical code. Rather we must bear in mind the literary function of the verb "to exchange" in vv. 25 and 26, which is to make graphic before the eyes of the reader the recoil unleashed by the fact that "they exchanged God for images" (v. 23).[119] Of the three instances of the expression "God gave them over to . . ." in Rom. 1:18-32, the only one that truly and in itself matters to Paul is the third (v. 28): God gave them over to the *adikia* described in vv. 29-31. Just as in the last movement of Rachmaninoff's Second Piano Concerto in C minor, the portents previous to the explosive theme (G-C-B^b-G-F-G) are important only as a preparation and yearning for the final explosion; anyone who tries to understand them independently of the final outburst is in error. Thus the cascade of the three "He gave them over" phrases (vv. 24, 26, and 28) begins after v. 23, that is, at the point where they exchanged God for images; and this is the idea which the third instance of "He gave them over" takes up again: "Since they did not deign to keep God in mind, God gave them over. . . ."

All commentators agree that Rom. 1:18-32 is inspired by Wisd. 13-15. Note this in Wisd. 14:24: "They no longer retain any purity in their lives or their marriages, one treacherously murdering the next or doing him injury [*odynē*] by adultery." The sexual effects of idolatry which are pointed out here are important only insofar as they are the means for men to afflict one another and make one another suffer. The *epithymiai* of Rom. 1:24 are instances of covetousness such that they always echo the "You shall not covet" of the Decalogue (Exod. 20:17; Deut. 5:21); regarding the meaning of this commandment as simple interhuman justice, see above p. 70. The focal point of Rom. 1:18-32 is the prevailing injustice and enmity among men. And Rom.2:1-3:20 extends the same description to the Jews. The purely interhuman dimension of Rom. 3:10-18 corroborates the meaning of 1:18-32, for it focuses only on this aspect. This means that in 1:18-32 this dimension was the only thing that mattered to Paul.

In summary, the first part of the Letter to the Romans (1:18-3:20) makes two seemingly inescapable specifications which affect in a determinative way the meaning of the whole letter and which, in my opinion, have not been sufficiently kept in mind by the Pauline exegetes: (1) the replacement of "doer of goodness" by "just man" in 3:10, which determines the Pauline meaning of "justice," a meaning which is, moreover, corroborated by other data which we have seen and more which we shall see shortly; (2) the structural importance of the base itself, namely, 1:18-3:20, whose meaning in the whole rest of the letter is condensed in the word "sin" in 3:9. Granted, the exegetical method which Conzelmann, Marxsen, Trilling, Strecker, Bornkamm, G. Barth, Held, Minette, and Walker have been so fruitfully applying to the Synoptics is not new with regard to Paul. The method deals with the redactor as a true author who reformulates things and really "composes" certain things with others; it no longer considers him as the simple compiler or archivist that we had for centuries imagined him to be. But even for the interpretation of Paul, the new method of *Redaktionsgeschichte* has sharpened our sense of the totality, our perception of the "complete work" which cannot be cut into pieces. No later chapter or verse of the letter can be understood if we forget what the author himself has told us previously. Paul is relying on the reader's keeping in mind the vision of the Gentile and Jewish world which he has drawn for us in 1:18-3:20; *it is in relation to this description that he continues to speak to us* in the following chapters. Any author who is truly an author would protest against those who try to interpret what he says in chapter 4 or 5 while forgetting what he has said in the previous chapters.

The thesis of the Letter to the Romans is in 1:16-17: Because in it the justice of God is revealed, therefore the Gospel is salvation. But the truth of this thesis depends on the truth of the demonstration (1:18-3:31), which has two parts: The anger of God is already operative in the world in the immanent punishment of interhuman injustice (1:18-3:20), but now the justice of God which saves from this anger has been made known (3:21-31). If we do not take seriously the demonstration in 1:18-3:20, we will have to resign ourselves to not taking seriously the thesis of the Letter to the Romans.

The term "deserving of death" in 1:32 seems to me to be intelligible only in terms of the new world which the entire Bible calls the kingdom of God. In it "all will be just" (Isa. 60:21) and they will no longer "commit injustice" (Zeph. 3:13); from it will be eliminated, as the Old Testament repeats so often, all the unjust, that is, precisely the oppressors, the proud, the envious, the ambitious, the arrogant, the unmerciful, whom Paul enumerates in 1:29-31 and 3:10-18. On this point the Old Testament passages are unequivocal. Ps. 145, thematically dedicated to Yahweh as king (v. 1), concludes by saying that "he destroys the unjust" (v. 20). Ps. 101, also a regal hymn, a program for the ideal kingdom, in v. 5 speaks to us of "destroying the man who slanders his neighbor, the man of haughty looks" (cf. Rom. 1:30) and concludes by saying that this means "to crush all the unjust of the earth" (v. 8). The same thing can be seen throughout Ps. 72, which is also programmatic of the ideal kingdom. Ps. 74 is dedicated to Yahweh "my king from the first" (v. 12), who saves "the poor and the needy" (v. 21); it ends by asking him to attack all oppressors because they are enemies of Yahweh (vv. 22-23), for, as it says in v. 12, he is "to accomplish salvation *in the midst of the earth.*" Ps. 146 describes for us in more detailed fashion the character of the reign of Yahweh:

> He who does justice to the oppressed,
> he who gives food to the hungry,

Yahweh is he who gives liberty to prisoners,
Yahweh is he who restores sight to the blind,
Yahweh straightens those who are bent over,
Yahweh loves the just,
Yahweh protects the stranger,
he who sustains the orphan and widow,
he who frustrates the unjust,
Yahweh reigns forever.

(Ps. 146:7-10)

The kingdom of God, which Paul tells us is "justice and peace and joy in the Holy Spirit" (Rom. 14:17), is described with these same terms (kingdom, peace, justice, spirit from on high) in the twenty verses of Isa. 32, including in vv. 6-8 the description of the unjust who will be destroyed. We can also see this in Isa. 9:3-6; Mic. 5:1-3; Amos 9:11-15; Isa. 11:1-5. See also Zech. 9:9-12; Mal. 3:5; Dan. 9:24; Isa. 60:17-22; 62:8-9; 65:21-25.

It seems to me that any nonevasive interpretation of "deserving of death" in Rom. 1:32 has to assume with Paul all this hope for the kingdom and at the same time the unequivocal earthiness of this kingdom and of the justice of God as a new reality with social dimensions in human history. I think the only alternative open is to attribute to "rhetoric" these first chapters on which Paul bases his entire message to the Romans. There does not seem to be any other explanation for the death penalty against the unmerciful, the ambitious, the envious, etc.

Otto Michel's affirmation that in Paul the "justice of God is at the same time judicial sentence and eschatological salvation"[120] is of utmost importance, provided that it is not understood juxtapositionally as "both the one and also the other." God's justice is a judicial sentence against the unjust precisely because it saves mankind from them; it is salvation because it is an effective sentence against the unjust. It is "the eschatological event which is now revealed."[121]

Eberhard Jüngel, who like Bultmann makes the formula *dikaiosynē ek Theou* (Phil. 3:9) his focal point, is completely correct when he wants "justice of God" not to be understood independently of the meaning of the word "justice."[122] Everything depends on the meaning of this word, and Jüngel's good beginnings are frustrated when he shuts himself up again in the Augustinian-Pelagian, Lutheran-Catholic questions regarding the word "justification"; he does this even though he believes, and rightly so, that the distinction between imputed justice and real justice no longer holds.[123] The Council of Trent had already insisted that "to justify" should be understood as effectively making men just. The agelong error in this regard revolves around the "forensic" appellative which objectively must be affirmed of the "justice of God" both in the Old Testament and in Paul. This relationship with God-Judge acquires its true meaning, dispelling all equivocation, only when we keep in mind that the Last Judgment is the definitive realization of justice on earth, real justice which mankind has tried to achieve and has not been able.[124]

The efficacy of faith in making man really and effectively just (that is, not an oppressor, not loveless, not unmerciful, etc.) is perhaps a point to which exegesis and theology have paid little attention, but it is of crucial importance, and indeed of definitive importance for Paul. In this matter Stuhlmacher is remarkably accurate when he points out that the gratuitousness of Pauline justice would again be entirely put in question if faith (which causes justice) were "works" and not the gratuitous gift of God,[125] for if justice is *ek pisteōs* (issuing from faith), then justice is as gratuitous or ungratuitous as its cause, which is faith. And this decisive problem is not resolved by the dogmatic-ontological thesis that everything real is caused by God, for Paul does not speak of such a thesis and the problem is exegetical. The gratuitousness of the faith must be explained by horizontal causation: It is evangelization, begun by Jesus and continued by the Church, which is God's instrument for causing faith and therefore justice in man. If Stuhlmacher and Lührmann had connected a deep understanding of this causation with the content itself of the *euangelion* (*nomen actionis*[126]), which is the death and resurrection of Christ, they would have moved Pauline exegesis much further ahead.[127] In any case the superseding of the merely forensic aspect of justice in both these authors is one of the greatest advances in modern exegesis, even though their reasons for struggling against the predominance of this forensic aspect often may have been based on an incomprehension of what the Bible understands by "Judgment" and by "Last Judgment." As Kertelge correctly observes, the salvific character does not replace but rather interprets the idea of Judgment.[128]

The most important step of modern exegesis in the interpretation of Pauline justice was, as I see it, the decision to look for its meaning in the Old Testament. This is due to the achievement of many authors, but perhaps Käsemann and Lyonnet are the most outstanding.[129] Unfortunately, both erred in separating "justice of God" from the meaning of the word "justice" itself, for neither the Old Testament nor Paul separates them. Lyonnet in particular suffers from the frequent error of *New* Testament exegetes who think that the Old Testament can be reduced to the covenant and who try to understand the justice of God as a function of the covenant. Such an error has been discarded by the most modern *Old* Testament exegesis.[130]

The most modern monographs, those of Müller, Stuhlmacher, and Kertelge, have produced very fertile results by basing the meaning of Pauline "justice" and "the justice of God" on the Old Testament, as Paul himself does, although there are still differences in the results of the three authors.[131] In particular it seems to me that Müller's insistent emphasis on Rom. 9-11 should be unrestrictedly borne in mind, and I shall do this shortly. But when he understands *dikaiosynē* as *Sieghaftigkeit* (triumph, victoriousness), Müller falls into the same impreciseness of content as the Old Testament translators who translate the *ṣidḳoth* of Yahweh as "victories"—without posing the question of why these triumphs, which they indeed are, should be called "justices."[132] Stuhlmacher and Kertelge emphasize, and rightly so, that the Pauline justice of God is equivalent, as Käsemann says, to "God's dominion over the world, a dominion which is eschatologically revealed in Christ."[133] Indeed God's justice is a new reality of worldwide dimensions in human history, and in this sense it dominates history and reigns within it. But why is it called "justice"? All these questions are identical for Paul and the Old Testament. It would be too much of a coincidence that the vocabulary itself should give rise to the same questions in both cases if they did not have something to do with each other. Scientifically speaking, the response given to the one must be valid for the other. The division of specialties between Old Testament scholars and New Testament scholars must be definitively overcome if exegesis is to achieve a truly deep understanding of the New Testament.

The clearest example of this is perhaps the phrase "deserving of death" in Rom. 1:32. A nonevasive explanation has to assume, with Paul, the imminent realization of the entire content of Old Testament hope. But such an understanding radically modifies the entire traditional interpretation of the Letter to the Romans.

We are forced to come to the same conclusion if we focus on another sensitive point in the letter, which in my opinion has in a similar way been to a greater or lesser degree avoided. It is true that Lyonnet says of Rom. 1:18-32 that "Paul does not claim that all these crimes are committed by each individual, but only by *the society* of the Gentiles in general."[134] And it is also true that Michel, with regard to the parallel description of the Jewish world in Rom. 3:10-18, observes that "the emphasis on collective guilt is striking."[135] Both Lyonnet's observation (where he himself italicizes the word "society") and Michel's seem to me to be not only accurate but of utmost importance. But these authors do not develop this point, nor do they realize that if Paul's concern is with societies, civilizations, and cultures, and not with individuals as exegesis and theology have generally supposed, the meaning of the Letter to the Romans changes completely.

It is also true that Kertelge agrees with Bultmann in rejecting, with regard to chapter 7 of the Letter, the subjectivistic and individualistic interpretation which the West has given to Pauline anthropology, that is, to the problem of man posed by Paul.[136] But neither Bultmann nor Kertelge draws from this accurate observation the revolutionary consequences which necessarily follow for the interpretation of the Pauline message as a whole. If the problem with which Paul is dealing is that of human civilization and not that of individuals as such, if what distresses Paul has dimensions much broader than those of the anthropological human subject, then the word "justice" acquires a meaning completely different from the one that customarily has been supposed.

The aporia of the traditional exegesis of the Letter to the Romans becomes extremely acute in Rom. 2:13-15 and 2:26-29, where Paul seems to contradict his central assertions that both Jews and Gentiles are under sin (3:9) and that by the works of the law no one will be just before God (3:20). This second point in particular seems to be expressly contradicted by Rom. 2:13: "Those who hear the law are not just before God, but those who keep the law will be justified." As Michel rightly observes, it is impossible to interpret this verse as if it expressed a merely fictitious or unreal possibility, for Paul continues thus: "For when Gentiles who do not have the law naturally fulfill what is prescribed by the law, without having the law they are the law for themselves, as those who show that they have the work of the law written in their hearts; their consciences and their conflicting judgments which accuse or defend are called as witnesses" (Rom. 2:14-15). As Michel says, "Paul supposes that there are Gentiles who are indeed obedient to God's demand."[137] And Lyonnet comments, "No reader who approaches this passage without preconceived ideas would think that here Paul is contrasting the Jew who 'sins under the law' (cf. v. 12) with already converted Christians whom he would present as 'Gentiles who do not have the law,' under the pretext that they come from paganism. Lyonnet continues, "The history of the exegesis of this passage shows that only reasons which are extraneous to exegesis in the proper sense of the word, that is, reasons of an apologetic or dogmatic order or on the authority of Saint Augustine, led to holding such an interpretation."[138]

Both the idea that Paul is speaking of Christians who have come from paganism as well as the idea that he is thinking of a purely fictitious possibility belong to the interminable series of *desperata tentamina* ("desperate attempts"; Lyonnet uses this term in describing the efforts of Kuss) which have been made to perform a disappearing act with the obvious and inescapable meaning of these verses. A few verses further on Paul refers again to the Gentiles and tells us that the uncircumcised who observe the law will judge the circumcised who transgress the law (vv. 26-27) because "the real Jew is the one who is inwardly a Jew, and the real circumcision is in the heart—something not of the letter but of the spirit. A Jew like that may not be praised by man, but he will be praised by God" (Rom. 2:28-29); here again it is impossible to understand superficially the above mentioned v. 13 and those following it as if they prescinded from the factual and total observance of the will of God by the "Gentiles," for the terminology of vv. 26-27 is that which Paul uses in 2 Cor. 3:6-7 to designate the interior transformation of the heart proper to the new covenant, as contrasted with the mere observance of the letter. This is authentic justice, the same which Paul promotes by means of the Gospel. And he asserts that there are Gentiles who have it.

Michel does not even perceive the apparent flagrant contradiction between Rom. 2:13-15, 26-29 on the one hand and Rom. 1:18-32; 3:9, 19-20, 27-30 (and the whole letter) on the other. Lyonnet turns his efforts to saving the dogma of Orange and Trent by observing that in Rom. 2:13-15, 26-29 Paul does not deny that in these genuinely just Gentiles God's grace obtained for us by Christ is operative. For the purpose of saving dogma this observation is very good. But the exegetical problem remains intact, and in this regard the "desperate attempts" of Kuss and the whole history of interpretation show greater perceptiveness than the tranquility of Lyonnet and Michel. They show greater perceptiveness and greater sensitivity, for although the dogma might be saved, on the exegetical level it seems that Rom. 2:13-15, 26-29 cannot be reconciled with the emphasis which Paul has given in his description of the Gentile world in Rom. 1:18-32 and with the whole message of his letter, namely, that faith is the only means for the salvation of the world. Why this great emphasis if there are Gentiles who are authentically just, with an interior transformation of the heart and all that Paul is trying to promote?

If Rom. 2:13-15, 26-29 move on the same level and deal with the same problem as the whole letter, then the contradiction seems to me to be irresolvable: In very express terms 2:13 affirms what 3:20 denies. Kuss simply admits that there is a contradiction.[139] But this does not prevent him, with regard to the spirit-letter contrast of Rom. 2:29, from "making the effort to reduce here the concept of 'spirit.' " Nor does it prevent him from adopting for Rom. 2:27 the insupportable hypothesis that these are merely hypothetical and fictitious cases dreamed up in the flight of an anti-Jewish argumentation.[140] But modern scientific rigor prohibits such subterfuges, no matter how traditional they might be. Moreover we cannot accept the notion that from one chapter to the next Paul contradicts the central thesis of his letter, for these are not secondary ideas more or less at the margin of the principal theme. If Rom. 2:13-15 and 26-29 are dealing with the same problem as the rest of the letter, then the contradiction would seem to me to be irresolvable.

But there is no contradiction. Rom. 3:9, 19-20 and the entire letter deal with the problem of society (as Lyonnet recognizes for 1:18-32), of human civilization. His anguish is over the injustice which reigns in the world, the collective slavery which has gained control of human history. His concern is not individual salvation. Isolated individuals can very well be just and fulfill, with an authentic transformation of the heart, the true will of God (Rom. 2:13-15, 26-29).

This interpretation is confirmed by another apparent contradiction which we would be forced to admit if this were not the meaning of the Pauline message. On the one hand, Rom. 2:11; Gal. 2:6; Eph. 6:9; and

Col. 3:25 tell us that "God has no favorites." On the other hand, Rom.
9:1-29 is the clearest possible history of God's choosing some people to
the exclusion of others "before they were born and had done anything
good or evil" (v. 11), for "when God wants to show mercy he does, and
when he wants to harden someone's heart he does so" (v. 18) and
"some are vessels of wrath prepared for perdition" and others "vessels
of compassion prepared for glory" (vv. 22, 23). But Paul has expressly
indicated in Rom. 9:3 that he is speaking of his brothers, the countrymen
of his own flesh and blood, the Israelites. That is, the problem is collective, the preference or nonpreference is national, of peoples, of nations.[141]
  Exegesis has not adequately considered that Rom. 9-11 responds to
a fundamental objection against the message of Rom. 1-8. Therefore
the dimensions of this message are collective, historical, pertaining to
peoples, to civilizations. Paul's gospel has nothing to do with the
interpretation which for centuries has been given to it in terms of
individual salvation. It deals with the justice which the world and
peoples and society, implicitly but anxiously, have been awaiting.
Otherwise, the basic objection to which Rom. 9-11 responds would not
be a real objection against Rom. 1-8.
  This interpretation is corroborated by still another apparent contradiction which we would be obliged to admit if the Pauline message were
not one of social dimensions, with the individual aspect entirely marginal or even ignored. On the one hand, it is obvious to Paul that before
Christ there was already faith in the world, the kind of faith that makes
one just. This is so much the case that Paul uses such a faith as an
example (Gal. 3:6; Rom. 4:1-25). On the other hand, Gal. 3:23 tells us,
"Before faith came, we were imprisoned under the law, confined for
the faith which was to be revealed." And Gal. 3:25 completes this idea:
"Now that faith has come, we are no longer under the guardian." Thus
to avoid contradiction we must admit that the faith with which Paul is
concerned, the faith which he has to stir up, the faith which came with
Christ, cannot be interpreted with an individualistic meaning; rather it
deals with social, historical, collective realities which pertain to the
whole of human civilization, to society. Without faith there is no
salvation. This is Paul's central message. But many individuals had faith
before Christ. What, therefore, is new about his message? What is the
meaning of the salvation and the justice whose existence, according to
Paul, depend on faith?

The question is closely connected with the first of the three contradictions which we have considered, namely, as to the real and true justice of the "Gentiles" without faith (Rom. 2:13-15, 26-29). As we have seen, this notion is apparently irreconcilable with the whole of the Letter to the Romans and really irreconcilable with the customary interpretation of the Letter, which has moved on an individualistic and not a social level. Regarding Rom. 5:19b ("By one man's obedience many will be made just"), Kertelge has recently pointed out, "In this verse nothing is said about the salvation of the individual."[142] But Kertelge refrains from examining the consequences to which such an assertion should lead concerning the entire chapter Rom. 5. If we keep in mind that the intention in 5:14 is to demonstrate (cf. the "because," *gar*, in v. 13) the assertion of 5:12 ("Sin entered the world through one man, and through sin death"), then the meaning of 5:14 is that "death reigned from Adam to Moses even over those who did not sin in the same way as Adam did," that is, even over those who simply did not sin.

What this passage really is trying to demonstrate is that "in this way death pervaded all men" (5:12c). We see this in the fact that 5:17 (after the indication in vv. 15-16 that the sin and the gift are not at all comparable) takes up again only the problem of death: "If because of one man's fall death reigned because of one man. . . ." In other words, the effectiveness of Adam's deed is shown by the death of all, even of those who did not sin (5:14). If everyone had sinned, there would be no demonstration, for the death of each one could be attributed to that individual's own sin. Paul supposes it to be completely taken for granted that not all individuals sinned, and he could not be unaware of the cases of Abraham, Noah, Moses, etc. Paul's problem is mankind, the whole of human civilization; it is to this that he wants to bring salvation and justice.

In previous editions of his commentary on Romans, Otto Michel had noted (for example, with regard to 2:14-15) that Pauline thought offers outstanding similarities to the Fourth Book of Esdras. Dodd has very emphatically insisted on this relationship.[143] By a meticulous comparison, Lyonnet has shown that the parallel is truly surprising, especially for Rom. 5:12-21, even in its division of human history into stages from Adam till the bestowal of the law, etc.[144] Even more recently, Kertelge has pointed out the similarity even in the most fundamental aspect of the doctrine on the freeness of grace.[145] Note, for example, this passage from the third chapter of 4 Esr., which is precisely the chapter which Lyonnet has found to be the most similar to Paul: "When have the inhabitants of the earth not sinned before you? Or, what nation fulfilled your commandments? You can find particular individuals who fulfill your commandments, but whole peoples you do not find" (4 Esd. 3:35-36, taken from Michel, *Brief an die Römer,* p. 79 n. 1). For the reasons which I have indicated it seems clear to me that this too is Paul's problem: that of peoples as such, not that of individual salvation and justice.

The injustice described in Rom. 1:18-3:20 leads to the conclusion that "Jews and Greeks are all under sin" (3:9), and we already have seen that Paul defines sin with regard to specific content by this interhuman injustice.[146] This does not mean that "injustice" and "sin" in Romans are interchangeable terms, but that *adikia* constitutes the qualitative characterization of what Paul understands by *hamartia* ("sin") in the whole rest of the letter.

It has already been frequently observed—and I know of no author who disagrees—that for Paul sin has something like its own subsistence. It is as if it were a mythical entity which enters into human history and takes control of it; the term "personification" has even been used. I think that really this is not a question of mythification or of personification, but these exegetical approaches to Paul's thought through the inadequate literary terms known to the West have the advantage of revealing at the same time three fundamental points: (1) According to Paul sin is a reality having obviously supraindividual dimensions and characteristics, a reality which by no means is reducible to the sum of individual sins; (2) nevertheless, far from being an abstract universal principle, a literary figure, or an imaginary model which helps us to understand or express realities which are difficult to grasp, sin is a reality as concrete as individuals, more powerful than they and more powerful than their properties, actions, and accidents; (3) in any case, negatively speaking, what Paul understands by sin does not coincide in any way with what philosophy and theology and the ordinary language influenced by them today understand by sin.

Without forgetting that the content of sin is specified by interhuman injustice, enmity, and mercilessness, we can say that for Paul sin is the kind of reality that, in history, does not become identified with men;

rather it enslaves them (cf. Rom. 6:16-20) and devastates the human species in every way. The "I" of the following passage is not the autobiographical nor the psychological I.[147] It is simply "man," like *ha'adam* of the Yahwist in Gen. 2:4b-4:1:[148]

> It is no longer I who am doing this [the evil], but sin living in me. The fact is, I know that good does not live in me, that is, in my flesh. For though the will to do what is good is in me, the performance is not, since I do not do the good things I want to do, but instead I carry out the evil that I do not want to do. And if I do what I do not want to do, it is not I who do it, but sin which lives in me.

> (Rom. 7:17-20)

Based on what we have already seen we can now affirm that according to Paul sin is incarnated in social structures, in the powerful wisdom of the world, in the human civilization which forces us to act in a determined way in spite of the contrary conscience which man still has regarding what is good and what is bad. But the fact that Paul repeats several times that the law serves as an instrument of sin (for example, Rom. 5:20; 7:10-11, 13; 1 Cor. 15:56; Gal. 3:19) leads us decidedly in the same direction: Sin, although it entered the world because of the guilt of one man, (Rom. 5:12a; cf. Rom. 5:15a, 17a, 18a; 1 Cor. 15:21-22) has become structured into human civilization itself, whose most characteristic and quintessential expression is the law. It seems to me that this is the only way we can understand how sin is a current within human history, a manifestly supraindividual force which gains control over peoples as such and increases its own power, even when men, trying to be conscientious observers of the law, believe they are struggling against sin.

This capacity for recuperative reabsorption is characteristic of the all-comprehensive cultural systems which our modern languages call "civilizations," although Paul is undoubtedly referring to all of human civilization when he speaks of "this world" or "this age."[149] He is speaking of all of human civilization, not in the abstract sense of what is defined and understood as "civilization as such," but rather the whole real, concrete human civilization which has existed and now exists. As the sociologists and philosophers of law know very well, law is the most symptomatic and concentrated expression of a culture and of a social system. As Talcott Parsons puts it, "Law is, as both Weber and his great French contemporary Émile Durkheim recognized, the primary structural focus of societies."[150] And bearing in mind the supraindividual, social character which modern exegesis recognizes in Paul's affirmations, note these words of Luis Recaséns Siches: "The juridical sphere represents the extreme form of the social sphere, the maximization of the social sphere, its most intense and most rigidly crystallized expression."[151]

In his commentary on Rom. 7:1 Otto Michel rightly observes, "Paul is referring not only to the knowledge of the Mosaic law, but also to the juridical thinking of antiquity."[152] And this is doubtless so, for the law to which this passage refers, namely, that with the death of one of the spouses the marriage is dissolved, is a juridical article found not only in the Mosaic law, but also in all other legislation. With regard to the summary of all law in Rom. 13:8-10 ("In this word it is summed up: You must love your neighbor as yourself" [v. 9]), Gratian as well as Thomas Aquinas and the entire tradition of Christian jurists have seen that this passage refers to the content not only of the Mosaic law, but also of law in general.[153] But what is important here is the formal aspect itself, the law insofar as it is law. As Lyonnet has shown, whenever he alludes to the Old Testament or to Mosaic law Paul uses the article before the word, but every time he uses the article, saying "the law," he is not necessarily referring to the Old Testament or Mosaic law.[154] "Law" without the article means all law, the law insofar as it is law. But even in the contexts in which it is clear that he alludes to Old Testament law, as in Rom. 3:27, "he is not speaking," Lyonnet says, "of the Mosaic law as specifically Mosaic and different from all other legislation."[155]

Schlier comments on Gal. 3:19 in this way: "For Paul the law, that is, the Torah and naturally—although he does not reflect on this—also the positive law of the Gentiles, is an episode which with Christ comes to an end."[156] This accurate assertion as it stands has enormous scope, although it seems to me that in Gal. 4:3, 9 and Col. 2:8, 20 Paul does indeed reflect on the fact that the law is one of the principal "elements of this world," the elements constitutive of the whole of human civilization which sin has made its instrument. As Gutbrod puts it, for Paul "the law is something which belongs to the essential constitution of this world."[157]

When Paul says in Rom. 4:15, "Where there is no law, neither is there transgression," he is clearly thinking of the law as law. Indepen-

dently of how such an assertion should be understood, it refers not
only to Mosaic law, but to all law, and similar Pauline assertions should
be studied as an authentic philosophy of law or theology of law. See,
for example, 1 Cor. 15:56: "The sting of death is sin, and the power of
sin is the law." In an assertion like this, the word "law" lays claim to as
much universality as the words "death" and "sin." We can even say that
a comparison of Rom. 13:3 with 1 Tim. 1:9 implies a juridico-
philosophical theory similar to that of the great jurist Kelsen concerning the identification between the State and law. The first passage tells
us that "those in authority are not to be feared by those who do good
works but by those who do bad works." And the second asserts the
same thing, not about those in authority, but about the law: "The law
is not framed for the just, but rather for the iniquitous and insubordi-
nate." In the same way as in this second passage, Gal. 5:23, after
enumerating the fruits of the Spirit, namely, love, goodness, etc.,
affirms, "Against such things there is no law." Let me repeat: The
comparison of this passage with Rom. 13:3 here too implies a juridical
philosophy in which the State and law are conceived as one and the
same thing. This seems to me to be of utmost importance, for if Paul, as
we shall see shortly, awaits an imminent age in which there will be no
law (and note Schlier's words on Gal. 3:19 which I have just quoted),
then he is referring to the State when in 1 Cor. 2:6 he speaks against
the wisdom of "the rulers of this age who are going to disappear," or
"the rulers of this age, who are on the way to destruction," as
Heathcote and Allcock translate it.[158] As is well known, Engels uses the
verb *absterben* when he speaks of what will happen to the State: It will
die out.

It seems to me that there can be no doubt concerning the universality of the Pauline assertions on law when we see that he conceives it
as the "law of works" (Rom. 3:20, 27; Gal. 3:2, 5, and passim) in
contrast with the law of the spirit or the law of faith. He is concerned
with the law as preceptive of works, a character inherent to all law by
the very fact of its being law; this is what he focuses on, not on whether
a law was promulgated by Moses or God or Solon. And when he says,
"If we had been given a law capable of giving life, then truly justice
would come from the law" (Gal. 3:21), he denies not only to Mosaic
law the power to achieve justice on earth; *a fortiori* he denies this
ability to all law. He denies that mankind's invention called law is

capable of achieving justice in the world—yet law claims that it is able to do this and it was for this that law was created. Contrasted with faith, "the law of works" is as universal as those laws in the world which are not identified with faith, namely, all the laws which exist now or have ever existed, the law as law, the law as the axis and quintessence of what we now call human civilization and Paul calls "this world" or "this age." Not without reason is it law and norm, because it tries to regulate the entire being and behavior of society, because it synthesizes in words and articles the manner of being and doing of a society.

In order to establish that Paul understands "this world" in the pejorative sense as meaning the way in which mankind is organized and stamped from within and from without—today we would call this "civilization"—we need only compare 1 Cor. 11:32 on the one hand and 2 Cor. 5:19 and Rom. 11:12, 15 on the other. But in 1 Cor. 11:32 he uses the verb *katakrinō*, whose exact meaning we should specify beforehand, not because the demonstrative force of this comparison depends on such a specification, but rather for reasons of exactness. The verb is customarily translated as "to condemn," but in the article in *TDNT* dedicated to it, Büchsel very rightly says, "Condemnation and its execution . . . can be seen as one, Mark 16:16; 1 Cor. 11:32; 2 Pet. 2:6."[159] Indeed, the text in 2 Pet. says that God "destroyed [*katekrinen*] the cities of Sodom and Gomorrah, reducing them to ashes."[160] The passages cited by Büchsel seem to me to be unequivocal: *katakrinō* means "to destroy." But even clearer is Rom. 8:3, for what the law could not do (*to adynaton tou nomou*) was to destroy sin (*katekrinen tēn hamartian*). It could indeed condemn it; in fact this was all that it had done. The destruction spoken of in all these passages is, undoubtedly, the effect of a sentence of condemnation and the execution of the same. But the accent proper to the verb is on the destroying, not on the sentencing. (This is of utmost importance for the meaning of the substantive *katakrima* in Rom. 5 and Rom. 8, but this is not the time for a consideration of this point.)

Having made this clarification, we can now translate 1 Cor. 11:32 in this way: "Judging us, the Lord corrects us so that we will not be destroyed with the world." According to this verse, the world is going to be destroyed (or condemned to destruction, if this translation is preferred; our demonstration does not depend on this point). On the other hand, Rom. 11:12, speaking of the Jews, says, "If their fall has meant richness for the world, and their disgrace richness for the Gentiles, how much more will their fullness mean." And Rom. 11:15 continues: "Since their rejection has meant the reconciliation of the world. . . . " And for its part 2 Cor. 5:19 asserts: "In Christ God was reconciling the world to himself, not holding men's faults against them, and putting in us the word of reconciliation." These three passages teach that God saves the *kosmos* identified manifestly with mankind. On the other hand, 1 Cor. 11:32 says that the world, no less clearly identified with mankind, will be destroyed or condemned to death. On the one hand, mankind will be destroyed or condemned to death; on the other, it will be saved and reconciled with God.

We can find no consistency in these two assertions if we do not understand *kosmos* as human civilization, that is, the manner in which mankind is organized and stamped from within and from without. It is all of civilization which will change. Paul uses the verb *katakrinō* only twice with God as the subject. In Rom. 8:3 the condemned and destroyed object is "sin"; in 1 Cor. 11:32 it is "the world." We must not forget that this "world" has its own "wisdom" (1 Cor. 1:20; 2:6; 3:19), which God "made foolish" (1:20), and of which Paul says that "the world by means of wisdom did not know God" (1:21); and this is the same "not knowing God" from which Rom. 1:18-32 derives the entire flood of injustices which inundated the world. And we also must not forget that the "reconciliation" of the world in 2 Cor. 5:19-20 consists, according to Paul, in our becoming "the justice of God in Christ" (2 Cor. 5:21).[161] And this is confirmed by the "reconcilation" of Col. 1:20, 22, whose meaning is intentionally specified by the contraposition in v. 21: "estranged . . . in wicked works" (a technical term in contrast with "good works").[162]

If we keep in mind, then, the apparent contradiction which exists between Rom. 11:12, 15 and 2 Cor. 5:19 on the one hand and 1 Cor. 11:32 on the other, it seems that *kosmos* must be understood as something very similar to what we today call human civilization as a whole, but taken in a concrete sense, not civilization because it is civilization nor because it is human. Otherwise, if this were not the meaning of "the world," then Paul would on the one hand be asserting that God saves the world and on the other be maintaining that God condemns and destroys the world. It seems to me inescapable that we understand things in this way: God will save mankind, but he will destroy without a trace the entire old civilizing, axiological, and organizational structuralization of mankind. Only in this way can we understand how God condemns-destroys the world and at the same time saves the world. In the first phrase the world is all of civilization; in the second the world is mankind.

A comparison of Gal. 1:4 with Gal. 4:5 (Gal. 3:23) shows that by "law" Paul understands not only the whole of law as law but also law as the normative quintessence of the entire cultural and social structure which we call human civilization and Paul calls *aiōn* or *kosmos*. With regard to Gal. 3:23 ("Before faith came, we were imprisoned under the law, confined for the faith which was to be revealed"), Schlier very rightly says that Paul is referring to "the prison which consists in the age dominated by the law."[163] For Paul law and faith are the determinants of two different epochs of history. Each one, law for its part and faith for its part, defines a world; each specifies the entire collective reality of mankind. There is a civilization of law and a civilization of faith, we might say. "To deliver us from this perverse present age" (Gal. 1:4) is synonymous with "to deliver those who were under the law" (Gal. 4:5).

Paul wants a world without law. Exegesis which avoids this fact makes an understanding of the Pauline message impossible. Neither Kropotkin nor Bakunin nor Marx nor Engels made assertions against the law more powerful and subversive than those which Paul makes. Paul is convinced not only that the law has failed in human history in its attempt to achieve justice, but that justice cannot be achieved in the world as long as law exists. In human history "law came so that sin might abound" (Rom. 5:20), so that "the power of sin is the law" (1 Cor. 15:56). If we bear in mind that the "I" of Rom. 7 is "man" in general, we will translate Paul's thesis in this way: "Thus the precept, given for life, was death for man, for sin, gaining momentum, by the precept deceived man and by it killed him" (Rom. 7:10-11). It is not that the law was evil or deadly, "but that sin, to show itself as sin, used the good to produce death for man, and thus through the precept sin became sinful to its fullest extent" (Rom. 7:13).

If Paul asserts of God's law that "the power of sin is the law" (1 Cor. 15:56), with all the more reason the Pauline subversion undermines the foundation of every human civilization needing laws. Any theology which seeks to justify such a civilization betrays Paul's message. Sin is incarnated in this civilization and in the ideology which supports it. "You have broken with Christ if you look for justice in the law; you have fallen from grace" (Gal. 5:4). All those who consider Paul's message to be utopian are keeping justice from coming to the earth; they are keeping mankind from reaching the maturity which Christ brought. They have not understood anything, because they do not hunger and thirst for justice. "It is through the law that sin became sinful to its fullest extent" (Rom. 7:13). When mankind was in its infancy and was irresponsible, "before we came of age, we were enslaved to the elements of the world; but when the fulness of time arrived, God sent his son, born of a woman, born under the law, to free those who were under the law" (Gal. 4:3-4).

That sin is incarnated in civilization is demonstrated nowhere more clearly than in the fact that Western theology has missed this message of Paul, and yet this is the only thing that Paul has to say. Otto Kuss formally insists again and again that Paul's teaching on justice came forth full-blown from the fact of the death of Christ.[164] And for his part Gutbrod asserts that "as concerns the material understanding of the Law in Paul, the cross of Jesus is decisive."[165] And Paul himself indicates, "During my stay with you, the only knowledge I claimed to have was about Jesus, and only about him as the crucified Christ" (1 Cor. 2:2). If Paul says that he knows nothing but Christ crucified, this implies that the law's incapacity to achieve justice on earth is a fact which Paul saw fashioned in Christ's crucifixion; in some way these two facts are identified, given that the only thing Paul can really talk about in his letters is that justice does not come by the law but by faith. In a brilliant study Fitzer has also "demonstrated that Paul sees Jesus' death primarily in relationship with the law."[166] And if there is anything on which Pauline exegesis can today fully agree it is that the object of faith—of that same faith which makes men just—is for Paul unequivocally the death and resurrection of Christ, although exegesis has not emphasized with equal force that it is precisely from this object that faith gets its ability to make men just.

I think that we must relate all this with Rom. 4:5 (chapter 4 is where the faith is intentionally thematized, and because of vv. 3, 23, and 24, I say the faith which counts as justice). Here, in contrast to the works of the law, the object of faith is delimited in this way: "He who does not do works but believes in him who justifies the impious one, his faith is considered as justice." Stuhlmacher rightly points out that this verse, precisely because it is theo-logical, constitutes "the polemical center of the Pauline teaching on justification."[167] In some way this object of the faith ("to believe in him who justifies the impious one") has to be identified with the object which Paul always indicates for the faith: Christ crucified and risen. In some way when God raised up the outlawed Jesus, he was justifying the impious one, him whom the whole of the law and human civilization crucified for being impious. This is the justice of the law: It crucified the only man "who knew no sin" (2 Cor. 5:21). The insurrection of authentic Christianity against all law and all civilization which has ever existed in history is a subversion which knows no limits.

This is so because, as Fitzer points out, the crucifixion of Jesus was not an error of human justice; it was not a lamentable mistake of the law. "Paul's vision, which since he was a Pharisee originated in his concept of the law, can be completely interpreted with the words of the Jews according to John 19:7: 'We have a law, and according to that law he must die.' "[168] According to Paul, to be followers of Christ is to join ourselves to the historical event called Jesus Christ, to incorporate ourselves into the outlawed Jesus: "Or perhaps you do not know that we who have been immersed into Christ Jesus have been immersed into his death?" (Rom. 6:3). And every Christian should say with Paul, "By means of the law I have died to the law to live for God: I have been co-crucified with Christ" (Gal. 2:19). For us to be free from the law it was necessary that the law crucify Christ before our eyes. Therefore Paul says to the Galatians who are tempted again to seek justice through the law: "If justice comes by means of the law, then Christ died in vain. Are you people in Galatia mad? Has someone put a spell on you, you before whose eyes they outlawed Christ, crucifying him?" (Gal. 2:21-3:1).[169]

Let me repeat: For us to be free from the law it was necessary that the law crucify Christ before our eyes; only in this way could we understand that justice does not come through the law. Therefore Paul says that he has nothing else to preach but Christ crucified (1 Cor. 1:23). But this is enough to subvert totally the order of this world. We need only join ourselves to the historical event called Jesus Christ: "Now we are delivered from the law, dying for that which held us prisoners" (Rom. 7:6). This is what Paul said in Gal. 2:19: "By means of the law I have died to the law . . .: I have been co-crucified with Christ." But in order for there to be conversion, the fact that God "made foolish the wisdom of this world" (1 Cor. 1:20) by raising up the outlawed Jesus must be granted all its unlimited radicalism. Since Paul understands this fact with all the unconditional extremism which in itself it contains, he therefore says, "Those who rely on the works of the law are under a curse" (Gal. 3:10), but "Christ redeemed us from the curse of the law, having been made a curse for our sake" (Gal. 3:13).

Paul considered the recoil immanent in not knowing God to be controlled from on high by the wrath of God (Rom. 1:18-32), which through intrinsic punishment throws men into a cascade of injustices; in the same way God reveals himself to us by directing from on high the crucifixion and resurrection of Christ. I want to emphasize this: He reveals himself to us. This is the whole point. In Paul's eyes the one who is active in all of this is God himself. Only if we understand this human history as the eloquent activity of God can God reveal himself to us by speaking through it. In "having been made a curse for our sake" (Gal. 3:13), which I have just cited, "having been made" is passive. God is supposed as the subject agent, just as God is the supreme agent in Rom. 1:18-32 ("he gave them over" in vv. 24, 26, 28) and in Rom. 4:25; Rom. 8:32; Gal. 4:4; Eph. 1:10 and in the very important passages Rom. 8:3 and 2 Cor. 5:21.

We saw that "to deliver us from this perverse present age" (Gal. 1:4) is synonymous with "to deliver us from the law" (cf. Gal. 4:5), because the age or world or civilization is specified by the law. But a third synonym is "to deliver us from sin" (cf. Rom. 6:18). It is not at all sufficient to say that according to Paul the age or epoch of sin has ended because in that epoch people sinned and now we are in an epoch in which there is no longer any sin. *Aiōn* is equivalent to *kosmos*; it is an imposing reality, with collective, social dimensions, not a mere empty space, of time, where things happen. *Kosmos* or civilization is sin incarnate, the institutional condensation that sin created to control men. The law, the generative segment of civilization, is now by its acquired and inextirpable essence the instrument of sin (cf. Rom. 5:20; 7:11, 13; 1 Cor. 15:56; Gal. 3:19). If sin is not identical to civilization specified by law, the supraindividual reality which Paul calls sin is then a myth in every way. And exegesis provides a pretty performance indeed when it gratuitously imputes a myth to Paul and then splendidly goes through the academic exercise of demythologizing it.

2 Cor. 5:21 refers to the sin which is condensed in history and in the civilization whose axis is the law. The idea is the same as in Gal. 3:13: "Christ redeemed us from the curse of the law, having been made a curse for our sake"; and here God is supposed as the supreme agent. "For our sake he made the one who knew no sin into sin, so that we might become the justice of God in him" (2 Cor. 5:21). Half a year later Paul reformulated this same event of the crucifixion of Christ in these other terms: "What the law could not do, because it was weakened by the flesh, God did by sending his own son in the likeness of the flesh of sin and in the place of sin; he *destroyed* sin in the flesh, in order that the content of justice of the law might be achieved in us who do not walk according to the flesh but according to the spirit" (Rom. 8:3-4).[170] If we do not forget that the content of "sin" in Rom. 3:9 is characterized by injustice[171] throughout the entire rest of the letter, then what we have in Rom. 8:3-4 and 2 Cor. 5:21 is Christ converted into the incarnation of all the human injustice which has been accumulated in civilization and the law.

When before our eyes the law crucifies as an outlaw the only man who did not know sin, God destroys sin and the law forever. At this point the justice of God begins in history and the "justice" of the law ends. "Now we are delivered from the law dying for that which held us prisoners" (Rom. 7:6). And this is the same as "to die for sin" (Rom. 6:2), for "sin will no longer reign in you *because now you are no longer under law* but rather under grace" (Rom. 6:14). The reason why we are freed from the reign of sin is that we are freed from the dominion of the law. Only by breaking with the civilization of the law and with its false justice can we make the definitive age of justice begin in the world. This is to join ourselves to the historical event called Jesus Christ. Thus Paul says, "so that we might become the justice of God *in him*" (2 Cor. 5:21).

Paul makes his whole point in the synonymy of two formulations of the object of faith: "to believe in the one [God] who justifies the impious one" (Rom. 4:5) and "to believe in the one [God] who raised Jesus our Lord from the dead" (Rom. 4:24). In Rom. 4:23 Paul expressly indicates that it is not only the faith of the first formulation which is counted as justice, but also that "counted as justice" (v. 24) was said also for the second. By raising him from the dead, God showed that the one whom the law and the civilization controlled by the law condemned as impious was indeed just. For Paul this action of God is God's supreme revelation. It is the revelation of the justice of God in absolute contrast with the justice of human civilization and law, in which sin has been incarnated. At this moment God breaks all our schemata, whether moral, legal, cultural, social, religious, cultic, etc. According to these schemata, Christ is the impious one, the personification of sin. Therefore Paul says that God "sent him in the likeness of the flesh of sin and in the place of sin," and thus he was able "to destroy sin in the flesh" (Rom. 8:3). It is a question of believing in this God more than in human civilization and law. Faith is an irreversible break: either . . . or.

Notes to Chapter 4

1. Exod. 18:16; 1 Kings 3:9; 1 Chron. 26:29; Job 21:22; Prov. 31:9; Joel 4:2, 12; Ezek. 17:20; 20:35, 36; 34:17, 20; 44:24.
2. These are the forty-eight instances: Exod. 21:1, 9, 31; 24:3; Num. 15:16; 36:13; Deut. 7:12; 33:10; 1 Sam. 2:13; 8:3, 9, 11; 10:25; 27:11; 30:25; 1 Kings 3:28; 8:45, 59a, 59b; 2 Chron. 6:35; Ps. 119:20; 140:12; Prov. 2:8; 8:20; 16:11; 17:23; 19:28; Isa. 61:8; Mal. 2:17; 3:22; Ezek. 11:20; 18:9, 17, 21a, 21b; 20:11, 13, 16, 18, 19, 21, 24, 25.
3. See above pp. 93-94.
4. Volkmar Herntrich, "krinō," *TDNT,* 3:927.
5. Ibid., *TWNT,* 3:922; cf. *TDNT,* 3:923.
6. See Wolfgang Richter, "Zu den 'Richtern Israels,' " *ZAltW* 77 (1965): 40-71; Otto Eissfeldt, *The Old Testament: An Introduction* (Oxford: Blackwell, 1965), pp. 258-60.
7. Cf. above pp. 88-89, on the technical meaning of this "outcry."
8. Cf. F. Charles Fensham, "Widow, Orphan, and the Poor in Ancient Near Eastern Legal and Wisdom Literature," *JournNESt* 21, no. 2 (April 1962): 129-39; cf. A. González, "Le Psaume LXXXII," *VT* 13, no. 3 (July 1963): 293-309.
9. Fensham, "Widow, Orphan," p. 135.
10. After the studies of Cross and Cooke the old benign interpretation which considered the *'elohim* to be human judges or angels does not deserve even to be discussed, nor does the interpretation which considered them to be Yahweh's heavenly court. There would be no reason to challenge the *'elohim* if they are

supposed to be servants and courtiers of Yahweh (Frank M. Cross, Jr., "The Council of Yahweh in Second Isaiah," *JournNESt* 12, no. 4 [October 1953]: 274-77; Gerald Cooke, "The Sons of (the) God(s)," *ZAltW* 76, no. 1 [1964]: 22-47). Cf. the Catholic Dahood: "The picture of God in the midst of the assembly of gods recurs again and again in the Psalter; cf. Pss. 29:1-2; 77:14; 89:6-9; 95:3; 96:4; 97:7; 148:2" (*Psalms II*, p. 269).

11. Cf. Th. C. Vriezen, "Prophecy and Eschatology," *VT Suppl* 1 (1953): 199-229, Festchr. Bentzen; Georg Fohrer, "Die Struktur der alttestamentlichen Eschatologie," *ThLitZ* 85, no. 1 (June 1960): 401-20.

12. Dahood, *Psalms I*, pp. 112-13.

13. Hermann L. Strack and Paul Billerbeck have shown this is their *Kommentar zum Neuen Testament aus Talmud und Midrasch* (Munich: C. H. Beck'sche, 1922-63), 4:536-58 and 559-610. And in an independent study the renowned Joachim Jeremias arrives at the same conclusion: "Die Salbungsgeschichte Mc. 14:3-9," *ZNeuW* 35 (1936): 77-78. See also Walter Grundmann, *Das Evangelium nach Matthäus*, ThHKomNT (Berlin: Evangelische Verlagsanstalt, 1968), 1:140 (concerning Matt. 5:16).

14. Michel, *Brief an die Römer*, p. 75.

15. Cf. Patrick D. Miller, Jr., "El the Warrior," *HarvThRev* 60, no. 4 (October 1967): 411-31; "Two Critical Notes on Psalm 68 and Deuteronomy 33," *HarvThRev* 57, no. 3 (July 1964): 240-43; "God the Warrior," *Interpretation* 19, no. 1 (January 1965): 39-46; and "The Divine Council and the Prophetic Call to War," *VT* 18, no. 1 (January 1968): 100-07; Gerhard von Rad, *Der Heilige Krieg im alten Israel* (Göttingen: Vandenhoeck, 1951); *Old Testament Theology*, 2:119-25; "The Origin of the Concept of the Day of Yahweh," *JournSemSt* 4, no. 2 (April 1959): 97-108; J. Alberto Soggin, "Der prophetische Gedanke über den heiligen Krieg, als Gericht gegen Israel," *VT* 10, no. 4 (1960): 79-83.

16. Von Rad, *Heilige Krieg*, p. 82.

17. As Kraus rightly points out, the idea of this verse is the same as that of Ps. 113:7-8; 145:14; 146:8-9; Isa. 40:29; and Luke's Magnificat (*Psalmen II*, p. 956).

18. Gottfried Quell, "dikē," *TWNT*, 2:177; cf. *TDNT*, 2:175.

19. *'ani* has the precise meaning of "poor"; there is no reason to translate it here in any other way, as Weiser and Dhorme do; cf. Dahood ("Indeed you are the Strong One who saves the poor") and Kraus ("Du hilfst dem armen Volk").

20. Von Rad, *Heilige Krieg*, pp. 74-75; and in *Studies in Deuteronomy*, pp. 55-56.

21. Norbert Lohfink, *Das Hauptgebot*, AnBi 20 (Rome: PIB, 1963), p. 203 n. 14.

22. See above p. 88-89.

23. Robinson, *Zwölf kleinen Propheten*, pp. 145ff.

24. Kuss, *Römerbrief*, p. 119.

25. Salvador Carrillo, "El Cántico de Moisés," *EstBi* 26, no. 4 (October-December 1967): 339; see also pp. 69-75; 143-85; 227-48; 327-52; 383-94 of the same volume.

26. Ibid., p. 341.

27. See above pp. 121-22.

28. Soggin, "Prophetische Gedanke," pp. 82-83.

29. Von Rad, *Old Testament Theology*, 2:125.

30. Bultmann, *Johannesbriefe*, p. 79; cf. above pp. 101-03.

31. Cf. above pp. 111-116.

32. Büchsel, "krisis," *TDNT*, 3:942.

33. Julius Schniewind, *Das Evangelium nach Matthäus*, 11th ed., NeuTestD 2 (Göttingen: Vandenhoeck, 1967), p. 157.

34. Günther Bornkamm, Gerhard Barth, Heinz Joachim Held, *Tradition and Interpretation in Matthew* (Philadelphia: Westminster, 1963), p. 128.

35. Robert Horton Gundry, *The Use of the Old Testament in St. Matthew's Gospel* (Leiden: E. J. Brill, 1967), pp. 110-16.

36. Cf. above p. 118.

37. Cf. above pp. 81-86.

38. André Feuillet, "Les *egō eimi* christologiques du quatrième évangile," *RechScR* 54, no. 1 (January-March 1966): 5-22; and 54, no. 2 (April-June 1966): 213-40.

39. Karl Heinrich Rengstorf, "sēmeion," *TDNT*, 7:243-57; Schnackenburg, *Johannesevangelium*, pp. 346-47.

40. Cf. above p. 125.

41. Carrillo, "Cántico," pp. 343-49 and passim.

42. Feuillet, "*Egō eimi*," p. 236.

43. Schnackenburg, *Johannesevangelium*, p. 349.

44. Ernst Haenchen, "Der Vater, der mich gesandt hat," *NTSt* 9, no. 3 (April 1963): 208-16.

45. Cf. above pp. 36-53.

46. Haenchen, "Vater."

47. See, for example, Walter Beyerlin, *Origins and History of the Oldest Sinaitic Traditions*, trans. S. Rudman (Oxford: Blackwell, 1965).

48. As Noth expresses well in his *Pentateuchal Traditions*, p. 62.

49. Julius Wellhausen, *Prolegomena to the History of Israel* (Edinburgh: Black, 1885), pp. 342ff.

50. Hugo Gressmann, *Mose und seine Zeit* (Göttingen: Vandenhoeck, 1913), p. 390.

51. Von Ràd, "Problem of the Hexateuch" (1938) in *Problem of the Hexateuch*, pp. 1-78; Noth, *Pentateuchal Traditions*.

52. Noth, "The Laws in the Pentateuch: Their Assumption and Meaning" (1940), *The Laws in the Pentateuch and Other Studies*, trans. D. R. Ap-Thomas (Philadelphia: Fortress Press, 1966), p. 40.

53. Noth, *Exodus: A Commentary* (Philadelphia: Westminster Press, 1962), pp. 173-74.

54. Albrecht Alt, "Die Ursprunge des israelitischen Rechtes" (1934), p. 30; English version: "The Origins of Israelite Law," in *Essays on Old Testament History and Religion*, trans. R. A. Wilson (Garden City, N.Y.: Anchor, Doubleday, 1968), p. 129.

55. Von Rad, *Old Testament Theology*, 1:204.
56. E. Gerstenberger, *Wesen und Herkunft des "Apodiktischen Rechts"* (Neukirchen: Neukirchener Verlag, 1965); Georg Fohrer, "Das sogenannte apodiktisch formulierte Recht und der Dekalog," *KerDog* 11 (1965): 49-74.
57. Von Rad, *Old Testament Theology*, 1:193
58. Noth, "Laws in the Pentateuch," pp. 91, 97, 102.
59. This question has been settled by the studies of Dennis J. McCarthy, *Treaty and Covenant*, AnBi 21 (Rome: PIB, 1963); R. Smend, "Die Bundesformel," *ThSt* 68 (1963); F. Nötscher, "Bundesformular und 'Amtsschimmel,' " *BiblZ* 9 (1965): 181-214; Fohrer, "Recht und Dekalog"; "Altes Testament— 'Amphiktyonie' und 'Bund'?" *ThLitZ* 91, no. 11 (November 1966): 801-15 and 893-904; T. Vriezen, "Exode 20, 2. Introduction au Décalogue: formule de loi ou d'alliance?" *RechBi* 8 (1967): 35-50; and the fundamental studies of Gevirtz and Kilian to which I shall refer shortly.
60. Norbert Lohfink, "Lectures in Deuteronomy," mimeographed notes (Rome, 1968), p. 117.
61. Ibid., p. 118.
62. George E. Mendenhall, *Law and Covenant in Israel and the Ancient Near East* (Pittsburgh: The Biblical Colloquium, 1955).
63. Fohrer, " 'Amphiktyonie' und 'Bund,' " p. 894 n. 59.
64. Lohfink, "Die Wandlung des Bundesbegriffs im Buch Deuteronomium," in *Gott in Welt: Festgabe für Karl Rahner* (Freiburg: Herder, 1964), 1:441.
65. Zimmerli, *Gesammelte Aufsätze*, pp. 205-16.
66. Noth, "Laws in the Pentateuch," p. 92.
67. Alt, *Ursprünge*.
68. Ibid., p. 39.
69. R. Bach, "Gottesrecht und weltliches Recht in der Verkündigung des Propheten Amos," in *Festschrift für G. Dehn* (Neukirchen, 1957), p. 29.
70. Ibid., pp. 26-27, n. 27.
71. Stanley Gevirtz, "West-Semitic Curses and the Problem of the Origins of Hebrew Law," *VT* 11, no. 2 (April 1961): 137-58; Rudolf Kilian, "Apodiktisches und kasuistisches Recht im Licht ägyptischer Analogien," *BiblZ* 7, no. 2 (July 1963): 185-202.
72. Von Rad, *Old Testament Theology*, 1:33.
73. Gevirtz, "West-Semitic Curses," p. 156.
74. Alt, *Ursprünge*, p. 16: "Origins of Israelite Law," p. 116.
75. Von Rad, "Problem of the Hexateuch," p. 15.
76. Ibid., pp. 11-12.
77. Ibid., pp. 5-6.
78. Von Rad, *Old Testament Theology*, 1:193.
79. Von Rad, "Problem of the Hexateuch," p. 19; cf. above pp. 88 and 79.
80. Noth, *Exodus*, p. 187.
81. Von Rad, "Problem of the Hexateuch," p. 15.
82. Cf. above pp. 139-40.
83. Alfons Deissler, *Psalm 119 (118) und seine Theologie* (Munich: Zink, 1955), p. 295.

84. Cf. above pp. 92-106.
85. See above pp. 146-47.
86. Cf. G. Baudissin, "Alttestamentliches *hajjim* 'Leben' in der Bedeutung von 'Glück,'" in *Festschrift Sachau* (1915), pp. 143-61. The best study of *'olam* is that of Ernst Jenni, "Das Wort *'olam* im Alten Testament," *ZAltW* 64 (1952): 197-248; 65 (1953): 1-35. One thing established here very clearly is that this is not a question of another life. Franz Mussner in his study, *Zoe: Die Anschauung vom 'Leben' im vierten Evangelium unter Berücksichtigung der Johannesbriefe* (Munich, 1952) was not aware of Baudissin's monograph, which is quite fundamental.
87. Cf. Ernst Käsemann, "Gottesgerechtigkeit bei Paulus," in *Exegetische Versuche und Besinnungen*, 5th ed. (Göttingen: Vandenhoeck, 1967), 2:181-93. Cf. Peter Stuhlmacher, *Gerechtigkeit Gottes bei Paulus* 2nd ed., FRLANT 87 (Göttingen: Vandenhoeck, 1966); Karl Kertelge, *"Rechtfertigung" bei Paulus* (Münster: Aschendorf, 1966); I am surprised by Bultmann's reaction in *JBL* 83, part 1 (March 1964): 12-16, when in *Glauben und Verstehen* he had said that the "justice of God" in Paul "is exactly the same as in Judaism" (1:200; cf. *Faith and Understanding*, 1:232).
88. Cf. above p. 120.
89. Rolf Knierim, "Exodus 18 und die Neuordnung der mosaischen Gerichtsbarkeit," *ZAltW* 73, no. 2 (1961): 146-71.
90. Cf. above p. 144.
91. Cf. Henri Cazelles, "Institutions et terminologie en Deut. 1:6-17," *VTSuppl* 15 (Leiden: Brill, 1966): 97-112.
92. Cf. above pp. 67-68.
93. Claude Tresmontant, *La doctrine morale des prophètes d'Israël* (Paris: Seuil, 1958), pp. 100-01.
94. Cf. above pp. 53-67.
95. Bach, "Gottesrecht," pp. 23-34.
96. Cf. above pp. 67-72.
97. Cf. above pp. 59-60.
98. E. Würthwein, "Amos-Studien," *ZAltW* 62 (1949-50): 47.
99. Hans Joachim Kraus, *Die prophetische Verkündigung des Rechts in Israel* (Zollikon: Evangelischer Verlag, 1957), p. 29.
100. Cf. above pp. 101-03.
101. Cf. above pp. 39-42.
102. Cf. above pp. 117-18.
103. Cf. above pp. 152-53.
104. Cf. Michel, *Brief an die Römer*, p. 70.
105. The series of evasive interpretations of "deserving of death" in Rom. 1:32 can be seen in Kuss, *Römerbrief*, p. 55.
106. "Von Rad scheint ... in der deuteronomischen Aussage vom unverbrüchlichen Bunde das zunächst im AT Legitime zu sehen. Die Propheten drohen von hier aus in das Licht charismatischer Schwärmer zu geraten" (Zimmeri, *Gesammelte Aufsätze*, p. 272).
107. Von Rad, *Old Testament Theology*, 2:395-97.

108. Würthwein, "Amos-Studien," pp. 47-48.
109. Cf. above pp. 153-55.
110. Cf. above pp. 148-49.
111. Von Rad, *Old Testament Theology*, 2:395.
112. Ibid., p. 401.
113. Cf. above p. 20.
114. Cf. above pp. 160-64.
115. The omission of the article in the Greek text is due to the preposition; cf. Max Zerwick, *Graecitas Biblica*, 4th ed. (Rome: PIB, 1960), n. 182, p. 56.
116. Cf. above pp. 101-03.
117. Cf. above pp. 39-42.
118. Cf. above p. 71.
119. Cf. Klaus Koch, "Gibt es ein Vergeltungsdogma im Alten Testament?" *ZThK* 52 (1955): 1-42.
120. Michel, *Brief an die Römer*, p. 254.
121. Ibid.
122. Eberhard Jüngel, *Paulus und Jesus*, 3rd ed. (Tübingen: Mohr, 1967).
123. Ibid., p. 46.
124. Cf. above pp. 109-37.
125. Stuhlmacher, *Gerechtigkeit Gottes*, pp. 78-84, including the notes.
126. Cf. Gerhard Friedrich, "euangelizomai ktl.," *TDNT*, 2:707-37.
127. Dieter Lührmann, *Das Offenbarungsverständnis bei Paulus und in paulinischen Gemeinden* (Neukirchen: Neukirchener Verlag, 1965).
128. Kertelge, *"Rechtfertigung,"* p. 306.
129. Ernst Käsemann, "Gottesgerechtigkeit bei Paulus," *ZThK* 58 (1961): 367-78. Stanislas Lyonnet. "De 'Iustitia Dei' in Epistola ad Romanos," *VD* 25 (1947): 23-24, 118-21, 129-44, 193-203, 257-62; cf. also Lyonnet, "De notione 'iustitiae Dei' apud S. Paulum," *VD* 42 (1964): 121-52.
130. Cf. above pp. 139-42.
131. Christian Müller, *Gottes Gerechtigkeit und Gottes Volk*, FRLANT 86 (Göttingen: Vandenhoeck, 1964); Stuhlmacher, *Gerechtigkeit Gottes*; Kertelge, *"Rechtfertigung."*
132. Cf. above pp. 124-27.
133. Käsemann, "Gottesgerechtigkeit," p. 377.
134. Lyonnet, *Exegesis epistulae ad romanos*, 1:148.
135. Michel, *Brief an die Römer*, p. 101.
136. Kertelge, *"Rechtfertigung,"* pp. 220-21; Bultmann, "Romans 7 and the Anthropology of Paul," in *Existence and Faith: Shorter Writings of Rudolf Bultmann*, trans. Schubert M. Ogden (New York: Living Age, Meridian, 1960), pp. 147-57.
137. Michel, *Brief an die Römer*, p. 82.
138. Lyonnet, Lecture on December 11, 1966, in the Biblical Institute on "Les fondements bibliques de la constitution pastorale 'Gaudium et Spes,'" p. 24.
139. Kuss says, "Dass sich ein Gedanke nicht nahtlos und lückenlos an den anderen fügt und dass die innere Einheit der paulinischen Theologie nicht mit systematischer Widerspruchslosigkeit im einzelnen identisch ist" (*Römerbrief*, p. 65).

140. Ibid., pp. 91, 90.
141. Cf. Müller's monograph, *Gottes Gerechtigkeit.*
142. Kertelge, *"Rechtfertigung,"* p. 145.
143. C. H. Dodd, *The Epistle of Paul to the Romans* (New York: Harper, 1959).
144. Lyonnet, "Péché Originel," *Supplément au Dictionnaire de la Bible,* 7:515-17.
145. Kertelge, *"Rechfertigung,"* pp. 35, 36, 40, 48, 60, 121, 188, etc.
146. Cf. above pp. 169-70.
147. Cf. Kertelge, *"Rechfertigung,"* pp. 220-21, and Bultmann, "Romans 7."
148. Cf. above p. 92; and Kuss, *Römerbrief,* p. 442: "von jedem Menschen schlechthin."
149. These two expressions are synonymous, as Hermann Sasse has pointed out in *TDNT,* 3:885, for "wisdom of the world" (1 Cor. 1:20), "wisdom of this world" (1 Cor. 3:19), and "wisdom of this age" (1 Cor. 2:6) are all interchangeable.
150. Talcott Parsons, *Sociological Theory and Modern Society,* 2nd ed. (New York: The Free Press, 1968), p. 97.
151. Luis Recaséns Siches, *Teoría general de filosofía del derecho,* 3rd ed. (Mexico, D.F.: Porrúa, 1965), p. 275.
152. Michel, *Brief an die Römer,* p. 166.
153. See Gratian, *PL* 187, col. 21; Thomas Aquinas, *Summa Theologica,* I-II, q. 94, art. 4 ad. 1; Francisco Suarez, *De legibus,* book 10, c. 2, no. 5.
154. Lyonnet, *Exegesis epistulae ad Romanos,* II, pp. 87-92.
155. Ibid., p. 87.
156. Heinrich Schlier, *Der Brief an die Galater,* 4th ed., MeyersKomm (Göttingen: Vandenhoeck, 1965), p. 155.
157. Walter Gutbrod, "nomos," *TDNT,* 4:1075.
158. Jean Héring, *The First Epistle of Saint Paul to the Corinthians,* 3rd ed., trans. A. W. Heathcote and P. J. Allcock (London: Epworth, 1966), p. 15.
159. *TDNT,* 3:951.
160. Aland, Black, Metzger, and Wikgren in their edition of *The Greek New Testament* omit *katastrophē,* following the Vatican, Ephraem, Seideliano II, and Bodmer P 72 codices. Max Zerwick is also inclined to omit it and adds that here the verb seems to signify the sentence and the execution together (*Analysis philologica novi testamenti graeci,* 2nd ed. [Rome: PIB, 1960]).
161. In *Gerechtigkeit Gottes,* n. 2, pp. 77-78, Stuhlmacher has shown, in opposition to Käsemann, that this verse is purely Pauline, while in vv. 19-20 Paul reelaborates and assumes previous material; therefore, v. 21 explains the meaning of "reconciliation."
162. Cf. above p. 118.
163. Schlier, *Brief an die Galater,* p. 167.
164. Kuss, *Römerbrief,* pp. 118-19, 121-22, 131, 161-74, 214, 275.
165. Gutbrod, "nomos," *TDNT,* 4:1071.
166. Gottfried Fitzer, "Der Ort der Versöhnung nach Paulus," *ThZ* 22, no. 3 (May-June 1966): 177.

167. Stuhlmacher, *Gerechtigkeit Gottes,* p. 227.
168. Fitzer, "Ort der Versöhnung," p. 176.
169. "Wir würden sagen: 'öffentlich anschlagen' " (Schlier, *Brief an die Galater,* p. 120).
170. Regarding *katakrino* 'destroy,' cf. above p. 185.
171. Cf. above pp. 169-70.

Chapter Five

Faith and Dialectics

What Bultmann and Käsemann say of the faith—namely, that it is completely falsified when it becomes a "conception of the world," a world view or a vision of history—Marcuse, Sartre, and Bloch say has happened in the same way, in remarkably the same way, to dialectics: It became petrified into a "conception of the world" and automatically ceased being dialectics.[1]

The concurrence of these two critiques is not a coincidence. Both stem from having understood faith and dialectics in much greater depth than that achieved by their respective official representatives. "In much greater depth" means with much greater fidelity to the original meaning. This leads us to suspect that between faith and dialectical thinking there is a common denominator considerably more serious than Western positivistic scientists disparagingly are accustomed to believe, those who claim to discredit authentic Marxism by saying that it is not science but faith. Both faith and dialectical thinking (of Hegel and Marx) accuse the "wisdom of this world" of total superficiality, indeed of blindness, in its knowledge of reality. The lords of this world respond to both: They not only dedicate to each, that is, to faith and to dialectics, an identical disdain; they also adduce as the reason for their disdain the fact that the two coincide.

There are too many convergences. There must be an underlying profound affinity which has not yet been brought completely to light.

The Faith of the Bible

The first and decisive affinity is that Marx believes that dialectics will produce justice in the world, and the Bible believes that faith will produce justice in the world—real justice, not fictitious justice, not a merely imputed justice as the Protestants of old sustained. Modern Lutherans today think in a very different way. Bultmann, for example, says this with regard to Rom. 5:19: "Just as certainly as Adamitic men were not 'merely regarded as if they were sinners,' but really were sinners, so are the members of the humanity founded by Christ really righteous."[2] And so too Schlatter says, "Imputation in Paul has nothing to do with the idea of 'appearance,' 'fiction,' 'title'. . . . Man *is* what the judgment of God says he is."[3] Jüngel states, "With this the alternative between imputed justice and efficacious justice in our understanding of justice is superseded."[4] We need say nothing of Stuhlmacher who believes that God's justice is not only efficacious but also really creative.[5] H. D. Wendland holds fundamentally the same thing in his commentary on 2 Cor. 5:17-21, when he shows that in his letters to the Corinthians Paul expresses the whole of his message without using the verb "to justify."[6] Heidland is of the same opinion in his article on the verb "to impute" (*logizomai*): "Man . . . becomes a new creature through God's *logizesthai*. Hence Gal. 3:2-6 can equate justification with the receiving of the Spirit and quote Gen. 15:6 in support of justification."[7] The list of modern Protestant exegetes who hold this view could be greatly extended. Among Catholic interpreters this point, namely, the reality of the justice for which the Bible yearns, needs no demonstration.

After what we have seen in chapter 4 and the previous chapters, there can be no doubt whether this real justice is strict justice in the social sense of the word. And this is true not only in the Old Testament and the four Evangelists, but also and especially in Paul. What caused doubt for many exegetes was the forensic reference, that is, the relationship to the Judgment of God. But such a reference or dimension of justice, far from rendering this justice unreal, accentuates to the extreme the strictly social meaning of this justice, as we have seen. This is especially true in Paul and his Letter to the Romans. Thus "to free from injustice" rigorously maintains the same meaning as in the Exodus, providing this liberation with the broad definitive scope which from the beginning it was meant to have, that is, to free man from the whole of human civilization which institutionalizes injustice.

The problem is posed when Paul, with that unlimited intransigence which we considered in the last section of the preceding chapter, asserts that justice comes to and is achieved in the world by means of (*dia*) the faith and stems from (*ek*) the faith.[8] To interpret these expressions as if faith were a mere condition for God to concede justice was, in my opinion, an exegetical idea very much linked to the declaratory theory of a purely imputed justice; it would never have occurred to anyone if the forensic reference of justice had been understood in accordance with the true meaning of the Last Judgment, which we saw in the first part of the preceding chapter. But the Greek prepositions *dia* and *ek* alone are enough to exclude such extrinsicist interpretations which fundamentally obfuscate the real problem, namely, the direct and efficacious causality of faith in making men really just.

If faith is a mere condition, believing becomes precisely a "work" meritorious before God, and all the lucubrations to avoid this are in vain. The Pauline expressions "before faith came" (Gal. 3:23) and "now that faith has come" (Gal. 3:25) undoubtedly suppose an understanding of the faith as a reality with social dimensions which entered into human history as the great gift and divine favor. This faith, propagated by means of evangelizing, is what causes justice in the world, and this whole process is the salvation which Christ brings to us. To think that this faith, granted by God, still has to "move" God so that he in turn produces justice in souls is speculatively to construct a contrivance of ascending vertical causality; the least that can be said of this idea is that it finds no basis at all in the Pauline texts.

On the contrary, it is by basing himself on this direct efficacy of faith to produce justice that Paul tries, by means of the summons of the Gospel, to arouse in the Gentiles the faith from which justice stems (Rom. 1:16-17); this is the justice "from faith to faith" (*ek pisteōs eis pistin*), and therefore the "justice of God," for the first of these faiths, the first link in this chain reaction, "entered into the world" introduced by God (cf. Gal. 3:23, 25). Thus we can understand why Paul, by means of this whole campaign to stir up justice, wishes to make the Jews envious (Rom. 11:14) and make them recall the multitudinous instances of the fact that "the Gentiles, who were not looking for justice, have found justice, but the justice which stems from faith; and on the other hand, Israel, looking for a law of justice, did not arrive at the law. Why? Because [it looked for it as stemming] not from faith, but from works" (Rom. 9:30-32), because it tried to achieve justice in the world by means of the law and not by means of faith. The authentic Jewish people was conscious that its mission in the world consisted in achieving justice. But it had not achieved it, and Paul believed that the many Gentiles who had been converted into achievers of justice would be for it a spectacle which would profoundly unsettle its categories and be the source of authentic *metanoia*.

The strictly causal meaning of the preposition *ek* is clear in Gal. 3:21: "If we had been given a law capable of giving life, then truly justice would come from the law."

Few things have done so much damage to exegesis as the interpretation of Paul's struggle against *kauchēsis* 'to be proud,' 'to boast' which holds that he is dealing with asceticism or virtue, as if he were trying to add another virtue, namely, humility. It would be as if in his battle to the death against the justice of the law something to do with "greater perfection" were at stake and not the entirety, the being or not being, of justice in the world. For Paul the history of mankind, not simply one virtue more or less, is determined here: "If justice comes by means of the law, then Christ died in vain" (Gal. 2:21); "you have broken with Christ if you look for justice in the law; you have fallen from grace" (Gal. 5:4); "those who rely on the works of the law are under a curse" (Gal. 3:10). Paul is convinced not only that the law has failed in human history in its attempt to achieve justice, but also that justice will not be achieved in the world as long as the law exists. On the other hand, the Gospel message "is the power of God for the salvation of every believer . . . *because in it the justice of God is revealed from faith to faith*" (Rom. 1:16-17).

Moreover, the ascetical interpretation of Paul's rejection of the works of the law is shown to be completely inadequate by the fact that in Phil. 2:16 Paul uninhibitedly boasts of the efficacy his evangelization has had among the Philippians. Also, according to 1 Cor. 9:15 his glory is to have preached without any payment or recompense; "I would rather die," he says, "than let anyone take away this glory." We see the same thing in 2 Cor. 11:10: "This glory will never be taken from me in the regions of Achaia."

To be supported by the law, not to break definitively with all law and with all the human civilization that is supported by the law, is not some little ascetical defect which hinders spiritual perfection; it is to nullify Christ's work and to frustrate completely the entire Gospel. The possibility of understanding Paul is excluded by those who do not see that Paul wants to eliminate *kauchēsis* so that justice be achieved in the world and that he desires this while fully conscious that the greatest obstacle is to maintain confidence in the law. It is a question of efficacy, of strictly horizontal causality: "If we had been given a law capable of giving life, then truly justice would come from the law" (Gal. 3:21). Therefore he says of the Jews, "I can swear to their fervor for God, but it is not in accord with understanding, for not recognizing the justice of God and wanting to establish their own, they did not incorporate themselves into the justice of God. Because the end of the law is Christ for the justice of every believer" (Rom. 10:2-4).

And how does Paul conceive of this rigorously horizontal efficacy of the faith in producing justice? I respond in anticipation: exactly as Christ and the four Evangelists conceive of it. But this crucial question obviously depends on what these six as well as the entire Bible understand by faith. It is on this point that we must focus.

It seems to me that the articles of Weiser and Bultmann on *pistis, pisteuein,* etc., all things considered, constitute the best study that there is on faith, although they suffer from the same defect as the other available exegetical studies: They juxtapose the various meanings of faith which, it seems, occur in the Bible.[9] There is a much more serious fault, nevertheless, from which their study is free, namely, the frequent dogmatic fault of choosing only those texts having one of the meanings of faith which occur in the Bible and then proceeding as if the other passages and meanings did not exist. Weiser and Bultmann at least accurately establish all the apparently diverse meanings of faith. They simply juxtapose them, but at least they establish them all.

Without denying the merit of their study, which is indeed a great step forward, it seems that we must still ask what was the original sense of "to have faith" and what relationship the other meanings have with it. Bultmann takes an initial step in this direction when he holds that "even where, according to specific Christian usage, *pistis* is faith in Christ, the character of faith as hope is maintained."[10] Bultmann does not explain to us how the meaning of faith = hope remains present in the other apparently different meanings. This leads us to suspect that on this insight would depend an understanding of the different biblical uses of *pisteuein* and *pistis* which would not simply juxtapose the various uses, including that of "to believe in Jesus Christ," which according to Bultmann is the specifically Christian meaning. It does not seem that this meaning itself can be understood in its true sense if we forget how it was generated out of the original meaning, in which faith is the same as hope.

To trust that God intervenes is another meaning of *pisteuō* which Weiser and Bultmann discover as absolutely fundamental in the Old Testament and the Synoptics. The importance of this abundantly documentable assertion is striking, because if the Old Testament has hope it is because it *believes* that God is going to intervene in our history as he intervened in the Exodus from Egypt. Thus to trust in God's intervention is a meaning which does not differ in the least from the sense that Bultmann recognizes as the original one, namely, faith = hope.

There is, moreover, a datum of special importance which cannot be equated with the others: Among the Synoptic expressions which employ *pistis* or *pisteuein* there are some which are the words of Jesus himself. I think that it is of utmost importance to discover how the historical Jesus understood what faith is, what it is to believe. And it is equally important to know the relationship this meaning has with the original and fundamental meaning which is to-have-hope-because-God-intervenes-in-our-history.

Let us begin with a negative example which allows us to distinguish among the various strata which the use of the terms "faith" and "to believe" reveals to us in the Gospel. "Those who believe in me" (Matt. 18:6) is *not* an authentic expression of Jesus himself, as can be seen by the Marcan parallel "those who believe" (Mark 9:42). The complement "in me" was added by Matthew or by the preredactional tradition which in the hands of Matthew provided a model for the work of Mark.[11] As far as I know, no modern exegete attributes this expression to Jesus himself. Now let us use a positive example: "Your faith has saved you" (Matt. 9:22; Mark 10:52; Luke 7:50; Luke 17:19; Luke 18:42). No one doubts the authenticity of this phrase as words of Jesus. As Herbert Braun says, "The explicit Christological reference of the faith does not pertain to the most ancient level of tradition; rather it was added to it in virtue of paschal faith. Jesus of Nazareth did not ask for (nor did he receive) belief in himself as the bearer of salvation."[12] The Catholic Schnackenburg holds the same opinion.[13] With regard to Matt. 9:22 Theodor Zahn had noted, "Jesus does not see the curing of the woman as his own work but rather as the work of the woman's faith."[14]

Indeed, if Jesus diverted attention from himself toward the grandeur of the faith of others (cf. Luke 7:9), it cannot be a faith whose center of attention is himself, unless we attribute to him a bizarre maneuver without any basis in the texts. Nor does Matthew believe that the faith to which he attributes the miracle in 9:22 is faith-in-Jesus-Christ, for Matthew, whose faith is indeed precisely to believe in Jesus Christ (cf. 18:6), would have affirmed this in some way in 9:22. And there is more. The redaction of Matt. 17:19-20, in which the Evangelist completely modifies the teaching of the curing of the epileptic (contrast this with Mark 9:29), clearly shows us that the reason why the disciples could not cure him and Christ could was that they did not have faith and Christ did. Here is the axis of Matthew's argumentation. But if this is a faith that Jesus himself has, it cannot be to-believe-in-Jesus-Christ. H. J. Held rightly rejects the interpretation of "supplicating faith" as "trust in the miraculous power of Jesus."[15]

Faith with a Christocentric reference (*pisteuein eis Christon,* with the preposition *epi,* or with the dative) belongs to a period which is not contemporaneous with Jesus Christ; we see it in Matthew, Paul, and John, as well as in Acts. We are not saying that this later faith has no importance and the primigenial faith does. Rather we want to proceed as one who truly wants to understand. The later formulations should be understood in terms of the primitive ones, as a development of them, not independently of them.

Everything leads us to believe that we have the connecting link in the formula of John 20:31; 1 John 5:1; and 1 John 2:22: "to believe that Jesus is the Messiah" (we see that this is the meaning of *ho Christos* here from John 1:41). Indeed, John uses the expression "to believe in him" or (in the words of Jesus) "to believe in me" innumerable times; since at the end of his Gospel (20:31) he tells us that he wrote it so that we might believe that Jesus is the Messiah, he assumes the previous formulations in this final one. And as Bultmann rightly observes, "In John especially 'to believe in . . .' and 'to believe that . . .' are constantly used interchangeably in the same sense. . . . 'To believe in . . .' is thus to be regarded as an abbreviation which in the language of the mission became formal."[16] "To believe that Jesus is the Messiah" has a very concrete historical meaning which should be clear from reading the Old Testament and John 1:41. It does not mean believing in a nontemporal attribute, as philosophy or dogmatics might understand it, but believing in a historical event. To believe that this man, Jesus of Nazareth, is the Messiah is to believe that with him the messianic kingdom has arrived. It is to believe that in our age the kingdom of God has arrived, an event which fulfills all hopes.

The formula "to believe in Christ Jesus" also occurs in Paul (Gal. 2:16), and here too it should be understood as an abbreviation of "to believe that . . .," as found, for example, in 1 Thess. 4:14 and Rom. 10:9. But the proposition-object, that event which one "believes that" happened, is not expressed as in John by saying that Jesus is the Messiah; rather it says that "God raised him up from the dead" (Rom. 10:9) or that "Jesus died and rose again" (1 Thess. 4:14). We find this same object of the faith in 1 Cor. 15:3-4 (the "to believe" is in vv. 2, 11). Fundamentally Pauline faith knows no other object, for when he says, "I knew nothing among you except Jesus Christ, and him crucified" (1 Cor. 2:2), he is referring to this unique event which faith "believes that" happened. Although it often occurs, it is superficial to allow ourselves to be diverted by the circumstance that Paul formulates the object of his "to believe that . . ." differently from the way that John formulates it. It is precisely this circumstance—that in both Paul and John "to believe in Jesus Christ" is a formal abbreviation for "to believe that something happened"—that should make us suspect that this "something" is for Paul the same as we have just seen in John, namely, to believe that Jesus is the promised and expected Messiah, that is, to believe that in the historical event of Jesus Christ the messianic kingdom has arrived.

Indeed Rom. 10:9 (cf. Rom. 10:10) tells us this very explicitly, if we bear in mind that, as many have pointed out, there is here a strict Hebrew synonymic parallelism.[17] Thus, "to believe that God raised him from the dead" is exactly synonymous with "to confess . . . that Jesus is the Lord," and therefore Jesus is the Lord precisely in virtue of his resurrection. In the words of Michel, "By means of the extraordinary and unique Easter event, God has made Jesus Lord and bestowed authority on the son."[18] The messianic sense of the title "Lord" in this context is as clear and unquestionable as that of the title "son of God" in Rom. 1:4: "constituted [by God] as son of God in power according to a spirit of holiness in virtue of the resurrection of the dead." Schweizer very rightly says of this passage, "To call this adoptionist Christology is not at all correct, for such a Christology implies a contrast with a different concept, but such a contrast does not exist yet. But it is true that the title 'son of God' indicates primarily a function of Jesus, for v. 4 expresses simply that in the paschal event Jesus entered into the functions of the messianic king of the community."[19] The object of the faith in Rom. 10:9—the event which "we believe that" has happened—is the same as in John, namely, that this man called Jesus of Nazareth is the promised Messiah, that is, that in the historical event Jesus Christ there has arrived the messianic kingdom anxiously expected for generations and generations. The meaning of Rom. 10:9 is the same as that found in the deliberate assumption of a pre-Pauline hymn in Rom. 1:3-4, for Paul makes the hymn issue into the "obedience of the faith" (Rom. 1:5).

What occurs is that for Paul the most outstanding sign and the unequivocal proof that the kingdom has arrived is the fact that the resurrection of the dead has begun. The accent is on the plural "dead": *anastasis nekrōn.* If it were a question of only Rom. 1:4, the plural could be attributed to the adoption of the pre-Pauline formula, but 1 Cor. 15:12, 13, 21, and 42 demonstrate that this plural is to be taken seriously (cf. Phil. 3:11). The resurrection of the dead in all these passages is a historical reality with supraindividual, social, collective dimensions, a completely new epoch in human history, a new reign which breaks with previous history. It is precisely the kingdom of God, for in the verb "to raise up," both in the active and the passive voice, God is explicitly stated or is understood as the agent.[20]

The Old Testament passages (2 Kings 20:5; Jon. 2:1; Ps. 16:10; Isa. 54:7) which Nestle and Merk cite with 1 Cor. 15:4 to document that Christ's resurrection was "according to the Scriptures" have nothing to do with a resurrection after death; nor does Hos. 6:2.[21] And good method would demand that we cite Old Testament passages at the margin of Rom. 1:4 as well (without being diverted by the "third day" of 1 Cor. 15:4), for in Rom. 1:2 it is expressly indicated that God "had promised [this message] long ago through his prophets in the sacred Scriptures." And as Paul adds with great precision, this message speaks "about his son" (Rom. 1:3); that is, in the hymn that is then cited Paul sees as foretold in the Scriptures precisely this: "constituted as son of God in power according to a spirit of holiness in virtue of the resurrection of the dead" (Rom. 1:4).

The Scripture passages which are customarily cited to document the Old Testament prediction asserted by Paul simply do not document it. And if they do not correspond it is because the search has been made with an individual resurrection in mind; yet it is clear that "resurrection of the dead" [in the plural] is taken with complete seriousness, as can be seen in 1 Cor. 15:12, 13, 21, 42. A true resurrection after death is spoken of in Isa. 26:19; Ezek. 37:12ff.; Dan. 12:2; and Hos. 13:14. But this resurrection has supraindividual, collective dimensions—a crucial constituent of the promised kingdom, an indispensable element of the justice of God foretold and expected for centuries. The Pauline argumentation in 1 Cor. 15:13 should suffice to dissuade us from thinking of an individual resurrection as we search through the Old Testament: "If there is no resurrection *of the dead* [plural], neither has Christ risen."

The linking of this resurrection with the Holy Spirit in Rom. 1:4 ("according to a spirit of holiness in virtue of the resurrection of the dead") is found precisely in Ezek. 37, which I have just mentioned: "You will know that I am Yahweh when I open your tombs and I make you come out of your tombs, my people: I will put my spirit in you and you will live" (Ezek. 37:13-14). We see that this is the eschatological conferral of the spirit of Yahweh in Ezek. 36:26 and 11:19. And we see in Rom. 8:11 that this linking of the Spirit with the resurrection in Rom. 1:4 is not cited only because it was mentioned in the earlier hymn, but rather because it is decisively important to Paul: "If the Spirit of him who raised Jesus from the dead is living in you, then he who raised Christ Jesus from the dead will give life to your own mortal bodies through his Spirit living in you" (see also Rom. 8:23).

What Paul saw in the resurrection of Christ was the resurrection of the dead which comes as a reality with social dimensions, as a new reign which breaks with all past history. Christ is only "the beginning, the first-born from the dead" (Col. 1:18); Christ was raised from the dead as the first fruits of all who have fallen asleep" (1 Cor. 15:20); "so that he might be the first-born among many brothers" (Rom. 8:29); "knowing that he who raised up the Lord Jesus will raise us with Jesus in our turn" (2 Cor. 4:14; cf. Rom. 6:8; 1 Cor. 6:14). As Luke splendidly puts it in his authentic interpretation of Paul's words to Agrippa: Christ is "the first of the resurrection of the dead" (Acts 26:23).

In no case may we think that Paul participates in the adoptionist Christology which some exegetes suspect in the pre-Pauline hymn assumed in Rom. 1:3-4 and which might also be presumed in Acts 2:36; Acts 13:33; and Luke 3:22. For Paul the preexistence of Christ seems certain (cf. Rom. 8:3; Gal. 4:4; Phil. 2:5-7). But then why does the resurrection of the dead make Jesus the Messiah (cf. Rom. 10:9; 1:4; Phil. 2:9-11)? It is because only the realization of the messianic kingdom gives meaning to the messiahship of Jesus; only the historical fact that the kingdom has come gives meaning to the statement that Jesus is the Messiah. This is not a matter of believing in an attribute, but of believing that the kingdom has come. The formula "to believe in Jesus Christ" (Gal. 2:16) or "the faith of Jesus Christ" (Rom. 3:22; cf. Rom. 3:26; Gal. 2:16; 3:22; Phil. 3:9) or their equivalents are conscious abbreviations of "to believe that. . . ." This is also true in John. But both in Paul and in John, the historical fact which it is "believed that" has happened is God's definitive intervention in human history. And just as in Rom. 4:24 the object of faith is "to believe in him who raised Jesus our Lord from the dead," so too in 2 Cor. 1:9 it is to trust and hope "in the God who raises the dead" and in Rom. 4:17 "to believe in the God who gives life to the dead and calls into being what does not exist." There is no dual object of Pauline faith which Bousset and Braun believed they found, with God as one object of faith and Christ as another.[22] The faith of the New Testament is to believe in the God who breaks into our history in the event called Jesus Christ.

"To believe that Jesus is the Messiah" is the connecting link. We have seen this in the phrase's connection with the later formulas "to believe in Jesus Christ" or "faith of Jesus Christ," etc. The latter formulas maintain perfectly operative the content of the former, namely, to believe that the kingdom of God has come. Let us now relate the first formula to the Synoptics. The obvious tie is in Mark 1:14-15: "preaching the Good News from God and saying, The time has been fulfilled and the kingdom of God has arrived. Be converted and believe in the Good News." The message in which it is necessary to believe, the good news whose content is the object of the faith, is precisely "that the time has come and the kingdom of God has arrived." The structure of this Marcan passage becomes quite transparent when we realize that the term "Good News" makes a bracketing: The first time it appears it indicates that the content of the news which Christ preached will be textually presented; once this textual content is made explicit word by word, we are told what our attitude or response to such a message should be: to be converted and believe in it. The Christocentrism which Marxsen discusses with regard to this passage seems to me to be entirely out of the question.[23] If anything is emphasized by Mark it is that this is the Good News *of God* and of the kingdom *of God.* Christ is the evangelizer (*m*[e]*basser*) as conceived by Deutero-Isaiah (Isa. 40:9; 41:27; 52:7; 61:1).

In any case the decisive importance of Mark 1:14-15 is that here faith is conceived of as a response to the "great news." This is a totally Pauline conception and we will have to come back to it, for at stake here is the whole power of the Gospel to save every believer through the realization of justice (cf. Rom. 1:16-17). Efforts have been made, with regard to the Greek perfect *ēngiken* ("has come," Mark 1:15), to reject the "realized eschatology" of C. H. Dodd[24] by asserting that *engizō* does not mean "to come"; but they seem useless to me when in any case we have the aorist *ephthasen* in Matt. 12:28 and Luke 11:20, whose meaning as "has arrived" is unquestionable. To keep the *eschaton* (the *ultimum*) perpetually in the future was precisely the recourse of Jewish stubbornness in order to reject Jesus Christ. And even today it is still the ironclad refuge of obduracy: "The view of Oscar A. H. Schmitz seems to me to be quite correct, . . . that the 'Pharisee takes upon himself the task of preventing anything, even the Messiah, from becoming real.' "[25] Mark 1:14-15 shows us that faith, as in John and Paul, consists in believing that with Christ the kingdom of God has come, God's definitive intervention in our history.[26]

Mark 1:14-15 is the first time that Mark speaks to us of faith. What is believed in is the definitive divine intervention in our history, the intervention which establishes the kingdom of God in the world, such as the kingdom is described innumerable times in the Old Testament.[27] This is why neither Mark nor Jesus himself nor the other Evangelists think it necessary to explain to us what is understood by the kingdom of God, although all of Jesus' preaching is summarized in proclaiming that the kingdom of God is arriving. Everybody understood. As Bultmann quite excellently expresses it, the problem was not what but that. . . . What the kingdom consisted in could not be a problem for any reader of the Old Testament. The only important thing was *the fact that* it was arriving. Not what, but that. As Friedrich asserts, "A new message is not expected with the dawn of God's kingdom. What will be proclaimed has been known from the time of Deutero-Isaiah. The longing is that it should be proclaimed. Hence [in contemporary literature], the messenger and the act of proclamation are much more important than the message. The new feature is not the message, but the eschatological act. Because all the emphasis is on the action, on the proclamation, on the utterance of the Word which ushers in the new age, *b^{e}sorah* [message] is less prominent than *m^{e}basser* [messenger, announcer, evangelizer] and *bisser* [to announce, to evangelize]."[28]

After proclaiming the coming of the kingdom, the next time that Mark speaks to us of faith is in Mark 2:5 (Matthew and Luke follow him here literally). This is a passage of enormous importance for grasping what "faith" means, for we must bear in mind that before the narration of this scene the verb "to believe" had been used only in Mark 1:14-15, where faith consists in believing the proclamation that the kingdom has arrived. Jesus sees four men approaching who are carrying a paralytic on a stretcher, and Mark describes Jesus' "seeing" in this way: "And Jesus, seeing their faith" (Mark 2:5). According to the Synoptics, in what could this faith consist unless in that these men effectively *believe* that the kingdom has arrived, the kingdom which will succor all those who suffer and help all the needy of the earth? This is the kingdom as it is described in the Old Testament. Although Mark 2:5 is not nor does it pretend to be the words of Christ, the historical Jesus was referring to this faith when he said, "Your faith has saved you,"[29] and when he spoke of the faith that moves mountains (Mark 11: 22-23; Luke 17:5-6; Matt. 21:21).

It is striking how much this faith in Mark 2:5 has to do with hope. But it is the collective hope of centuries, the hope of all the human generations which have suffered illness, injustice, and death. This is the faith that Jesus "sees" in the four men. There is obvious homogeneity between this faith-hope, whose meaning goes back to Jesus himself, and the faith which according to Paul consists in "believing in the God who gives life to the dead" (Rom. 4:17), whose content of hope Paul tries to express through a kind of reiterated internal accusative, which is very difficult to translate: "against hope with hope he believed" (*par' elpida ep' elpidi episteusen,* Rom. 4:18). But there is also evident continuity between this faith and the faith of the Old Testament.

As Weiser and Bultmann observe, the importance of the Hebrew verb *he'ᵉmin* for our understanding of New Testament faith is deduced from the fact that the Septuagint uses *pistis* only to translate this root, and it uses *pisteuein* only (with the exception of Jer. 25:8, *šm'*) to translate this root. The exception itself is only an apparent one, for there they use *pisteuein* only for variation; in Jer. 25:7 they had just translated *šm'* by *akouein* and they did not want to repeat the same verb immediately after this. Paul not only tries to preserve the meaning of Old Testament faith; he is also conscious that his central message regarding justice by faith would founder if the argumentation of Rom. 4, Gal. 3, Rom 9:33, and Rom. 10:11 should use the verb "to believe" in a sense different from that of the faith of the Old Testament.

Deutero-Isaiah is, of course, as we might have supposed, the one who carries Old Testament faith again to new hopes,[30] with his staunch faith in the God who intervenes and who would definitively break into our human history to establish justice and life (cf. Isa. 40:27-31, etc.). But as Weiser quite accurately points out, "The fact that most of the instances of *he'ᵉmin* refer to the relationship with God in the days of Moses (Exod. 4:8f.; 14:31; 19:9; Num. 14:11; 20:12; Deut. 1:32; 9:23; 2 Kings 17:14; Ps. 78:22, 32; 106:12, 24) shows plainly enough the close connection between the special use of *he'ᵉmin* and the sacral tradition from the very beginnings of Yahweh religion in Israel."[31] All these passages refer to the great liberating act by which Yahweh destroyed the Egyptian slavery. Israel's original faith is to believe in the God who intervenes to do justice in our human history. It is therefore superfluous to emphasize that in this faith there is the certain hope that one day justice will reign on our earth.

Weiser himself points out that Deutero-Isaiah takes up the Proto-Isaianic concept of faith, which can be seen in Isa. 28:16-17.[32] And it is commonly admitted that Proto-Isaiah is where we find the purest concept of biblical faith, valid both for the Old Testament as well as the New. The passage reads:

> [16] That is why the Lord Yahweh says this:
> Behold that I lay as a foundation in Zion a chosen stone,
> a precious cornerstone, a foundation stone;
> he who has faith in it will not waver.

[17] I will make right [*mišpaṭ*] the measure
and justice [*ṣᵉdaḳah*] the plumb line.

It is universally acknowledged that Paul is alluding to Isa. 28:16 in Rom. 9:33 and 10:11 with the Septuagint formula: "He who believes in him will not be confounded" [will not be deceived]. But v. 17 should not be overlooked, for what Paul is trying to explain is, as it says right there (Rom. 9:30), "the justice [which stems] from faith." If we prescind from Isa. 28:17, Paul has no basis for connecting faith with justice, for v. 16 mentions only faith. He supposes that the readers of the letter know the passage from Isaiah in its entirety and that to evoke it he need only cite its most relevant words. According to Isaiah faith does not deceive because the new foundation of the city of men will be the justice of God, "justice and right" which Yahweh himself establishes.[33] Paul's whole point is this: Faith does not deceive because the new human civilization will have as its foundation the justice of God (cf. Rom. 10:3), not the justice of men (cf. Rom. 10:3), which is the justice of the law (cf. Rom. 9:31). The justice (which stems) from faith is the justice of God.[34]

Kertelge insinuates that in his principal and absolutely central reference to Old Testament faith (Rom. 4), Paul interprets the faith of Abraham in his own way and for his own purposes.[35] In exegesis we quite often find this insinuation, which serves to escape the impact of the Old Testament. But it cannot be sustained before the modern method of *Redaktionsgeschichte,* which regards the Yahwist not as an archivisit or a collector, but as a true author of a work structured with authentic literary unity.[36] For the Yahwist, Abraham is the very incarnation of all human hope. We need only read the Yahwist's work as it really is, namely, a work. Abraham is presented in Gen. 12, but this is after Gen. 4-11, which is the description of human history in which Cain is the protagonist and in which "Yahweh saw that the wickedness of man was great on the earth, and that the thoughts in his heart fashioned nothing but wickedness all day long. And Yahweh regretted having made man on the earth, and he became angry in his heart" (Gen. 6:5-6). (The theological and literary similarity between Gen. 6:5-6 and Gen. 18:17-19 is striking.) In this regard von Rad quite rightly says:

> It is therefore misleading to find in ch. 11 that conclusion to the primeval history, as is usually done; for then the primeval history has a much too independent and isolated importance. Rather, its conclu-

sion, indeed its key, is ch. 12:1-3, for only from there does the theological significance of this universal preface to saving history become understandable.[37]

This redactional intention of the Yahwist is especially sharpened at the end of his narrative on the tower of Babel (Gen. 11:1-9): Yahweh's previous punitive irruptions into human events had been followed by the calming of his anger so that the human race might be preserved. This time, however, the punishment is carried out without qualification. The compositional redaction raises this unavoidable question for the reader: Is God rejecting mankind forever? With chapter 11 the narrative ends on a deliberately dissonant note. Only then is the reader prepared to meet the man "in whom all the tribes of the earth will be blessed" (12:3). Abraham, who represents the people of Israel, is the very incarnation of all mankind's hope. This is the man, Paul tells us, "who against all hope with hope believed" (Rom. 4:18). And no one has understood this better than Paul of Tarsus.

The works of men were not able to achieve justice. This is the thesis of the Yahwist in Gen. 2-11; Abraham, however, believed that Yahweh would achieve justice by intervening in our history (Gen. 15 and 18). (We must not forget that in Gen. 18:17-19 the Yahwist takes up again and deepens what, in accord with the preredactional tradition, he had told us in Gen. 12:3[38]). Otto Michel very rightly points out, "The passage Rom. 4:17-22 is decisive for grasping what Paul understands by 'to believe.' "[39] It should be noted that, more strictly speaking, the very pregnant expression in Rom. 4:18 should be translated in this way: *"against all hope he believed in hope"*; this is the meaning of *pisteuein* with the preposition *epi* whenever it occurs in the New Testament (Matt. 27:42; Luke 24:25; Acts 9:42; 11:17; 16:31; 22:19; Rom. 4:5, 24; 9:33; 10:11; 2 Thess. 1:10b; 1 Tim. 1:16; 1 Pet. 2:6), independently of whether the preposition is with the accusative or, as it is here, with the dative (It is also with the dative in Luke 24:25; Rom. 9:33; 10:11; 1 Tim. 1:16; and 1 Pet. 2:6).

In the existential structure of biblical faith there is an absolutely fundamental element which is common to both the faith of the Old Testament and of the New. Without it, it is not possible either to believe that God intervenes in our history or to believe that his intervention occurs in Jesus Christ. This element or existential moment is a faith which consists in *believing* that our world is not past

recovery. Over the issue of believing or not believing that our world is
not past recovery mankind is divided into two groups with a deeper
cleavage than over any other issue which men dispute and fight over. It
is necessary to gauge accurately this fundamental "having faith." Not
all those who say that they believe really believe in this. Those who
have projected (against the direction of the Old and especially the New
Testament) salvation and glory solely in another world, in a beyond, do
not believe that our world is remediable.

I repeat what I said above: "They will inherit the world" is denied
by Paul to those who observe the law, but so that he might assure it to
those who through faith become just: "The promise of inheriting the
world was not made to Abraham and his descendants on account of the
law, but on account of the justice of faith" (Rom. 4:13).[40] When
Matthew says, "Blessed are the gentle because they will possess *the
earth*" (Matt. 5:5), it is simply impenitent escapism to interpret this by
saying that it refers to "the land of their hearts." The two groups into
which the above-mentioned absolutely basic element of faith divides
the world are here seen as irreconcilable. Marx is on the same side as the
biblical authors: He does believe that there is hope for our world. When
Matthew tells us that Christ will return to the earth in order to "gather
out of his kingdom all scandals and all those who do injustice" (Matt.
13:41), there is no way he could tell us more clearly that the kingdom
is on earth, that "the field is the world" (Matt. 13:38). Only those
possessed with this irreducible worldliness can take seriously and thrill
with the Pauline hope that death too will finally be overcome (1 Cor.
15:26). In Spanish and French damage has been done especially by the
lack of a preposition *ex* to translate John 18:36: "My kingdom is not
(derived) of this world." Rev. 5:10 says this of believers: "You have
made of them for our God a kingdom and priests, and they will reign
on earth." [In English the Greek of John 18:36 can be rendered more
faithfully than in Spanish or French by the use of the preposition
"from." In fact, however, the English translations have traditionally
used the preposition "of" (Translator's note).]

I wonder where there is more faith and hope: in believing "in the
God who raises the dead" (Rom. 4:17) or in believing like Luke in the
God who "filled the hungry with good things and sent the rich away
empty" (Luke 1:53)? In any case Nestle and Merk are incontrovertibly
correct when they cite Gen. 18:18 in connection with Paul's comment

that "the promise of inheriting the world was not made to Abraham and his descendants on account of the law, but on account of the justice of faith" (Rom. 4:13). Indeed only in Gen. 18:18-19 is the promise of Gen. 12:3—that in Abraham all the nations of the earth will be blessed—related with "justice" and with Abraham's descendants. Only in Gen. 18:18-19 does the Yahwist express in terms of justice his authentic interpretation of the meaning of that promise which he formulates for the first time in 12:3: How will all the nations of the earth be blessed in Abraham? "By keeping the way of Yahweh, that is, by observing justice and right in order that Yahweh might carry out for Abraham what he has promised him." To inherit and possess the whole world means that Abraham's descendants will teach all nations to achieve justice on earth. Toward this are directed all the promises that were made to Abraham, beginning, naturally, with that of having descendants (cf. Rom. 4:18-21; Gen. 15:2, 5, 6).

The correctness of citing Gen. 18 in preference to Gen. 12 is confirmed by the formulation of Gal. 3:8b, where Paul literally cites the promise "in you all nations will be blessed"; he follows the meaning of the Septuagint in Gen. 18:18 (Paul does not say "all the tribes" as Gen. 12:3 says, both in the Hebrew and the Septuagint). But a problem arises in Gal. 3 which has been curiously minimized by exegesis but which we must face here. The promise mentioned in Gal. 3:8b reappears in v. 14 in these words: "so that the blessing of Abraham should fall on the nations in Jesus Christ, so that by means of faith we should receive the promise of the Spirit." This is the Spirit of which he has been speaking from the beginning of chapter 3, but with what basis does Paul suppose that the promise made to Abraham was the promise to confer the Spirit on men? His basis is twofold: (1) the identification of authentic justice with the spirit of Yahweh; (2) that the justice promised (Gen. 18:18-19) was authentic justice, that is, social justice, for all peoples. The problem is very serious, and by no means is it sufficient to declare with Schlier, "The blessing of Abraham is interpreted as Spirit," although what Schlier says is obviously true.[41] The strength of Gal. 3:14 lies in the fact that the identification between authentic justice and the spirit of God is here considered to be completely taken for granted. No matter how much we might like to play it down, it is indeed serious that the biblical authors take completely for granted something which Christian theology has not even considered.

We have just touched on chapter 28 of Isaiah because Paul cites it twice in his Letter to the Romans to demonstrate the justice of faith; as we have seen, the key to the chapter is v. 17: "I will make right the measure and justice the plumb line." In this same chapter Isaiah's hope is also formulated in this way: "Yahweh will be [or will become] the spirit of justice for those who preside over *mišpat*" (Isa. 28:5-6). Duhm comments, "This indeed can be called an infelicitous expression."[42] Instead of drawing this conclusion we might rather carefully investigate what the spirit of God is according to the Bible, in order not to confuse it with what our Greek ontological categories have made us think it is. If we bear in mind that Num. 11:14-30 is the Yahwistic version of Exod. 18:13-27[43] and that the instituting of seventy men to help Moses has as its purpose "to judge [= do justice] between a man and his neighbor" (Exod. 18:16), then we can understand quite well why "Yahweh puts his spirit upon them" (Num. 11:29).

We have already seen that Yahweh's essential character, what distinguishes him from the other gods, is the unlimited sense of justice which makes him intervene in human history to eliminate oppression; his spirit is this. And the heart of Old Testament revelation is reached by the so-called infelicitous expression of Isaiah: "Yahweh will be the spirit of justice for those who preside over *mišpat*" (Isa. 28:5-6). This is what he had said in Isa. 1:26: "I will restore your judges as of old, your counsellors as in the beginning; then you will be called city of justice, faithful city." But in 28:5-6 this is eschatologically attributed to the fact that they will have the spirit of Yahweh; thus we are given an indication for understanding the spirit of Yahweh in a qualitative way, as the Yahwist undoubtedly understood it in Num. 11:17, 25, 29: It was the same spirit that was in Moses.

But note that Micah also understood the spirit of Yahweh as a characterization, as a distinctive manner of being and acting:

Not so with me, I am full of strength
of the spirit of Yahweh,
of justice [*mišpat*] and courage
to declare Jacob's crime to his face
and Israel's sin to it.
Now listen to this, you leaders of Jacob,
rulers of Israel,
you who loathe justice
and pervert all that is right;

you who build Zion with blood,
and Jerusalem with injustice.

(Mic. 3:8-10)

Within v. 8 the synonymic parallelism between the spirit of Yahweh and justice leaves no room for doubt. And this is confirmed in vv. 9-10 when we see the kind of transgressions for which Micah needed the spirit of Yahweh to denounce. According to Weiser, the *miŝpaṭ* of v. 8 means "a clear sense of right and of justice."[44] And indeed, to have this is to have the spirit of Yahweh. We need not deny or doubt the substantiality or ontic status of the Holy Spirit to affirm that this is not what the Bible is concerned with; rather it is concerned with qualitative characterization. The meaning of "spirit" here is something like our meaning when we today speak of the spirit of Teilhard de Chardin or we assert that a given initiative is or is not according to the spirit of John XXIII.

The Old Testament passages which mention the charismatic conferral of the spirit of Yahweh on a man or a group of men are relatively few. We are not concerned here with the passages in which Yahweh infuses his spirit as a mere breath of life, as in Gen. 6:3. This is clearly something else.

Let us keep in mind Isa. 11:1-9: On the descendant of David "the spirit of Yahweh will rest" (v. 2), and the descendant of David "will defend the poor with justice and the needy with equity; he will strike down the violent with the rod of his mouth and will kill the unjust with the breath of his lips; justice will be his loincloth and goodness the belt around his hips" (vv. 4-5). This is exactly the same characterization of the spirit of Yahweh as that which we saw in Num. 11, in Isa. 28, and in Mic. 3.

In Isa. 32:15ff. the infusion "of the spirit from on high" means without any doubt the conferral of the spirit of Yahweh which is predicted in Joel 3:1ff. and Ezek. 36:26. This prediction is fulfilled, according to Luke, in Acts 2:4 and 4:31 with the result, intentionally repeated, which is described in Acts 2:44-45 and 4:32. Let us see how Isa. 32:15-17 describes this infusion:

When the spirit from on high is poured out on us,
the desert will be a garden and the garden will
    appear as a forest:
in the desert justice [*miŝpaṭ*] will dwell
and in the garden right [*ṣᵉdaḳah*] will live,

the work of justice will be peace,
the result of justice will be security and
confidence forever.

We could not ask for greater explicitness. The spirit of Yahweh is the spirit of interhuman justice—definitive, total justice. Luke describes such justice in this way: "The whole group of believers had one heart and one soul, and no one called his own anything that he had; rather they held everything in common" (Acts 4:32). As this description is a substantial repetition of Acts 2:44-45, we see that Luke was especially concerned with showing the effect of the coming of the Holy Spirit; therefore he put the description immediately after 4:31. In Acts 2 he had had to insert Peter's pentecostal discourse and thus the connection between 2:4 and 2:44-45 was not sufficiently clear. In Acts 10:38 it is clear that Luke sees man's unlimited giving of himself to his neighbors as the distinctive effect of the conferral of the Spirit: "As God anointed him with the Holy Spirit and with power and he went about doing good." Here the reference is doubtless to the citation Luke 4:18 makes of Isa. 61:1; there Trito-Isaiah offers us a testimony as unequivocal as Micah's and Isaiah's (28; 11; 32) regarding the Bible's understanding of the spirit of Yahweh. This spirit is understood as a manner of being and acting, as a qualitative characterization, more than as a hypostasis or an entity or a person, even though it might be quite logically legitimate to deduce the affirmation of these ontological categories. Trito-Isaiah says this:

The spirit of the Lord Yahweh is upon me,
for Yahweh has anointed me to announce the
good news to the poor;
he has sent me to bind up hearts that are broken,
to proclaim liberty to captives
and liberation to those in prison.

(Isa. 61:1)

Both the texts taken as a whole as well as each text taken in particular make this conclusion inescapable: The Bible understands the spirit of Yahweh as the spirit of justice, the spirit of love of the needy and afflicted. And I say the Bible, both the New Testament and the Old. As a testimony to the uninterrupted continuity between the Old Testament and the New, see the Psalm of Solomon 17. V. 37 asserts of the Messiah that "God made him powerful in the holy spirit" and therefore, according to v. 32, "in his days there will no longer be injustice among them," but rather (vv. 3, 15, 19, 23, 27, 29) an abundance of justice and compassion (*eleos*). Also we see in the intertestamental Test. XII Patr. in Sim. 4:4: "But Joseph was a good man, and having the spirit of God in himself, compassionate and merciful he held no rancor for me, but rather loved me like the other brothers." The qualitative meaning, prescinding from any ontological problem, is clear. We see also in Qumran that this understanding of the spirit of Yahweh was never interrupted:

> The soul of your servant has detested every
> work of injustice;
> I have known that man is not just outside of you,
> I have appeased your face by the spirit which
> you have placed (in me).

(1 QH 16:10-11)

The same can be seen in 1 QH 4:31. But the connection between the Old and the New Testaments is direct, as can be seen in the relationship which we studied above between Luke and Trito-Isaiah, and very especially by the relationship between Matthew and Deutero-Isaiah, which merits much study with respect to Matt. 12, without losing sight of Matt. 8:17. We have already seen that the *krisis* of Matt. 12:18, 20 (where he is citing almost in its entirety the First Servant Song of Deutero-Isaiah) is justice on behalf of all the helpless and needy and that Matthew emphasizes this very strongly.[45] Bultmann has observed that Matt. 8:17 contains a true and proper interpretation of the mission of the Servant of Deutero-Isaiah; this interpretation contradicts the customary idea, based on expiation, which we have fashioned regarding the Fourth Song (Isa. 52:13-53:12).[46] And Ellen Flesseman-van Leer has shown how doubtful and improbable is the expiative meaning which we are accustomed to read there.[47]

In any case, Matthew has read and understood the four songs as a unified work and he rightly interprets the fourth in light of the first: The mission of the servant is *krisis,* that is, justice for all those who suffer. Therefore in Matt. 8:17 it is not a question of Jesus taking upon himself our sufferings but rather of his eliminating them from the face of the earth. What deserves greater attention is the fact that Matt. 12 deliberately attributes this work of Christ to the circumstance that God "places his spirit upon him" (Matt. 12:18). Therefore he immediately adds "and he will proclaim justice to the nations" (ibid.). And the dispute which the Evangelist then introduces in Matt. 12:22-30 deals precisely and solely with whether the works of Christ are the effect of the spirit of God or not (see 12:28, where he modifies Q to say "By the spirit of God I cast out devils," while Q says, "By the finger of God I cast out devils"; cf. Luke 11:20). Both mentions of the spirit of God (Matt. 12:18, 28) are redactionally added by Matthew. In this way he makes the dispute of Mark 3:22-27 (assumed in Matt. 12:24-26), which did not mention the spirit of God at all, lead with perfect coherence into the question of the sin against the Holy Spirit (Mark 3:28-30; assumed and amplified in Matt. 12:31-37). With the introduction of the spirit of God in Matt. 12:18, 28, Matthew succeeds in giving perfect sense to Mark's thesis that the sin against the Holy Spirit consists in attributing Christ's works to the "impure spirit" (Mark 3:30) and not to the Spirit of God.

But it is not only the Synoptics who understand the spirit of God as a qualitative characterization, as an acute sense of justice on behalf of the needy and dispossessed. If we bear in mind that, as we have seen,[48] Johannine love is not the vastly universal (rationalistic or romantic) love of neighbor, but the love-justice for "the brother in need" (1 John 3:17), then John offers us a testimony of this very ancient tradition as unequivocal as that of Isaiah, Micah, Deutero-Isaiah, Trito-Isaiah, the Psalms of Solomon, Qumran, Test. XII Patr., and the Synoptics.

No one has ever seen God;
(a) if we love one another,
(b) God dwells in us and his love is complete in us.
(b) In this we know that we dwell in him and he in us:
(a) in that he has given us *of his spirit.*

(1 John 4:12-13)

Note that 4:13 takes up again the theme of "he dwells in us" from 4:12 and that therefore the two verses should not be separated. The last four lines are structured in chiasmus (a-b-b-a), and if 4:13 causes a "strange impression" for Schnackenburg, so strange that he tends to consider it a gloss,[49] it is precisely because Christian theology does not take for granted what the Bible does, namely, that "the spirit of God" is the qualitative characterization of him who gives himself completely to his neighbor. The argument of 1 John 4:12-13 is closeknit and essentialistic like few others in the Bible. *The goal of God's intervention in our history is not that we should see God; God is not seen. It is rather that God be in us, and this consists in our loving one another.*

John wants to shout this at the top of his lungs, for this is the only revelation of the true God. And he reinforces his argument by adding very strongly: How could our love of our neighbor not be the sign that God is in us if love of neighbor is the very spirit of God? It is his spirit, his own manner of being, that is in us when we love our neighbor: In this we know that God is in us and that we are in him: in that we have his own spirit. God is already here. The tragedy of Christianity is that it has not dared to take this revelation seriously.

Only by taking this step can we understand why for the biblical authors it was absolutely necessary that death be definitively overcome (cf. 1 Cor. 15:26; and cf. Rev. 21:4: "And he will wipe every tear from their eyes and there will be no more death, nor will there be mourning nor outcry nor pain") and that all the just who have died should return to participate in this life. "We know that we have passed from death to life because we love our brothers" (1 John 3:14). But "he who believes in me, although he has died, yet he shall live" (John 11:25); "I shall raise him up on the last day" (John 6:40, 44, 55). And we cannot attribute this to ecclesiastical redaction. If we understand what the only revelation of God is, then this is eternal life, and it is this life which demands the resurrection of the dead and the definitive defeat of death.

Like John, Paul also takes for granted the understanding of "the spirit of God" as the qualitative characterization of the spirit of justice, as we see very clearly in Gal. 3:14;[50] here he translates the promise of the Spirit as the promise of justice which was made to Abraham. What is serious, what is disturbing for Western theology, is the very high level of "taking for granted" that this identification has here, just as in 1 John 4:12-13.

Paul is more explicit in Gal. 5:22: "The fruit of the Spirit is love." And if we refer to Isa. 32:15-17 as background[51] we can better understand Rom. 14:17: The kingdom of God is "justice and peace and joy in the Holy Spirit."

We find the same idea in Rom. 8:4, "in order that the content of justice of the law might be achieved in us who do not walk according to the flesh but according to the spirit." But we must make no mistake about what it means to walk according to the spirit, which Paul immediately explains to us: "You are not in the flesh, but in the spirit, *provided that the spirit of God dwells in you*" (Rom. 8:9). If we are to understand Pauline faith-hope, it is extremely important that we not separate these two verses. H. D. Wendland has made this precise observation: "When Paul says 'spirit,' he always means 'the spirit of God.' "[52] And commenting on Rom. 12:9, Otto Michel adds this distinction: "Only when we qualify the *pneuma* as agape is the *pneuma* in the full sense the Spirit of God."[53] And Bultmann says, "The new being is characterized by the Spirit as a walking in justice."[54]

If we do not wish to confuse Paul with dichotomous Greek anthropology and with Stoic ascetics, then this point is decisive. Indeed, Gal. 5:13-25 makes it clear that "to walk in the spirit" (v. 25) means precisely "by means of love serve one another" (v. 13), as Schweizer has already observed.[55] I cannot emphasize enough the importance of this assertion. In the Bible the epithet "carnal" was not coined primarily because of the flesh, but rather in contrast with the spirit of Yahweh. This is so much the case that according to Gal. 3:1-5, *the irreproachable observance of the law is a carnal attitude!* The least we can say is that Western morality, so repressive of the body, of material things, and of joy, is quite inadequate to transmit the Gospel message in this regard; this is an understatement. For Paul it is the same to say "carnal" (*sarkikoi*) as to say "psychic" (compare 1 Cor. 2:14 with 3:1). And in the same passage (3:3) "to be carnal" is the same as "to walk according to the man" (*kata anthrōpon peripatein*).

The true meaning of these terms is given in 1 Cor. 2:12: "We have not received the spirit of the world, but rather the spirit [which comes] from God." The biblical understanding of the "spirit of God" as a qualitative characterization is here quite apparent; and the spirit of the world is the "jealousy and dissension" (cf. 1 Cor. 3:3) which has been structured into human civilization, as we saw above.[56] Oettinger quite rightly says, "Carnality is where the ways of God end."[57] In 1 Cor. 3:3 Paul characterizes "being carnal" by the fact that "there is still jealousy and discord in you"; this is corroborated by the definitional contrast which Gal. 5:13 makes of the flesh: "Give no opportunity to the flesh, but rather by means of love serve one another." And because 1 Cor. 3:1-3 identifies "jealousy and discord" with the puerile immaturity of "being infants" (*nēpioi*), then Eph. 4:13-16 offers us a corroboration when it says that we shall "no longer be infants" (*nēpioi,* v. 14), but rather "build up Christ in charity" (v. 16). I repeat: Carnality is a concept coined in contrast with the spirit of God. Paul makes this explicit in Rom. 8:6-7: "The aspiration of the flesh is death; the aspiration of the spirit is life and peace, because the aspiration of the flesh is contrary to God." Kertelge sums it up very well: "For Paul flesh means the manner of existence of man insofar as he belongs to the old age."[58]

With regard to the body, Paul is diametrically opposed to Platonism. He desires and expects the liberation of our bodies (Rom. 8:11, 13). The body must be a weapon of justice (Rom. 6:13). And this is so not only of our bodies; all creation is in anxious expectation of liberation (Rom. 8:19, 21). Paul does not derive evil from the flesh nor from what is corporeal. Even more, as Althaus emphasizes, he does not even derive it from nature.[59] Sin is not deduced from the human essence nor from creation nor from contingency nor from finitude. Paul is completely biblical: "It was good" in Gen. 1:9-31 from the beginning to the end of the creation of all things. Sin and death *entered* the world (Rom. 5:12). They were not there at the beginning. They do not naturally belong to mankind. They entered because of one man, and because of one man both sin and death are destroyed. Far from being a "nonentity," as those who deduce it from finitude have to conclude, sin is a reality which enters the world and causes death. But "because of one man death and because of one man the resurrection of the dead" (1 Cor. 15:21). This verse is more than sufficient to dismiss those who claim that in Rom. 5:12-21 and in Romans in general death means some sort of spiritual death. The death which is contrasted, as the work of Adam, to the resurrection of the dead, as the work of Christ, is real, physical death. But here there is at stake that absolutely fundamental existential element of biblical faith, which is common to both the Old and the New Testaments.[60]

"Against all hope he believed in hope" (Rom. 4:18). The essence of the faith that becomes justice is described in Rom. 4; it could not be more intentionally spelled out. The worldliness, the hereness, of this faith is explicit in Rom. 4:13-16. The question of whether or not in Jesus Christ God has intervened in our human history has importance only when we believe that our human history and our world have importance, that is, when we suffer with it and in it. Otherwise, it does not matter whether God intervenes or not. Matthew unsurpassably expresses this idea in his fourth Beatitude: Those who hunger and thirst for justice, they will be filled when the kingdom comes (Matt. 5:6). Rom. 4 is not a comparison; rather it assumes in their entirety Abraham's history and hope, making them completely its own; and in so doing it eliminates Jewish exclusivity. On this crucial point, Paul is limitlessly faithful to Jesus Christ; the salvation of the world comes from the Jews (John 4:22; Rom. 9:4-8); *quam olim Abrahae promisisti et semini eius.* This is not simply a question of demonstrating with an example or with biblical authority that true justice is that of faith. Faith is not a Platonic essence which is realized in isolated "cases," atomized into different moments and places, independent of each other. This would be the individualistic conception in which faith has been falsified by being reduced to a "virtue."

Paul's faith is the assumption of Abraham's history and of the promise which was made to him; it is a total incorporation into this hope: that the whole world would be transformed by Yahweh's intervention which makes men just and raises the dead. This is Abraham's faith which was considered as justice (Gen. 15:6). Because it is justice. Because effectively to hunger and thirst for the realization of justice in the world is already justice. The Yahwist's intention in all these chapters is for us to have a historical perspective. No one can judge Paul's fidelity to the Yahwist if he does not feel—together with Paul and the Yahwist—human history as his own, as his affair, as his hope, as his tragedy, as his only church. Individualism of salvation is the very negation of the faith of Jesus Christ. And Catholicism as a discriminatory denomination is etymologically the negation of Catholicism.

Biblical faith understands itself as hope, but truly as hope that recognizes no limits. We will see this shortly, and indeed the fact that this faith is described as believing in the God who raises the dead demonstrates this limitlessness quite abundantly. In this sense we can schematically distinguish three existential elements in New Testament faith; the first two of these are common to Old Testament faith, though this does not mean that the third element is foreign to Old Testament faith: (1) Faith is believing that there is hope for our world;[61] (2) faith is believing that there is hope for our world because God intervenes in human history; (3) faith is believing that there is hope for our world because God intervenes in our history precisely in the historical event called Jesus Christ. It bears repeating that anyone who lacks the first element cannot believe in the other two. And in this sense the words of Teilhard the Jesuit cited by Garaudy the Marxist are very true:

I wonder if mankind today is not really at the point of being divided between those who believe and those who do not believe in the future of the universe. And I feel more determined than ever to join the former in the conquest of the world.[62]

Before proceeding let us establish that the identification of faith with unlimited hope is found in the very definition of faith offered to us in Heb. 11:1, a definition on which dogmatics literally "fixed itself" as if the Gospels did not exist:[63] "Faith is the firmness of what we hope for, the conviction of what we [still] do not see." I have interpolated "still" because in 11:7 the author again uses in a negation the neuter plural participle *blepomenōn*, clarified with a "still," and precisely in order to exemplify in Noah the faith which in 11:1 he has just defined. In fact, "the conviction of what we still do not see" is in parallel with "the firmness of what we hope for."

The word *hypostasis*, which I have translated as "firmness" (cf. Otto Kuss: "ein Stehen zu Gehofftem"), although others render it as "pledge" (Otto Michel), "guarantee," "certain security," etc., is in Heb. 3:14 intimately linked to the idea of hope: "We have come to be participators in Christ, provided that we keep the firmness of the beginning strong until the end" (cf. Heb. 3:6: "provided that we keep the confidence and exultation of hope strong until the end"). Independently of the exact meaning of the substantive *hypostasis*, its radical and explicit connection with hope leads us to think that the definition of 11:1 means this: What makes hope indomitable is faith. This does not mean that hope and faith are two different things, for the one enters into the definition of the other, and, although faith seems to surpass hope, it surpasses it precisely in order to be able to keep on having hope.

In this case we can improve upon the translation of Rom. 4:18 even further and postulate this Pauline verse as the best definition of faith: *"Beyond hope he believed in hope."* In fact, the preposition *para* with the accusative has as its genuine and proper meaning "on the margin of," "beyond," *praeter.*[64] This is more apparent in Paul than in other authors, as can be seen especially in 2 Cor. 8:3 and Rom. 12:3. Faith is the limitlessness of hope.

This is the meaning of "faith" on the lips of Jesus, both in the phrase "Your faith has saved you" as well as when he spoke of the faith that moves mountains.[65] We have also seen that authentic faith is exercised by "believing that."[66] It is clear that not simply any fact can be "believed to have happened" by a faith which is identified with hope. Not simply any truth-in-itself can be "believed" by a faith which is identified with hope. I am speaking of existential conditions of possibility, against which no dogmatism stands up. "That the kingdom has come" does indeed have meaning for the hope that "believes" that our world is remediable. That Christ, the first born of many brothers, has been raised up, does indeed have meaning for hope. For faith, history is not a conglomeration of bald facts; it focuses only on those which have relevance for the hope of mankind, and whoever does not perceive these does not know the true reality and meaning of history. Faith is soteriology. And a soteriology which can be understood without hope has no reason for existing.

Dialectics of the Faith

Let us confirm the faith=hope indentification by the use of the verb *kataischynein* in the Letter to the Romans. It appears only three times: twice to say that the faith will not be confounded or deceived (Rom. 9:33; 10:11)[67] and once to say that hope does not deceive (Rom. 5:5). This coincidence seems quite eloquent.

Even more eloquent, nevertheless, is the fact that Rom. 5:1-5 is an intense treatise on hope (*elpis* in vv. 2, 4, 5), in which Paul assumes ("justified, *then*, by faith," v. 1) all that he has said in Rom. 4 regarding faith. This confirms our conviction that 4:18 (the only verse in chapter 4 in which hope is explicitly mentioned) was the hinge of chapter 4, for this is the idea which Paul takes up again, with the words "faith" and "hope," in 5:1-5. This is especially apparent when we see the development of Rom. 4:19-21, in which the meaning of hope is clear: "unshaken in faith" (v. 19), "since God had promised it, Abraham refused even to deny it or even to doubt it, but grew strong in faith, gave glory to God, and was strongly convinced that he who promises also has the power to fulfill; *therefore* it was considered as justice for him" (vv. 20-22). If we bear in mind that all this is a development and an elaboration of 4:18—"beyond hope he believed in hope"—then the aforementioned identification is clear. And what Paul means is that this is precisely the faith which is considered as justice, for he had already told us in 4:3 that "Abraham believed in God and this was considered as justice for him," and he did not have to repeat it. Vv. 18-22 undertake to explain *why* faith is considered as justice, and the explanation is reducible to this: because this faith is true hope.

But the greater importance of Rom. 5:5 is that it tells us why hope does not deceive. In Gal. 3:6-14 Paul was not able to explain without reference to the conferral of the Spirit of God why or how the promise of justice made to Abraham is fulfilled in us. In Rom. 4 this explanation through reference to the conferral of the Spirit was still pending. Therefore Rom. 5:1-5 constitutes a unit with Rom. 4 (though I do not mean to say that the unit ends in 5:5). It says, "And hope does not deceive, *because* the love of God has been poured out into our hearts by the Holy Spirit who was given to us" (Rom. 5:5).

To tell the truth, Gal. 5:22 ("The fruit of the Spirit is love") should have been sufficient from the very start to settle the old question concerning the meaning of "the love of God" in Rom. 5:5, for there is no doubt that Gal. 5:22 is speaking of love-of-neighbor (because of the unequivocal context). Gal. 5:22 affirms an essential, definitional link; thus a love that has been poured into our hearts by the Holy Spirit (Rom. 5:5) can be only love-of-neighbor. Moreover, the old question concerning the meaning of "the love of God" was posed as a dilemma between the subjective genitive (Origen, Chrysostom, Ambrosiaster, Althaus, Sanday-Headlam, etc.) and the objective genitive (Augustine, Theodoret, Photius, many Catholics). Posed in this way the dilemma can be conclusively surmounted if we bear in mind v. 8, which takes up the issue again by saying, "God demonstrates the love that he has for us. . . . " But what caused perplexity is that the love of which God is the subject is poured out into our hearts. To resolve the problem it would have been necessary not to be led astray by the fatally ontologizing Greek mentality, but rather to grasp that in the Bible "the spirit of God" is a distinctive characterization before it is anything else.[68] Looking at the question in the Greek way, it was as absurd for the spirit of God to be conferred on us as it was for God's love for men to be poured into us. According to Rom. 5:5 it is this love with which God loves men which has been poured into our hearts, and *precisely for this reason (hoti)* we now have a hope that cannot fail.

The thesis is exactly the same as that of 1 John 4:12: "If we love one another, God dwells in us and his love·is complete in us."[69] Note the qualitative meaning of "the spirit of God" in the following broadly synonymic enumeration: "in magnanimity, in goodness, in the holy spirit, in love free from affectation, in the true word, in the power of God" (2 Cor. 6:6); see too Rom. 12:9-11). Therefore I have insisted on the very high level of "being taken for granted" that the meaning of "the Spirit" has in Gal. 3:14; it is identified completely with an acute sense of justice and self-giving to one's neighbor.[70] *This is because the foundation of hope consists in the fact that this justice of God is already on earth and that it is this which is going to transform the world* and all its civilizing structures—including bodies: "The spirit is life by means of justice" (Rom. 8:10),[71] "so that, just as sin reigned in death, so too grace should reign by means of justice for everlasting life through Jesus Christ our Lord" (Rom. 5:21).

That the "love" of Rom. 5:5 is love-of-neighbor is also confirmed by 5:9 ("much more, then, justified in his blood now, through him we will be saved from wrath"), which repeats 5:1 ("justified, then, by faith . . . ") and expressly gives us the logical connection between *the unit 3:21-5:11* and the "wrath" described in *the unit 1:18-3:20*. The justice of faith, explained and demonstrated in 3:21-5:11, is what saves us from the wrath described in 1:18-3:20. It rescues us by making us just, that is, by making us cease to belong to the *adikia* in which God's wrath is immanently concretized (cf. 1:18) as a reality with social dimensions in human history.[72] As we saw, this *adikia* involved enmity, envy, pride, mercilessness, etc. (and no one is fundamentally unaware that with these things we do our neighbor the deepest injustice). It is clear that only love-of-neighbor takes us out of this magma of injustices into which God's wrath is condensed. If then 5:9 summarizes what went before (5:1-8) by saying that we will be saved from wrath, the love of 5:5 is the love of neighbor.

Moreover, it is on the presence of love that Rom. 5:5 bases the hope mentioned in 5:2 in this way: "Let us exult in the hope of the glory of God." And here it becomes absolutely indispensable to make a clarification concerning "the glory of God," just as we had to do in the preceding section with "the spirit of God." In my opinion erroneous methodological principles have in both cases prevented us from seeing clearly. In the case of the spirit, it has been the placing of the ontological question before the qualitative one; in the case of the glory of God, it has been the placing of the chronological question first, that is, whether the glory is present or future, instead of discovering first what the Bible understands by "the glory of God." The eschatological "now," with its present-future dialectic, must be our concern, and not only with respect to "glory," for the whole subversive power of the Gospel is involved in this question.

Just as Gal. 3:14, in the way it takes for granted the meaning of "Spirit," required of us a specific inquiry, so too with "the glory of God" the first and decisive consideration is required of us by Rom. 3:23. Here Paul summarizes the description which he has made of the *adikia* of the world, both that of the pagan world (1:18-32) and that of the Jewish world (2:1-3:20), but he summarizes all the world's injustice in these words: "There is no difference; everyone has sinned and lacks the glory of God." He obviously takes for granted a very specific meaning of "glory of God" when he says that everyone lacks the glory of God, that everyone urgently needs the glory of God. His preceding description would lead us to say that everyone needs justice, that everyone urgently requires the coming of justice to the world. And in fact the description in 1:18-3:20 intentionally leads into the contrasting statement, "But now, without the law, *the justice of God* has been made known" (3:21). This is what the preceding description led us to sense that everyone needed, so that when he goes on to repeat the same idea by saying that "because there is no difference, for everyone sinned and needs the glory of God," the synonymy between the justice of God and the glory of God is clear.

Since this is the case, neither glory nor justice is understood as a property in God, but rather as a concrete, comprehensive reality with supraindividual dimensions pervading human history and the earth. We cannot hope to discover the qualitative content, the characterization of this reality, in the word "glory." Nor can we hope to discover it in the philology of the Greek substantive *doxa*, for the New Testament takes this term from the Septuagint, and the translators of the Septuagint, when they translated the Hebrew *kabod* by *doxa*, achieved "a recasting of the Greek term so strong that a stronger one could not be imagined."[73] This is the most paradigmatic case known of the modification of a language. And the distance between the meanings becomes insurmountable especially in the term "the glory of God," much more than in the other uses of the word. The classical definition—*clara cum laude notitia*—is of absolutely no use to us here. If the Hebrew etymology of *kabod* ("gravity," "weight," in the metaphorical sense of these words) were a trustworthy indication, the philological study could still be of some value, bearing in mind that *doxa=ḳabod* by the decision of the translators of the Septuagint. But this is not so either. As von Rad has rightly pointed out, "the glory of Yahweh" is simply a "technical term in OT theology."[74] Indeed in Rom. 3:23 the technical character of the term is very apparent.

This verse, as we have said, requires an understanding of "the glory of God" as synonymous with "the justice of God." Let us use this as a working hypothesis and see if it is confirmed. If it fits, the meaning of the glory of God will be one more corroboration of the meaning of the justice of God to which we have come from various directions.

Provisionally, the synonymy is well attested to:

Justice will go before you,
and the glory of Yahweh behind you.

(Isa. 58:8b)

The peoples will see your justice,
and all the kings your glory.

(Isa. 62:2a)

The heavens proclaim his justice,
and all the peoples see his glory.

(Ps. 97:6)

Wrap around you the cloak of the justice that comes from God,
put on your head the diadem of the glory of the Eternal.

(Bar. 5:2)

Your name will be "Peace of justice and glory of piety."

(Bar. 5:4)

They give glory and justice to the Lord.

(Bar. 2:17 and 2:18)

They will be called the plants of justice,
the planting of the Lord for glory.

(Isa. 61:3b [LXX])

To praise God for his justice,
the Most High for his glory.

(1 QS 11:15)

The standards in 1 QM 4:6 are these: "Goodness of God, justice of God, glory of God, *mišpaṭ* of God."

Salvation is near those who fear him,
so that *glory* will dwell on our earth.
Compassion and goodness meet,
justice and peace embrace.
Goodness blossoms forth from the earth,

and justice looks down from heaven.
Yahweh will bestow well-being on us,
and our earth will bear its fruit.
Justice will go before him,
and peace following his footsteps.

(Ps. 85:10-14)

In this passage the fact that Yahweh's glory dwells on our earth is a reality which, taken as a whole, is described as compassion, goodness, peace, and above all justice (three times). It is impossible to deny that this correlates perfectly with what Rom. 3:23 tell us. This is so, first, because both passages speak of the glory of God as a concrete, comprehensive reality, which comes to dwell *on our earth*. And second, this glory consists in justice, goodness, compassion, and peace. Thus we can understand very well why, according to Paul, both the Jews and the Gentiles "need the glory of God," why they urgently require the coming of the glory of God. And in fact, in accord with the passages cited above, the peoples will be able to see this glory, the kings will be able to witness it. It is something collective, social, notably supraindividual; it is certainly not an attribute or property in the essence of God.

By the characteristics which describe it, one begins to suspect that the glory of Yahweh is the same collective reality, like a new epoch or a new reign of justice, which other biblical passages call "the kingdom of God."

Ps. 96:4-5 develops the same idea as Ps. 82 regarding the superiority of Yahweh with respect to other gods.[75] And the last verse gives us the same reason for this superiority as the last verse of Ps. 82: because Yahweh is he who judges the world with justice. But it is important to note that Ps. 96 is dedicated to "singing the glory of Yahweh among the nations" (v. 3); the glory of Yahweh is the central theme (vv. 3, 7, 8). The superiority of Yahweh's justice provides the foundation for asserting the glory of Yahweh; this glory therefore seems to consist in Yahweh's manifesting his justice (in the sense of Ps. 82: to save the poor and the weak from the hands of the unjust).

Ps. 57 is the outcry of an oppressed person (vv. 1, 4, 5), who in order to be saved (v. 4) appeals to Yahweh's commiseration (v. 2), to his compassion and goodness (vv. 4, 11). But it is striking that the manifestation of Yahweh's glory is the refrain which structures the Psalm (vv. 6, 12), and it is understood that this manifestation of Yahweh will consist in the compassionate intervention which saves the oppressed. Methodologically it is noteworthy that the glory of God constitutes the common denominator of this Psalm and Ps. 96, without there being any mention at all of Yahweh the Judge in Ps. 57. Thus to do justice to the oppressed is directly related with the glory of God.

Ps. 138, compressed into eight verses, seems to identify the glory of Yahweh (v. 5) with his "compassion and goodness" (v. 2) and with the fact that Yahweh saves man from misfortune (v. 7). The same can be seen in Ps. 63 (cf. v. 3), as well as in Ps. 62 (cf. v. 6) and Isa. 35:1-7 (note the end of v. 2, which is quite expressive).

We have already seen the synonymic parallelism of Ps. 97: "The heavens proclaim his justice, and all the peoples see his glory" (v. 6). But note that as in Pss. 82 and 96, in Ps. 97:6-9 the superiority of Yahweh over the other gods seems to consist in the justice of v. 6. This is all the more apparent when we consider that v. 10 completes the idea by affirming that Yahweh "delivers from the hand of the unjust" and v. 2 provides unity to the Psalm by saying, "Justice and right are the base of his throne" (with the hendiadys *s^edakah umišpat*). This Psalm attests, then, to the same conception of the glory of God as Ps. 96. But what is striking is that Ps. 97 is a poem dedicated to Yahweh the King (v. 1). This confirms our suspicion that the glory of God, as a comprehensive reality which establishes itself on our earth, is exactly the same as the kingdom of Yahweh.

On the level of form, Ps. 24:8-10, with its insistent "king of glory" (four times), shows that both these themes are closely related. On the level of content, the gates, which according to v. 9 must open to let the king of glory come in, signify the entrance to the kingdom to which only the just described in vv. 3-4 will have access.[76] The message of the Psalm is essentialistic, which is our concern here. As Dhorme and Weiser note, the gates of v. 9 must be related to the "gates of justice" of Ps. 118:19-20: "For this is the gate of Yahweh; through it enter the just." The cultic procession in which all this materialized should not prevent us from understanding the idea of a kingdom of justice, whose this-worldliness is clear in Ps. 118:17-18; 24:1; this justice too is called the glory of Yahweh. All otherworldly interpretations are invalidated when we see that "the glory dwells on our earth" (Ps. 85:10), that "his glory fills the whole earth" (Ps. 72:19). I repeat, Pss. 24 and 118 are important because of the essential relationships which they reveal, even though the projection toward an epoch or age at the end of history may not seem certain or explicit. The title "king of glory" implies that glory is a kingdom whose king is Yahweh.

Ps. 145 is dedicated to singing the glory of Yahweh (vv. 5, 11, 12), but a careful reading shows that this glory consists in Yahweh's being just and compassionate (v. 17), in his destroying the unjust (v. 20) and saving the humble (v. 14). As we have seen the *mišpaṭ* and the kingdom of Yahweh also consist in this. Thus a Psalm dedicated to singing the glory of Yahweh "proclaims his justice" (v. 7), proclaims his goodness, mercy, and compassion (vv. 7-9). But what is most striking is that formally and expressly the Psalm is devoted from its initial dedication to Yahweh as king: "I will exalt you, God my king" (v. 1). Thus the identification between the glory and the kingdom of God is clearer than ever. And with the splendid formulation "Your kingdom is a kingdom from age to age" (v. 13) we find "the glory of your kingdom" (v. 11); this phrase is comparable to "king of glory," which we saw in Ps. 24:8-10.

The messianic intention of Ps. 72 is debated.[77] However, v. 5 asserts that the king or the kingdom or the justice described will last "like the sun, and like the moon from generation to generation"; thus it should not be doubted that the Psalm refers to the definitive reign of God (through the Messiah) on earth. Although Oesterly's idea, which reduces the Psalm to a description of a reign "ideal for all times," seems to me to be unsupportable, even in this minimalistic thesis it is recognized that Ps. 72 indicates the essential relationships, the qualitative content, without which a kingdom cannot be the kingdom of God. And, indeed, the Psalm says that the king will "do justice to the poor of the people, and save the children of the needy, and crush their oppressors" (v. 4; cf. v. 2). Vv. 12-14 say the same. This kingdom is the realization of justice (vv. 1, 2, 3, 7) and of peace (vv. 3, 7). But what is most significant is that this entire description is directed toward the last verse (19); thus when it says "that his [Yahweh's] glory fills the whole earth" this glory consists in all that has gone before.

The working hypothesis which Rom. 3:23 forces us to formulate— namely, that the glory of God is the justice of God as a comprehensive reality which fills the whole earth—is confirmed most abundantly, then, by the Old Testament. It is the very same kingdom of God in which goodness, compassion, right, and justice reign, a kingdom from which all the unjust are eliminated. In chapter 2 we saw that for the Priestly text (as well as for the Yahwist) the intervention by which Yahweh delivered the Israelites from Egyptian slavery eminently signified justice and compassion; it is therefore quite understandable that this same text should regard the glory of Yahweh as condensed in the cloud which protected them from the sun during the day as they crossed the desert and in the cloud of fire which illuminated their way at night (cf. Exod. 40:34-38; 13:21-22; 14:19-24). It even happens that, prescinding from these initial instances, the cloud in which Yahweh's glory is incarnated or materialized appears when they are about to be miraculously saved from dying of thirst (Num. 20:6; cf. vv. 7-11) or of hunger (Exod. 16:10; cf. vv. 11-16). The meaning is the same as in the other Old Testament passages which we have considered: "They have seen my glory and my signs, what I did in Egypt and in the desert" [*tēn doxan mou kai ta sēmeia*] (Num. 14:22).

The meaning is also the same in John: "This beginning of signs Jesus did in Cana of Galilee. He manifested his glory, and his disciples believed in him" (John 2:11). And after narrating the whole series of "signs" (*sēmeia*), he refers to the Jewish people when he says at the end, "Although he had done such great signs before them they did not believe in him" (John 12:37). And he adds that thus was fulfilled the obstinacy foreseen by Isaiah: "He has closed their eyes and hardened their hearts," etc. (v. 41). But "Isaiah said these things when he saw his glory" (v. 41). This tradition regarding the concrete meaning of "glory" powerfully confirms the meaning that we have already seen for "works" and "signs" and "judgment" in John; it also confirms that the obstinacy and failure to believe are rooted in the fact that the Jews did not grasp the qualitative identification of Jesus' works as characteristic of Yahweh: unmistakable works of justice, compassion, and goodness.[78] It is in these that the glory of God consists, according to all the Old Testament passages which we have seen.

John 12:37-43 closes a great compositional arc that had begun not in John 2:11 but rather at the end of the prologue: "And we saw his glory, the glory that is his as the only Son of the Father, a glory full of compassion and goodness" (John 1:14). This glory, characterized by compassion and goodness, correlates perfectly with the entire Old Testament tradition which we have just considered. Many exegetes have already seen in the Greek pair *charis kai alētheia* of John 1:14 an attempt (like the "goodness and philanthropy" of Titus 3:4) to translate the famous Hebrew pair *ḥesed w'ᵉmeth*.[79]

It was difficult to translate this Hebrew hendiadys into Greek, just as it is difficult today to translate it into any of our languages.[80] But 2 Sam. 2:6; Gen. 24:49; 19:19; 39:21; 47:29; and Josh. 2:12 are enough to demonstrate that the term refers to interhuman relationships and that the expression of Titus 3:4 is the closest to the original meaning. See also Prov. 3:3; 14:22; 16:6; 20:28. It is in synonymic parallelism with the hendiadys *mišpaṭ uṣᵉdaḳah* in Ps. 89:15; Ps. 40:11 Isa. 16:5; Zech. 7:9 (cf. Hos. 2:21-22).[81] And according to Exod. 34:6 it is the *ḥesed wᵉᵉmeth* of Yahweh that Moses sees in fulfillment of the promise made to him in Exod. 33:22, namely, that he would see that glory of God pass by. And Ps. 85, after saying "so that glory might dwell on our earth" (v. 10), adds "compassion and goodness [*ḥesed wᵉᵉmeth* meet; justice and peace embrace" (v. 11).[82] Likewise in Ps. 57:11-12 the glory of Yahweh is synonymous with *ḥesed wᵉᵉmeth*.[83] And this pair had already appeared in v. 4 before the refrain of v. 6 (on the glory of Yahweh), with which the Psalm also concludes in v. 12. Therefore when John 1:14 says that the glory of the Son was full of compassion and goodness he is only continuing this same tradition in applying it to the Son. This is the same meaning of glory which according to the Old Testament was proper to the Father. Therefore John insists, "the glory that is his as the only Son of the Father."

When John repeats the idea of 1:14 in 1:17 ("The law was given through Moses; compassion and goodness came to be through Jesus Christ"), he adds incisively, "No one has ever seen God; it is the only Son, who is nearest to the Father's heart, who has made him known" (v. 18). This confirms the meaning of love-of-neighbor which John wants to express by *charis kai alētheia,* for whenever he repeats his decisive thesis that God is not seen (1 John 4:12; 1 John 4:20; 3 John 11), it is to speak of love of neighbor.[84] This is of interest to us in the present context, because in John 1:14 this expression gives us the qualitative meaning of glory (whether the adjective *plērēs* 'full' refers to "glory" or "son").

The sense of the glory of God as goodness toward men is also clear in the *corpus Paulinum.* In the following passages the key is the word "richness":

The richness of his goodness.

(Rom. 2:4)

The richness of his glory on the recipients of his compassion.

(Rom. 9:23)

The richness of his grace in goodness.

(Eph. 2:7)

According to the richness of his glory.

(Eph. 3:16)

The richness of his grace (or goodness).

(Eph. 1:7)

The richness of the glory of his inheritance

(Eph. 1:18)

The richness of the glory of this mystery.

(Col. 1:27)

My God will fulfill all your needs according to his richness in glory in Christ Jesus.

(Phil 4:19)

The almost exclusive use of the word "richness" to say either "richness in glory" or "richness in goodness" is striking; glory and goodness seem to be interchangeable. This is all the more apparent when we see that in Eph. 3:16 and Phil 4:19 the context would indicate that there should be an appeal to God's goodness instead of God's glory; the passage deals with God's granting certain benefits according to the richness of his goodness, as we would say. But the author can say just as well, "according to the richness of his glory." This is all very good, but we must also bear in mind that Rom. 3:23 and the entire Old Testament oblige us to conceive of the glory of God as a comprehensive, supraindividual reality which comes into human history and establishes itself there, constituting in it a new age, a universal reign of goodness and justice.[85]

Otherwise we cannot understand Rom. 6:4: "so that just as Christ was raised from the dead through [*dia*] the Father's glory, so we too may walk in the newness of life." When Paul mentions some instrument (*dia*) of the action by which the Father raises Christ or will raise us, he mentions the force or power of God (*dynamis*: 2 Cor. 13:4; 1 Cor. 6:14; Phil. 3:10; Rom. 1:4; Eph. 1:19). He would have had no reason to mention glory as an instrument in Rom 6:4 if there were not some deliberate intention. The reason is that the resurrection of Christ makes manifest the fact that the glory of the Father has at last arrived on earth. As is apparent from the Old Testament texts we have considered, this glory consists in a life of justice and goodness and compassion and love of neighbor, which for the world is completely new.[86] In this verse there is a convergence of the biblical concept of "life" with the concept of the "glory of God," which we have just delineated. The concept of "life" also converges here with Paul's notion that the unequivocal sign that the kingdom has come is the resurrection of Jesus.[87]

As Althaus rightly perceived with regard to Rom. 6:4, "The end of the verse is surprising. The first thing one would expect is that Paul would continue, 'As Christ was raised up, so too we will be raised up for a new life,' or, 'So too we will be raised up (on the last day).' "[88] And in fact when Paul uses the resurrection of Christ as the first part of a comparison, the second part is generally our resurrection (2 Cor. 4:14; 1 Cor. 6:14; Rom. 8:11). On the other hand, as Michel also perceived with regard to Rom. 6:4, "the thought is diverted from its logical consequence, namely, that like Christ man will be raised up."[89] Likewise Lyonnet says, "What would be expected now is 'We will be raised up.' "[90] By no means is it sufficient to say that this is a "moral application," as Lyonnet so facilely resolves the problem,[91] except in the sense that the total moral revolution of mankind is the center and the only theme of the Letter to the Romans. Newness of life is the theme of Rom. 8, a chapter which no one would characterize as a simple moral application. Here we are at the very nucleus of the dialectics of the Gospel, of the dialectics of the faith. But before getting into this let us go back to Rom. 5:2, which obliged us to make this long but indispensable clarification of the biblical meaning of "the glory of God."[92]

The surprising thing about Rom. 6:4 is that it anticipates for the present the newness of life which our Western theology would preserve for that tranquil day on which the resurrection of the dead might arrive. In a similar way, Rom. 5:5 bases the infallibility of hope on the present and contemporary fact of love of neighbor. Since it speaks of the "hope of the glory of God" mentioned in Rom. 5:2, the meaning of "glory of God" described in the Old and New Testaments requires that the "love" of 5:5 must be understood as love of neighbor. But, independently of and beyond this, the problem which exegesis has for the most part been avoiding is that glory on the one hand seems to be future (Rom. 5:2; 1 Cor. 15:43; Rom. 8:17, 18, 21, etc.), and on the other it is clear that it has already arrived (Rom. 6:4; 8:30). Regarding Rom. 8:30, Michel says, "We are struck by the aorist *edoxasen* instead of a future *doxasei*, which properly was to be expected."[93] The solutions which generally are proposed are tantamount to asserting that Paul regards glory "as if" it were already present. But by the same token we could hold that in the other passages he regards it "as if" it were future. And then exegesis is not to be taken seriously, for it arrogates to itself the right to decide when Paul is speaking seriously and when he is being "carried away."

The matter is too important to be dismissed with a stroke of the pen, saying that "for Paul it is legitimate to be so sure of the last act, glorification, that he can speak of it in the manner of something which has already happened, in the past tense."[94] Justice is also present on the one hand (e.g., Rom. 5:1, 9, 17; 8:10, 30; 9:30; 1 Cor. 6:11) and future on the other (Rom. 2:13; 5:19; Gal. 5:5). So too "life" is future (Rom. 1:17; 2:7; 5:17-18; 8:13; Gal. 6:8) and present (Rom. 6:4, 11, 13; 8:10). Likewise salvation is future (Rom. 5:9, 10; 10:9, 13; 11:26; Phil. 1:19) and present (1 Cor. 1:18; 2 Cor. 2:15; Eph. 2:5, 8; Titus 3:5; Rom. 11:11; cf. 2 Cor. 6:2; Phil. 2:12; 1 Thess. 5:8). Also sonship is future (Rom. 8:23) and present (Rom. 8:15; Gal. 4:5, 6). When we find this same apparent bipolarity in "glory," we cannot resolve the problem with recourse to some emotional Pauline anticipation of glory, as if this were not a question which invests the whole message of Paul. Attributing the cause of this bipolarity to emotionalism or to mythology does not resolve anything for an exegesis which wants to take Paul seriously.

As we saw in the previous section, Pauline faith and the faith of the whole New Testament consist in believing that the definitive kingdom of justice and life has arrived. From Rom. 6:4 we can say that for Paul the resurrection is just as much *eschaton*, just as much *ultimum*, as is the new life of justice that all of human history has been awaiting. Therefore, when he sees that Jesus Christ has risen, he sees that glory has arrived, the same glory which consists in our "walking in the newness of life." The exegetes' surprise at Rom. 6:4 depends as much on their prescinding from the qualitative and terrestrial meaning of the "glory of God" according to the Bible as it does on their not taking seriously the total presentness of the Pauline *eschaton*. Let us consider this *eschaton* in relationship with justice, for the texts referring to the latter term offer greater basis for an evaluation. The apparent antithesis between present and future is no less strident with regard to justice than it is with regard to life or glory or sonship or salvation.

God's justice which was made known through the law and the prophets has now been revealed without the law.

(Rom. 3:21)

For by the spirit which stems from faith we are in expectation of the justice which we hope for [or of the hope of justice].

(Gal. 5:5)

Heinrich Schlier tries to understand this bipolarity by saying that the latter verse reveals "a characteristic of the internal structure of justice or justification."[95] He explains this characteristic by adding that the hope of justice "is always also a justice ... which still awaits within itself its realization."[96] Heidegger's existential categories, which Bultmann and after him many others have used to interpret Paul, have precisely the disadvantage of being nontemporal although they deal with time. In them the future is no longer future and becomes futureness as an "internal structure" of the present, as a "human possibility" constitutive of the present.[97] And in the same way the present becomes nontemporal presentness, indifferently repeatable in every moment of history and in every human generation.

Whether the Pauline *eschaton* is called "present" with these categories, or whether it is called "future," in either case it loses its unrepeatableness and is detemporalized; it is really taken out of time. Such a disconnection from physical time permits Bultmann to take the Pauline *eschaton* either as present[98] or future.[99] His reason for this is genuinely biblical: that Christ's "now" be ours, because if it is not, then it does not concern me. The only truly real time is my "now." The others are not real times for me, but rather conceptual times. I can very well, through a supposed faith and through a *sacrificium intellectus,* "affirm" of them whatever I like, and still remain unaffected. This is a spectator's faith which leaves me undaunted and which is, therefore, false. As Käsemann says, in authentic faith "it is not a question of affirming salvation but of encountering it."[100] This encounter is the unrenounceable objective of Paul and John. It responds to Kierkegaard's problem concerning simultaneity. And the anti-Bultmannian opposition would do well to grasp first that this is something without which Christian faith is not biblical faith but rather Greek faith.

To grasp our "now" with all the implacability with which Paul grasped his, we are afforded valuable help by the existential categories ("existential" is to "existentiel" something like "ontological" is to "ontic"). These separate presentness and futureness from physical history and make them "possibilities" of every moment of history.

But we need only think of such a detemporalization applied to the historical event of the crucifixion and resurrection of Christ to see that it is irreconcilable with the mind of Paul. The present of which Paul speaks ("but now without the law the justice of God has been made known . . . ," in Rom. 3:21) is not mere presentness, but rather the authentic historical present. "When the fulness of time arrived, God sent his Son . . . " (Gal. 4:4) is an expression which takes history very seriously and the moment of Christ as an unrepeatable "now." When Bultmann, following Barth on the resurrection of the dead, makes the *eschaton* always in the future, he is saying, against the intention of Paul and Christ and the whole Bible, that history really does not have an *ultimum.* An *eschaton* which is always future really is not an *eschaton,* even existentially speaking. History does not come *to completion.* If the future and the present are transformed into "internal structures," into mere existential categories of futureness and presentness, then we again have the eternal return of all things, in spite of the sincerity of the effort to take seriously the difference between the biblical approach and the Greek.

Neither Heidegger nor Bultmann is able to free himself from Aristotle, although Bultmann walks much further along the path of liberation than all the Western Christian schools of thought. The eternal return of all things is inseparable from categories. No matter how existentially these are conceived, they are just as eternal and nontemporal as the Platonic ones, repeatable in an indefinite number of cases and applications; there is nothing new under the sun; everything was already contained in essences. To keep the *eschaton* perpetually in the future was the obstinate recourse of this world in its rejection of Jesus Christ. "The view of Oscar A. H. Schmitz seems to me to be quite correct, . . . that the 'Pharisee takes upon himself the task of preventing anything, even the Messiah, from becoming real.' "[101] The decisive point is not *what* but *that.* And nevertheless the shackles in which the wisdom of this world holds us have caused Bultmann himself to change the "that" into a "what." This shows quite clearly the insulating power that Western culture exercises, a power decidedly greater than the good will of individuals. Only authentic biblical faith can free us: believing that with Christ the kingdom has come.

What happened to the existential categories is, as Bloch very rightly points out, what happened to Bergson's life philosophy:

Because of it there arose the rigidity (only this time of a different kind) of a surprise which is always the same, . . . so that the dawn, the *incipit vita nova,* in the so-called life philosophy remains a *fixum.* And the concept of the new turns out to be in Bergson nothing more than the abstract contrast of repetition, at times the simple reverse of mechanical uniformity. At the same time the new was attributed to every moment of life without exception and was therefore invalidated.[102]

In Paul, as in the entire New Testament, the *eschaton* is physically and existentially the *ultimum* of history, something really new and definitive: "The time has been fulfilled and the kingdom of God has arrived. Be converted and believe in the good news" (Mark 1:15).

In rejecting the solution provided by existential categories, we have certainly not made the interpretation any easier. We are still faced with the contrast between the present justice of Rom. 3:21 and the expectation of justice in Gal. 5:5.[103] And it is quite clear that in both cases Paul refers to the *eschaton,* a one and only *ultimum.* The Pauline parallel of Mark 1:15 is Gal. 4:4 ("When the fulness of time arrived God sent his Son . . . "), and here it is clear that for Paul the *ultimum* of history is already present. The justice of Rom. 3:21 and of the many passages which proclaim justice as present is the *eschaton.* By no means can it be asserted that only the passages referring to the future speak of the *eschaton.* On the contrary, the contrast which we are considering between present justice and future justice (as between life in the present and life in the future, glory in the present and glory in the future, etc.) can be seen as the sharp and piercing message it is only when we see that both series speak of one and the same *ultimum* of history. Kertelge's solution gives every impression of being subjectivistic: "The eschatological character of the Pauline concept of justification consists in faith's feeling [or experiencing or living, *erfahren*] justification as the eschatological action of God."[104] It seems as if one could individualistically and subjectively "by faith" leave the old eon. On the contrary, according to Paul the death and resurrection of Christ are really the *eschaton.* Because of this fact faith is born, and not vice versa.

And nevertheless it is true that according to Paul eschatological justice arrives and is achieved in the world by means (*dia*) of faith and causatively stems from (*ek*) faith,[105] provided we do not take this idea in some imaginary or subjective sense. The reason that Rom. 1:16-17 gives (*gar*) for the Gospel's being "the power of God for the salvation of every believer" is that in the Gospel "the justice of God is revealed from faith to faith." This "power" or "force" (*dynamis*) of God to save the world consists in the revelation of the justice of God by means of the proclaiming word which works stemming from faith and causing faith in others (*ek pisteōs eis pistin*). The spirit of God, understood as a qualitative and real characterization, as the spirit of justice,[106] is according to Gal. 5:5 conveyed by faith: "By the spirit which stems from faith [*pneumati ek pisteōs*] we are in expectation of the hope of justice."

The possession of this spirit which has been produced in us by faith is what makes us have certain hope that justice is coming. And the following verse explains why: "Because [*gar*] of faith which works through love." This is the same reason that Rom. 5:5 gave us to explain why hope does not deceive.[107] It has been an error to explain these expressions psychologically and individualistically. It is the working of love in the world which makes us have certain hope for the achievement of justice on earth. Evangelizing is really efficacious by virtue of the faith which it arouses. The *proclamation* that the kingdom *is arriving* has to *make* the kingdom *arrive*. Therefore Paul believes that the multitudinous instances of the justice of the Gentiles, produced by Paul's evangelization, will make the Jews "envious" (Rom. 11:14).

Involved here is the whole apparent antinomy between objective redemption and subjective redemption, between present *eschaton* and future *eschaton*, between "indicative" and "imperative." There is no more penetrating imperative than the indicative "the kingdom has arrived" (Mark 1:15; Matt. 12:28; Luke 11:20), which was clearly uttered by Jesus of Nazareth. When one is convinced that the moment of justice has arrived for the whole earth, this conviction (which is New Testament faith-hope) causes the *eschaton* effectively and really to come. They were perfectly right in accusing Jesus of subversion (cf. Luke 23:2). Likewise in 1 Cor. 2:6 Paul speaks of "the rulers of this age who are going to disappear." And in Rom. 4:13-15 he alludes to an imminent world in which there will no longer be any laws because the just will take possession of the earth (the law belongs—v. 15—to the wrath described in Rom. 1:18-3:20; it is a factor in this wrath, an effective cog of its gears). And in 1 Cor. 6:1-6 he reproaches the Christians for not having understood that the new humanity no longer has any need for courts.[108]

It is true that until the end of his life Paul was even expecting that the parousia might occur at any moment (cf. 1 Thess. 1:9-10; 4:13-17; 5:1-2; Phil. 4:5; 1 Cor. 7:29-31; Rom. 13:11b). And thus we can explain certain precepts which moral theology has commited the error of detemporalizing (e.g., 1 Cor. 7:17-24, 26, 29-35; 11:3-16; 14:34-35; Rom. 13:1-7), erecting them into an eternal norm, as if they implied an absolute hierarchy of values. But this proximate expectation of the parousia does not explain why justice and life and glory and salvation and sonship were for Paul, precisely because they were constitutive of the *eschaton*, both present and future.[109]

For John as well judgment is both present and future,[110] and John does not await the parousia as imminent. And also for Matthew the resurrection of the dead is both present (cf. 27:52-53) and future, and Matthew does not have a proximate expectation of the parousia.[111] Scientifically the explanation must be valid for the three authors, since for all three the *eschaton* is both present and future. In particular it should be noted that in John and Matthew the certainty of a future parousia does not in the least prevent the *eschaton* from being unequivocally and physically present (cf. Matt. 12:28; John 5:24; 12:31; etc.). It is not that the imminent proximity makes the *eschaton* seem to feel present. Bultmann himself recognizes that in Matt. 11:5-6 and Luke 7:22b-23 the "that" is there.[112]

It is faith, enkindled by the proclamation called Gospel, which makes the *eschaton* arrive, not in fantasy but in reality. The evangelizers summon; what they require is the now-achievement of what Christ came to achieve. And to be sure this is done by identifying our "now" with that of the historical Christ, not through a detemporalizing prestidigitation of concepts or of the imagination, but rather through the most acute sense of real history that can be conceived: Christ came to achieve justice, the hour awaited by all mankind has tolled. The subversion is limitless. The more realistic our sense of history is, the more the message is directed to us: All human history has been awaiting this moment. *Idou nyn hēmera sōtērias* 'Now is the propitious moment; now is the day of salvation' (2 Cor. 6:2). In the Letter to the Romans alone we see this "now" twenty times (Rom. 3:21, 26; 5:9, 11; 6:19, 21, 22; 7:6, 17; 8:1, 18, 22; 11:5, 31a, 31b; 13:11; 15:23, 25; 16:26). The word *euangelion* ("the great news") makes absolutely no sense if we are not yearning, with all the hope of mankind, for the definitive liberation, the total realization of justice. Only with this expectation of one who *does indeed believe* that there is hope for our world[113] is there great news in the fact that Christ "destroyed in his flesh the law of the commandments and decrees" (Eph. 2:15). The evangelizing word is creative only if it is eschatological, that is, only if it makes us *believe* that the *eschaton* has arrived. Only then are the death and the resurrection of Christ really, not imaginarily, present to us. This is eternal life, which at last has begun. The only hard-heartedness (*pōrōsis tēs kardias*), the true blindness-before-reality, is antimessianism.

The ontological affirmation of metaphysics (whether or not a "transcendental" prologue precedes metaphysics is not important) indicates something so different from the "that," that I openly refuse to designate this "that" as "being," that is, I refuse to describe the difference by saying, as the Heideggerians do, that we have changed the concept of being and discovered another being. Even the transcendentalists (Maréchal, Rahner, Lotze, Marc, Coreth, and even Lonergan) grasp the "that" as quiddity, as a being-in-general which is really not a "that." Both the Greeks and the Scholastics have their faithful culmination in illuminism, in Lessing, Spinoza, Descartes, and Leibniz: the necessariness of concepts and essences. No "that" ever stems from this outlook, nor will it ever be possible to know a "that" with quiddities. The very fact that they say that existing is in the essence of God is a clear sign that they do not understand the "that," for they consider it as reducible to essence or quiddity. They allege that we know only through propositions, that Christ himself comes to us converted into language. Thus they show that they grasp neither the "that" nor speech. They overlook precisely the one central point of language: the fact that I am speaking to you.

The translation of the "that" in language is not in any word or combination of words, but rather in the fact of language, in the enjoinder. Bultmann very rightly points out, "*What* he says, [Christ] does not say as something new, as something not heard before. But *that* he says it, that he is saying it *now,* is the decisive event."[114] And Friedrich says, "*Dabar* can mean 'thing,' 'history,' 'event,' as well as 'word.' "[115] On the contrary, however, *logos,* the word of the Greeks, "is anything but an address or a powerful creative word."[116] Moreover with the Greek word, "one must prescind from its injunctive character: He who hears the words of the philosopher should assent not to him but to the *logos*." "What constitutes the Greek word is its content, not the fact of being uttered."[117] The etymology of the Greek word is "to gather," "to glean," and figuratively "to count," "to explain."[118] He who perceives the *logos* does not encounter a demand stemming from the situation. The Greek man does not need to hear; he wants "to see."

Greek knowing is achieved in a regarding that keeps its distance. It is "objective" to the extent that the participation of the knower in the known is reduced to "seeing." The result must be that the known should be "obvious" (*dēlon*), "manifest" (*phaneron*). Both *eidōs* and *idea* have a visual origin, and for Greek understanding the *eidōs* is the real element of things. What is real is conceived as eternal and untemporal, that which in the midst of all alterations is always there and is seen by the *omma psychēs* (eye of the mind). The knower really "has" it; he "disposes" of it.[119] On the contrary, biblical understanding is far from thinking that the reality of the known is better grasped when the interpersonal relationship between the knower and the object are eliminated and that the knowing must be reduced to regarding from a distance; rather, for the Bible not-knowing is sin, not simply error, and knowing is achieved only when the meaning and demand of the known is grasped and has effect.[120]

The biblical communication of understanding, the word, evangelizing, does not proclaim eternal and general truths, but rather a historic fact. But it does not do this in such a way that the word becomes dispensable when it has transmitted the news and the information concerning the fact to the hearer, as if the function of the word were merely one of transmission and mediation. The word itself pertains to the fact.

> Therefore it is itself revelation and it brings death and life to the world, because the decision for death or for life is made when it is heard (2 Cor. 2:14-16; 4:1-6). It is addressed, not to the curiosity or "interest" of the hearers, but to their conscience (2 Cor. 4:2; 5:11).[121]

But existentialism itself, although superior to metaphysics for having grasped the "that," is insufficient if it does not realize that the only decisive "that" is the *eschaton*. Social conservatives do not realize the exceedingly deep level of systematization and organicity with regard to world view in which the West has them enclosed. The categorial repeatability of the eschatological dimension reduces the faith to "phenomenological experiences." "And all this is in the last analysis rotten subjectivism," as Bloch says of Heidegger.[122] If I refuse to describe the difference between the "that" and being as the appearance of a new concept of being, it is not because in such a description the Heidegggerians are not correct with regard to the metaphysicians. They are correct, very, very correct. Rather it is because the difference is much greater than they indicate. The generative nucleus of all solipsism, the true ironclad refuge of the "I," consists in keeping the *eschaton* perpetually in the future. There is no authentic, enjoining otherness if the moment of justice for the entire world has not arrived. Only this unrepeatable and uncategorizable fact constitutes an "other." Only this can deliver us from the chains in which "this world"[123] has us captive. "This is the victory which has overcome the world: our faith. Who overcomes the world but he who believes that Jesus is the son of God" (1 John 5:4-5)?[124] The true immorality is antimessianism, and there is nothing that the West fears so much as our being convinced that the kingdom of God has come. To the extent that we should realize that Jesus is the Messiah the kingdom of God would be achieved. The "outcry" of the oppressed would cease forever, that "outcry" which caused Yahweh to intervene in our history.

"To overcome the world" in 1 John does not mean only, as it is generally interpreted, not to be overcome by the world, as if the term referred to ascetical contests in the spiritual inwardness of subjectivism and as if what were at stake were of merely individual importance. In this subjectivization of the Gospel, which serves to rationalize and justify twenty centuries of real antimessianism, calling it Christianity, there fraternally coincide the "experiences" of the existentialists and the "spiritual lives" of the rankest metaphysical conservatism. What else does this enslaving world want than for us to replace faith with the Stoic nihilism of despair, which the existentialists teach as a heroic position in the face of nothingness, or to project on "another world" or on "the land of our hearts" the subversive biblical hope which says that the just "will reign on earth" (Rev. 5:10)! Heidegger is involuntarily—but with great effectiveness—the great ideologue of the bourgeoisie and the establishment. That he should dominate Rahner, disconnected as Rahner stands from the Bible, is not at all surprising. But that in the last analysis he has been able to bridle the efforts of Bultmann to escape the "wisdom of this world" constitutes an unsurpassable demonstration of how the enslavement in which the world holds us reaches its greatest effectiveness when it makes this slavery not even able to see that it is slavery.

The decisive step in human liberation was taken by the biblical authors when they intuited that evil consisted in an organic and cohesive totality, that sin had a unity, that it was structured into civilization and therefore had gained control of the very essence of the law. Only in future centuries will we be able to evaluate the meaning for man's history of understanding (Christ in person was the one who did it) that death and sin are united and the law with them. The best formulation of this is Rom. 5, but the four Gospels implacably insist on the same thing. It is the end of reformism when it is seen that the law was already inseparably yoked to sin. All reformism, even in the present day, even the "best intentioned," would have said that it was a question of improving the legislation, of making laws with a greater sense of justice and with more scientific understanding of reality. The world revolution is summed up in this sentence: "The law came so that sin would reach its apex" (Rom. 5:20), or in this: "Everything which does not stem from faith is sin" (Rom. 14:23).

Marx and Dialectics

Marx and Paul coincide in their intuition of the totality of evil: Sin and injustice form an all-comprehensive and all-pervasive organic structure. Paul calls this totality *kosmos.* Marx calls it "capitalism." But if Marxism does not recognize that capitalism is the consummation and the deepening of the oppression which was inherent to human civilization since biblical times, then it is denying dialectics and attributing the birth of capitalism to exterior causes, exactly as metaphysics and mechanistic materialism would do it. Mao Tse-Tung asks, "Why is it that the Chinese revolution can avoid a capitalist future and be directly linked with socialism without taking the old historical road of the Western countries, without passing through a period of bourgeois dictatorship?"[125] And he can ask this precisely because the structuralization of injustice into total civilization already existed before capitalism. And in the *Communist Manifesto* Marx himself asserts:

The modern bourgeois society that has sprouted from the ruins of feudal society has not done away with class antagonisms. It has but established new classes, new conditions of oppression, new forms of struggle in place of the old ones.[126]

In the same work, he argues in this way against the legitimists or promoters of "feudal socialism":

In pointing out that their mode of exploitation was different from that of the bourgeoisie, the feudalists forget that they exploited under circumstances and conditions that were quite different and that are now antiquated. In showing that, under their rule, the modern proletariat never existed, they forget that the modern bourgeoisie is the necessary offspring of their own society.[127]

Marx's thesis at the very beginning of the *Manifesto* is that the "civilizing" structuralization of oppression does not go back only to the medieval order: "The history of all hitherto existing society is the history of class struggles."[128] It is, then, pure mechanistic dogmatism, proper to a "conception of the world" and not to dialectical thought, to assert that before capitalism it was not possible to discover human society's totalitarian organicity in its oppression and that therefore the determinism of history itself afforded Marx the merit of such a discovery. The intention of this dogma is adialectically to absolutize the economic factor, but it inevitably runs up against the problem of the origin of the primitive accumulation of capital in a few hands, without which the capitalistic system as such could not have begun to exist. As Calvez very rightly points out, "Once capital is acquired, exploitation occurs in conformity with an established mechanism. But for the acquisition of the first capital it is necessary to establish the mechanism. In whose name is it established, unless by a personal will of power? And no matter how much this will finds support in the new productive forces it does not therefore cease to be a *choice* which was not determined.[129] The *possibility* of extorting the surplus value was given in the fact called trade, in the fact of the mercantile economy and in money, but from the possibility to the decision to take advantage of the possibility there is a great distance. The very words of Marx exclude the economic determinism of his adialectical followers:

In actual history it is notorious that conquest, enslavement, robbery, murder, briefly force, play the great part. In the tender annals of Political Economy, the idyllic reigns from time immemorial. Right and "labour" were from all time the sole means of enrichment, the present year of course always excepted. As a matter of fact, the methods of primitive accumulation are anything but idyllic.[130]

Whether or not this Marxist explanation is consistent with the reduction which Marx himself makes, sooner or later, of all alienations to economics, is quite another matter. But the primitive accumulation of capital, without which the capitalistic mechanism is not established in history, is attributed by Marx precisely to causes like those described by Paul in Rom. 1:28-31 and 3:10-17.[131]

One of Paul's central theses is that all these factors form an organic unity in which some things condition others in such a way that there is no escape from this iron circle without a total break with the *kosmos* or civilizing age which is made up of them.[132] Moreover, the dialectical character of this unified, supraindividual reality described by Paul is clear in Rom. 7, among other passages: The sin which has been structured as a supraindividual reality in history controls man and is stronger than he, although it initially entered history by the work of man (Rom. 5:12-21). Even more, it controls man in such a way that he is not released from personal blame and responsibility (Rom. 1:20, 32; 2:12-16; 3:5-8; etc.). The law, the functional and quintessential axis of this *kosmos,* had been originally invented for well-being and life (Rom. 7:10, 13), but it has inextricably become the crystallization point of this *kosmos* of evil. Even more, the very historical development of this totality causes evil to reach its apex (Rom. 7:8, 13; 5:20-21; Gal. 4:4-5) and inescapably demands the break with the whole past (Gal. 3:10a; 2:21b; 5:4; 4:9).

Anticommunism has fixed on the more or less real inconsistencies in Marx or Marxism, but it deceives itself when it says that because of scientific objectivity and a desire for logical consistency the West rejects Marxism. If this were the reason, the West would have had to reject itself long before Marx was born. The reason behind the Western anti-Marxist rejections is in reality all that in which Marx coincides with the Bible, not his systematic inconsistencies. In the first place there is the denunciation of the indissociable unitary character which evil has acquired. Structured into a total civilization,[133] it is able to "co-opt" for its own reinforcement even the best intentioned attempts and initiatives for justice, for these accept the rules of the game imposed by the system. Clear perception in this point is intolerable to the West. The West abhors few biblical passages as much as it does this: "No one tears a piece from a new cloak to put it on an old cloak; if he does, not only will he have torn the new one, but the piece taken from the new will not match the old" (Luke 5:36; Mark 2:21; Matt. 9:16). Compare this with Marx's reproach of Proudhon's reformism:

By changes in the material conditions of existence, this form of socialism by no means understands abolition of the bourgeois relations of production, an abolition that can be effected only by a revolution, but administrative reforms, based on the continued existence of these relations; reforms, therefore, that in no respect affect the relations between capital and labor, but, at the best, lessen the cost, and simplify the administrative work, of bourgeois government.[134]

The Jesuit Calvez very accurately paraphrases this idea in this way: Reintegration into the world of "having" is not a solution to social malaise. It is not a solution which brings with it the elimination of the proletarian condition, because it is precisely "having," taken as a manner of human existence, which engenders social alienation, the division of society into radically hostile classes, the proletariat.[135]

This clarity concerning the "co-optive," "reabsorbent" power which reformist initiatives exercise in the name of the prevailing system has been analyzed in recent times by no one better than Marcuse.[136] But this clarity is derived entirely from the intuition regarding the organic, all-pervasive total character which evil comes to acquire by being structured into civilization, precisely into a cosmos, as Paul calls it. Compare the Pauline description of "sin"[137] with the Jesuit Bigo's accurate comments on Marx:

For Marx capital is not only a combination of means or a combination of rights. It is a combination which takes on life in a certain way, gaining strength in a fantastic movement, putting thousands of men to work and pursuing with an implacable logic its ultimate objective, which is, not the satisfaction of human needs, but rather "the appropriation and capitalization of surplus value" (*Das Kapital*, VIII, 172). This is a reality totally penetrated by intentions and calculations, a reality which seems to be possessed by a substitute for the human soul and which, endowed with a prodigious dynamism, raises itself before real man to control him and submit him to its ends. It is a mythical being whose dramatic adventures Marx describes in the course of the ninety-eight chapters of his unfinished work.[138]

Bigo exaggerates a little here, as do those who speak of a personification of evil in Paul. Anyone who would today write the history of injustice in the world, or the history of mercilessness, etc., would have to establish that there is a supraindividual reality involved, a totality which controls men, whose constitutive elements condition and inter-relate with each other like the parts of an organism. More than one reader would get the impression of a mythological personification, but it is not so. It will be necessary to trace the same parallel between Paul and Freud with regard to "death."

What is clear is that the totality and organicity of injustice struc-tured into civilization was pointed out by Paul eighteen centuries before Marx, and, as we have just seen, those who think that the totality called capitalism grew up like a mushroom without roots or precedents in history betray Marx's dialectical thought. The indubitable fact that in the first century Paul denounced this civilizing totality of sin and enmity objectively obliges us to assert that the capitalism denounced by Marx is the consistent development of human civilization and oppression. It is the culture of injustice and of the crushing of men carried to extreme perfection and systematic refinement. It has such a capacity for reabsorption that it was able to co-opt and assimilate for its own advantage and reinforcement even the power of Christianity itself, dulling its edge through a reduction to the Greek world view. ·

Marx and the Bible coincide in this affirmation of incalculable impor-tance: Sin's achievement of an institutional systematization in a flaw-less civilizing structure is what was historically needed before mankind could change its epoch. This exacerbation of sin to an extreme, this *reductio peccati ad absurdum,* is, for both Paul and Marx, the total maturation of history, the breaking point which mankind needed to become aware of the infernal machinery which it has assembled and to be definitively delivered from it. Not every abstract moment is the moment; there is an *eschaton.* Calvez as well as Marcuse and Bloch have accurately insisted that the Marxian denial of abstract moral ideals does not in the least way imply determinism. Rather it implies a precise and free increase in consciousness brought about by the same historical facts as are carried to an extreme in this system. And this system itself produces the conscious men who will be its subverters.

But in both Marx and the Bible the possibility of this definitive liberation is absolutely the basis of all the thinking. The most revolu-tionary historical thesis, in which, in contrast with all Western ideol-ogies, the Bible and Marx coincide, is this: Sin and evil, which were later structured into an enslaving civilizing system, are not inherent to mankind and history; they began one day through a human work and can, therefore, be eliminated. The entire West has relegated this conviction to the archive of utopias. In Christian theology itself one can find apologies for private property established, as if on objective data, on an allegedly natural and essential tendency to "have," as if individualism and the desire for gain were essential attributes of human nature. This amounts to asserting that there is no hope for our world. In few things do we see as clearly as in this that Greek thought is the annihilation of faith and hope. There can be no news for the Greek mind, which thus shows itself to be inextirpably the ideology of the status quo. The argumentation claims to have deduced a "natural" law. Therefore it believes it is touching on "human nature" when it speaks of the propensity to "have." Various corrections clarify that this is "fallen nature," but then we cannot see how they can derive from this "fallen" nature the "natural" law of ownership and the "natural" necessity that the State should exist. Both for the Bible and for Marx selfishness and the State are precisely "fallen" facts, not natural ones.

Precisely for this reason we believe that man can cease being selfish and merciless and self-serving and can find his greatest fulness in loving his neighbor. We reject the imposition of an allegedly unchangeable nature, in virtue of which man will be a wolf to man as long as there is history. The acquisitive motivation which *Populorum progressio* (no. 26) rejects and denounces as the main support of the capitalist system can be eradicated. If the West calls Marx utopian, it must first give up its pretense and call the Gospel utopian. And let the forces be separated by drawing the line where it really is; let us not continue to defend the West under the pretext of the eternal values of Christian culture. The Gospel is war to the death against this motive of acquisition without which Western civilization collapses. There is nothing in strict exegesis which authorizes us to postpone its elimination to another world or another life. The ridiculing of hope which is made by qualifying it as "utopian" constitutes, in the first place, ignorance of reality and history and, in the second place, a mordic defense of the status quo, ideological in the strongest sense of the word.

The interpretation of the "new creation" in Gal. 6:15 and 2 Cor. 5:17 in terms of invisible ontology has been an error of incalculable consequences. The latter passage interprets itself in v. 21, where it says that the new creation consists in our becoming "the justice of God in

Christ." And as Schlier and Bultmann have very accurately pointed out, Gal. 6:15 is synonomous with Gal. 5:6:

Neither circumcision nor uncircumcision matter, but rather the new creation.

(Gal. 6:15)

Neither circumcision not uncircumcision matter, but rather faith which works through love.

(Gal. 5:6)[139]

Thus, just as 2 Cor. 5:17 and 21 describe the new creation as our being the justice of God present in the world, so Gal. 5:6 and 6:15 make it consist in the faith which is operative in the world through love. This is the love and the justice which mankind had not been able to achieve before Christ; therefore Paul is so conscious of the radical human transformation that the advent of justice implies. Not even in Marx do we find such a strong expression of this total transformation as that coined by Paul in the term "new creation." The faith which is effective through love cannot be interpreted in terms of invisible and undemonstrable ontology; and much less can it be asserted that Paul is referring to another world or another life. This is the new world that the whole history of mankind has been yearning for. "If anyone is in Christ he is a new creation; the old has passed away and the new has been made" (2 Cor. 5:17). Moreover, the aforementioned equivalence between Gal. 6:15 and Gal. 5:6 is explicit in Eph. 2:10, if we bear in mind that "good works" is a technical term:[140]

We are his handiwork, created in Christ Jesus for the good works that God prepared so that we might walk in them.

It is precisely because Paul believes in this new creation that he believes in a new world of justice in which there will be no laws (cf. Rom. 4:15 in the context of 4:13-22); and the greatest obstacle to the coming of this new world is to continue trusting in the law to achieve justice.[141] For this "new creation" clearly neither circumcision nor uncircumcision matters (Gal. 6:15); "the old has passed away and the new has begun" (2 Cor. 5:17). What matters is "the faith which works through love" (Gal. 5:6). With this we are the justice of God (2 Cor. 5:21) present in the world as an entirely new reality. Law and government are not only superfluous; they are an obstacle:

To be a Jew is not just to look like a Jew,
and circumcision is more than a physical operation.
The real Jew is the one who is inwardly a Jew,

and the real circumcision is in the heart—
something not of the letter
but of the spirit.

(Rom. 2:28-29)

The meaning of "circumcision of the heart" is the most radical transformation which makes man able to love the helpless spontaneously.[142] Thus Rom. 2:28-29 corroborates the meaning which the rejection of the circumcision of the flesh has in Gal. 5:6 and 2 Cor. 5:17, 21. Let us accuse Marx of being utopian all we want, but let us be aware that with greater reason we must use this term to qualify the central message of Christianity. The designation of the law as "letter" (Rom. 7:6; 2 Cor. 3:3, 6; Rom. 2:29) indicates the scope of the word "law" when Paul rejects the law—every written or formulated law. If the term refers even to the law of God, much more does it refer to the law of men. This must be understood seriously without restriction. There is no way to turn it around. Paul believes in a world without law and without government because he believes in an entirely new man who constitutes an authentic "new creation": "Put on the new man, created according to God in justice and in true holiness" (Eph. 4:24).

Do not lie to each other;
strip off the old man with his works,
and put on the new man
who according to the image of his creator
is renewed for knowledge,
where there is neither Greek nor Jew,
circumcision nor uncircumcision,
barbarian nor Scythian,
slave nor freeman,
but Christ all in all;
put on, then—as chosen ones, holy and beloved of God—
a heart of mercy, goodness, humility, gentleness, patience,
supporting one another and pardoning one another
if one has a complaint against another,
just as the Lord pardoned you.
But over all these things, put on love. . . .

(Col. 3:9-14)

There can be no doubt concerning what "the new man" means for Paul. "All will be just," Isa. 60:21 had said. When in Rom. 13:13-14 Paul tells us "not in discord and envy, but put on our Lord Jesus Christ and do not comply with the flesh's intention for greed," he is only expressing in a great synthesis what he has just said in Rom. 13:8-10, namely, that the fulness of the law is brotherly love, the brotherly love which was incarnated in Jesus Christ as the inaugural event of the new world.[143] Jesus Christ, qualified in this way and in this way very faithfully understood, is the new event in history (cf. Rom. 15:2-3; 15:7; Eph. 5:1-2; 5:25; Phil. 2:1-8; Mark 10:35-45; Matt. 20:20-28; 1 John 3:16; 4:10-12; 4:19). To be in Christ means to join this new current, to incorporate oneself into this new world which yearns to be born in history. Therefore 2 Cor. 5:21 tells us, "so that we might become the justice of God *in Christ.*" Therefore the "put on our Lord Jesus Christ" in Rom. 13:14 is the conclusion after "the fulness of the law is love" in Rom. 13:10. What Rom. 13:11-14 adds is all the power of the *eschaton*: "The fulness of the law is love. And in this we are conscious of the moment: that now is the time for us to arise from sleep. . . ." As we have already seen, only the messianic *eschaton* bursts forth with true otherness which disrupts all subjectivism.[144] But if the *eschaton* consists in the total demand of justice in the outcry of the neighbor, the absolute Other is revealed only there.[145]

We said that both Marx and the biblical writers believe that man can cease being selfish and merciless and self-serving and can find his greatest fulness in loving his neighbor. We can see that this is Marx's hope in this passage from the *Manuscripts of 1844*:

> Not only *wealth,* but likewise the *poverty* of man—under the assumption of socialism—receives in equal measure a *human* and therefore social significance. Poverty is the passive bond which causes the human being to experience the need of the greatest wealth—the *other* human being.[146]

Let us hear it more clearly expressed by Calvez, an impartial witness:

> In all this the highest good is man, with whom man is related by a sole need which summarizes all the other needs and is called the need of man. Basing himself on these assertions of Marx, Mascolo has been able to define communism as a need for "communication."[147]

Let us listen to another Jesuit, a no less impartial witness. Pierre Bigo says that according to Marx

> the antagonism of individuals, which is already present in barter, is transformed by the salary system into an antagonism of class, which rests on a fundamental inequality among men and on a disguised

form of slavery. The confiscation of surplus value is the direct consequence of this state of affairs. Capitalism is at the same time the elimination of men's freedom, of some men's freedom with respect to others, and of their equality. It means that man is no longer a man for man. And here the idea is not secondary, but rather predominant. It controls all reasoning. Without it nothing has meaning in Marxist political economy.[148]

It is an ideological caricature to assert that the historical primacy of the economic realm held by Marx implies the submission and debasement of man. If Marx struggles against anything it is against the slavery into which man has fallen with respect to the economic world. In the words of Bigo:

In whatever form it is expressed—fetishism, abstraction, objectification, materialization, fraud, inversion of the relationship between things and man—the idea runs through the whole of Marxist political economy: the idea of a kind of debasement of man by the primacy which the economic world has gained over him. And this idea is not adventitious. It is fundamental. If this is not an affirmation of man, then we must give up hope of seeing clearly.[149]

It has been very easy for the ideologues of the Western establishment to take advantage of the common ignorance of the meaning of "dialectics" and to propagandize against "dialectical materialism," as if this term had anything to do with what the West understands by "materialism." People tend to become fixed only on what they understand. Since this ignorance of the meaning of "dialectics" also plagues the overwhelming majority of Marxists, they themselves have facilitated such a great falsification of Marx's thought. To refute this mistaken notion we need only point out that Marx combats the materialism of the Encyclopedists and Feuerbach with as much force as he does idealism and spiritualism. He reproaches them mainly for their lack of dialectics and their ignorance of Hegel (cf. the *Theses on Feuerbach*). What some might understand, without dialectics, by "materialism," not only cannot be attributed to Marx; it also constitutes one of the adversaries against which Marx struggles. It is disconcertingly simplistic to adduce the fact that the word "materialism" is found both in the designation of mechanistic and metaphysical materialism and in the designation of dialectical materialism; notwithstanding what the propaganda might say, these two are not species of the same genus.

The fact is that to understand dialectics we must take it seriously and to take dialectics seriously is a step which would demand abandoning the moral color blindness which is essential to the epistemology of Western science inherited from the Greeks. This epistemology, as "the ideal of objectivity," has succeeded in penetrating down to popular, unscientific levels, that is, to the man in the street. Max Weber's famous *Werturteilsfreiheit* (science free from value judgments) is the Western ideal of knowledge, to the measure that the West remains faithful to the Greeks, a measure which continues to be quite high and which impenitently continues to constitute a goal to be reached.

Morality as separate knowledge was impossible for Marx, because he practiced this knowledge with enormous profundity and intensity in all his understanding of reality. And his unsurpassable merit is to have shown that a science which does not take this approach knows only appearances and not reality, that is, it is no longer science. Very few affirmations have come to my attention as brilliant as this in the *Manuscripts of 1844*: "Political economy . . . carries to its logical [that is, mental] conclusion the denial of man."[150] Marx refers to economic science created by the West, which is the only one there is. This science knows nothing of the most important element of economic reality, namely, the crushing of man. But this science, brought into the world by Quesnay, Smith, and Ricardo, was simply the application of Western epistemology to a new object: economic reality. As we shall see, the "hardness of heart" of which the Bible speaks found its great instrument and rationalization in the "wisdom of this world" (and Paul is undoubtedly referring to the Greeks). "This world" has used this wisdom to tame and nullify the revolutionary impact of the Gospel.

> The function of political economy consists in tearing down the veils and dispelling the enchantment, in casting down the idols. The earth does not produce rent. Capital does not produce profit. The wage-earner produces much more than his wage. These are all blasphemies to the ears of the ordinary economist. Enclosed in a kind of fetishism, he believes, on the contrary, that rent blossoms forth from the land and profit from capital as if by sorcery. And the form of parthenogenesis which impresses him most is that which he finds in capital which produces interest, "the most absolute fetish."[151]

In Marx's opinion, the ordinary economists get lost in the multiplicity of phenomena and "under the pretext of harmonizing everything, they eliminate the contradictions inherent in capitalism."[152]

"It is a characteristic of ordinary economy to confine itself to recording facts as they are given in immediate experience, after the fashion of the empiricists, and then to establish the relationship between them."[153] In the same way pre-Copernican astronomy was unaware of the real movement of the heavenly bodies, without which their apparent movement is unintelligible, even if it is established with mathematical precision. The astronomer was held prisoner of appearances. On the other hand, the dialectical method "consists in seeking, beyond the supposed 'data' of experience, the human relations hidden beneath the 'appearance' of things,"[154] and with dialectics Marx "discovers in human relationships the very origin of appearances, products, institutions and things."[155]

When the equivalence of value and work is asserted, one aligns oneself with the point of view of production. When it is asserted that value is determined in wages, profits, and rents, one aligns oneself with the point of view of distribution and circulation. All Marxism is affirmed in becoming aware of this distinction. . . . It is not denied that the land and the instruments of labor *materially* have a function. It is simply denied that they have a *social* function, a function in the formation of value, that is, it is denied that they confer on their deforcers a valid title to the product. Value is determined in labor.[156]

In the calculations of the employer, there is indeed no difference between these subdivisions under cost price: *wages paid* or *raw materials purchased*. . . . Thus the transformation of the capitalist process of production into a complete mystery is happily accomplished and the origin of the surplus-value existing in the product is entirely withdrawn from view. . . . In political economy the positivist reluctance to advance beyond appearances has a definite class bearing, for in this domain appearances are a function of the class viewpoint of the observer.[157]

Perhaps the greatest triumph of conservatism in the history of thought was when empirical verifiability became the criterion of truth. This was to abide by appearances, and since the datum which could be experienced was the prevailing situation, the status quo was set up as the criterion of truth and rationality. Any thought which might go beyond or transcend the status quo was automatically relegated to the catalogue of the irrational. With this "the conceptual effort to sustain the tension between 'is' and 'ought' and to subvert the established universe of discourse . . . is . . . eliminated from all thought which is to be objective, exact, and scientific."[158] To the conservative mind it is very important to affirm that reality is not contradictory; thus it assures that reality cannot change. There exists, of course, for so-called "common sense" and for Western science, an objective "world," definable as if it were not seen from any angle. But all knowledge has an intention (this thesis of Husserl is one of the most relevant discoveries of philosophy), and this "world" is what the Greek point of view taught us to conceive. This is the "world" of the intention of Greek culture, the intention of avoiding all responsibility for what happens. But woe to us if reality were not contradictory; there would be no hope.

As Max Scheler especially has pointed out, the "in itself" is thus relative, relative to a given manner of knowing and wishing.[159]

It is not that reactionary Western sciences gave to Greek epistemology, logic, and metaphysics a conservative usage that they did not naturally have. By no means. Classical Greek science was born to neutralize reality, so that it would not enjoin me, so that it would not affect me. It was born to "objectify" reality. And from the beginning it constituted an aristocratic wisdom for free privileged people in the midst of a population of which five-sixths were slaves. Aristotle sums it all up in his classic thesis: Truth is incompatible with the condition of the slave.

Even prescinding from other considerations, simply by its method it is a priori much more likely that dialectical thought rather than classical thought should be able to deal with reality. Classical thought *starts from the presupposition* that there are no contradictions in reality. This presupposition is not demonstrated. It originates in the fact that there are no contradictions in the mind; from here this thinking takes the fatal step, saying that "therefore" there are no contradictions in reality either. That something, to the extent that it is, cannot, at the same time and under the same aspect, not be: Where do they find this principle unless in a pure analysis of concepts? They do not find it in realities.

They strip a concept down until on their mental screen they leave a single differentia of dazzling purity, and then they say that this one-dimensional differentia is not accompanied by more than itself. (Of course. This is how they set it up on the basis of their intellectual procedure of isolating it.) They go on to say that therefore it is not accompanied by its own negation. And then they universalize this merely intramental "experience" through the principle of non-contradiction. Once they have projected the principle onto reality, naturally they will make every effort to "dissolve" with their thinking any contradiction which reality might try to cast into their eyes; they will hold that it is a merely apparent contradiction. For the establishment there is nothing so disturbing as knowing that present reality is contradictory.

As Francette Arnault says, the passage from contrary to contrary, from a quality to its negation, "classical logic cannot be unaware of, but it lays aside this difficulty by isolating the different moments of a thing. It matters little that a thing becomes not-A after it has been A. The essential point is that it cannot be A and not-A at the same time. We know that to explain this fracture of the principle of the stability of things classical logic will have recourse to an external cause, to an accidental disturbance."[160] On the other hand, as Marcuse lucidly observes, "Dialectical logic cannot be formal because it is determined by the real, which is concrete. And this concreteness, far from militating against a system of general principles and concepts, requires such a system of logic because it moves under general laws which make for the rationality of the real. It is the rationality of contradiction, of the opposition of forces, tendencies, elements, which constitutes the movement of the real and, if comprehended, the concept of the real."[161]

Thus to the following very accurate statement of Bigo we should add that the classical economists are mere followers of the method of the Greeks and the Scholastics, although neither the followers nor the followed are aware of their approach:

> The only difference between the Marxists and the classical economists is that the latter do not challenge a manner of distribution and production which, on the contrary, is for the Marxists full of paradoxes and contradictions.[162]

The difference between those who do not challenge the present reality and those who regard it as full of contradictions and absurdities dates from long before the birth of economic science. This is the very ancient contrast between the mode of knowing of those who have a sense of justice and the mode of knowing of those who, with hardened hearts, have a vested interest in the preservation of the present system. The latter naturally antedate the Greeks, but they found in classical epistemology an undoubtedly excellent systematization.

Marx's path has been perfectly described by Bigo in his *Marxisme et humanisme*:

He does not resort to the abstraction of an unreal world which controls the real world—whether the unreal world of the theologians, the philosophers, or the jurists; he does not leave the real world. Rather, by the mere force of the elements included in this world, he nevertheless interprets, not as a verbal protest but as a real contradiction, man's rebellion against the domination which material beings make him suffer and against the exploitation of which he is the object at the hand of his neighbors.[163]

Thus I said above that morality as separate knowledge was impossible for Marx because he practiced this knowledge in all his understanding of reality. Those who sustain that in the strictly philosophical realm Marx's contribution was nil have to face the fact that if anything was radically revolutionized by Marx it was philosophy as such. With him we began to see that the reality itself analyzed by science is in itself moral and that not to perceive it as such is to lack depth, objectivity, and realism. Garaudy exemplifies this in a concrete case with regard to the elaboration-correction which Marx makes of the law of value discovered by Ricardo:

> Just at the point where he comes close to making the crucial discovery later made by Marx, i.e., that wages are determined by the cost of production of labor power, Ricardo overlooks that this law results from *the transformation of labor into a commodity, from its fetishization into an object,* from the very principle of the capitalist system which reduces everything to the common denominator of commodity value.[164]

In passing let us say that the idea of the incarnation of injustice, immorality, and sin into a civilizing system could not be better expressed. Garaudy continues: Ricardo

> attributes this phenomenon to what is actually only a secondary effect of the system—the competition of the workers and the law of supply and demand. From the viewpoint of his own doctrine, this is inconsequential. His ambition had been to reduce all economic categories to labor value, and to achieve the merit of putting himself at the standpoint of production; now he passes over to the point of view of distribution and circulation to account for wages.[165]

When science does not grasp the moral substance of facts, it stops halfway down the road to understanding reality.

A very similar case is observed by Bigo with regard to Marx's attitude toward Adam Smith's law concerning fixed capital and circulating capital, a law which compares labor with merchandise:

To find an analogy between these elements it is necessary deliberately to adopt the capitalistic viewpoint and consent to reducing everything to objective value. The entire Marxist doctrine consists in the rejection of this point of view.[166]

And it is right in rejecting this, for this approach is voluntarily blind; in a systematic and rationalizing way it undertakes to not perceive what in reality is happening, which is the crushing of man. If the technocrats of our century have betrayed the workers it is because the science with which they identified themselves was structured in a manner contrary to the cause of the poor. As Domergue correctly says in his summary of Galbraith, "This is without a doubt a profound indoctrination, a seizing of the human spirit which is intimately persuaded that the great social truths are economic growth, financial stability, technological development, etc. These dogmas are accepted as such with no possibility of critique: To question them is to go against the natural order of things."[167]

Epistemology and the very concept of science have been brainwashing the world for twenty-five centuries, preventing it from hearing the outcry of the poor because it is unscientific to hear their outcry; they have insulated the world from the most profound and most serious aspect of the reality that is before us. Domergue continues,

By means of this "belief" the technostructure exercises a power which is less direct than that of the "entrepreneurs," but this is due to the much greater influence which in the last analysis it has at its disposition. The State has become the bureaucratic organism of its right functioning. There is an absolute correspondence between their objectives. The State and the technostructure are inseparable allies, permanent promoters of a "belief" which they need in order to exist.[168]

This observation gets much closer to the root of the matter than Marshall McLuhan's diagnosis: "[The intellectuals'] great betrayal was that they had surrendered their autonomy and had become the flunkies of power, as the atomic physicist at the present moment is the flunky of the war lords."[169] What McLuhan says is true, but in reality "the game is played on the level of man's spirit, in the possibility that he will have or not have of criticizing the aforementioned 'belief.' In a society which has come to the stadium of technostructure, politics becomes religion."[170] We need only add that this game has been played since the invention of the great ideology of the "natural order of things," to which Domergue himself alludes. This natural order is the status quo, and to postulate it as "natural" has the same reactionary function as the undemonstrable postulate of classical logic, namely, that the present reality is not contradictory.[171] The iron law of wages, discovered by Ricardo and Lassalle, was also postulated as "natural": The fact that the workers died of hunger and malnutrition seemed to the classical economists to be the most natural thing in the world. We have already seen that both Marx and the Bible reject the imposition of an alleged unchangeable "nature," in virtue of which man will be a wolf toward man as long as there is history.[172]

The "natural" balance of supply and demand, which so fascinated the classical economists combated by Marx, is nothing more than the application to the economic realm of the "natural order" deprived of contradictions which was postulated by Greek metaphysics. This esthetical pleasure of self-contentment and tranquilization of the soul produced by the "system" of a cosmos perfected in self-preserving totality is characteristic of "contemplation." Naturally it does not demand praxis. On the other hand, dialectical knowledge and biblical knowledge demand praxis to the point of being identified with it: "He practiced justice and right; this is good. He defended the cause of the poor and the needy; this is good. Is this not what it means to know me? It is Yahweh who speaks" (Jer. 22:15-16). The epistemology of contemplation is the tranquil knowing characteristic of self-assured amorality. It was born to neutralize reality and keep it from disturbing me. As Levinas says, "A philosophy of power, ontology, as a fundamental philosophy which does not call into question the self, is a philosophy of injustice."[173]

In this supposedly natural balance of reality there originates the circular thinking that characterizes classical economics: If we "artificially" interfere with the natural order of the economy, for example by raising salaries above the level indicated by the free play of supply and demand, the preestablished harmony of the natural order will cause salaries to return to this level. (If they earn more, the working masses reproduce more prolifically; the supply of labor thereby increases without an equivalent increase in the demand, and therefore there is a decrease in the price of labor, that is, wages.) This is the total rationalization and justification of "leaving things as they are." But let us be aware that this circular thinking has been extended to the man in the street; it has become so connatural to him that he does not even suspect that he is thinking in exactly the same way as Western sciences. A very frequent example is this: "If so-and-so's idea were as clear and important as he claims, it would have already occurred to many others before him; if it is neither clear nor important, there is no reason for us to pay it any mind." This is hermetically sealed armor plate. There is no way anything new can get through. There is nothing new under the sun.

Another example is this: "Everything has its pros and its cons; if we do what you propose, we do indeed obtain certain good results; but there are also bad results which counterbalance them; do not think that our predecessors were so stupid that they would not have done what you now propose; if they did not do it, it is because they saw that there would follow both good and bad effects." This door is equally closed. We must not interfere in the already established "natural" balances, for in the long run the "natural" laws will prevail (which are the ones which have no contradiction). This argumentation on behalf of the status quo is incessant in the West. Its applications are innumerable in daily life and in the mini-theoretical conversations over coffee.

Thus we see that "the eternal return of all things" is inseparable from classical logic, epistemology, and metaphysics. Those who, through Christian obedience, have thought that they could adopt these disciplines without professing the eternal return as a concept of history have remained on a superficial level of consciousness. The existence of history and of the *eschaton* is incompatible with Greek epistemology.

Even Marx's most adverse commentators will have to recognize the truth of the following assertion which I will express in Bigo's words:

> None of the economists before Marx had discerned the birth of a new world or a new man. . . . Only after Marx is capitalism presented as a period of history.[174]

The point pertains to the very essence of dialectics: It is the contradiction inherent in reality which makes all fixity and stabilization impossible and therefore requires that there be history. Hope and faith are here in their entirety, not projecting on reality entelechies which it does not have, but rather achieving in the very center of what happens a perception of the moral substance which classical, Western epistemology prevents us from perceiving.[175]

In our times it is alleged (and this is another example of the circular thinking which I mentioned above) that revolution is useless because once the revolutionaries have come into power they will become exploiters like the human beings they deposed; there could be no clearer indication of a total absence of hope and the total presence of the "eternal return of all things" than this notion. Here we see that it was obstinate Greek epistemology which forced Christians to project a solution onto "another world," for without some appearance of hope they could not continue to call themselves Christians. But they thereby took all hope out of their conception of the history of this world, considering it as the eternal return of all things. The fact that no history occurs when one does not perceive the moral substance of what happens is quite tangible in this objection of Marx to classical economic science: "Political economy starts with the fact of private property, but it does not explain it to us."[176] It is precisely this moral perception, this unquelled sense of justice, which obliges Marx to penetrate the historical origin of private ownership, not to accept this as an untemporal datum after the Greek fashion or as an essence. The most essential element of facts, Garaudy quite rightly says, is that "they have taken place."

In what sense is all dialectics liberation? It is liberation from a repressive, evil, and false system—whether this is an organic system, or social, mental, or intellectual: It is liberation through the forces which develop within such a system. This is a decisive point. This is a liberation in virtue of the contradiction created by the system, precisely because it is an evil and false system. . . . I think that—in Marx as well—socialism *should* be. This "should" pertains to the very essence of scientific socialism.[177]

When he opposes communist society to capitalism, Marx designates it as a society in which men will work under conditions "more worthy of their human nature and more suitable to it" [Marx-Engels, *Works,* in Russian, vol. 25, part 2, p. 387], and where man's labor, no longer being simply the means of assuring his biological existence, will again find its specific original meaning.[178]

Thus Calvez lacks depth when he asserts that it is inconsistent with dialectics to speak of an *eschaton* in which there are no contradictions.[179] It is inconsistent with mechanistic materialism and with a Marxism which has degenerated into a "world view," but it is not inconsistent with authentic dialectical thought. Calvez himself, discussing the interpretations which have been given of Marx's theory on economic crises as contradictions inherent to capitalism, indicates Marx's authentic thought:

What is much more important is that the crises, like the laws of capitalist development in general, engender situations of a nature such that men can become aware of their own inhuman situation and decide to take control of the blind mechanism which develops with such severe paroxysms.[180]

For the Marxist the catastrophic result of capitalism is not the unleashing of a natural catastrophe.[181]

It is a matter of eliminating the "alienated form of communication, in which men are controlled by their own social relationships in the form of blind and elemental forces."[182] What Calvez objects to in Marx is precisely that in which Marx coincides with the Bible: an *eschaton* here below. The Christian, anti-Greek conception of history does not consist solely in a line instead of a circle, as Cullmann and Danielou seem to sustain.[183] Rather it consists in the incomparable and unsuppressable messianism of an *eschaton* which the Western mind will ever designate as utopian. Mao Tse-Tung quite rightly says, "Not only should contradictions be resolved, but they definitely can be."[184] And Paul of Tarsus says, "The promise of inheriting the world was not made to Abraham and his descendants on account of the law, but on account of the justice of faith" (Rom. 4:13).

The ontological tension between essence and appearance, between "is" and "ought" becomes historical tension, and the "inner negativity" of the object-world is understood as the work of the historical subject—man in his struggle with nature and society. Reason becomes historical Reason. It contradicts the established order of men and things on behalf of existing societal forces that reveal the irrational character of this order—for "rational" is a mode of thought and action which is geared to reduce ignorance, destruction, brutality, and oppression.[185]

This is true dialectical thought. When Marx speaks of "tendential law," Bigo objects to his equivocation: "Is this a purely positive tendency or a tendency which rests on the intervention of conscience?"[186] Clearly this law is not something which can be established by Western positivistic science, which methodically blinds itself to the most profound dimension of reality—precisely the conscience of humankind which yearns for liberation. This "object" is impervious to classical epistemology, but the "intervention of conscience" *is in the object* and in the subject of dialectical knowledge. History exists to the extent that conscience intervenes; without conscience there is only eternal return. Levinas rightly says about this foundation which is invisible to Western science,

What is above all invisible is the offense universal history inflicts on particulars. To be I and not only an incarnation of a reason is precisely to be capable of seeing the offense of the offended, or the face.[187]

Dialectics does see this reality and very rightly accuses of blindness those who do not see it.

When he criticizes economic science, Marx does not want to replace it with a more alert economic science. Rather he replaces it in fact with a "science" pure and simple. This science will be intimately linked to praxis, and Marx will not recognize the autonomy of an alleged economic science which would have its own method and its own laws understandable by induction and deduction.[188]

Joseph Gabel has discovered that the basic recourse of schizophrenia is to detemporalize and devaluate, that is, to eliminate history and with this the axiological imperative which arises from it.[189] Greek wisdom (*sophia*) and its continuation in Western science has therefore been really a centuries-long schizophrenia; it does not allow itself to be affected by reality, for reality consists above all in the outcry of the poor who have been crushed by history and in the very dialectics of the history which yearns to heed this outcry in a definitive way. The historical hermeneutic must at last understand that it is fulfilling an obligation which has been delayed for centuries, and this delay has been criminal. It must understand that for centuries we have been acting deaf and that the victims of injustice relied on the following generation to understand their appeal. Interpreting, understanding, is a "judgment" to which those crushed by the civilizing structure appeal. We understand reality to the measure that we identify with the conscience of humankind, which is the true subject of history. Instead of simply accepting a reality dogmatically "given" and deprived of a subject, it is necessary, from within this object-subject identification, to understand reality as a product and activity of this object-subject which is unified. And this unity is praxis.

The approach of Western science in general is reproduced in the approach of psychoanalytic science: Explain the phenomenon by its causes; thus it does not disturb; there is nothing new; everything is mechanistic combinations of known things. In his critique of Freud, Adler, and Jung, Bloch rightly points out, "The unconscious of psychoanalysis never is a not-yet-conscious, an element of progressions. Rather it consists of regressions. . . . That is, in the Freudian unconscious there is nothing new."[190] The trick is to reduce you to a "case," to catalogue you. As for Plato and Aristotle, for psychoanalysis you are a mere concretization (*quantitate signata*) of already known essences, that is, the eternal return of all things. The idea is that they make you represent a role whose actions and reactions they have already studied very well. Thus you do not summon them; you are a mere spectacle. If there were something really new in the psychoanalyzed person, a new world would be beginning which would demand a decision of the scientist, as it would of all men. A new world cannot be controlled by categories and catalogues. These are no longer competent; the bearers of the new world take command.

At its core Western science is an evasion of reality through taking refuge in "the more known." It is better that what is not reducible to the *magis notum* should not exist. Such a flight from reality is inevitably linked to the approbation and support of the prevailing situation. If we want to be tranquilized, the best thing we can do is to interpret the phenomenon as a thing of the past. (This is what the *explicatio per causas* does.) If the phenomenon tries to be a thing of the future, it must be crushed. If in the psychoanalyzed person there should dawn a world of true liberation and not of "adaptation to reality" (which is a euphemism for enslaving oneself to social structures and to their agelong taboos), this would demand both of the psychoanalyst and the psychoanalyzed effective rebellion against the existing world. The "personality," which has been so idealized as a goal, "is but a 'broken' individual who has internalized and successfully utilized repression and aggression," which all of Western culture imposes.[191] The present structure gains much in making—by means of psychology—rebellion and nonconformity to be channelled toward the realization of such a "personality."

In contrast with all this, dialectical thought does grasp the contradiction and instead of disguising and domesticating this contradiction, dialectical thought identifies with it. And this is because dialectical thought believes in hope. If for Greek science to understand is to reduce to the known, for dialectics to understand is to identify with what breaks with the known and transcends it.

"Merely contemplative knowledge necessarily refers to what is concluded, that is, past; it is defenseless before what is present and blind before what is future."[192] On the other hand dialectical knowledge is pledged to the good that advances, to the real process of that which is worthy-of-man, struggling to be realized. "It is superfluous to add that this manner of knowing is the only objective one, the only one that reproduces the reality of history."[193] Both ways of knowing seek "to make the world perfect," but the former in thought, the latter in reality. Therefore the former creates the reactionary illusion that everything is all right, and the latter is revolutionary praxis.

Marx's criticism of the classical economists[194] is the same criticism which Marx, in another form, directs against Western thought in general: "Philosophers have only *interpreted* the world, in various ways; the point, however, is to *change* it."[195] Here Marx touches upon the original sin of Greek epistemology: To contemplate is to leave things as they are. And he likewise criticizes the materialistic "world view": "The chief defect of all hitherto existing materialism—that of Feuerbach included—is that the thing, reality, sensuousness, is conceived only in the form of the *object* or of *contemplation*, but not as *human sensuous activity, practice*; not subjectively."[196] Except for those superficialities which have been perpetrated with the Gospel, I think that the greatest one of recent centuries has been to interpret these theses of Marx in a pragmatistic sense. What they really say is that objectifying, standing at a distance and distinguishing oneself from the object, are operations which cannot be performed when the object is human history, mankind, because I really am identified with it and it is the original and immediate datum, the primary evidence. Only by an artificial, secondary mental operation do we construct a knowing subject who imagines himself not to be part of historical humanity but a kind of untemporal point, like a Platonic essence, which is outside of mankind and history. Descartes and Kant greatly deceive themselves when they think that such a distilled subject is the immediate indubitable datum.

Freud has had to dismantle this subject, and with his exhaustive material of analysis, show that its "ego" as well as its "id" and its "superego" are the crystallization of the entire history of mankind. The disincarnate transcendental "ego" of Greco-Western epistemology is, despite illusions to the contrary, an abstraction. My knowing is part of the human activity in which, and only in which, human history consists. It is before this history that the transcendental subject claims to situate itself as if before an object distinct from itself. The true subject is identified with the movement of history, with the great march toward liberation, with human praxis. And all knowledge which abstracts from this praxis is indeed abstract and therefore false.

Such is contemplative cognition, for to contemplate is to remove oneself from the great human march toward justice. To prescind from the moral imperative which arises with history, to separate theory from ethical praxis, is to keep this theory from being realistic. This is what Paul calls "the injustice of the men who by their injustice are suppressing the truth" (Rom. 1:18). Kant's merit was to have discovered that the subject is active. Hegel took this seriously: The activity of the subject pertains not only to the representation of the object, but also to the reality of the object. Feuerbach corrected this: not the subject, but man; not the philosopher, but man. Marx carried this great conversion of Western thought to its conclusion: Man is an abstraction if he does not signify suffering, working, struggling mankind. Such is the subject, but such too is the object of knowing.

History itself moves toward justice, toward love of neighbor. It does this not through determinism, but by creating an intolerably acute conscience of the necessity of this justice, of its possibility, and its urgency. This is the conscience truly produced by history. No knowing which prescinds from this conscience can correspond to reality. But Western science claims in principle and in method to prescind from it, to be impartial, to be amoral. No wonder dialectical knowledge wishes to be precisely the opposite.

> If Marx says that the working class must not achieve ideals, this anathema does not refer to concrete tendential goals, but to abstract ideals imposed without contact with the process of history. . . . With Marx's militant optimism, abstract ideals are not realized, but rather the oppressed elements of the new humanized society; the elements of the concrete ideal are set free.[197]

We can very correctly say that Marx denies morality in the sense that Paul denies the law, that is, "in order that the content of justice of the law might be achieved in us" (Rom. 8:4) and because love is already operative in history. The error of the anti-Marxists who are scandalized by the importance which Marx attributes to matter is that they believe that Marx's matter is identical to space, when in reality it is identical to time, that is, to history, which is the only real and concrete time. Neither the Western definition of matter nor that of time help us to understand Marx. Particularly inadequate is the definition of matter, which in Newton's hands is reduced to the pure abstraction of quantity. Such unreal distillates are the necessary consequence of the merely contemplative approach of Western science. On the other hand, dialectics has to conceive of matter in such a way that it includes in matter the existence of love, of heroism, of unselfish dedication, and of intuition, especially the intuition of the absolute moral imperative. Marx says,

> Among the qualities inherent in matter, motion is the first and foremost, not only as mechanical and mathematical but even more as impulse, vital spirit, tension, or—to use Jakob Böhme's expression—the anguish and torment of matter.[198]

It is very important to bear in mind the critique which Marx makes here of Hegel's notion: The Hegelian conception of history is nothing but "the speculative expression of the Christian-Germanic dogma of the antithesis between spirit and matter."[199] These passages prove that everything the West understands by "spirit" is included in what Marx calls "matter" and Marx's understanding indeed has very little to do with what Greece and the West understand by "matter." Marx clearly denies the existence of a spirit as an entity different from the body. But the spiritual, profoundly spiritual character of the whole man and of the social relationships which are the axis and engine of history is affirmed by Marx explicitly or implicitly on every page of his writings.

In the first of the passages from "The Holy Family" which I have just cited (the one which adopts Böhme's expression), the similarity with Rom. 8:19-23 is striking:

> For the created universe awaits with eager expectation for God's sons to be revealed. It was made the victim of frustration, not by its own choice, but because of him who made it so; yet always there was hope, because the universe itself is to be freed from the shackles of mortality and enter upon the liberty and splendor of the children of God. Up to the present, we know, the whole created universe groans in all its parts as if in the pangs of childbirth. Not only so, but all of us who possess the first fruits of the Spirit, we too groan inwardly as we wait *to be sons* and for our bodies to be set free.

Where Marx speaks of *Qual der Materie* ("the anguish and torment of matter" as I have improvably translated it), Paul speaks of "the groans and pains of childbirth" of a creation which is obviously material, since our bodies form a part of it.

To understand correctly the Pauline passage it is well first to specify the meaning of "sonship" (*huiothesia*), for three times in this passage Paul says that the transformation of material creation depends on the achievement of this divine sonship of man. The first and decisive point which should be noted is v. 14, which in this same chapter 8 had just said, "Whoever are moved by the spirit of God, these are the sons of God." The intention of the verse is clearly one of definition. As Otto Michel observes, "The verse states who is a son of God and who is not."[200] The resistance of Cándido Pozo to a "direct influence" of human activity on the transformation of the cosmos originates first in his failing to perceive that "spirit of God" is a qualitative characterization in the Bible and very especially in Paul and in John.[201] Second, it originates in his belief that the defenders of the direct influence idea necessarily understand by human activity any type of "progress," whereas the activity characterized by the Spirit, an activity of limitless justice and love, is a total break with what human civilization has up until now called "progress." As Lyonnet faithfully interprets the passage, "Given that the redemption of the universe and of the body depends on the redemption of man himself, it follows that every human effort is vain which is directed to prepare and as it were to commence the redemption of the universe if it is not ordered to the redemption of man."[202]

A dazzling corroboration of the meaning of "to be sons of God" is found in 1 John 2:29 and 4:7, if we bear in mind that, as Schnackenburg has shown, "to be born of God" is synonomous with "to be son(s) of God."[203] The perfect equivalency between these formulas can be seen in 1 John 3:9-10; 2:29-3:1; and 5:1-2, three passages in which the interchangeability of the expressions is clear. But according to 1 John 2:29, "Everyone who does justice is born of God," and according to 4:7, "Everyone who loves is born of God." This is exactly the same meaning that Rom. 8:14 obliges us to adopt for divine sonship, since "the spirit of God" always has the intention of qualitative characterization, as we have seen.

The key is in a phrase of Jesus which at the same time constitutes a powerful confirmation of what we have said: After teaching us his unsurpassable "Love your enemies" (Luke 6:35), he tells us in apodosis, "And you will be sons of the Most High, for he himself is kind to the ungrateful and the wicked" (v. 35b). And then he recapitulates, "Become compassionate as your Father is compassionate" (v. 36).

Being sons of God consists in this. Matthew grasped the thought with the most exact fidelity: "Love your enemies and pray for those who persecute you so that you might be sons of your heavenly Father" (Matt. 5:44-45). "Blessed are the peacemakers, for they will be called sons of God" (Matt. 5:9). And if we bear in mind that "good works" is a technical term,[204] Matt. 5:16 teaches us the same thing: "Your light must shine in the sight of men, so that they see your good works and glorify your heavenly Father." The meaning of this sentence is reduplicative: On seeing your "good works" men will recognize God as your Father, that is, they will realize that you are sons of God. As in the case of the "spirit of God,"[205] so too in that of divine sonship, theology has been misled by centering its attention on the ontological problem, when the clear intention of the biblical authors is one of qualitative characterization by action, by behavior, by attitude. The thought is very simple and obvious: We recognize the son as such by his likeness to the father.

Once we have clarified the precise meaning of "sons of God," we see that in Rom. 8:19 ("The created universe awaits with eager expectation for God's sons to be revealed") the transformation of the cosmos clearly depends on the realization of justice on earth. Let us withhold for a moment the incredulity and skepticism with which Greece and the West have made modern man scorn anyone who might assert the influence of morality and love and justice on matter. (Naturally a matter conceived as mere abstract mathematical extension, as *positio partium extra partes*, is a pure abstraction and has nothing to do with man; if concrete matter should be grasped, this reality obviously would have to do with man.) Let us withhold our skepticism and not allow the Western mind to prevent the Bible from asserting something that the Western mind considers absurd a priori. First let us establish what the Bible says; then we will see if the West accepts this message or not, or if the West is even capable of accepting it.

In one of the most central theses of his entire message, Paul affirms that "through sin death entered the world" (Rom. 5:12), that "because of the transgression of one (man) many died (Rom. 5:15; cf. 14, 17), and that it was "in death that sin reigned" (Rom. 5:21); therefore we should not be surprised that for him the transformation of material creation and even the resurrection of bodies depends on justice: "Thus grace will reign *by means of justice* for life without end" (Rom. 5:21);

"all of us who possess the first fruits of the Spirit, we too groan inwardly as we wait *to be sons* and for our bodies to be set free" (Rom. 8:23). (The two italicized expressions are synonymous; cf. above.) And Paul is not original in his unrenounceable thesis of the efficacy of justice or injustice in the transformation or corruption of the cosmos. We saw it in the Yahwist when Yahweh, after the disobedience of Adam (who is simply "the man"[206]), says to him, "Cursed be the earth because of you" (Gen. 3:17). And likewise Yahweh exclaims after the flood, "Never again will I curse the earth because of man" (Gen. 8:21). The exegetical and theological efforts to marginate and evaporate this absolutely central point of biblical hope all seem to me to be dictated by the desire, which is indeed utopian in the worst sense of the term, of reconciling the Bible with Greek philosophy, which from its birth persistently regarded matter—to say the least—as something irrelevant and foreign to the so-called "true man."

As Christians we really have to choose. The Marxist hope is that the world be transformed when the relationships among men become true bonds of love and justice. If this seems utopian to the Western intellect, what must this intellect think of biblical hope, which expects exactly the same thing, but also includes in the transformation of the world nothing less than the resurrection of the dead—something which Marx did not have the dialectics sufficient to reach? Let us take the bull by the horns: Is it truly more utopian to hope for the transformation of the world through justice than it is to hope for the definitive elimination of sin in the world? Is it more utopian to believe in the resurrection of the flesh than in the abolition of all the injustices, enmities, and cruelties in the world? Above we saw that in both Marx and the Bible the basis for all thought is this thesis which is the most revolutionary imaginable: Sin and evil are not inherent to humanity and history; they began one day through human work and they can, therefore, be eliminated.[207] "Because of one man sin entered the world and because of sin death" (Rom. 5:12). When Paul believes in the transformation of the world through justice ("The spirit is life through justice," Rom. 9:10), he is only being consistent with this fundamental conviction; it is not a conviction invented by him, but rather was present in a part of the Bible which is as difficult to ignore as is the work of the Yahwist. In reality it is all summed up when John calls Christ "the lamb who *takes away* the sin of the world" (John 1:29), for in John the verb *airō* means

"to take away" (10:18; 17:15; 19:15, 31, 38a, 38b; 20:1), "to raise" in
the sense of *tollere* (5:8, 9, 10, 11, 12; 8:59; etc.).

Returning to Marx, it is well by way of contrast to note that the
mechanistic concept of matter, both in Democritus and the Greek
classics, necessarily leads to the conclusion of the eternal return of all
things, for the history of "here below," being in some way linked to
matter, could consist only in combinations and permutations of the
same elements as always. The moment that the eternal return is rejected
as a conception of history, it becomes indispensable to understand
matter as a reality susceptible to true novelty in its development. This is
dialectics. What we must reproach Marx for when he avoids the problem of death and therefore does not even glimpse the possibility of the
resurrection of the dead is that he was not sufficiently dialectical. The
difference among the diverse Greek conceptions of matter is of little
importance (even though some might refuse to be called mechanistic);
this is demonstrated precisely by the neccessity that they all, with variations, have of arriving at the eternal return.

We do not mean to conceal the abysmal difference between Marx
and the biblical authors, a difference stemming from the fact that the
latter believe in God and his intervention and Marx does not. It is God
who curses the earth because of man, according to Gen. 3:17 (cf. 8:21).
It is the wrath of God which "gives men over" to the immanent
cataract of injustice of which they have made themselves guilty, according to Rom. 1:28-32.[208] But what God's intervention does is precisely
to set in motion the immanent and horizontal causality of human
history itself. What the biblical authors want to highlight is precisely
the immanence of this mechanism, the causal link intrinsic to history,
by which a certain type of event brings certain other types with it. "A
synthetic vision of life," Koch has called it.[209] I do not know if the
expression is the happiest, but what is affirmed is, as von Rad says, "the
closest possible correspondence between action and fate: What is in
question is a process which, in virtue of a power proper alike to all that
is good and all that is evil, comes to a good or evil end. Israel regarded
this as a basic order of her whole existence, to which Yahweh had given
effect and over whose functioning he himself kept watch."[210]

The certainty that God directs history and intervenes in it in no way
causes the biblical authors to overlook the dialectic which is inherent to
history. On the contrary, they emphasize it: "Because of one man

death and because of one man the resurrection of the dead" (1 Cor. 15:21). Paul's thesis is precisely this. If not, he would have said, "Because of one man death and because of the work of God the resurrection of the dead." As the sin of one man unleashed a history of death, so the justice of another man (cf. Rom. 5:18b) unleashed the dialectics that results in the definitive realization of justice and the abolition of death (Rom. 5:12-21). It is not faithful to the Bible to attribute a really new *eschaton* exclusively to the fact that God intervenes from outside of history. This is not what the Bible teaches. According to Paul, the real, concrete possibility of something truly new and unprecedented comes from the immanent development of history itself, directed, it is true, by God. "Hope does not deceive *because* (already) the love of God has been poured out *into our hearts* by the Holy Spirit who was given to us" (Rom. 5:5).[211] "Just as the crime of one brought death to all men, so the justice of one brings justice and life to all men" (Rom. 5:18).[212]

I repeat: When Marx avoids the problem of death and therefore does not even glimpse the possibility of resurrection, it is not precisely his lack of faith in God but rather insufficient dialectics for which we must reproach him. Here we have only to follow a truly consistent Marxist, Ernst Bloch.

When the petit bourgeois began to be edified as he looked on the Alps and to chatter about the wonders of the mountains and the majesty of the peaks, what he was doing was putting into poetic form his mechanistic world view. This view had left him only... colorless, soundless atoms, and death meant to be dissolved into them. ... For Kant reality coincided with the object of Newtonian science. What went beyond this was either evil or a purely reflective postulate. For dialectical-materialistic thought, which does not recognize such a dualism but rather grasps in reality itself a postulating (an unfinished tendency) and in the postulating a possible reality, the world does not end with Newton's mechanics. The world does not have a "beyond" (materialism continues to be an understanding of the world in itself). But neither does it have barriers in its "here below." Or better, it has no barriers but those that the direction of the dialectical process sets, ... for no one knows yet if the process of life contains and tolerates a mutation, no matter how invisible it might still be now. A simple "no," although up to the present it would be quite an empirical response, does not settle the question. It is the "no" of a purely blind necessity, not that of a necessity penetrated and therefore dominated and therefore nuanced with the reign of human designs. ... In contrast to mechanistic materialism, dialectics knows no limits in its "here below." Therefore it knows no nothingness predetermined beforehand and imposed by an order supposedly desired by nature.[213]

At its core the avoiding of the problem of death implies the same opiatic resignation which Marx very rightly calls a capitulation before injustice. No matter how positivistic science might prattle about the lack of a foundation for hope in the resurrection, it is incapable of hiding the fact that this science stems from vile resignation, pure abdication. Bloch perspicaciously observes this about the stoicism of the existentialists:

> The precarious profession of nothingness would with difficulty suffice to enable us to hold our head high and work as if there were no end. On the contrary, there are clear indications that, in the subconscious, there still perdure the robust previous ideals and that these are what sustain man. ... Thanks to them, even without knowing it, modern man preserves security-in-himself. Thanks to them the impression is formed, not that man perishes, but that the world, one fine day, decides not to appear before him any longer. ... He lives on previous hopes and the security that they once provided.[214]

The case of existentialism, at least that of an Albert Camus, is not the same as that of positivistic science. The latter does indeed impose nothingness at the end of the route. But its authority is meagre, because it does not know realities but rather abstractions, for neither defining nor measuring nor seeing nor contemplating is really knowing. "Contemplative knowing. .. can, *per definitionem*, refer only to what has been."[215] It has not the least authority concerning the future; its concern is the *res finitae*, the finished things. Therefore it does not know reality, for it begins by proclaiming the dogma that these things are already finished, that they are already *facta*. But this is precisely what is in question. Positivism does not have a consciousness of the *fieri* of reality and, therefore, of the process which continues. Above we established that both the Bible and authentic dialectical thought reject the imposition of an alleged unchangeable "nature of things."[216] And this is all the more true when it is a question of man. It simply does not follow from the fact that all the men who have existed until today have died that death will never be conquered.

Life itself is a qualitatively new irruption outside the mechanical order of entropy. The new qualities of the energetic order constitute planes in which entropy alone (let us say with Freud, "death instinct") can no longer be all-powerful. And it cannot because negentropy—in contrast with entropy—organizes itself and transcends itself and grows. . . . *If there is life*—and its existence, although improbable that it should occur, has become a necessary fact—if there is life which has unfolded consciousness from itself, then *there will necessarily have to be a transcending [Aufhebung] of death* as the goal of the self-transcending of the vital process.[217] The entropy of a system is the indicator of its disorder, and this disorder will increase if it is abandoned to itself. Thus this law does not have an unlimited force in the realm of biology, since "the fundamental property of a living thing is to struggle against chance. This struggle is carried to the world by man: Man changes the world."[218]

The causal relationship which in Rom. 5:12-21 Paul asserts between sin and death constitutes, in my opinion, one of the most important realities for the future of mankind. If we do not forget that the meaning of "sin" in Rom. 3:9 is specified as interhuman injustice for the whole rest of the letter,[219] then the elimination of injustice in mankind will bring with it the definitive defeat of death (cf. 1 Cor. 15:26, "the last enemy to be destroyed is death"). Marx suspected something when he said, "Men have defended themselves until now against death in various ways, but they have still not undertaken the struggle against it."[220] I must, then, slightly modify my affirmation that Marx avoided completely the problem of death. But the causal relationship between interhuman injustice and death, although consistent dialectical thought should have seen it, was not, it seems, perceived by Marx.

The first step, in recent science, was taken in all likelihood by Sigmund Freud. After much hesitation and contradiction, in his work of 1923 titled *The Ego and the Id*, he established that the death instinct focuses, on the one hand, on other beings through the muscular system as a special organ, and, on the other hand, on the interior of the individual, establishing itself in the superego: "What is now holding sway in the superego is, as it were, a pure culture of the death instinct."[221] As is well known, in the superego there is all of human civilization with its structures, its taboos, its laws, its ideologies. This is the same human civilization which Paul calls "cosmos" or "eon,"[222] and in which "sin" has come, as it were, to be incarnated and condensed. Indeed, the person's psyche, where in one or another form the whole history of mankind comes to settle, offers an exceptional field of analysis for knowing historical reality. If we bear in mind that for Paul the law is the quintessence of the cosmos or civilization and that the Freudian superego is the prism of the whole of repressive civilization, Freud's discovery is what Paul had expressed in Rom. 7:10: "The law, which was for life, turned out to be death for man."

Still in 1917 in "On the History of the Psycho-Analytic Movement," Freud was angered by this argumentation of Adler: "If you ask where repression comes from, you are told, 'From civilization'; and if you ask where civilization comes from, you are told, 'From repression.' "[223] In reality, both Adler and Freud should have continued their questioning, for its character of repression and death comes to civilization from the injustice of men, that is, from what Paul calls "sin": "The law intervened so that sin might abound" (Rom. 5:20); "man at one time lived without the law, but when the law came sin took on life and man died" (Rom. 7:9); "for sin, gaining strength through the law, deceived man and through it brought death to him" (Rom. 7:11). If Freud had heeded Marx and his thesis that the State and legislations are instruments of oppression and injustice against some social classes by other social classes, he could have arrived at the same conclusion as Paul: The character of repression and death, which human civilization has, comes from sin, that is, from men's injustice. Repression is oppression and it is injustice. And death is the extreme form of repression. Paul, Freud, and Marx coincide in holding that by means of the law and of "morality" and of ideologies, civilizing oppression comes to be interiorized in the individual man and causes, within the psyche, some elements to exercise this oppression against others and against the entire man. Therefore this extrasystematic observation by Freud in his *Beyond the Pleasure Principle* of 1920 acquires incalculable importance: "It may be, however, that this belief in the internal necessity of dying is only another of those illusions which we have created." And so too this observation in one of the last annotations he ever wrote: "The individual perishes because of his own conflicts."[224]

All these observations point in this direction: In a world in which there is no longer oppression or enmity or mistrust or injustice, death too will disappear. As Paul says, "The last enemy to be destroyed is death" (1 Cor. 15:26). This certainty is inescapable once we have clearly understood that "death entered the world because of sin" (Rom. 5:12; 1 Cor. 15:21).

In other words, this certainty is inescapable once we have clearly understood that in the beginning there was not death but life. Caruso's thought is authentically dialectical: "The path which leads to the overcoming of death is thus a *necessity* postulated by the existence of life."[225] Dialectical thought, as Bloch says, "grasps in reality itself a postulating (an unfinished tendency) and in the postulating a possible reality."[226]

In his psychoanalysis of today's man, Caruso finds that separation, sadism, masochism, enmity, impotence, and noncommunication all seem to be the anticipated presence of death in the life of man. ("In the animals we nowhere see the presence of death in life, masked behind intraspecies oppression, self-destruction, and forced separation."[227]) Caruso's conclusions indicate the intelligent experimental basis for the Pauline affirmation of the causal relationship between death and injustice. But if the causal influence which Caruso finds goes from death to injustice, this is because the relationship is perceived in this way by the man of today. This insight still has not penetrated the fact that injustice, by bringing death into the picture, has made of death its instrument. It is in this way that death produces enmity and injustice.

The skepticism with which the modern scientist (and, under his influence, modern man) approaches the idea of the defeat of death and the triumph of life in resurrection has absolutely nothing modern and scientific about it. It is a fatalistic capitulation typically inherited from Greece. Out of all the possible places Luke situates this scene in Athens: "But when they heard of the resurrection of the dead some mocked him and others said, 'We will hear you out on this at another time' " (Acts 17:32). Let Bultmann not tell us that modern man can no longer accept these utopias.[228] This is not a question of the modern man nor of the modern image of the world. The man who makes the prevailing situation and the status quo his criterion of truth and his norm for distinguishing the possible from the impossible is a man who has always existed and who found his best ideological systematization in Greek thought, that is, in that same thought which Bultmann, without meaning to, shares. It is a thought in which, as Richard Stith says, "Observation takes the place of vocation."[229] What Marcuse says of Galilean science is completely valid for Greek epistemology:

Now precisely because Galilean science is, in the formation of its concepts, the technic of a specific *Lebenswelt*, it does not and cannot *transcend* this *Lebenswelt*. It remains essentially within the basic experiential framework and within the universe of ends set by this reality. . . . At stake [here is this] : . . . the inherent limit of the established science and scientific method, by virtue of which they extend, rationalize, and insure the prevailing *Lebenswelt* without altering its existential structure—that is *without envisaging a qualitatively new mode of "seeing"* and qualitatively new relations between men and between man and nature.[230]

The aforementioned skepticism arises from the artificial subject which the Western mind literally "adopts" (as an unnatural posture is "adopted") when it exercises what it calls objective knowledge. We have already seen that only by an artificial mental operation can we construct a knowing subject who imagines himself not to be part of historical humanity but rather a kind of untemporal point, like a Platonic essence outside of mankind and history.[231] The true subject of knowing, the real subject, he who is identified with the movement of history and with the great march toward liberation, cannot be skeptical when it is a question of the defeat of death and the triumph of life in the resurrection.

If the martyr's name has an altar in the heart of the working class, this does not restore to this name either his eyes or his corporal presence. As a cadaver he too remains far from the goal for which he struggled. How far from and outside of future justice remains the martyrdom which he suffered. This justice will be enjoyed, perhaps, by other entirely different men. The world is full of massacred good men and successful criminals with a long and peaceful old age. . . . In both cases everything becomes irreparable with death.[232]

The Stoics "have made the nothingness of the capitalist future into an absolute and inevitable nothingness in order that the glance which looks toward a transformable world, toward the socialist future, might be radically blocked."[233] For the real and concrete man this nothingness—the true opiate of the people—continues to be nothingness if he is promised only an altar in the heart of the working class; a so-called "generic" survival in the liberated "human race" is also reduced to this nothingness. The negation of the resurrection of the dead is an ideology defensive of the status quo; it is the silencing of the sense of justice that history objectively stirs up; it is to kill the nerve of the real hope of changing this world. The authentically dialectical Marxist and the

Christian who remains faithful to the Bible are the last who will be able to renounce the resurrection of the dead.

Notes to Chapter 5

1. Bultmann, *Faith and Understanding*, 1:63. Ernst Käsemann, *Der Ruf der Freiheit*, 4th ed. (Tübingen: Mohr, 1968), pp. 98 and passim; English version: *Jesus Means Freedom* (Philadelphia: Fortress Press, 1970). Herbert Marcuse, *Soviet Marxism: A Critical Analysis* (New York: Columbia University Press, 1958), pp. 136-59. Jean-Paul Sartre, *Crítica de la razón dialéctica* (Buenos Aires: Losada, 1963), pp. 176-77, 193, passim; original French version: *Critique de la raison dialectique* (Paris: Gallimard, 1960). Ernst Bloch, *Das Prinzip Hoffnung* (Frankfurt: Suhrkamp, 1969), pp. 273, 296-97, 300, 311, passim.
2. Bultmann, *Theology of the New Testament*, 1:277.
3. Adolf Schlatter, *Gottes Gerechtigkeit* 3rd ed. (Stuttgart: Calwer, 1959), p. 162.
4. Jüngel, *Paulus und Jesus*, p. 46.
5. Stuhlmacher, *Gerechtigkeit Gottes*, pp. 227 and passim.
6. Heinz Dietrich Wendland, *Die Briefe an die Korinther*, NeuTestD 7 (Göttingen: Vandenhoeck, 1968), p. 207.
7. H. W. Heidland, "logizomai," *TDNT*, 4:294
8. "By means of the faith," in Rom. 1:12; 3:22, 25, 27, 30; Gal. 2:16 (3:14) (3:26); Phil 3:9; etc. "Stemming from the faith," in Rom. 1:17; 3:26, 30; (4:16a, 16b); 5:1; 9:30, 32; 10:6; Gal. 3:8, 11 (3:7, 9), 24; 5:5; etc.
9. Artur Weiser and Rudolf Bultmann, "pistis," *TDNT*, 6:174-228.
10. Bultmann, "pistis," *TDNT*, 6:207.
11. Cf. Walter Grundmann, *Das Evangelium nach Matthäus*, ThHKomNT 1 (Berlin: Evangelische Verlagsanstalt, 1968), p. 415.
12. Herbert Braun, "Glaube im NT," *RelGG*, 3rd ed., 2:1592.
13. Rudolf Schnackenburg, "Glaube," *Lexikon für Theologie und Kirche*, 2nd ed., 4: col. 915.
14. Theodor Zahn, *Das Evangelium des Matthäus* 2nd ed. (Leipzig: A. Deichertsche, 1905), p. 383.
15. In Held's excellent monograph "Matthew as Interpreter of the Miracle Stories," in Günther Bornkamm, Gerhard Barth, and Heinz Joachim Held, *Tradition and Interpretation in Matthew*, pp. 279-81.
16. Bultmann, "pistis," *TWNT*, 6:204; cf. *TDNT*, 6:203-04.
17. Cf. Michel, *Brief an die Römer*, p. 259; Paul Althaus, *Der Brief an die Römer*, NeuTestD 6 (Göttingen: Vandenhoeck, 1966), p. 109: "Der Inhalt des Glaubens und des Bekenntnisses ist im Grunde ein und derselbe"; Bultmann, "pistis," *TDNT*, 6:209; Kertelge, *"Rechtfertigung,"* p. 175; etc.
18. Michel, *Brief an die Römer*, p. 259.

19. Eduard Schweizer, *TWNT* (1969), 8:368; cf. *TDNT*, 8:367.

20. Albrecht Oepke, *TDNT*, 2:335: "The idea of the self-resurrection of Jesus is first found in Johannine theology."

21. Cf. Rudolph, *Hosea*, pp. 136-37; Wolff, *Dodekapropheton I*, pp. 150-51.

22. Wilhelm Bousset, *Kyrios Christos*, trans. John E. Steely (Nashville: Abingdon, 1970), pp. 204-05. Herbert Braun, "Der Sinn der ntl. Christologie," *Gesammelte Studien Zum Neuen Testament und Seiner Umwelt* (Tübingen: Mohr, 1962), pp. 244-45.

23. Willi Marxsen, *Mark the Evangelist*, trans. James Boyce et al. (Nashville: Abingdon, 1969), pp. 131-34.

24. C. H. Dodd, *The Parables of the Kingdom* (New York: Scribner's, 1961).

25. Bultmann, *Glauben und Verstehen*, 1:210, n. 1; cf. *Faith and Understanding*, 1:243.

26. Regarding *ēngiken*, cf. Paul Joüon, "Notes philologiques sur les Évangiles," *RechScRel* 17 (1927), p. 538; Feuillet, *"Egō eimi,"* pp. 234-35; Matthew Black, *An Aramaic Approach to the Gospels and Acts*, 3rd ed. (Oxford: Clarendon, 1967), pp. 208-11. For me it is more than probable that the origin is in the Hebrew verb *Ḳareb* and precisely in the Deutero-Isaianic usage of Isa. 46:13; Isa. 51:5; 55:6; and 56:1, which the Septuagint translates with the verb *engizō*. The change to the intransitive perfect seems intentional in the Synoptics, precisely so to bring out that the justice which God was causing to draw near, according to Deutero-Isaiah, with Christ "has already come."

27. Cf. above pp. 172-73.

28. Gerhard Friedrich, "euangelion," *TDNT*, 2:726.

29. Cf. above pp. 206-07.

30. Cf. Weiser, "pisteuō, pistis ktl," *TDNT*, 6:194-95.

31. Ibid., p. 192.

32. Ibid., p. 195.

33. Regarding the strictly social sense of this justice, cf. above pp. 93-94

34. Althaus has seen very clearly that 10:1-3 cannot be separated from 9:30-33 (*Brief an die Römer*, pp. 105-07).

35. Kertelge, *"Rechfertigung,"* pp. 192-93.

36. Cf. above pp. 88-99.

37. Von Rad, *Genesis*, p. 150.

38. Cf. above pp. 94-95.

39. Michel, *Brief an die Römer*, p. 126.

40. Cf. above p. 104.

41. Schlier, *Brief an die Galater*, p. 141.

42. Duhm, *Jesaja*, p. 196.

43. Cf. Noth, *Pentateuchal Traditions*, p. 128, n. 360. Regarding the meaning of Exod. 18, cf. above pp. 144-45 and 155-56.

44. Weiser, *Zwölf Kleinen Propheten*, p. 259.

45. Cf. above pp. 128-29.

46. Bultmann, *Glauben und Verstehen*, 2:165.

47. Ellen Flesseman-van Leer, "Die Interpretation der Passionsgeschichte

vom Alten Testament aus," in *Zur Bedeutung des Todes Jesu* (Gütersloh, G. Mohn, 1967), pp. 89-90.

48. Cf. above pp. 63-64.

49. Schnackenburg, *Johannesbriefe*, p. 241.

50. Cf. above p. 218.

51. Transcribed above, pp. 220-21.

52. Wendland, *Briefe an die Korinther*, p. 29.

53. Michel, *Brief an die Römer*, p. 302, n. 1.

54. Bultmann, *Glauben und Verstehen*, 1:171; cf. *Faith and Understanding*, 1:203.

55. Schweizer, "pneuma," *TDNT*, 6:431.

56. Cf. above pp. 181-92.

57. The text is cited in Wendland, *Briefe an die Korinther*, p. 52.

58. Kertelge, *"Rechtfertigung,"* pp. 214-15.

59. Cf. Althaus's study "Fleisch und Geist bei Paulus," in his *Brief an die Römer*, pp. 87-89.

60. Cf. above pp. 216-17.

61. Cf. above pp. 216-17.

62. Garaudy, *Perspectivas del hombre*, p. 205.

63. Cf. above p. 205.

64. Cf. Bauer, "para," *Greek-English Lexicon*, p. 616. Zorell, *Lexicon*, col. 981-82 (III).

65. Cf. above pp. 206, 213.

66. Cf. above pp. 207-12.

67. Cf. above p. 215.

68. Cf. above pp. 218-26.

69. Cf. above p. 223.

70. Cf. above pp. 218-26.

71. This refers to the spirit of God. Cf. Michel, *Brief an der Römer*, p. 193; Kuss, *Römerbrief*, pp. 503-04; Lyonnet, *Exegesis epistulae ad romanos*, pp. 193-94.

72. Cf. above pp. 160-64 and 169-84.

73. Gerhard Kittel, "doxa," *TWNT*, 2:248; cf. *TDNT*, 2:245.

74. Von Rad, "doxa," *TDNT*, 2:239.

75. Cf. above p. 115.

76. Independently of later liturgical symbolization, concerning which cf. Kraus, *Psalmen I*, pp. 197-205.

77. Kraus, *Psalmen I*, pp. 499-500.

78. Cf. above pp. 127-37.

79. Cf., for example, C. K. Barrett, *The Gospel According to St. John* (London: SPCK, 1955), p. 139; Henri van den Bussche, *Jean* (Paris: Desclée, 1967), p. 102; Raymond E. Brown, *The Gospel According to John (I-XII)*, Anchor Bible 29 (New York: Doubleday, 1966), p. 14; B. F. Westcott, *The Gospel According to St. John* (London: Murray, 1908), p. 13; etc.

80. Cf. Paul Joüon, "Notes de lexicographie hebraïque," *Mélanges de la*

Faculté Orientale 5 (1911-12): 407; Felix Asensio, *Misericordia et veritas* (Rome: Gregoriana, 1949).

81. Cf. above pp. 93-94.
82. Cf. above pp. 233-34.
83. Cf. above pp. 234-35.
84. Cf. above p. 223.
85. Cf. above p. 236.
86. Cf. above pp. 233-36.
87. Indicated above pp. 208-11.
88. Althaus, *Brief an der Römer*, p. 62.
89. Michel, *Brief an die Römer*, p. 153.
90. Lyonnet, *Exegesis epistulae ad romanos*, c. 5 ad 8, p. 31.
91. Ibid.
92. Cf. above p. 231.
93. Michel, *Brief an die Römer*, p. 212.
94. Althaus, *Brief an die Römer*, p. 95.
95. Schlier, *Brief an die Galater*, p. 233.
96. Ibid., p. 234.
97. Kertelge, *"Rechtfertigung,"* p. 136.
98. Bultmann, *Theology of the New Testament*, pp. 274-79.
99. Bultmann, "Karl Barth, The Resurrection of the Dead," *Faith and Understanding*, 1:66-94.
100. Käsemann, "Die Heilsbedeutung des Todes Jesu nach Paulus," in the collective work *Zur Bedeutung des Todes Jesu*, p. 27.
101. Cf. above p. 212.
102. Bloch, *Das Prinzip Hoffnung*, p. 231.
103. Cf. above p. 241.
104. Kertelge, *"Rechtfertigung,"* p. 159.
105. Cf. above p. 203.
106. Cf. above pp. 218-26.
107. Cf. above p. 230.
108. Cf. above pp. 182-92.
109. Cf. above p. 241.
110. Cf. above pp. 127-37.
111. Cf. Georg Strecker, *Der Weg der Gerechtigkeit*, 2nd ed., FRLANT 82 (Göttingen: Vandenhoeck, 1966), pp. 236-42.
112. Bultmann, *Faith and Understanding*, 1:237.
113. Cf. above pp. 216-18 and 226-29.
114. Bultmann, "The Concept of the Word in the New Testament," *Faith and Understanding*, 1:237.
115. Gerhard Friedrich, *TDNT*, 2:721 n. 3.
116. H. Kleinknecht, "logos," *TWNT*, 4:78; cf. *TDNT*, 4:80.
117. Bultmann, *Glauben und Verstehen*, 1:275; cf. *Faith and Understanding*.
118. Cf. Kleinknecht, "logos," *TDNT*, 4:77.
119. Cf. Bultmann, "ginōskō," *TDNT*, 1:691-92.
120. Cf. ibid., pp. 697-98.
121. Bultmann, *Faith and Understanding*, 1:242.

122. Bloch, *Das Prinzip Hoffnung*, p. 79.
123. Cf. above pp. 181-92.
124. Cf. above pp. 206-18.
125. Mao Tse-Tung, "On Contradiction," in *Selected Readings from the Works of Mao Tse-Tung* (Peking: Foreign Languages Press, 1967), p. 100.
126. Marx and Engels, "The Communist Manifesto," *Essential Works of Marxism*, ed. Arthur P. Mandel (New York: Bantam, 1961), p. 14.
127. Ibid., p. 34.
128. Ibid., p. 13.
129. Jean-Yves Calvez, *La Pensée de Karl Marx* (Paris: Seuil, 1959), p. 331.
130. Marx, *Capital: A Critique of Political Economy* (New York: International Publishers, 1967), vol. 1, part 8, ch. 26, p. 714.
131. Cf. above pp. 160-64.
132. Cf. above pp. 181-92.
133. Cf. Marx, *Capital*, in its entirety.
134. Marx, "Communist Manifesto," pp. 39-40.
135. Calvez, *Pensée de Karl Marx*, p. 233.
136. I refer to four of Marcuse's books: *Eros and Civilization* (Boston: Beacon, 1966); *One-Dimensional Man*; *Soviet Marxism*; *Essay on Liberation* (Boston: Beacon, 1969).
137. Cf. above pp. 181-192.
138. Bigo, *Marxismo y humanismo*, p. 171.
139. Schlier, *Brief an die Galater*, p. 283; Bultmann, *Faith and Understanding*, 1:203.
140. Cf. above p. 118.
141. Cf. above pp. 181-92.
142. Cf. above pp. 67-72.
143. On the meaning of "covetousness" as interhuman injustice, cf. above pp. 69-70. On the meaning of "flesh," cf. above pp. 224-26.
144. Cf. above pp. 246-50.
145. Cf. above pp. 60-65.
146. Cited by Calvez, *Pensée de Karl Marx*, pp. 518-19; cf. Karl Marx, *Economic and Philosophic Manuscripts of 1844*, trans. Martin Milligan (New York: International Publishers, 1964), p. 144.
147. Ibid., p. 518.
148. Bigo, *Marxismo y humanismo*, p. 234.
149. Ibid., pp. 233-34.
150. Cited by Roger Garaudy in *Karl Marx: The Evolution of His Thought* (New York: International Publishers, 1967), p. 126; cf. Marx, *Manuscripts of 1844*, p. 129.
151. Bigo, *Marxismo y humanismo*, pp. 76-77, summarizing Marx.
152. Ibid., p. 78.
153. Garaudy, *Karl Marx* (Paris: Seghers, 1964), p. 161; cf. English translation, p. 112.
154. Ibid., English translation, p. 56.
155. Ibid., p. 113.

156. Bigo, *Marxismo y humanismo*, pp. 81-82.
157. Garaudy, *Karl Marx*, English translation, pp. 55 and 112-13.
158. Marcuse, *One-Dimensional Man*, p. 140.
159. H. G. Gadamer, *Wahrheit und Methode*, 2nd ed. (Tübingen: Mohr, 1965), p. 426.
160. Francette Arnault, *Lecciones de filosofía marxista* (Mexico, D. F., 1966), p. 294.
161. Marcuse, *One-Dimensional Man*, pp. 140-41.
162. Bigo, *Doctrine sociale*, p. 189.
163. Bigo, *Marxismo y humanismo*, p. 232.
164. Garaudy, *Karl Marx* (French version), p. 169; cf. English version, p. 117; the italics are mine.
165. Ibid.
166. Bigo, *Marxismo y humanismo*, p. 195.
167. Domergue, *Frères du monde* (May-June 1968), p. 14.
168. Ibid., p. 15.
169. Marshall McLuhan, *Understanding Media* (New York: McGraw-Hill, 1964), p. 37.
170. Domergue, *Frères du monde* (May-June 1968).
171. Cf. above pp. 262-63.
172. Cf. above pp. 254-55.
173. Levinas, *Totalité et infini*, p. 14; cf. *Totality and Infinity*, p. 46.
174. Bigo, *Marxismo y humanismo*, p. 107.
175. Cf. above pp. 262-64.
176. Marx, *Manuscripts of 1844*, p. 106, cited by Garaudy, *Karl Marx*, p. 56.
177. Marcuse, *Sociedad carnívora* (Buenos Aires: Galerna, 1969), p. 30.
178. Koschelava, *El mito de los dos Marx*, p. 52.
179. Calvez, *Pensée de Karl Marx*, passim.
180. Ibid., p. 465.
181. Ibid., pp. 464-65.
182. Koschelava, *El mito de los dos Marx*, pp. 50-51.
183. Oscar Cullmann, *Christ and Time*, trans. F. V. Filson (Philadelphia: Westminster Press, 1950); Jean Daniélou, *The Lord of History* (Chicago: Regnery, 1958).
184. Mao Tse-Tung, "On the Correct Handling of Contradictions Among the People," in *Selected Readings*, p. 373.
185. Marcuse, *One-Dimensional Man*, pp. 141-42.
186. Bigo, *Doctrine sociale*, p. 188 n. 2.
187. Levinas, *Totality and Infinity*, p. 247.
188. Calvez, *Pensée de Karl Marx*, p. 263.
189. Joseph Gabel, *Ideologie und Schizophrenie, Formen der Entfremdung* (Frankfurt: Fischer, 1967).
190. Bloch, *Das Prinzip Hoffnung*, p. 61.
191. Marcuse, *Eros and Civilization*, p. 257.
192. Bloch, *Das Prinzip Hoffnung*, p. 227.
193. Ibid., p. 228.

194. "To say that the act of production is an act of exploitation which divides man within himself and from other men is the equivalent of putting the economists on trial as well, for they have very rarely found such great evil in the act of production" (Calvez, *Pensée de Karl Marx*, p. 262).

195. Marx, "Theses on Feuerbach," no. 11, in Karl Marx and Friedrich Engels, *On Religion* (New York: Schocken Books, 1964), p. 72; italics in the original.

196. Ibid., no. 1, p. 69.

197. Bloch, *Das Prinzip Hoffnung*, pp. 198-99 and 229.

198. Marx, "Die Heilige Familie," in *Ausgewählte Schriften*, pp. 233-34; cf. "The Holy Family," in *Writings of the Young Marx on Philosophy and Society,* trans. and ed. Loyd D. Easton and Kurt H. Guddat (Garden City, N. Y.: Anchor, Doubleday, 1967), p. 391.

199. Marx, *Ausgewählte Schriften*, p. 218; *Writings*, p. 382.

200. Michel, *Brief an der Römer*, pp. 196-97.

201. Cándido Pozo, *Teología del más allá*, 4th ed. (Madrid: BAC, 1968), pp. 127-35; cf. above, pp. 218-26.

202. Stanislas Lyonnet, "Redemptio 'cosmica' secundum Rom. 8, 19-23," *VD* 44, nos. 5-6 (1966): 240.

203. Rudolf Schnackenburg, in his excellent presentation "Gotteskindschaft und Zeugung aus Gott," in his *Johannesbriefe*, pp. 175-83.

204. Cf. above p. 118.

205. Cf. above pp. 218-26.

206. Cf. above p. 92.

207. Cf. above pp. 254-55.

208. Cf. above pp. 160-64.

209. K. Koch, "Gibt es ein Vergeltungsdogma im Alten Testament?" *ZThK* 52 (1955): 1-44.

210. Von Rad, *Old Testament Theology*, 1:265.

211. Cf. above pp. 230-32.

212. Regarding *katakrima* (death), cf. above p. 185.

213. Bloch, *Das Prinzip Hoffnung*, pp. 1357, 1303, 1382.

214. Ibid., p. 1361.

215. Ibid., p. 7.

216. Cf. above pp. 254-55.

217. Igor Caruso, *La separación de los amantes* (Mexico, D.F.: Siglo XXI, 1969), pp. 205-06; italics in the original.

218. Ibid., p. 205, summarizing Albert Ducrocq in n. 39.

219. Cf. above pp. 169-70.

220. Cited by Rolf Denker in *Aufklärung über Aggression* (Stuttgart: Kohlhammer, 1966), p. 128.

221. Freud, *The Ego and the Id*, trans. James Strachey (New York: Norton, 1960), p. 72; cf. Caruso, *Separación*, p. 156.

222. Cf. above pp. 181-92.

223. Freud, *Collected Papers* (New York: Basic Books, 1959), 1:346; cf. Caruso, *Separación*, p. 155.

292 Marx and the Bible

224. Freud, *Gerke W.* 17:152; cf. Caruso, *Separación*, p. 157; cf. *Beyond the Pleasure Principle*, trans. James Strachey (New York: Liveright, 1950), p. 59.
225. Caruso, *Separación*, p. 204.
226. Bloch, *Das Prinzip Hoffnung*, p. 1303.
227. Ibid., p. 207.
228. Cf. Bultmann, "Die Entmythologisierung der neutestamentlichen Verkündigung als Aufgabe," in his study "Neues Testament und Mythologie" in H. W. Bartsch, ed., *Kerygma und Mythos I* (Hamburg: Reich, 1960), pp. 15-48.
229. Richard Stith, "Lettre à un professeur sur la connaissance calculatrice," *Esprit* 8-9 (1968): 85.
230. Marcuse, *One-Dimensional Man*, pp. 164-65; italics in the original.
231. Cf. above p. 272.
232. Bloch, *Das Prinzip Hoffnung*, p. 1300.
233. Ibid., p. 1364.

Epilogue

Paul uses the expression "new covenant" in 2 Cor. 3:6 to synthesize his whole task and everything that the preacher of the Gospel must achieve in the world; in relation to this expression, Jer. 31:31-34 (LXX, 38:31-34) is often cited, and rightly so, for here the expression *kainē diathēkē* appears for the first time in the Septuagint.[1] From the Qumran scrolls we have learned that the expression coined by Jeremiah came to constitute a very rich synthesis of everything that the Old Testament expectation awaited. The Qumran group uses it in CD 8:21; 19:33; 20:12; 1 QpHab 2:3.[2] And in Paul it effectively has this same extremely pregnant meaning. According to Jeremiah in the passage we have cited, the new covenant will consist in an interiorization of the content of the law of such a kind that—and the consecutive force must be borne in mind—all men will know Yahweh, "then all will know me, from the smallest to the greatest. It is Yahweh who speaks."

What Paul's commentators usually do not recall is that nine chapters earlier Jeremiah himself had defined with an almost scholastic precision what he understands by "to know Yahweh": "He practiced justice and right; this is good. He defended the cause of the poor and the needy; this is good. Is not this what it means to know me? It is Yahweh who speaks" (Jer. 22:15-16).[3] For Jeremiah the new covenant consists in "knowing Yahweh," but this "knowing Yahweh" in turn consists in doing effective justice to all the poor and needy of the earth. If we keep in mind what the genuine Exodus and prophetic tradition understands by "law,"[4] we can thoroughly understand the consecutive force of the Jeremian passage: Because of the acute sense of justice, interiorized in the hearts of human beings, "they will know Yahweh" (taking this expression in the precise meaning already mentioned). Ezekiel saw this

293

very clearly when, upon adopting Jeremiah's hope of a new "covenant" (cf. Ezek. 34:25; 37:26), he described it as a conferral of the "spirit of Yahweh" on the hearts of men (Ezek. 36:24-28).[5] In the same passage Ezekiel links this notion to the authentic meaning of the law: "my commands and my *mišpaṭim*" (v. 27). Paul is thinking of both Ezekiel and Jeremiah when he says, "in order that the content of justice of the law might be achieved in us who do not walk according to the flesh but according to the spirit" (Rom. 8:4), for in 2 Cor. 3:6 he linked the "new covenant" (an expression taken from Jeremiah) with the "spirit" (an expression which is not in the passage in Jeremiah, but is in that of Ezekiel). As Rom. 13:8-10 summarizes the whole content of the law in "love your neighbor," it is clear that this passage moves in the same Exodus and prophetic tradition.

But Jeremiah's description of the "new covenant" (Jer. 31:31-34), *before* it asserts that all will know Yahweh, has Yahweh say, "And I will be (or I will become) their God and they will be (or will become) my people" (Jer. 31:33), a likewise exceedingly pregnant expression that Ezek. 37:37 takes up again and Paul also adopts in 2 Cor. 6:16. The heart of the matter is that men will not have Yahweh as their God unless they love their neighbor and achieve justice completely on the earth. God will not be God until then. The God whom we claim to affirm when we prescind from the realization of justice is simply an idol, not the true God.[6] The true God is not; he will be.

"I will be who I will be," Yahweh says to Moses when Moses asks him his name (Exod. 3:14). Michel Allard has shown that the Septuagint and the Vulgate erred when they translated this as "I am who I am."[7] As Joüon establishes in his grammar, in the stative verbs the imperfect expresses only future, and there is nothing in the context of Exod. 3:14 that suggests that the verb *hayah* should cease to be stative and should become active.[8] In fact the Septuagint always translates the first person singular of the imperfect of *hayah* as "I will be" (*esomai*), except in this verse and in Hos. 1:9, where it intentionally alludes to Exod. 3:14.[9] As Allard shows, the other two exceptions, Job 7:20 and 2 Sam. 15:34, really are not exceptions, the former because it has a consequential and not a temporal nuance, and the latter because it clearly has to do with the preterite.[10]

"I will be who I will be" (Exod. 3:14) is indeed the explanation of the name "Yahweh" (Hebrew: *Yahweh*), as Allard and Noth rightly point out.[11] "Yahweh" is the third person of the imperfect (= future) of the verb "to be," and all those who are not God had to designate God in the third person; on the other hand in "I will be who I will be," it is Yahweh himself who speaks, in the first person. In the very name "Yahweh" the essential futureness of the God of the Bible is unequivocally expressed. If there is any interpretation of Exod. 3:14 radically excluded by the context, it is the one proposed by Loisy, who suggests that by the response "I will be who I will be" God refused to give a response and evasively concealed his name. As Noth indicates, "The context lead[s] us to understand that the name Yahweh is disclosed to Moses as a real divine name."[12] The force of this name is in the future, for Yahweh goes on to say to Moses in the most abbreviated form: "Thus you will speak to the sons of Israel, ' "I will be" has sent me to you' " (Exod. 3:14b).

As Horst Dietrich Preuss has shown in a series of converging observations not based specifically on Yahweh's name itself, " 'To know that I am Yahweh' is always, from its own greatest depths, an eschatological affirmation."[13] Contrary to everything we can include within our ontological categories, Yahweh is not, but rather will be. He will be when there is a people who fulfill certain conditions. Thus we are able to understand expressions like this: "Because of his name, Yahweh will not reject his people, for Yahweh has wanted to make you his people" (1 Sam. 12:22). Yahweh is essentially an eschatological God, and all his intervention in history is directed toward forming a mankind in which he is finally able *to be*. In 1 Sam. 12:22 there is implied an understanding of the meaning of the "great name" of Yahweh: the God who will be. It is in virtue of his name that Yahweh must have patience and continue to form a people as the seed of future humanity, in which, and only in which, he finally will be able *to be*.

Before presenting to us his conception of the new covenant through the conferral of the spirit of Yahweh, Ezekiel has Yahweh indicate to us, "I do not do this because of you, house of Israel, but because of my holy name" (Ezek. 36:22). I do not believe that there is any basis for asserting that this is a formulistic, stereotyped expression. Everything leads us to believe that in such formulations there exists a full awareness of the original significance of the name "Yahweh":

Do not hold our ancestors' crimes against us,
may your compassion quickly reach us,

we can hardly be crushed lower.
Help us, God of our salvation,
for the honor of your name;
deliver us and pardon our sins,
for the sake of your name.

(Ps. 79:8-9)

In order for Yahweh to come to be he must save a germ of the future humanity, notwithstanding the faults and betrayals of the people whom Yahweh chose as the seed of the future world. Deutero-Isaiah shows that he has this same understanding of the meaning of the name of Yahweh when he has God say, "Because of my name I will hold off my rage" (Isa. 48:9). We find the same thought in Jer. 14:7; Ezek. 20:8-9; Josh. 7:9; Ps. 106:8; Ezek. 20:13-14; Ps. 25:11; Ezek. 20:21-22; etc.

After what we saw in chapter 2 above, we should not be surprised at this characteristic futureness of the God of the Bible. According to Western ontology ("a philosophy of injustice," as Levinas says), first the object exists and then it is known, and it exists independently of whether it is known or not. Like a brick, like a thing, like an . . . object, precisely. Anyone would say that we cannot think of existence in any other way. And yet the biblical authors implacably insist that a god who is conceived as existing outside the interhuman summons to justice and love is not the God who revealed himself to them, but rather some idol. Moreover the whole Bible is directed toward creating a world in which authentic interhuman relationship is possible and is a reality.

God will be only in a world of justice, and if Marx does not find him in the Western world it is because he is indeed not there, nor can he be. As Freud attests, "There is no longer any place in present-day civilized life for a simple natural love between two human beings."[14] All our rebellion against Western civilization and against its acute extreme called capitalism is the attraction exercised on us by a future world in which justice, authentic love, is possible. Then, in the societal relationship of justice, and not before, the authentically dialectical mind will have to see if God exists or does not exist. Anything else would be vulgar materialism and dogmatism.

Notes to Epilogue

1. See, for example, Stanislas Lyonnet, *La storia della salvezza nella lettera ai romani* (Naples: D'Auria, 1967), pp. 131-66; and Wendland, *Briefe an die Korinther*, p. 179. Cf. Heb. 8:8; 12:24.

2. Cf. C. Spicq, "L'Épître aux Hébreux, Apollos, Jean-Baptiste, les Hellénistes et Qumran," *Revue de Qumran* 1, no. 3 (February 1959): 365-90; and Herbert Braun, *Qumran und das Neue Testament* (Tübingen: Mohr, 1966), 1:198-99.

3. Cf. above pp. 44-53.

4. Cf. above pp. 137-60.

5. Cf. the qualititative significance of "spirit of God," above pp. 218-26.

6. Cf. above pp. 53-67 on the anticultus of the prophets.

7. Michel Allard, "Note sur la formule 'ehyeh aser' ehyeh,'" *RechScR* 45 (1957): 79-86.

8. Joüon, *Grammaire*, no. 113a.

9. Cf. Wolff, *Hosea*, pp. 7 and 24; cf. Rudolph, *Hosea*, p. 54.

10. Allard, "Note," p. 80.

11. Ibid., p. 83; Noth, *Exodus*, pp. 43-44.

12. Noth, *Exodus*, p. 44.

13. Horst Dietrich Preuss, *Jahweglaube und Zukunftserwartung*, BWANT 87, (Stuttgart: Kohlhammer, 1968), p. 28.

14. Sigmund Freud, *Civilization and Its Discontents*, p. 77, note, cited by Marcuse, *Eros and Civilization*, p. 264.

Abbreviations

AAS	Acta Apostolicae Sedis	HarvThRev	Harvard Theological Review
AnBi	Analecta Biblica	HAT	Handkommentar zum Alten Testament
ATDeut	Das Alte Testament Deutsch	HBAT	Handbuch zum Alten Testament
Bi	Biblica	JBL	Journal of Biblical Literature
BiblZ	Biblische Zeitschrift		
BiKomm	Biblischer Kommentar	JournNESt	Journal of Near Eastern Studies
BWANT	Beiträge zur Wissenschaft vom Alten und Neuen Testament	JournSemSt	Journal of Semetic Studies
BZAltW	Beiheft zur Zeitschrift für alttestamentliche Wissenschaft	KerDog	Kerygma und Dogma
		KommAT	Kommentar zum Alten Testament
BzFöchrTh	Beiträge zur Förderung der christlichen Theologie	MeyersKomm	Kritisch-Exegetischer Kommentar über das Neue Testament, begründet von H. A. W. Meyer
CBQ	Catholic Biblical Quarterly		
EstBi	Estudios Bíblicos	NeuTestD	Das Neue Testament Deutsch
EvTh	Evangelische Theologie	NT	Novum Testamentum
EVZ	Evangelischer Verlag Zürich	NTSt	New Testament Studies
ExpTim	Expository Times	PG	Patrologiae cursus ... Series graeca
FRLANT	Forschungen zur Religion und Literatur des Alten und Neuen Testamentes	PIB	Pontificio Istituto Biblico
		PL	Patrologiae cursus ... Series latina

RB	Revue Biblique	ThStKr	Theologische Studien und Kritiken
RechBi	Recherches Bibliques		
RechScR	Recherches de Science Religieuse	ThSt	Theologische Studien
		ThZ	Theologische Zeitschrift
RelGG	Die Religion in Geschichte und Gegenwart	TWNT	Kittels Theologisches Wörterbuch zum Neuen Testament
ScJourTh	Scottish Journal of Theology	VD	Verbum Domini
StBiFr	Studi Biblici Franciscani	VT	Vetus Testamentum
		VTSuppl	Vetus Testamentum Supplement
StdZ	Stimmen der Zeit		
TDNT	Kittel's Theological Dictionary of the New Testament	ZAltW	Zeitschrift für alttestamentliche Wissenschaft
ThHKomNT	Theologischer Handkommentar zum Neuen Testament	ZNeuW	Zeitschrift für neutestamentliche Wissenschaft
ThLitZ	Theologische Literaturzeitung	ZThK	Zeitschrift für Theologie und Kirche

Bibliography

Allard, Michel. "Note sur la formule "ehyeh aser 'ehyeh.' " *RechScR* 45 (1957):79-86.

Allaz, Tomás G. "El derecho de los postergados." In *La Iglesia, el subdesarollo y la revolución*. Mexico, D.F.: Nuestro Tiempo, 1968.

Alt, Albrecht. *Die Ursprunge des israelitischen Rechtes* (1934). English version: "The Origins of Israelite Law." In *Essays on Old Testament History and Religion*. Trans. R. A. Wilson. Garden City, N.Y.: Anchor, Doubleday, 1968.

Althaus, Paul. *Der Brief an die Römer*. NeuTestD 6. Göttingen: Vandenhoeck, 1966.

Arnault, Francette. "Leyes de la dialéctica." In Roger Garaudy et al. *Lecciones de filosofía marxista*. Mexico, D.F.: Grijalbo, 1966.

Asensio, Félix. *Misericordia et veritas*. Rome: Gregoriana, 1949.

Bach, R. "Gottesrecht und weltliches-Recht in der Verkündigung des Propheten Amos." In *Festschrift für G. Dehn*. Neukirchen, 1957.

Balscheit, B. "Alter und Aufkommen des Monotheismus in der israelitischen Religion." *BZAltW* 69 (1938).

Barrett, C. K. *The Gospel According to St. John*. London: SPCK, 1955.

Barth, Gerhard. "Das Gesetzesverständnis des Evangelisten Matthäus." In Günther Bornkamm, Gerhard Barth, Heinz Joachim Held. *Überlieferung und Auslegung im Matthäus-Evangelium*. 4th ed. Neukirchen: Neukirchen Verlag, 1965. English version: "Matthew's Understanding of the Law." In *Tradition and Interpretation in Matthew*. Philadelphia: Westminster, 1963.

Barth, Karl. *Die Auferstehung der Toten*. Zurich: Evangelischer Verlag, 1953. English version: *The Resurrection of the Dead*. Trans. H. J. Stenning, New York: Revell, 1933.

_____. *Der Romerbrief*, 1919. Zurich: Evangelischer Verlag, 1963. English version: *The Epistle to the Romans*. Trans. Edwyn C. Hoskyns. 6th ed. New York: Oxford, 1933.

Baudissin, G. "Alttestamentliches *hajjim* 'Leben' in der Bedeutung von 'Gluck.' " In *Festschrift Sachau* (1915).

Beaucamp, E. "La justice de Yahve et l'économie de l'alliance." *StBiFr* 2 (1960-61).

Beyerlin, Walter. *Herkunft und Geschichte der ältesten Sinaitraditionen*. Tübingen: Mohr, 1961. English version: *Origins and History of the Oldest Sinaitic Traditions*. Trans. S. Rudman. Oxford: Blackwell, 1965.

Bigo, Pierre. *La doctrine sociale de l'Église.* Paris: Presses Universitaires de France, 1965.

_____. *Marxismo y humanismo.* Madrid: ZYX, 1966. French version: *Marxisme et humanisme.* 3rd ed. Paris: Presses Universitaires de France, 1961.

Black, Matthew. *An Aramaic Approach to the Gospels and Acts.* 3rd ed. Oxford: Clarendon, 1967.

Blass, F., and Debrunner, A. *A Greek Grammar of the New Testament.* 3rd ed. Trans. Robert W. Funk. Chicago: University of Chicago Press, 1967.

Bloch, Ernst. *Das Prinzip Hoffnung.* 2nd ed. Frankfurt: Suhrkamp, 1969.

Bonnard, Pierre. *L'Évangile selon Saint Matthieu.* Neuchatel: Delachaux, 1963.

Bornkamm, Günther. See above Barth, Gerhard.

Botterweck, G. Johannes. *"Gott Erkennen" im Sprachgebrauch des Alten Testaments.* Bonn: Peter Hanstein, 1951.

Bousset, Wilhelm. *Kyrios Christos.* 3rd ed. FRLANT 22. Göttingen: Vandenhoeck, 1926. English version: *Kyrios Christos.* Trans. John E. Steely. Nashville: Abingdon, 1970.

Braun, Herbert. "Glaube im Neuen Testament." In *RelGG.* 3rd ed. 2:1590-97.

_____. *Qumran und des Neue Testament.* Tübingen: Mohr, 1966.

_____. "Der Sinn der ntl. Christologie." In *Gesammelte Studien zum Neuen Testament und seiner Umwelt.* Tübingen: Mohr, 1962.

Bright, J. "Isaiah-I." In *Peake's Commentary on the Bible.* Matthew Black and H. H. Rowley, eds. London: Nelson, 1962.

Brown, Raymond E. *The Gospel According to John (I-XII).* Anchor Bible 29. New York: Doubleday, 1966.

Büchsel, Friedrich. "ileos." *TWNT* 3:311-18, 320-24. English version: *TDNT* 3:310-18, 319-23.

_____. "krisis." *TWNT* 3:933-55. English version: *TDNT* 3:933-54.

Buis, Pierre, and Leclercq, Jacques. *Le Deutéronome.* Paris: Gabalda, 1963.

Bultmann, Rudolf. "Dikaiosyne Theou." *JBL* 83, part 1 (March 1964): 12-16.

_____. *Die drei Johannesbriefe.* MeyersKomm. Göttingen: Vandenhoeck, 1967.

_____. *Das Evangelium des Johannes.* Göttingen: Vandenhoeck, 1964. English version: *The Gospel of John: A Commentary.* Trans. G. R. Beasley-Murray et al. Philadelphia: Westminster, 1971.

_____. *Die Geschichte der synoptischen Tradition.* Göttingen: Vandenhoeck, 1957. English version: *The History of the Synoptic Tradition.* Trans. John Marsh. Oxford: Blackwell, 1963.

_____. "ginōskō." *TWNT* 1:688-719. English version: *TDNT* 1:689-719.

_____. *Glauben und Verstehen.* Tübingen: Mohr, 1954. English version (vol. 1): *Faith and Understanding.* Trans. Louise Pettibone-Smith. New York: Harper & Row, 1969.

_____. *History and Eschatology.* Edinburgh: University Press, 1957.

_____. "Neues Testament und Mythologie." In H. W. Bartsch, ed. *Kerygma und Mythos I.* Hamburg: Reich, 1960. English version: *Kerygma and Myth.* New York: Harper, 1961.

_____. "pistis." *TWNT* 6:175-82, 197-230. English version: *TDNT* 6:174-82, 197-228.

_____. "Römer 7 und die Anthropologie des Paulus." *Imago Dei, Festschrift Krüger.* Giessen: Töpelmann, 1932. English version: "Romans 7 and the Anthropology of Paul." In *Existence and Faith: Shorter Writings of Rudolf Bultmann.* Trans. Schubert M. Ogden. New York: Living Age, Meridian, 1960.

_____. *Theologie des Neuen Testaments.* 2nd ed. Tübingen: Mohr, 1954. English version: *Theology of the New Testament.* Trans. Kendrick Grobel. New York: Scribner's, 1970.

van den Bussche, Henri. *Jean.* Paris: Desclée, 1967.

Calvez, Jean-Yves. *La pensée de Karl Marx.* Paris: Seuil, 1959.

_____, and Perrin, Jacques. *Église et société économique.* Paris: Aubier, 1959. English version: *The Church and Social Justice: The Social Teachings of the Popes from Leo XIII to Pius XII (1878-1958).* Chicago: Henry Regnery, 1961.

Carrillo, Salvador. "El cántico de Moisés." *EstBi* 26 (1967):69-75, 143-85, 227-48, 327-52, 383-94.

Caruso, Igor. "Prolegómenos para un diálogo entre religión y psicoanálisis." *Comunidad* (Mexico, D.F.) 4 (1969):279-89.

_____. *Psicoanálisis dialéctico.* Buenos Aires: Paidos, 1964.

_____. *La separación de los amantes.* Mexico, D.F.: Siglo XXI, 1969.

Cazelles, Henri. "À propos de quelques textes difficiles relatifs à la justice de Dieu dans l'Ancien Testament." *RB* 58, no. 2 (April 1951):169-88.

_____. "Institutions et terminologie en Deut. 1:16-17." *VTSuppl* 15 (1966): 97-112.

Cooke, Gerald. "The Sons of (the) God(s)." *ZAltW* 76, no. 1 (1964):22-47.

Cottier, Georges M. Martin. *L'athéisme de jeune Marx.* Paris: J. Vrin, 1959.

Cross, Jr., Frank M. "The Council of Yahweh in Second Isaiah." *JournNESt* 12, no. 4 (October 1953):274-77.

Cullmann, Oscar. *Christ et le temps.* Neuchatel: Delachaux, 1957. English version: *Christ and Time.* Trans. F. V. Filson. Philadelphia: Westminster, 1950.

_____. *Heil als Geschichte.* Tübingen: Mohr, 1965. English version: *Salvation in History.* New York: Harper & Row, 1967.

_____. *Der Staat im Neuen Testament.* 2nd ed. Tübingen: Mohr, 1961. English version: *The State in the New Testament.* New York: Scribner, 1956.

Dahood, Mitchell. *Psalms I.* Anchor Bible 16. New York: Doubleday, 1966; and *Psalms II.* Anchor Bible 17. New York: Doubleday, 1968.

Daniélou, Jean. *Essai sur la mystère de l'histoire.* Paris: Seuil, 1953. English version: *The Lord of History.* Chicago: Regnery, 1958.

Dawson, Christopher. "Karl Marx and the Dialectic of History." In *The Dynamics of World History.* New York: Sheed and Ward, 1956, pp. 354-65.

Deissler, Alfons. *Psalm 119 (118) und seine Theologie.* Munich: Zink, 1955.

Denker, Rolf. *Aufklärung über Aggression.* Stuttgart: Kohlhammer, 1966.

Dewart, Leslie. *The Future of Belief.* New York: Herder, 1966.

Dobbie, Robert. "Deuteronomy and the Prophetic Attitude to Sacrifice." *ScJourTh* no. 1 (March 1959):68-82.

Dodd, C. H. *The Epistle of Paul to the Romans.* New York: Harper, 1932.

_____. *Historical Tradition in the Fourth Gospel.* Cambridge: University Press, 1963.

_____. *The Interpretation of the Fourth Gospel.* Cambridge: University Press, 1953.

_____. *The Parables of the Kingdom.* New York: Scribner's, 1961.

Duhm, Bernard. *Das Buch Jesaja,* 5th ed. Göttingen: Vandenhoeck, 1968.

Dupont, Jacques. *Études sur les Actes des Apôtres.* Paris: Cerf, 1967.

_____. *Gnosis.* 2nd ed. Paris: Gabalda, 1960.

_____. *Syn Christoi. L'union avec le Christ suivant saint Paul.* Bruges: DDB, 1952.

Eichrodt, Walther. *Der Prophet Hesekiel.* ATDeut 22. Vol. 1, 2nd ed., 1965; vol. 2, 1966. English version: *Ezekiel: A Commentary.* Philadelphia: Westminster, 1970.

_____. *Theologie des Alten Testaments.* Stuttgart: Klotz; vol. 1, 7th ed., 1962; vol. 2, 5th ed., 1964. English version: *Theology of the Old Testament.* Trans. J. A. Baker. London: SCM Press, 1961.

Eissfeldt, Otto. *The Old Testament: An Introduction.* Trans. Peter R. Ackroyd. Oxford: Blackwell, 1965.

Elliger, Karl. *Das Buch der zwölf Kleinen Propheten II.* 6th ed. ATDeut 25. Göttingen: Vandenhoeck, 1967.

_____. *Kleine Schriften zum Alten Testament.* Munich: Kaiser Verlag, 1966.

Fensham, F. Charles. "Widow, Orphan, and the Poor in Ancient Near Eastern Legal and Wisdom Literature." *JournNESt* 21, no. 2 (April 1962):129-39.

Feuillet, André. *Le Christ sagesse de Dieu.* Paris: Desclée, 1966.

_____. "Les *egō eimi* christologiques du quatrième évangile." *RechScR* 54, no. 1 (January-March 1966):5-22 and 54, no. 2 (April-June 1966):213-40.

_____. "Mort du Christ et mort du chrétien d'après les Épîtres Pauliniennes." *RB* 66 (1959):481-513.

_____. *Le prologue du quatrième évangile.* Paris: Desclée, 1968.

Fitzer, Gottfried. "Der Ort der Versöhnung nach Paulus." *ThZ* 22, no. 3 (May-June 1966):161-83.

Flesseman-van Leer, Ellen. "Die Interpretation der Passionsgeschichte vom Alten Testament aus." In *Zur Bedeutung des Todes Jesu.* Gütersloh: G. Mohn, 1967, pp. 79-96.

Fohrer, Georg. "Altes Testament—'Amphiktyonie' und 'Bund'? *ThLitZ* 91, no. 11 (November 1966):801-15 and 893-904.

_____. "Das sogenannte apodiktisch formulierte Recht und der Dekalog." *KerDog* 11 (1965):49-74.

_____. "Die Struktur der alttestamentlichen Eschatologie." *ThLitZ* 85, no. 1 (June 1960):401-20.

Friedrich, Gerhard. "euangelizomai." *TWNT* 2:705-35. English version: *TDNT* 2:707-37.

_____. "keryx." *TWNT* 3:682-717. English version: *TDNT* 3:683-718.

Gabel, Joseph. *Ideologie und Schizophrenie, Formen der Entfremdung.* Frankfurt: Fischer, 1967.

Gadamer, Hans-Georg. *Wahrheit und Methode.* 2nd ed. Tübingen: Mohr, 1965.

Garaudy, Roger. *Karl Marx.* Paris: Seghers, 1964. English version: *Karl Marx: The Evolution of His Thought.* New York: International Publishers, 1967.

_____. *Perspectivas del hombre.* Buenos Aires: Platina, 1965. French edition: *Perspectives de l'homme.* 3rd ed. Paris: Presses Universitaires de France, 1961.

_____, et al. *Lecciones de filosofía marxista.* Mexico, D.F.: Grijalbo, 1966.

García Máynez, Eduardo. *Introducción al estudio del derecho.* 16th ed. Mexico, D.F.: Porrúa, 1969.

Gerstenberger, E. *Wesen und Herkunft des "Apodiktischen Rechts."* Neukirchen: Neukirchener Verlag, 1965.

Gevirtz, Stanley. "West-Semitic Curses and the Problem of the Origins of Hebrew Law." *VT* 11, no. 2 (April 1961):137-58.

González, A. "Le Psaume LXXXII." *VT* 13, no. 3 (July 1963):293-309.

Gramsci, Antonio. *Scritti politici.* Rome: Editori Riuniti, 1967.

Grundmann, Walter. *Das Evangelium nach Lukas.* 3rd ed. ThHKomNT. Berlin: Evangelische Verlagsanstalt, 1966.

_____. *Das Evangelium nach Markus.* 3rd ed. ThHKomNT. Berlin: Evangelische Verlagsanstalt, 1968.

_____. *Das Evangelium nach Matthäus.* ThHKomNT. Berlin: Evangelische Verlagsanstalt, 1968.

_____. "kalos." *TWNT* 3:539-53. English version: *TDNT* 3:536-550.

Gundry, Robert Horton. *The Use of the Old Testament in St. Matthew's Gospel.* Leiden: Brill, 1967.

Gunkel, Hermann. *Genesis.* 7th ed. Göttingen: Vandenhoeck, 1966.

_____, and Begrich, J. *Einleitung in die Psalmen.* 2nd ed. Göttingen: Vandenhoeck, 1966.

Gutbrod, Walter. "nomos." *TWNT* 4:1029-84. English version: *TDNT* 4:1035-1091.

Haenchen, Ernst. *Die Apostelgeschichte.* 5th ed. MeyersKomm. Göttingen: Vandenhoeck, 1965. English version: *Acts of the Apostles: A Commentary.* Philadelphia: Westminster, 1971.

_____. "Historie und Geschichte in den johanneischen Passionsberichten." In *Zur Bedeutung des Todes Jesu.* Gütersloh: G. Mohn, 1967, pp. 55-78.

_____. "Der Vater, der mich gesandt hat." *NTSt* 9, no. 3 (April 1963):208-16.

Harper, William Rainey. *Amos and Hosea.* International Critical Commentary 19. Edinburgh: Clark, 1936.

Heidland, H. W. "logizomai." *TWNT* 4:287-95. English version: *TDNT* 4:284-92.

Hentschke, R. "Die Stellung der vorexilischen Schriftpropheten zum Kultus." *BZAltW* 75 (1957).

Héring, Jean. *The First Epistle of Paul to the Corinthians.* 3rd ed. Trans. A. W. Heathcote and P. J. Allcote. London: Epworth, 1966.

_____. *La seconde Épître aux Corinthiens.* Neuchatel: Delachaux, 1958. English version: *The Second Epistle of Paul to the Corinthians.* Trans. A. W. Heathcote and P. J. Allcock. London: Epworth, 1967.

Herntrich, Volkmar. "krinō." *TWNT* 3:920-33. English version: *TDNT* 3:921-33.

Hertzberg, Hans Wilhelm. "Die Entwicklung des Begriffes mišpaṭ im AT." *ZAltW* 40 (1922):256-87; 41 (1923):16-76.

_____. *Prophet und Gott.* BzFöchrTH 28/3 (1923).

Hoffmann, Paul. *Die Toten in Christus.* Münster: Aschendorff, 1966.

Jenni, Ernst. "Das Wort 'olam im Alten Testament." *ZAltW* 64 (1952):197-248; 65 (1953):1-35.

Jepsen, Alfred. "Beiträge zur Auslegung und Geschichte des Dekalogs." *ZAltW* 79 (1967):277-304.

306   *Marx and the Bible*

_____. *"Sdk* und *sdkh* im Alten Testament." In *Festschrift Hertzberg* (1965), pp. 78-97.

Jeremias, Joachim. "geenna." *TWNT* 1:655-56. English version: *TDNT* 1:657-58.

_____. "hadēs." *TWNT* 1:148-49. English version: *TDNT* 1:148-49.

_____. *The Parables of Jesus.* New York: Scribner's, 1963.

_____. "Die Salbungsgeschichte Mk. 14:3-9." *ZNeuW* 35 (1936):77ff.

Joüon, Paul. *Grammaire de l'hébreu biblique.* 2nd ed. Rome: PIB, 1947.

_____. "Notes de lexicographie hébraïque." *Mélanges de la Faculté Orientale* 5 (1911-12):405-15.

_____. "Notes philologiques sur les Évangiles." *RechScRel* 17 (1927):537-40.

Kaiser, Otto. *Der Prophet Jesaja, Kap. 1-12.* 2nd ed. ATDeut 17, 1963. English version: *Isaiah 1-12: A Commentary.* Philadelphia: Westminster, 1972.

Käsemann, Ernst. *Exegetische Versuche und Besinnungen.* 5th ed. Göttingen: Vandenhoeck, 1967.

_____. "Die Heilsbedeutung des Todes Jesu nach Paulus." In *Zur Bedeutung des Todes Jesu.* Gütersloh: G. Mohn, 1967.

_____. *Jesu letzter Wille nach Johannes 17.* 2nd ed. Tübingen: Mohr, 1967. English version: *The Testament of Jesus: A Study of the Gospel of John in the Light of Chapter 17.* Philadelphia: Fortress, 1968.

_____. *Der Ruf der Freiheit.* 4th ed. Tübingen: Mohr, 1968. English version: *Jesus Means Freedom.* Philadelphia: Fortress Press, 1970.

Kelsen, Hans. *Teoría general del estado.* Mexico, D.F.: Nacional, 1965. English version: *General Theory of Law and State.* Trans. Anders Wedberg. New York: Russell, 1961.

_____. *Teoría pura del derecho.* Buenos Aires: Eudeba, 1960. English version: *The Pure Theory of Law.* Trans. Max Knight. Berkeley and Los Angeles: University of California Press, 1967.

Kertelge, Karl. *"Rechtfertigung" bei Paulus.* Münster: Aschendorff, 1966.

Kilian, Rudolf. "Apodiktisches und kasuistisches Recht im Licht ägyptischer Analogien." *BiblZ* 7, no. 2 (July 1963):185-202.

Kittel, Gerhard. "doxa." *TWNT* 2:245-58. English version: *TDNT* 2:242-55.

_____. "eidōs." *TWNT* 2:371-73. English version: *TDNT* 2:373-75.

_____. "eikon." *TWNT* 2:380-86. English version: *TDNT* 2:383-88.

_____. "eschatos." *TWNT* 2:694-95. English version: *TDNT* 2:697-98.

Knierim, Rolf. "Exodus 18 und die Neuordnung der mosaischen Gerichtsbarkeit." *ZAltW* 73, no. 2 (1961):146-71.

Koch, Klaus. "Gibt es ein Vergeltungsdogma im Alten Testament?" *ZThK* 52 (1955):1-42.

Kraus, Hans-Joachim. *Die prophetische Verkundigung des Rechts in Israel.* Zollikon: Evangelischer Verlag, 1957.

_____. *Psalmen.* 3rd ed. BiKomm 15. Neukirchen Kreis Moers: Verlag der Buchhandlung des Erziehungsvereins, 1966.

Kuss, Otto. *Auslegung und Verkundigung.* Regensburg: Pustet; vol. 1, 1963; vol. 2, 1967.

_____. *Der Brief an die Hebräer.* 2nd ed. Regensburg: Pustet, 1966.

_____. *Der Römerbrief.* 2nd ed. Regensburg: Pustet, 1963.

Leenhardt, Franz-J. *L'Épître de saint Paul aux romains.* Neuchatel: Delachaux, 1957. English version: *The Epistle to the Romans: A Commentary.* Cleveland: World, 1961.

Lenin, V. I. *Obras escogidas.* Moscow: Progreso, 1969. In English see *Selected Works of V. I. Lenin.* New York: International Publishers, 1971.

Levinas, Emmanuel. *Totalité et Infini: Essai sur l'exteriorité.* 2nd ed. The Hague: Nijhoff, 1965. English version: *Totality and Infinity: An Essay on Exteriority.* Trans. Alphonso Lingis. Pittsburgh: Duquesne University Press; The Hague: Nijhoff, 1969.

Lohfink, Norbert. *Bibelauslegung im Wandel.* Frankfurt: Knecht, 1967.

_____. *Das Hauptgebot.* AnBi 20. Rome: PIB, 1963.

_____. "Lectures in Deuteronomy." Mimeographed notes. Rome: PIB, 1968.

_____. *Das Siegeslied am Schilfmeer.* Frankfurt: Knecht, 1965. English version: *The Christian Meaning of the Old Testament.* Milwaukee: Bruce, 1968.

_____. "Die Wandlung des Bundesbegriffs im Buch Deuteronomium." In *Gott in Welt: Festgabe für Karl Rahner.* Freiburg: Herder, 1964, pp. 423-44.

Lohmeyer, Ernst. *Das Evangelium des Markus.* 17th ed. MeyersKomm. Göttingen: Vandenhoeck, 1967.

_____, and Schmauch, Werner. *Das Evangelium des Matthäus.* 4th ed. MeyersKomm. Göttingen: Vandenhoeck, 1967.

Löwith, Karl. *Weltgeschichte und Heilsgeschehen.* 4th ed. Stuttgart: Kohlhammer, 1961.

Lührmann, Dieter, *Das Offenbarungsverständnis bei Paulus und in paulinischen Gemeinden.* Neukirchen: Neukirchener Verlag, 1965.

Lyonnet, Stanislas. *Exegesis Epistulae ad Romanos Cap. I-IV.* 3rd ed. Rome: PIB, 1963.

_____. *Exegesis Epistulae ad Romanos Cap. V-VIII.* 2nd ed. Rome: PIB,1966.

_____. *De Peccato et Redemptione.* Rome: PIB; vol. 1, 1957; vol. 2, 1960.

_____. "Le péché." *Supplément au Dictionnaire de la Bible* 7:481-567.

_____. *Quaestiones in Epistulam ad Romanos.* Prima series. 2nd ed. Rome: PIB, 1962.

_____. *Quaestiones in Epistulam ad Romanos.* Series altera. 2nd ed. Rome: PIB, 1962.

_____. A long series of articles in *VD* and *Bi.*

McCarthy, Dennis J. *Der Gottesbund im Alten Testament.* Stuttgart: Katholisches Bibelwerk, 1966.

_____. *Treaty and Covenant.* AnBi 21. Rome: PIB, 1963.

McLuhan, Marshall. *Understanding Media.* New York: McGraw-Hill, 1964.

Mao Tse-tung. *Quotations from Chairman Mao Tse-tung.* Peking: Foreign Languages Press, 1968.

_____. *Selected Readings from the Works of Mao Tse-tung.* Peking: Foreign Languages Press, 1967.

Marcuse, Herbert. *Eros and Civilization.* Boston: Beacon, 1966.

_____. *Essay on Liberation.* Boston: Beacon, 1969.

_____. *One-Dimensional Man.* Boston: Beacon, 1964.

_____. *Soviet Marxism: A Critical Analysis.* New York: Columbia University Press, 1958.

Marx, Karl. *Ausgewählte Schriften.* Munich: Kindler, 1962.

Marxsen, Willi. *Der Evangelist Markus.* 2nd ed. Göttingen: Vandenhoeck, 1959. English version: *Mark the Evangelist.* Trans. James Boyce et al. Nashville: Abingdon, 1969.

Meinertz, Max. *Theologie des Neuen Testamentes.* 2 vols. Bonn: Hanstein Verlag, 1950.

308   *Marx and the Bible*

Mendenhall, George E. *Law and Covenant in Israel and the Ancient Near East.* Pittsburgh: The Biblical Colloquium, 1955.

Messner, Johannes. *Kultur-Ethik.* Innsbruck: Tyrolia Verlag, 1954.

_____. *Das Natur-Recht.* 4th ed. Innsbruck: Tyrolia Verlag, 1960. English version: *Social Ethics: Natural Law in the Western World.* Rev. ed. Trans. J. J. Doherty. St. Louis and London: Herder, 1965.

_____. *Die Soziale Frage.* 6th ed. Innsbruck: Tyrolia Verlag, 1956.

Michaelis, Wilhelm. "horaō." *TWNT* 5:315-68. English version: *TDNT* 5:315-67.

Michel, Otto. *Der Brief an die Hebräer.* 6th ed. MeyersKomm. Göttingen: Vandenhoeck, 1966.

_____. *Der Brief an die Römer.* 4th ed. MeyersKomm. Göttingen: Vandenhoeck, 1966.

Miller, Jr., Patrick D., "El the Warrior." *HarvThRev* 60, no. 4 (October 1967): 411-31. And cf. *HarvThRev* 57, no. 3 (July 1964):240-43.

_____. "God the Warrior." *Interpretation* 19, no. 1 (January 1965):39-46. And cf. *VT* 18, no. 1 (January 1968):100-07.

Montefiore, C. G. *The Synoptic Gospels.* London: Macmillan, 1927.

Moran, William L. "The Ancient Near Eastern Background of the Love of God in Deuteronomy." *CBQ* 25 (1963):77-87.

_____. "The Conclusion of the Decalogue (Ex 20, 17=Dt 5, 21)." *CBQ* 29 (1967):543-54.

_____. "Moses und der Bundesschluss am Sinai." *StdZ* 170 (1961):120-33.

Mowinckel, Sigmund. *Die Erkenntnis Gottes bei alttestamentlichen Propheten.* Oslo: Universistets-Forlaget, 1941.

_____. *Erwägungen zur Pentateuch-Quellenfrage.* Oslo: Universistets-Forlaget, 1964.

_____. *The Psalms in Israel's Worship.* Trans. D. R. Ap-Thomas. Oxford: Blackwell, 1962.

Müller, Christian. *Gottes Gerechtigkeit und Gottes Volk.* FRLANT 86. Göttingen: Vandenhoeck, 1964.

Mussner, Franz. *Zoe: Die Anschauung vom "Leben" im vierten Evangelium unter Berücksichtigung der Johannesbriefe.* Munich, 1952.

Navarrete, Ifigenia M. de. *La distribución del ingreso y el desarrollo económico de México.* No. 10. Mexico, D.F.: Ediciones de la UNAM, 1960.

von Nell-Breuning, Oswald. "Katholische Kirche und marxistische Kapitalismuskritik." *StdZ* 180 (1967):365-74.

_____. *Wirtschaft und Gesellschaft heute.* 3 vols. Freiburg: Herder, 1956-60.

_____. Numerous articles in *Herders Wörterbuch der Politik*, 1952.

North, Christopher R. "Sacrifice in the Old Testament." *ExpTim* 47, no. 6 (March 1936):250-54.

_____. *The Second Isaiah.* Oxford: Clarendon, 1964.

_____. *The Suffering Servant in Deutero-Isaiah.* 3rd ed. New York: Oxford, 1963.

Noth, Martin. *Das dritte Buch Mose.* 2nd ed. ATDeut 6. Göttingen: Vandenhoeck, 1966. English version: *Leviticus: A Commentary.* Philadelphia: Westminster, 1965.

_____. *Gesammelte Studien zum Alten Testament.* Munich: Kaiser, 1966. English version: *The Laws in the Pentateuch and Other Studies.* Trans. D. R. Ap.-Thomas. Philadelphia: Fortress Press, 1966.

_____. *Geschichte Israels.* 6th ed. Göttingen: Vandenhoeck, 1966. English version: *The History of Israel.* 2nd ed. New York: Harper and Row, 1960.

_____. *Überlieferungsgeschichte des Pentateuch.* Stuttgart: Kohlhammer, 1948. English version: *A History of Pentateuchal Traditions.* Trans. Bernhard W. Anderson. Englewood Cliffs, N.J.: Prentice-Hall, 1972.

_____. *Das vierte Buch Mose.* 2nd ed. ATDeut 7. Göttingen: Vandenhoeck, 1966. English version: *Numbers: A Commentary.* Trans. James D. Martin. Philadelphia: Westminster, 1969.

_____. *Das zweite Buch Mose.* 3rd ed. ATDeut 5. Göttingen: Vandenhoeck, 1965. English version: *Exodus: A Commentary.* Philadelphia: Westminster, 1962.

Nötscher, F. "Bundesformular und 'Amtsschimmel.'" *BiblZ* 9 (1965):181-214.

Oepke, Albrecht. "egeiro." *TWNT* 2:332-37. English version: *TDNT* 2:332-39.

Ouellette, Jean. "Le deuxième commandement et le rôle de l'image." *RB* 74, no. 4 (October 1967):504-16.

Parsons, Talcott. *Sociological Theory and Modern Society.* 2nd ed. New York: The Free Press, 1968.

Perrin, Norman. *Rediscovering the Teaching of Jesus.* London: SCM Press, 1967.

Pitarque, Felipe. *Curso de sociología pontificia.* 3rd ed. Barcelona: Casulleras, 1961.

Pozo, Cándido. *Teología del más allá.* 4th ed. Madrid: BAC, 1968.

Preuss, Horst Dietrich. *Jahweglaube und Zukunftserwartung.* BWANT 87. Stuttgart: Kohlhammer, 1968.

von Rad, Gerhard. "Aspekte alttestamentlichen Weltverständnisses." *EvTh* 24 (1964):57-63. English version: "Some Aspects of the Old Testament World-View." In *The Problem of the Hexateuch and Other Essays.* Trans. E. W. Truman Dicken. New York: McGraw-Hill, 1966, pp. 144-65.

_____. *Deuteronomiumstudien.* 2nd ed. FRLANT 40. Göttingen: Vandenhoeck, 1948. English version: *Studies in Deuteronomy.* Trans. David Stalker. London: SCM, 1953.

_____. "doxa." *TWNT* 2:240-45. English version: *TDNT* 2:238-43.

_____. *Das erste Buch Mose.* 7th ed. ATDeut 2-4. Göttingen: Vandenhoeck, 1964. English version: *Genesis: A Commentary.* Trans. John H. Marks. London: SCM, 1961.

_____. *Gesammelte Studien zum Alten Testament.* Munich: Kaiser, 1965.

_____. *Der Heilige Krieg im Alten Israel.* Göttingen: Vandenhoeck, 1951.

_____. "The Origin of the Concept of the Day of Yehweh." *JournSemSt* 4, no. 2 (April 1959):97-108.

_____. *Theologie des Alten Testaments.* 4th ed. Munich: Kaiser; vol. 1, 1962; vol. 2, 1965. English version: *Old Testament Theology.* Trans. D. M. G. Stalker. 2 vols. New York: Harper, 1962.

_____. "zaō." *TWNT* 2:844-50. English version: *TDNT* 2:843-49.

Recaséns Siches, Luis. *Teoría general de filosofía del derecho.* 3rd ed. Mexico, D.F.: Porrúa, 1965.

Renckens, Henricus. *La Bible et les origines du monde,* 1964. English version: *Israel's Concept of the Beginning.* New York: Herder, 1964.

310   *Marx and the Bible*

Rendtorff, Rolf. "Die Offenbarungsvorstellungen im Alten Testament." *KerDog* 1 (1961):21-41.

Rengstorf, Karl Heinrich. *Das Evangelium nach Lukas.* 12th ed. NeuTestD 3. Göttingen: Vandenhoeck, 1967.

Richter, Wolfgang. "Zu den 'Richtern Israels.' " *ZAltW* 77 (1965):40-71.

Robinson, Theodore Henry, and Horst, Friedrich. *Die zwölf kleinen Propheten.* 3rd ed. HBAT 14. Tübingen: Mohr, 1964.

Rowley, H. H. "The Antiquity of Israelite Monotheism." *ExpTim* 61, no. 11 (August 1950):333-34.

Rudolph, Wilhelm. *Hosea.* KommAT. Gütersloh: Mohn, 1966.

_____. *Jeremia.* 3rd ed. HBAT 12. Tübingen: Mohr, 1968.

Sarna, Nahum. *Understanding Genesis.* New York: McGraw Hill, 1966.

Sartre, Jean-Paul. *Crítica de la razón dialéctica.* Buenos Aires: Losada, 1963. French version: *Critique de la raison dialectique.* Paris: Gallimard, 1960.

Sasse, Hermann. "aiōn." *TWNT* 1:197-209. English version: *TDNT* 1:197-209.

_____. "kosmeo." *TWNT* 3:867-98. English version: *TDNT* 3:867-98.

Schlatter, Adolf. *Der Glaube im Neuen Testament.* 4th ed. Stuttgart, 1927.

_____. *Gottes Gerechtigkeit.* 3rd ed. Stuttgart: Calwer, 1959.

Schlier, Heinrich. *Besinnung auf das Neue Testament.* Freiburg: Herder, 1962. English version: *The Relevance of the New Testament.* New York: Herder, 1968.

_____. *Der Brief an die Epheser.* 6th ed. Düsseldorf: Patmos, 1968.

_____. *Der Brief an die Galater.* 4th ed. MeyersKomm. Göttingen: Vandenhoeck, 1965.

_____. *Die Zeit der Kirche.* 3rd ed. Freiburg: Herder, 1962.

Schmid, Josef. *Das Evangelium nach Lukas.* 3rd ed. Regensburg: Pustet, 1955.

_____. *Das Evangelium nach Markus.* 3rd ed. Regensburg: Pustet, 1954. English version: *The Gospel according to Mark.* New York: Alba, 1968.

_____. *Das Evangelium nach Matthäus.* 3rd ed. Regensburg: Pustet, 1956.

Schnackenburg, Rudolf. "Glaube. Die Aussagen der Schrift." In *Lexicon für Theologie und Kirche.* 2nd ed. 4:913-17.

_____. *Die Johannesbriefe.* 3rd ed. Freiburg: Herder, 1965.

_____. *Das Johannesevangelium.* Freiburg: Herder, 1965. English version: *The Gospel According to St. John.* Trans. Kevin Smyth. New York: Herder, 1968.

_____. *The Moral Teaching of the New Testament.* London: Burns and Oates, 1964.

Schniewind, Julius. *Das Evangelium nach Matthäus.* 11th ed. NeuTestD 2. Göttingen: Vandenhoeck, 1967.

Schweizer, Eduard. *Das Evangelium nach Markus.* Göttingen: Vandenhoeck, 1967. English version: *The Good News According to Mark.* Richmond: Knox, 1971.

_____. "hyios." *TWNT* 8:355-57 and 364-95. English version: *TDNT* 8:354-57 and 363-92.

Skinner, John. *Prophecy and Religion.* London: Cambridge University Press, 1926.

Smend, R. "Die Bundesformel." *ThSt* 68 (1963).

_____. "Das Nein des Amos." *EvTh* (1963):404-23.

Soggin, J. Alberto. "Der prophetische Gedanke über den heiligen Krieg, als Gericht gegen Israel." *VT* 10, no. 4 (1960):79-83.

Bibliography 311

Spicq, C. "L'Épître aux Hébreux, Apollos, Jean-Baptiste, les Hellénistes et Qumran." *Revue de Qumran* 1, no. 3 (February 1953):365-90.

Stählin, Gustav. *Die Apostelgeschichte*. 2nd ed. NeuTestD 5. Göttingen: Vandenhoeck, 1966.

———. "orge." *TWNT* 5:419-48. English version: *TDNT* 5:419-47.

Stamm, Johann Jakob. "Ein Vierteljahrhundert Psalmenforschung." *Theologische Rundschau NF* 23 (1955):1-68.

———, and Andrew, M. E. *The Ten Commandments in Recent Research*. Naperville, Ill.: Allenson, 1967.

Stith, Richard. "Lettre à un professeur sur la connaissance calculatrice." *Esprit* 8-9 (1968):81-88.

Strack, Hermann L., and Billerbeck, Paul. *Kommentar zum Neuen Testament aus Talmud und Midrasch*. 6 vols. Munich: C. H. Beck'sche, 1922-63.

Strecker, Georg. *Der Weg der Gerechitigkeit*. 2nd ed. FRLANT 82. Göttingen: Vandenhoeck, 1966.

Stuhlmacher, Peter. *Gerechtigkeit Gottes bei Paulus*. 2nd ed. FRLANT 87. Göttingen: Vandenhoeck, 1966.

Tresmontant, Claude. *La doctrine morale des prophètes d'Israël*. Paris: Seuil, 1958.

———. *Essai sur la pensée hébraïque*. Paris: du Cerf, 1953. English version: *A Study of Hebrew Thought*. New York: Desclee, 1960.

Trilling, Wolfgang. *Das wahre Israel*. 3rd ed. Munich: Kösel, 1964.

Vriezen, T. C. "Exode 20,2. Introduction au Décalogue: formule de loi ou d'alliance?" *RechBi* 8 (1967):35-50.

———. "Prophecy and Eschatology." *VTSuppl* 1 (1953):199-229.

Walker, Rolf. *Die Heilsgeschichte im ersten Evangelium*. FRLANT 91. Göttingen: Vandenhoeck, 1967.

Ward, William Hayes. *Habakkuk*. International Critical Commentary 20. Edinburgh: Clark, 1911.

Weiser, Artur. *Das Buch der zwölf kleinen Propheten*. 5th ed. ATDeut 24. Göttingen: Vandenhoeck, 1967.

———. "pisteuō." *TWNT* 6:175-97. English version: *TDNT* 6:175-96.

———. *Die Psalmen*. 2 vols. 7th ed. ATDeut 14 and 15. Göttingen: Vandenhoeck, 1966. English version: *The Psalms: A Commentary*. Philadelphia: Westminster, 1962.

Wendland, Heinz Dietrich. *Die Briefe an die Korinther*. NeuTestD 7. Göttingen: Vandenhoeck, 1968.

Westcott, B. F. *The Gospel According to St. John*. London: Murray, 1908.

Westermann, Claus. *Das Buch Jesaja Kap. 40-66*. ATDeut 19. Göttingen: Vandenhoeck, 1966. English version: *Isaiah 40-66: A Commentary*. Philadelphia: Westminster, 1969.

———. *Forschung am alten Testament* (Gesammelte Studien). Munich: Kaiser, 1964.

Wolff, Hans Walter. *Hosea*. 2nd ed. BiKomm 14/1. Neukirchen: Neukirchener Verlag, 1965.

———. *Joel-Amos*. BiKomm 14/2. Neukirchen: Neukirchener Verlag, 1969.

312 Marx and the Bible

_____. " 'Wissen um Gott' bei Hosea als Urform von Theologie." *EvTh* 12 (1952-53):533-34.

Würthwein, E. "Amos-Studien." *ZAltW* 62 (1949-50).

Zahn, Theodor. *Das Evangelium des Matthäus.* 3rd ed. Leipzig: A. Deichertsche, 1910.

Zerwick, Max. *Analysis philologica novi testamenti graeci.* 2nd ed. Rome: PIB, 1960.

_____. *Graecitas Biblica.* 4th ed. Rome: PIB, 1960.

Zimmerli, Walther. *Gottes Offenbarung: Gesammelte Aufsätze zum Alten Testamenten.* Munich: Kaiser, 1963.

_____. " 'Offenbarung' im Alten Testament." *EvTh* 22 (1962): 15-31.

Zimmermann, L. J. *Geschichte der theoretischen Volkswirtschaftslehre.* Cologne: Bund Verlag, 1954.

Note: This bibliography does not include all the dictionaries and critical editions of the Bible.

Index of
Hebrew and Greek Terms

'adam, 92
adikia, 161, 162, 169-70, 181, 231, 232
agapē, 118
agapōmen allēlous, 61
'ahab, 119
aiōn, 187, 190
aiōnios, 152
airō, 277
akouein, 214
alēthōs, 136
anastasis nekrōn, 209
'ani, 120, 193
'ani-hu, 86, 132
'aw^elah, 108 n.47, 151
'awen, 100, 101, 103

ba'^abur, 146
b^e, 49, 106 n.2
ben, 112
b^e'ohaleyka teseb, 73 n.21
b^eris'ath, 121
b^esorah, 213
b^esedek, 106 n.2
bisser, 213
blepomenōn, 228

charis kai alētheia, 237, 238
chrēstotēta, 162

dabar, 247
dak, 120
dal, 101

debarim, 39
dēlon, 248
dia, 203, 239, 244
diakrinein, 111
dikaiōma, 41
dikaiōma tou Theou epignontes, 41
dikaiosynē, 15, 94, 111, 112, 175
dikaiosynē ek Theou, 173
dikastēs, 111
dikazein, 111
din, 83
doxa, 232, 233
doxasei, 240
dynamis, 239, 245

'ebyon, 120
edoxasen, 240
egō eimi, 132
eidōs, 248
eis ton aiōna, heōs aionos, 152
ek, 203, 204, 244
ekdikein, 111
ek pisteōs, 174
ek pisteōs eis pistin, 203, 245
eleēmosynē, 15
eleos, 15, 46, 47, 63, 122, 222
'^elohim, 192 n.10
elpis, 229
emataiothēsan en tois dialogismois
   autōn, 42
en, 72 n.8
ēngiken, 212, 286 n.26

313

Index of Scriptural References

Old Testament

316

New Testament

Apocrypha and Other Writings

Index of Authors

Adler, Alfred, 270, 282
Aland, Kurt, 198 n.160
Allard, Michel, 294, 297 n.7, 297 n.10
Allaz, Tomás G., O.P., 1, 21, 32 n.1, 32 n.3
Allcock, P.J., 184, 198 n.158
Alt, Albrecht, 139, 142, 143, 144, 194 n.54, 195 n.67, 195 n.74
Althaus, Paul, 72 n.8, 226, 230, 240, 285 n.17, 286 n.34, 287 n.59, 288 n.88, 288 n.94
Ambrose, Saint, 16, 32 n.15, 32 n.16
Ambrosiaster, 230
Andrew, M.E., 38, 72 n.4
Aristotle, 16, 31, 38, 243, 262, 271
Arnault, Francette, 263, 290 n.160
Asensio, Felix, 287 n.80
Augustine, Saint, 16, 32 n.17, 177, 230

Bach, Robert, 143, 144, 158, 195 n.69, 196 n.95
Bakunin, Mikhail, 187
Balscheit, B., 74 n.41
Barrett, C.K., 287 n.79
Barth, Gerhard, 129, 171, 194 n.34, 285 n.15
Barth, Karl, 243
Basil the Great, Saint, 15, 32 n.14
Baudissin, G., 195 n.86

Bauer, Walter, 72 n.6, 287 n.64
Beaucamp, E., 83, 106 n.14
Bergson, Henri, 243-44
Beyerlin, Walter, 194 n.47
Bigo, Pierre, xiv, xix n.3, 1, 2, 21, 31, 32 n.1, 32 n.5, 33 n.25, 62, 75 n.48, 253, 258, 259, 263, 264, 267, 269, 289 n.138, 289 n.148, 289 n.151, 290 n.156, 290 n.162, 290 n.163, 290 n.166, 290 n.174, 290 n.186
Billerbeck, Paul, 193 n.13
Black, 198 n.160
Black, Matthew, 286 n.26
Blaise, Michel, xv, xxi n.5
Blass, F., 61, 75 n.42
Bloch, Ernst, 44, 73 n.11, 201, 243, 249, 254, 270, 279, 280, 283, 285 n.1, 288 n.102, 289 n.122, 290 n.190, 290 n.192, 291 n.197, 291 n.213, 292 n.226, 292 n.232
Böhme, Jakob, 274
Bonnard, Pierre, 159
Bornkamm, Günther, 171, 194 n.34, 285 n.15
Botterweck, G. Johannes, 45, 51, 73 n.13, 73 n.28
Bousset, Wilhelm, 211, 286 n.22
Braun, Herbert, 206, 211, 285 n.12, 286 n.22, 297 n.2
Bright, J., 101
Brown, Raymond E., 287 n.79
Büchsel, Friedrich, 128, 185, 194 n.32

333

Oepke, Albrecht, 286 n.20
Oesterley, William Oscar Emil, 108
n.43, 236
Oettinger, 225
Origen, 230
Ouellette, Jean, 38, 72 n.4

Packard, Vance, 8
Parsons, Talcott, 182, 198 n.150
Paul VI, Pope, xv, 30, 33 n.24
Perrin, Jacques, 31, 33 n.25
Perrin, Norman, 18, 33 n.18
Photius, 230
Pitarque, Felipe, 31, 33 n.25
Pius IX, Pope, xv
Pius X, Pope, xv, xxi n.4
Pius XI, Pope, xiii, 30
Pius XII, Pope, xv, 1, 24, 27, 32 n.4,
33 n.21
Plato, 31, 271
Pozo, Cándido, 275, 291 n.201
Preuss, Horst Dietrich, 295, 297 n.13
Proudhon, Pierre Joseph, 253

Quell, Gottfried, 119, 193 n.18
Quesnay, François, 260

von Rad, Gerhard, 38, 72 n.4, 74
n.41, 77, 78, 90-93, 106 n.1, 106
n.3, 107 n.27, 107 n.29, 107 n.34,
119, 121, 126, 138-40, 143, 145,
147-50, 155, 157, 164, 167, 168,
193 n.15, 193 n.16, 193 n.20, 194
n.29, 194 n.51, 195 n.55, 195 n.57,
195 n.72, 195 n.75, 195 n.78, 195
n.79, 195 n.81, 196 n.106, 196
n.107, 197 n.111, 215, 233, 278,
286 n.37, 287 n.74, 291 n.210
Rahner, Karl, 247, 249
Recaséns Siches, Luis, 183, 198 n.151
Renckens, Henricus, 107 n.26
Rendtorff, Rolf, 80, 106 n.10
Rengstorf, Karl Heinrich, 133, 194 n.39

Ricardo, David, 260, 264, 266
Richter, Wolfgang, 192 n.6
Robinson, Theodore Henry, 73 n.22,
73 n.30, 74 n.32, 124, 193 n.23
Rowley, H. H., 74 n.41
Rudolph, Wilhelm, 50, 73 n.15, 73
n.21, 73 n.23, 73 n.24, 73 n.26, 74
n.37, 107 n.22, 286 n.21, 297 n.9

Sanday, William, 230
Sarna, Nahum, M., 89, 90, 107 n.25,
107 n.26, 107 n.28
Sartre, Jean Paul, 44, 73 n.11, 201,
285 n.1
Sasse, Hermann, 198 n.149
Saydon, P., 126
Scheler, Max, xix, 262
Schlatter, Adolf, 202, 285 n.3
Schlier, Heinrich, 183, 184, 187,
198 n.156, 198 n.163, 199 n.169,
218, 242, 256, 286 n.41, 288 n.95,
289 n.139
Schmid, Josef, 75 n.51, 159
Schmitz, Oscar A. H., 212, 243
Schnackenburg, Rudolf, 75 n.42,
75 n.44, 75 n.52, 133, 136, 194
n.39, 194 n.43, 207, 223, 275, 285
n.13, 287 n.49, 291 n.203
Schniewind, Julius, 129, 194 n.33
Schweizer, Eduard, 209, 225, 286
n.19, 287 n.55
Skinner, John, 74 n.37
Smend, R., 60, 74 n.37, 74 n.38, 141,
195 n.59
Smith, Adam, 260, 264
Soggin, J. Alberto, 126, 193 n.15,
194 n.28
Speiser, E.A., 107 n.30
Spicq, C., 297 n.2
Spinoza, Benedictus de, 247
Stamm, Johann Jakob, 38, 72 n.4,
108 n.43
Stith, Richard, 283, 292 n.229
Strack, Hermann L., 193 n.13
Strecker, Georg, 171, 288 n.111